GNOSTIC APOCALYPSE

GNOSTIC APOCALYPSE

Jacob Boehme's
Haunted Narrative

CYRIL O'REGAN

STATE UNIVERSITY OF NEW YORK PRESS

Cover image: Corbis Images

Published by
State University of New York Press, Albany

For information, address State University of New York Press,
90 State Street, Suite 700, Albany, NY 12207

Production by Judith Block
Marketing by Patrick Durocher

Library of Congress Cataloging-in-Publication Data

O'Regan, Cyril
    Gnostic apocalypse : Jacob Boehme's haunted narrative / Cyril O'Regan.
        p. cm.
    Includes bibliographical references and index.
    ISBN 0-7914-5201-8 (alk. paper)—ISBN 0-7914-5202-6 (pkb. : alk. paper)
        1. Bèhme, Jakob, 1575–1624. I. Title.

    BV5095.B7 O73 2002
    230'.044'092—dc21   2001049420

10 9 8 7 6 5 4 3 2 1

Dedicated to Niall Meehan O'Regan

This breathing in the dark sheds
no light. Its catch and release
opens like a bedroom door
on a swollen carpet until its arc
achieves the gaiety of swing.

This is familiar, familial, a now
of sound inflected by desire
between the stasis of hesitations,
a dream that wants to worry the stars.

September's blue of recall flames
furiously purple. You rise from
the wound red, perfect. I run

into beauty's trip-wire, my mind
falling into a shout.

Tugged by an invisible moon
you bring my ancestors, humors
and sweat and hope routing
their lives. But more you are

the plan I cannot read, the sketch
whose outline is not formed,
the boat to the future

the aftermath of the barque
tumbling over the edge of the world.

Contents

Acknowledgments

While my interest in the seventeenth-century German speculative mystic Jacob Boehme dates back to my undergraduate days in Dublin, and while I spent considerable time charting the relation between Boehme and Hegel in *The Heterodox Hegel*, at no time did I think that I would write a book on this figure. There was neither the time nor the need. Or so I thought. Need, however, gave birth to time. As the Gnostic return project got under way it became obvious that an examination of Boehme was inescapable, since, arguably, it is his discourse that represents the site of introduction of Gnosis into the field of modern discourse. In its birth I am grateful to a number of people. I owe much to two Irish friends, to John Doyle for first introducing me to a thinker whose opacity made Hegel and Heidegger look positively lucid, and to Brendan Purcell for his unfailing support for this strange interest. I am deeply indebted to Louis Dupré who encouraged my interest in the mystical traditions. My study with him, both as a student and colleague of his at Yale, of Eckhart, Cusa, and Pseudo-Dionysius, as well as the Kabbalah and Eastern forms of mysticism not only proved illuminating and fruitful, it was also exciting, pursued as it was under the assumption that these discourses were both philosophically and religiously important. Such study created a space for reexamining even more marginal speculative mystics of the Christian tradition, as well as providing a vocabulary and the outlines of a syntax of the discourse of the Christian mystical tradition that if it could not fit all occasions, was appropriate to many. John Jones, editor at Crossroad, was an early cheerleader in my first attempts to write on Boehme in the Gnosticism project, although he had been equally enthusiastic about my earlier unpublished work. Denying anything like an elective affinity with speculative mysticism, colleagues at Yale such as David Kelsey, Wayne Meeks, and Gene Outka were deeply reassuring in their openness to entertaining a claim for importance that had little prima facie plausibility. As was the case with *Gnostic Return in Modernity*, Gene Outka was supererogatory in playing the role of grammatical steward to my latest raid on the inarticulate. I say thanks to him twice. At Notre Dame, where the final draft of the book was written, I am especially indebted to Cyril Gorman, O.S.B. He exemplified in the manner of the very best of monk-scholars the virtues of patience and attention to details of grammar and punctuation that I do not possess. I am grateful for his painstaking reading of the entire manuscript including the notes. My gratitude to the readers at State University of New York Press of the original manuscript of *Gnostic Apocalypse* is enormous. All three readers read the manuscript charitably as well as deeply. Their probing comments have helped in no small way to make this a much better book than otherwise it might have been. I am especially grateful to one of these readers, David Walsh, who voluntarily surrendered his incognito as a reader. He has continued to be a discussion partner with regard to the texts of Boehme in which he is expert. But he has also continued to be a discussion partner with respect to the entire project of mapping the return of Gnostic discourse in the modern period of which this is only the second installment. Throughout I have been marvelously treated by SUNY Press. Jane Bunker, the acquisitions editor could not have been more supportive; Judith Block, the production editor, could not have been more efficient; and Patrick Durocher, the marketing manager, could not have been more helpful.

Introduction

This is a book on the post-Reformation, German speculative mystic Jacob Boehme (1575–1624).[1] In one sense at least, it shares the universe of commentary and criticism with works by Ernst Benz, Hans Grunsky, Alexandre Koyré, John Joseph Stoudt, and Andrew Weeks.[2] In it, I am no less convinced of the historical importance of Boehme and of his religious and metaphysical depth, no less intent on rescuing Boehme's thought and discourse from the oblivion into which it has fallen, and no less interested in persuading that the archaic discourse and thought of this obscure Silesian shoemaker, who is a devout Lutheran, is important in ways we do well to recognize.

This is also a book in which the "history of effects" of Boehme's work is central, even if I postpone much of the discussion of such effects for future volumes. Thus, at least in an anticipatory mode, it belongs in the same interpretive space as the explorations in English, German, and French of the influence of Boehme on philosophical, religious, and literary thought and discourse from the seventeenth century onward. It belongs in the same interpretive space as the various studies on the influence of Boehme on the philosophical discourse of Hegel and Schelling,[3] but also on the philosophical discourse of Leibniz, and even the scientific discourse of Newton.[4] At the same time this text belongs in the same interpretive space as studies on the history of effects of Boehme's discourse on religious thought in general—for example, in esoteric thought of the eighteenth century with particular reference to the eccentric figures of John Pordage and Jean Lead, on the one hand, and Swendenborg and Louis Claude de Saint Martin on the other.[5] This text belongs in the same interpretive space as discussions on the influence of Boehme on the more speculative wing of eighteenth-century Pietism, both German and English,[6] and reflections on the Boehme retrievals prosecuted in the nineteenth century by the Roman Catholic religious thinker Franz von Baader and somewhat later by Bishop Martensen, Kierkegaard's bête noir.[7] And again, this text belongs in the same interpretive space as studies in the relationship of Boehme to the literary tradition—for example, his influence on Milton and Romantic and post-Romantic poetry in German and English.[8] Ultimately, however, this book represents a genre with very few instances—that is, a genre in which Boehme's corpus is named as a privileged site of the return of a Gnostic modality of thought in modernity— what I have called *Gnostic return*. Precisely as such, Boehme is a point of origin for other better known discourses: religious (e.g., Thomas Altizer and Jürgen Moltmann), philosophical (e.g., Hegel and Schelling), and even literary (e.g., William Blake and Harold Bloom).

In this sense, the main interpretive company this text keeps is that of nineteenth-century German theologians, who saw in Boehme a post-Reformation discursive event with consequences that could be traced into Romanticism and Idealism. The classic expression of this view is provided by Ferdinand Christian Baur in his magisterial *Die christliche Gnosis* (1835).[9] And later texts of the great Protestant historian of dogma, particularly his work on the Trinity,[10] fill out the claim made in his earlier text. The other major German theologian who interests himself in making such a claim is the admittedly derivative, and largely forgotten, Roman Catholic theologian, Franz Anton Staudenmaier (1800–1856).[11] Staudenmaier accepts the main lines of Baur's analysis, specifically his views that there exists a line of thought in the post-Reformation and post-Enlightenment fields of discourse that give evidence of Gnostic return, and that Boehme and Hegel respectively represent the origin and culmination of Gnostic return in the modern field. Staudenmaier, however, mourns what Baur celebrates. Granting to Baur, and not to Staudenmaier (who at every turn presupposes him) the patent on a Gnostic return that features the seventeenth-century theosophist, I argue here that Baur is right to claim that Boehme can be regarded as the proximate origin of the emergence of Gnosticism in modern discourse, which emergence signifies a reemergence after an eclipse. But I do so with a tone that is more nearly that of Staudenmaier than Baur himself. That is, I argue Baur's case with a tone more of mourning than celebration, where this tone suggests that Christian thought has not been delivered from authority, but endured a catastrophe that amounts to something like a Babylonian captivity. I will return to the evaluative dimension of my Baurian claim later in the introduction.

At the outset it should be admitted that Baur's claim about the unique importance of Boehme has seemed implausible to many. Yet, it is interesting that this claim continues to be entertained both without and within theology. It gets voiced in the ruminations of students of the political theorist Eric Voegelin.[12] To a somewhat more limited extent it is touched on by theologians such as Hans Urs von Balthasar and John Milbank.[13] It should be confessed up front that no *quod erat demonstrandum* has been hung by any advocate of Boehme as a privileged site of Gnostic return. In general among its supporters argumentation seems to give way quickly to assertion and rhetoric, thereby suggesting that the Baurian claim is not only not proved, but is in principle unprovable. As

Gnostic Return in Modernity,[14] the companion text to the present text shows, the latter conclusion is itself peremptory without a more methodological sorting through of the difficulties that face a Gnostic return thesis, which puts an emphasis on the originary role of Boehme on the threshold of modernity. One should not rule out beforehand that concerted reflection on the methods of Baur and others, who support such a claim, might show the interpreter a way out of what can only be acknowledged as *cul-de-sacs*, even if a finally satisfying proposal will look considerably different from that of Baur.

In any event, I accept that serious difficulties beset a *Gnostic* or *Valentinian* ascription of Boehme's discourse. These come from the side of Boehme's discourse itself and its interpretation. These also come from the side of Gnostic return proposers, whose method, whether following Baur or emending him, shows serious signs of flaw. But these different kinds of difficulty are not hermetically sealed from each other. In distinguishing them I should not be understood to imply that difficulties in one area have no effect on the other. Indeed, I wish to assert just the opposite. Difficulties in Boehme interpretation at the very least exacerbate the general difficulties of the Gnostic return claim. Conversely, difficulties in the Gnostic return hypothesis exacerbate the difficulties of Boehme interpretation. Recognizing the interdependence of these two difficulties, I can procedurally, however, separate them.

I begin with the nontrivial, but more tractable difficulties that beset the interpretation of Boehme himself. I wish to comment on four difficulties that inhibit an adequate interpretation of Boehme. These make him essentially unavailable for genealogical use in general and for Gnostic genealogical use in particular.

The first and, arguably, the least of the difficulties with respect to the interpretation of Boehme himself is the notorious opacity of Boehme's expression, commented on influentially by Hegel,[15] repeated by Baur,[16] and suffered—but usually not without complaint—by later commentators. If the texts of Boehme are powerful enough to exert fascination—to encourage still "the mingling of lives; worlds simmering/in the entranced interval,"[17] to cite the modern Irish poet, Thomas Kinsella, in a very Gadamerian moment—it is equally true that to approach Boehme's texts is to approach a form of discourse that is encapsulated famously in another modern poet's figure, that is, Paul Claudel's figure of "cyclone figé."[18] In Boehme the interpreter comes upon the coagulated cyclone of language, a form or nonform of linguistic implosion that repels and excludes.

As the following passages from *Sex Puncta Mystica* and *De Signatura Rerum* indicate, Boehme is simply one of the most difficult reads in the history of Christian thought. In the former text Boehme writes:

> Magic is the mother of eternity, of the being of all beings; for it creates itself, and is understood in desire. It is in itself nothing but a will, and this will is the

great mystery of all wonders and secrets, but brings itself into imagination or figuration itself by the imagination of the desireful hunger into being. It is the original state of Nature. Its desire makes an imagination, and imagination or figuration is only the will of desire. But desire makes in the will such a being as the will in itself is. (Point 5.1–3)[19]

In the latter text, we read:

> Outside of nature God is a mystery, understand in the nothing, for outside of nature is the nothing, which is the eye of eternity, an abyssal eye that stands or sees in the nothing, for it is the abyss; and this same eye is a will, understand a desire for manifestation, to find the nothing. But now there is nothing before the will, where it may find something, where it might have a place of rest. Therefore, it enters into itself, and finds itself through nature. (*SR* 3.2)

Nothing is semantically clear in either of these texts, certainly not the relation of desire to will, nor the relation of either to nothing and something. Moreover, how appropriate is the anthropomorphic language of desire and will, and the language of "magic" and "mother" to the topic, which seems to be nothing less than reality in its most total extension and its most complete dynamic intension?

The opacity charge then is sustainable; the habits of Boehme's expression lie well beyond the infelicities commonplace in theological and philosophical writing. Nevertheless, while this opacity may be due to a lack of intellectual training, it is most certainly not due to a poverty in reading. It is now obvious that the profile of an 'unlettered' Boehme is largely a Romantic fiction.[20] It proves dangerous to the extent to which Boehme's 'genius' is held to support a fundamentally native German aptitude for thought.[21] And while lack of culture might well be explained by a Christianly driven commitment to the vernacular and the colloquial, it does not account for Boehmian neologism and the continuous straining after something like technical precision.

This straining suggests that a tension exists between expression and meaning, and that a gap exists between the declared transparency of reality and its rendering in language (which is perhaps all the more ironic given Boehme's belief in an Adamic language that discloses the essence of things and is fundamentally untouched by the fall). In any event, the tension between expression and meaning may in part account for Boehme's incredible repetitiousness. It is only a slight exaggeration to say that the texts of Boehme's mature period (1619–1624) seem to constitute one text written over and over again.[22] It is as if relatively constant subject matter always needed to be dealt with one more time. And with Boehme, it is not, as it is with others in the Baroque period, simply a matter of a montage of perspectives,[23] where one can think of a multitude of perspectives being equally sharp. With Boehme it is the straining after and failing to achieve the one truly adequate perspective.

Now while obscurity of expression is never a virtue in itself, it is possible that it is a function of the difficulty of the subject matter, which is nothing less than a description of all reality as an expression of the divine drive toward self-manifestation. Boehme himself suggests as much. And if this is rationalization and alibi, it has a checkered history. For it is a commonplace of modern philosophy of the continental stripe to make just such an appeal, with Heidegger, and in a sense deconstruction, representing but the latest examples. Nevertheless, even if one is sympathetic to Boehme's plea for understanding, obscurity of expression is not the most inviting quality in the figure on whom one wishes to place the burden of the unlikely genealogical thesis that his thought represents something like the return of a Gnostic or Valentinian form of speculative religious discourse, but whose last hurrah was essentially in the fourth century.

I fully understand the reluctance to invest time and energy in interpretation where one cannot guarantee the outcome, but I submit that the difficulty of style may itself suggest something productive both with respect to the interpretation of Boehme and the genealogical project as a whole. That is, obscurity itself may be a literary mark of Gnosticism, which together with other literary marks, and in concert with definite content commitments, may indicate the effective presence of a presumptively dead discourse and thus a *haunting* of a Christian discourse by another discourse, or better, the haunting of a Christian discourse by its *other*.

A second, and plausibly more genuine difficulty, revolves around the essentially mixed or impure nature of Boehme's discourse, which is at once theological and philosophical, biblical and speculative. A typical complaint lodged against the discourse of Boehme is that it fails to keep the discourses of theology and philosophy apart. While a philosophical exigence has to be granted to texts in which questions such as, Why is there something rather than nothing? and Whence evil? figure prominently, these questions are couched in a theological language that owes much to the medieval mystical traditions and intramural developments within Lutheranism that have become unfamiliar.[24] The hermeneutic concern here is practical. Given the general separation of philosophy from theology in the modern period, even the most general knowledge of the history of theology is beyond the reach of most philosophers, not to mention relatively specialized knowledge. If the objection against Boehme's discourse here is contingent, it is nonetheless assertive: the theological envelope detracts from the philosophical content precisely because its unfamiliarity distracts.

Heidegger, however, offers a stronger and more theoretical objection to the mixed discourse of Boehme, despite his well-known penchant for the 'religious' dimension of human existence. In his powerful (re)reading of Schelling's *Essay on Human Freedom*,[25] Boehme is dismissed as a real influence on Schelling precisely because of the presence of the theological element in his thought and discourse, which, according to Heidegger, makes authentic philosophy impossible.[26] If Schelling is an authentic philosopher who asks the primordial question of being, it follows axiomatically that he is uninfluenced by any view that holds that the being of beings and the highest being are one and the same. Stated otherwise, Schelling escapes the sin of ontotheology, superbly instanced in the discourse of Boehme, where the being of beings (*Wesen des Wesens*) is identified with the ground of being.[27] This ground of being is further identified by the one who is revealed in and by the biblical text.

What is troublesome about this reading, which theoretically commits itself to the theologically sanitized view of philosophy, is not that Boehme is dismissed as a nonphilosopher, and thus is held out of the sacred modern line that runs from Descartes, through Kant and Hegel to Nietzsche. Philosophers fairly typically engage in such exclusions. Conceptual analysts, for example, routinely dismiss the whole continental tradition as being nonphilosophical or as being prephilosophical. Phenomenologists regularly object to traditional metaphysics as being unrigorous and unscientific. And metaphysicians often refuse to include rhetorical and "loose" thinkers like Kierkegaard and Nietzsche, and latterly Derrida, in their philosophy club. What is objectionable about the stronger and more theoretical objection to the impure character of discourse is the binary opposition between philosophy and theology that functions to stipulate what a discourse should be rather than record what a discourse is. Most commentators and critics of Schelling would agree that not only is his discourse ontotheological in a fairly formal sense, but that it is ontotheological in a much more material sense in that it is theologically aspirated with Christian symbols, with Christ figuring very prominently.[28]

The consensus on the mixed nature of Schelling's discourse, which suggests that there may be other such instances, is important genealogically. It is the condition of the possibility for claiming that Boehme in particular is a major influence in the thought of Schelling after his early transcendental and identity-philosophy phases. The concession that Schelling's discourse is impure, that it is not simply philosophical but also theological, obviously has broad ramifications. It suggests that other nineteenth-century discourses, for example, the discourse of Hegel, might be similarly impure and similarly affected by the mixed discourse of Boehme's speculative form of Christianity. Certainly, for a Gnostic return thesis, which features Boehme, to have real significance, a trajectory from Boehme to speculative philosophers such as Schelling and Hegel, who are both interested in the viability of Christianity and its reinterpretation, should remain thinkable, essentially because of, not despite, the mixed nature of Boehme's discourse.

The insistence on discursive purity, which is the other side of the contamination thesis, obviously, can have other kinds of application. Not only the visionary aspect of Boehme's discourse, but also its extratheological metaphysical aspect may encourage dismissing it from the history of theology. Indeed, this is precisely what has happened not only in the narratives of thought constructed by theologians who identify with the mainline traditions, but also in interpreters sympathetic to him who judge him to be outside the mainline theological tradition as this tradition has come to be defined by insiders. But dismissed from both the history of philosophy and theology, Boehme's discourse then becomes confined within the history of esoteric thought, and the history of the effects of his discourse is similarly confined.

At one level there is nothing wrong with the explanation of Boehme's discourse being part of an esoteric tradition of discourse. It is clear that Boehme calls upon relatively marginal religio-philosophical traditions such as alchemy and the Kabbalah, and it is equally clear that Boehme's discourse has real effects in mystical and philosophical circles from the seventeenth century onward. Antoine Faivre, Desiree Hirst, Nils Thune, and Francis Yates among others have traced this influence.[29] Pushed too strongly, however, the esoteric taxonomy of Boehme's discourse, and his role in the genealogy of such a tradition in the modern period, may prove a straitjacket. For it would concede beforehand the marginal character of Boehme's discourse, as it points to the tradition of discourse defined as just the opposite of the mainline traditions of discourse in the modern period. But this is not to see what Hegel, and what Baur after him saw, in the discourse of Boehme—namely, that it is nothing less than a revolution in discourse different than, but of the same order as, the revolution in discourse enacted in Descartes and Bacon. And it is not to see that Boehme's discourse is not simply other than mainline discourses, but also their other, what affects them, infects them, and by so doing effects them. Without denying the real and important effects of Boehme's discourse on a whole host of nonmainline thinkers, I want to suggest that Boehme's discourse has effects in mainline theological discourses such as those of Moltmann, as well as philosophical discourses such as those of Hegel and Schelling. And I also want to suggest that Boehme's discourse further disseminates itself in literary discourses as important as Romanticism, thereby once again pointing to the impurity of this originary discourse—which thus may have literary and aesthetic as well as philosophical elements—by appeal to its presence in quite different discourses,

A third difficulty is constituted by the sheer eclecticism of Boehme's symbols. To biblical and mystical symbols Boehme adds the symbolism of alchemy, apocalyptic, Kabbalah, and indeed, just about any esoteric symbolism available at the beginning of the seventeenth century. Without some knowledge of alchemical speculation of sixteenth-century Germany, the following passage from *Sex Puncta Theosophica* (SPT) cannot be properly elucidated, even if the obscurity of the language has not prevented some comprehension of the general drift of sense.

> The principle of fire is the root, and it grows in its root. It has in its proprium sour, bitter, fierceness and anguish. And these grow in its proprium in poison and death into the anguished stern life, which in itself gives darkness, owing to the drawing in of the harshness. Its properties make sulphur, mercury, and salt; though the fire's property makes not Sul in sulphur, but the will of freedom makes Sul in sulphur, while the principle goes forward. But what advances into its properties is only Phur, viz. sternness, with the other forms in the center. This is the chief cause of life and of the being of beings. Although it is bad in itself, yet it is the most useful of all to life and the manifestation of life. (1.42–43)[30]

Understanding Boehme, then, means among other things understanding alchemical as well as other symbolisms in their own right, the way in which they elaborate and subvert Reformation Christianity, and how they play in Boehme's texts. Hacking one's way through symbolic forests and wading through mythological swamps is not every scholar's idea of interpretive amusement. They are, however, absolutely necessary in the case of Boehme. Even in hermeneutical situations in which Enlightenment critique has been replaced by a critique of the Enlightenment, there tends to be a demand for a less foliating symbolism and a more manageable mythic terrain. On both counts Boehme fails to oblige. Finally, a discourse as symbolically heterogenous as Boehme's is not only difficult to track down, but its value is also inherently questionable on the grounds that symbolic density and heterogeneity somehow reflect a failure of discursive integrity and coherence.

The eclecticism objection relates to the first in that it concerns the difficulty of Boehme's discourse. Yet it differs from it in bearing on the complexity rather than the obscurity or opacity of Boehme's discourse. Against an interpretive default line that privileges univocal determination of a discourse as well as clarity, it is obvious that Boehme's eclecticism functions to discourage any genealogy, not excluding a Gnostic genealogy. For if discursive complexity makes it difficult to determine in any precise fashion whether and in what way Boehme's discourse is integral and coherent, it becomes all the more difficult to plot a trajectory that has Boehme's discourse as a point of departure.

But again as with the opacity objection, it is possible not only to resist the presupposition that symbolic density and heterogeneity is privative, but also to embrace them as a taxonomic, and even more importantly, as genealogical opportunities. For the heterogeneity of symbols, and the heterogeneous narratives these symbols subserve, may itself be something of a tip-off regarding the Gnostic character of Boehme's discourse, and one marker among others of the Gnostic character of post-Enlightenment discourses that can be plotted in a discursive line that begins with Boehme. As suggested in *Gnostic Return in Modernity*, literary features such as obscurity, impurity, and symbolic density and heterogeneity are anything but extraneous to a definition of Gnostic. With Irenaeus as a guide, the text proposes that at least in concert with a content criterion that centers on narrative, such literary features perform a vital taxonomic and even genealogical service,

The fourth and final difficulty that I will briefly comment on is the individualist interpretation of Boehme. Rightly assuming that no discourse that has genuine claims to intellectual attention is simply the sum of previous discourses, the individualist interpretation goes further in focusing on the eccentric aspects of the character of the author and the experiential occasions that are taken to be the ground for explaining discourses and texts. Boehme seems to provide an especially good opportunity to showcase and even legitimate this methodology. Interpreting Boehme then can take the form of focusing on the visionary experiences Boehme had in 1600 and 1611 respectively, and determining that his speculative discourse is without remainder an exegesis of these discrete theophanic events. I will have more to say about the hermeneutic adequacy of this style of interpretation in Part I, but the way in which it undermines genealogical exploration should be noted at the outset.

The resolving of Boehme's discourse into states of mind or experience, takes away the kind of public access enjoyed, when discourse, no matter how obscure and complex, remains the object of interpretation. For by the nature of the case, this experience is both private and contingent, even if the interpreter is dependent on the communication of discourse to reach such judgment. But this means that the problem of a Boehme taxonomy is effectively dissolved, for discourse is only as important as the occasion that incites it. And with the dissolution of taxonomy goes the dissolution of genealogy, for the reduction to experience provides insufficient motive to follow lines of discourse as such. Correspondences between discourses may come in for discussion, but if they do, they do so because of some suspected similarity in the occasions for discourse and the existential conditions. Thus there is the anomaly that discourses from different historical periods and from different cultures and religious traditions evidence correspondences in excess of discourses from within the same cultural and religious tradition. The basic wrongheadedness of this procedure has been exposed in recent years by William Christian, Paul Griffiths, George Lindbeck, and Joseph DiNoia among others.[31] The flaws in this hermeneutic suggest that at least one is on safer ground reflecting on the properties of Boehme's discourse with a view to an adequate taxonomy. And, of course, what is good for an adequate taxonomy is necessarily good for an adequate genealogy.

Pointing back in interpretation to state of mind and experiential occasion functions then as the avoidance of discourse, just as the obscurity, impure nature of discourse, and symbolic density and heterogeneity of Boehme's discourse, gives rise to interpretation rather than providing reasons to shut down its operation. Correcting both for the avoidance of discourse and unrealistic expectations in interpretation, there is a sense in which Boehme becomes more rather than less fascinating, for the challenges presented by his discourse to modernity, but more importantly Christianity become more evident.

The challenges presented to a claim of Gnostic return, from the side of method, are equally pressing and equally central to my enterprise of taxonomically identifying Boehme's discourse with a view to arguing that it inaugurates a particular line of discourse that justifies the ascription of Gnostic return. Simplifying and abbreviating a very complicated discussion prosecuted at length in *Gnostic Return in Modernity*, four challenges seem especially urgent. First, there is the problem of whether any discourse in modernity, or on its threshold, could repeat an ancient discourse—a possibility, for example, Baur simply assumes in *Die christliche Gnosis*. Second, there is the problem of rival genealogical claims, with Boehme being regarded throughout the literature of commentary and criticism as a transit site and a point of origin for apocalyptic, Neoplatonic, and Kabbalistic thought as well as Gnostic or Valentinian thought. Third, there are flaws in the way Baur and his successors, who serve as prototypes for the genealogical investigation that begins here, conjugate Gnosis or Gnosticism. Fourth, emendations of Baur, particularly those that come from the direction of Eric Voegelin or his followers, are less rather than more likely to sustain a strong claim of Gnostic return in modernity that is ushered in by Boehme. I will elucidate each of these difficulties in turn.

a) In *Gnostic Return in Modernity*, I spend a great deal of time exploring the challenge posed by Hans Blumenberg for a Baurian view of Gnostic return.[32] As I point out in that text, what makes Blumenberg an extraordinarily interesting interlocutor is that he thinks that mythological discourse at least striates the modern discursive landscape in which critical reason is in the ascendancy,[33] that he views Boehme's mythic agonistic discourse as both interesting in itself and from the point of view of its history of effects,[34] and that he even flirts with a Gnostic return thesis of his own.[35] But ultimately he does not integrate these "talking points." The Gnostic return proposal is not serious in the sense that it has nothing to do with the continuity of patterns of thought that could be identified with the mythic discourses of the first centuries of the common era. Finally, of course, he rules out all notions of discursive repetition, all possibility of a discourse being *haunted* by an earlier discourse. The discourses of the past are as irrecoverable as the past itself. Medieval discourses function essentially as a wall dividing and protecting modern discourses from contamination by ancient discourses, this protection in turn being a condition of the autonomy and thus legitimacy of modern discourses, narrative or otherwise. Although Blumenberg's general historiographic principles suffice to rule out Gnostic return, in a supporting move, Blumenberg reinforces the exclusion of the possibility of Gnostic return by contrasting what he finds in Gnosticism with the dramatic process ontotheological discourse he finds in Boehme, and following him in Hegel and Schelling.[36] This contrast between the discourses from different historical periods makes it even harder to question Blumenberg's axiom of discontinuity.

Yet, if Blumenberg is a solvent, he is at the same time indispensable to the formulation of a viable Gnostic return model. He is so because he reminds us that discontinuity cannot be soft-pedaled in renditions of Gnostic return, and that remythologization is an indelible part of the landscape of modern discourse characterized generally, and perhaps fundamentally, by critical rationality. Nevertheless, Blumenberg has been rightly criticized on three counts. One, he is incomplete: one is often not sure to which side of the hiatus between the premodern and the modern, various thinkers, including Boehme, are assigned. Two, he is inconsistent: from time to time in his corpus, especially in *Work on Myth*, he avows more than functional continuity between premodern and modern discourse. Three, he is apriorist and reductive: discourses are held to verify simultaneously his historicist view that they simply replace other discourses[37] (or in his language, "reoccupy" them) and his opponents' view that modern discourses show signs of being transformations of premodern religious discourses, from which they gain their authority. Thus, Blumenberg can claim only a partial victory over the theorists of secularization, especially those who emphasize the secularization of eschatology.[38] He chastens theoretical ambitions in genealogical construction. Still, I take this critical function to be essentially positive in any attempt to resurrect a view of Gnostic return, whether this view includes or excludes Boehme as an essential part of the plot.

b) Not only are there challenges in principle to *any* genealogy of prominent modern discourses, especially of prominent narrative ontotheological discourses in modernity where Boehme is regarded as originary, but there are also factual genealogical challenges. That is, other genealogies are offered that feature Boehme as a *terminus a quo*. Boehme has been charted as a transit and originary point for Neoplatonism, Kabbalah, and most influentially, apocalyptic. These genealogies too have to be taken seriously.

As an inheritor of late medieval German mysticism, Boehme simply cannot avoid Neoplatonism, which is Christian mysticism's *lingua franca*. Indeed, the very same nineteenth-century figures who propose Gnostic return in Boehme—that is, Baur and Staudenmaier[39]—also suggest "Neoplatonic return," and point to the Neoplatonic figuration of the Boehme-influenced Hegel as major evidential support. At the same time, it is documented that Boehme interacts with thinkers familiar with the Kabbalah, so that patent Kabbalistic recalls pervade his texts. We find relatively persuasive arguments in the secondary literature to the effect that Boehme commences a new line of Christian Kabbalah that makes its way into Romanticism and Idealism.[40] In short, we cannot dismiss a Kabbalistic genealogy. And then there are apocalyptic genealogies that come in essentially two forms. The first is offered by Henri de Lubac. He understands Boehme to reprise essential elements of the symbolism and thought of Joachim of Fiore, and as such comes to serve as a foundation for the apocalyptic discourses of Romanticism, Idealism, and beyond.[41] The second is suggested by Thomas Altizer. He proposes that Boehme uncovers the ancient apocalyptic dispensation of Christianity, while unfolding a specifically modern form of apocalypse that thinks of the divine as manifestation, and manifestation as erotic, kenotic, and agonistic.[42] Boehme's texts do show sufficient recall of Joachim-style apocalyptic and the narrative features mentioned by Altizer that neither of these apocalyptic genealogies can be ruled out of court. Of course, we must allow that noncanonic and canonic texts of biblical apocalyptic are powerfully present in the discourse of Boehme, supplying his discourse with its visionary apparatus and not a little of its content.

Sustaining a thesis of Gnostic return will necessarily, therefore, involve showing how the Gnostic return hypothesis accounts for features not accounted for by any of these other three genealogical models. More importantly, the explanatory power of the Gnostic return model is demonstrated if it can account for the very presence of Neoplatonic, Kabbalistic, and apocalyptic strands of narrative discourse in Boehme's texts, each of which could plausibly define it. Such a demonstration is one of the key aims of my text.

c) The third major genealogical difficulty is presented by Baur's own prosecution of the case of Gnostic return in *Die christliche Gnosis*. One grants to Baur the nontrivial nature of his thesis or hypothesis of Gnostic return through Boehme, and celebrates how it distinguishes itself from the historicist position that in principle no discourse from the past returns, and from a position that holds the matter of fact judgment that a Gnostic form of discourse does not return in modernity, and certainly not through Boehme. Because the discourses of Gnosis are as disparate in the Hellenistic world as Hermeticism, Marcionism, Neoplatonism, and Valentinianism, *Gnosis* functions indeterminately in Baur from a categorial point of view. Baur's own asseveration lacks the force of an assertion of Gnostic return that focuses on the texts of Nag Hammadi and the heresiological sources, for historical and textual anchoring definitely aids taxonomic determinacy. *Gnostic Return in Modernity* corrected Baur by specifying Gnostic as Valentinian, and specifying Valentinian primarily by means of those texts of Nag Hammadi identified by scholars of Gnosticism as belonging to the Valentinian school. Thus, Valentinianism is distinguished not only from non-Gnostic discourses such as Marcionism, Hermeticism, and Neoplatonism, but also from other forms of Gnostic thought.

In Baur's analysis the indeterminacy of the categorial function of Gnosticism and Gnostic is linked to another systemic weakness. In line with Hegel,[43] Baur thinks that the link between ancient Gnosis and pneumatic forms of modern religious thought is narrative—indeed, encompassing narrative of an ontotheological kind, in which the properties of struggle and development stand out. This is a valuable insight, and one I embrace in *Gnostic Return in Modernity* as potentially providing a publicly verifiable criterion for diagnosing the presence of Gnosticism in modern discourses. Unfortunately in his magisterial text Baur compromises this insight by often deploying a much broader criterion of pneumatic religion that includes nonnarrative as well as narrative species of ancient and modern thought under the rubric of Gnosticism.[44]

But it is not only that Baur cannot decide between a broader and narrower criterion of inclusion-exclusion, his articulation of the narrower and more determinate narrative criterion is also not without flaw. The basic problem is that he implies that Gnostic narrative is invariant in both the ancient and modern contexts, and thus obviously invariant across history, although history itself is interrupted, with Catholicism itself being an interregnum between two periods of Gnosis. His predilection for an *Urnarrative* encourages Baur to go in precisely the opposite direction from Blumenberg, who on the basis of an apriori commitment to discontinuity determines that the dynamic and developmental modern narratives of Boehme, as well as German Idealism, are just the opposite of the static narrative ontotheology of classical Valentinianism.

Specifically, Baur suggests that as the Boehmian narrative and the modern narratives, which have their origin in Boehme, are dynamic and developmental, so also are the heterogeneous band of narratives in the Hellenistic field that he subsumes under the category of Gnosis. But this is (1) to propose an absolute form of continuity that seems thoroughly unbelievable and to grant nothing to the specific contexts of ancient narratives and narrative ontotheologies in both the post-Reformation and post-Enlightenment periods, and (2) to pay almost no attention to the difficulty of sustaining a dynamic reading of ancient narrative ontotheologies, and especially those that are Valentinian. As I argue in the *Gnostic Return in Modernity*, one can sustain a dynamic, developmental, and even agonistic reading of classical Valentinianism, but only by reading its texts against their surface implications. But as Hans Jonas and Hans Urs von Balthasar have suggested,[45] and my own analysis in *Gnostic Return in Modernity* (Chapter 3) of the third-century Valentinian text the *Tripartite Tractate* has demonstrated, such a reading is possible. Modern Valentinian narratives are different, then, precisely because there is nothing inchoate about their dynamic, developmental, and agonistic commitments. These narrative features, which are real but quite recessed in classical Valentinian paradigms, are dominant features in the modern narrative ontotheologies, that represent Gnostic return, beginning with Boehme.

d) The fourth obstacle to a Baurian genealogy in which Boehme is a privileged site of Gnostic return is presented by scholars as different as Harold Bloom, the early Hans Jonas, Carl Gustav Jung, and Eric Voegelin, all of whom, in different ways, prosecute a version of Gnostic return thesis. In *Gnostic Return in Modernity*, I comment both on what is different as well as common between these modes of analysis that broadly speaking are existential-psychological in character. I pay particular attention to the Voegelinian version, not because this version necessarily enjoys more currency, but because it is from within the ranks of those whose intellectual debts are primarily to Voegelin rather than from within the ranks of those whose heritage is that of Bloom, Jung, or even the early Jonas that a Gnostic genealogy of discourses has emerged that centrally features Jacob Boehme. The most important example for my present purposes is David Walsh. In his fine book on Boehme, *The Mysticism of Innerworldly Fulfillment: A Study of Jacob Boehme*,[46] one notices a slide from a narrative criterion by which to assess whether Boehme does or does not represent a crucial moment of Gnostic return to an existential set of criteria in which Boehme's discourse is plumbed for signs of epistemic hubris and ego inflation. The effect of this shift is that Gnostic then becomes an ascription that Boehme effectively shares with just about every other esoteric discourse in modernity, and especially with apocalyptic and millenarian forms of thought, but also with premodern esoteric forms of thought that are quite heterogeneous.

The slide into an existential-psychological mode of analysis is problematic on both formal and material grounds. On the formal front the two main issues are the lack of verifiability of the supposedly Gnostic existential state, on the one hand, and a mode of argument that seems basically to be circular, on the other. How do we know, and if we do know, how can we be sure that we know that a Gnostic existential state is revealed in and through a discourse or particular set of discourses? And how can we guarantee against circularity if the verdict of Gnostic pneumapathological state is never seriously put into question? On the material front the slide into the existential-psychological mode of analysis, no less than in the case of Jung and the early Jonas, leads to a dehistoricization that is at odds with the express Voegelinian principle that history is the constitutive medium of and for human beings. Human beings symbolize their wonder and desire in historically specific ways, which if not incommensurate, nevertheless, are different. To be fair to Walsh, however, in some significant respects he proceeds on the basis of the historical principle, for he does not argue that Boehme repeats in any exact way the basic tenets of classical Gnosticism. Moreover, in his prognostications about the effect of Boehme's thought in modernity, and especially the effect of Boehme's thought on Hegel, Walsh invokes a discursive and narrative (and thus more public) criterion than sometimes he allows himself.

Now while Walsh methodologically may be at odds with himself, the narrative discursive side of his interpretation of Boehme represents a real opening. His fine description of the dynamic, agonistic narrative of divine becoming that Boehme shares with Hegel highlights the need to ask the question of the relation-difference between Boehme's form of narrative ontotheology and that illustrated in the texts of classical Gnosticism. Specifically, it points to the question of whether both can be included under the common category of Gnostic. Walsh vacillates, sometimes answers yes, sometimes no. Ultimately, however, this vacillation itself is productive, for it points to the need for a theory that accounts for both what is continuous and discontinuous between classical Gnostic thought and those discourses such as Boehme's and Hegel's that are candidates for Gnostic ascription.

Serious as the above four difficulties are with respect to a view of Gnostic return that starts at least with Baur's formulation and accepts his view of the pivotal role of Boehme, they do not make it impossible. The reconstructed Baurian model I propose in *Gnostic Return in Modernity* gives determinacy to Gnosticism by insisting that Gnosticism and especially Valentinianism be allowed to define itself primarily through the texts of Nag Hammadi in a threefold manner of objectivity, credibility, and plausibility: (1) objectivity by proposing narrative structure as the basic criterion for labeling a discourse Gnostic, (2) credibility by proposing a narrative grammar as opposed to *Urnarrative* understanding of what is key in Valentinian speculative discourse, and (3) plausibility by acknowledging that the classical Valentinian paradigms such as *Ptolemy's System*, the *Gospel of Truth*, and the *Tripartite Tractate* do not show in any obvious way the dynamic, developmental narrative impulse of Boehme's speculative texts nor those of Romanticism and German Idealism that the interpreter takes seriously as candidates for Gnostic ascription. It is just as important to show how Boehme's discourse, and narrative ontotheologies in his line, are discontinuous with the narrative discourses of ancient Gnosticism as to show that they are continuous. In addition, as I indicated earlier, *Gnostic Return in Modernity* removes Blumenberg's historicist roadblock by showing the possibility at least of substantive continuity, and argues for the distinctiveness of Gnosticism from Marcionism, Middle Platonism, Neoplatonism, Hermeticism, and the belated discourse of the Kabbalah. Without claiming that these non-Valentinian discourses do not return in modernity, I make the case specifically with respect to Valentinianism.

Beyond the presentation of conceptual needs that must be satisfied for any account of Gnostic return to be viable, it is necessary to give a brief account of the conceptual apparatus presented in detail in *Gnostic Return in Modernity*. The primary conceptual pair generated in the prolegomenon to a Gnostic genealogy, which begins in this text, is *Valentinian narrative grammar* and *rule-governed deformation of classical Valentinian genres*. *Valentinian narrative grammar* refers to the rules of formation of Valentinian narratives by contrast with the rules of formation of narrative for canonically oriented Christianity, for apocalyptic modalities of Christianity, and Marcionism, on the one hand, and for Middle Platonism, Neoplatonism, Hermeticism, and the Kabbalah, on the other. Generating such a grammar through an examination of classical Valentinian texts, which show extraordinary variety with respect to narrative episode and style, I suggest in *Gnostic Return in Modernity* that a significant band of discourses from Boehme to twentieth-century theologians such as Tillich, Moltmann, and Altizer operate in terms of this basic narrative grammar.

More specifically, Valentinian narrative grammar articulates a six-stage narrative that recounts the movement from a realm of divine perfection that is the proper place of the knower of the narrative, back to the realm of divine perfection through the detour of the catastrophe and alienation of fall from the divine that is the fall of the divine. The six stages, which are parsed differently from text to text, and communicated in quite different styles, are: (i) the realm of undisturbed divine perfection or pleroma; (ii) the introduction of fault into the realm of divine perfection, and fall of a part of the divine that generates the other of the divine and is responsible for the demiurge who is the proximate cause of the material universe; (iii) the creation of the physical world and the creation of material and psychic human being; (iv) the fall of spiritual human being who is irreducible to the physical and psychical conditions of existence; (v) the appearance of a savior figure, who comes from the pleroma and who is associated with Christ, whose purpose is to enlighten human beings and in no sense to atone for their violation of the law; (vi) an eschatological verdict that without denying the possibility of salvation to the psychics, privileges those who are enlightened by holding in reserve for them alone a realized eschatology.

The construct of *rule-governed deformation of classical Valentinian genres* is at once coordinate with and subordinate to the construct of *Valentinian narrative grammar*. With respect to narrative ontotheologies in the modern period that are candidates for Gnostic ascription, it suggests that in their dynamic, developmental, and agonistic tendencies, modern narrative ontotheologies move beyond the classical paradigms, but they do so in ways allowed by Valentinian narrative grammar. Specifically, I argue that in select postreformation and postenlightenment narrative ontotheologies erotic, kenotic, and agonistic features recessed in classical Valentinian genres become dominant. As Hegel provides *the* example of this phenomenon in the post-Enlightenment situation, Boehme provides *the* example in the postreformation situation. Relatedly, I argue that the very symbolic oppositions of light and darkness, death and life, and so forth, that move the Valentinian story along in the classical texts function quite differently in the narrative ontotheologies of the modern period. Whereas in the classical texts of Valentinianism these symbolic oppositions occlude the erotic, kenotic, and agonistic dimensions of Valentinianism's narrative commitment, in the narrative ontotheologies of the modern period they come to support and reveal precisely such narrative dimensions, or perhaps better narrativity dimensions.[47]

A third important construct is that of *metalepsis*. This construct is inspired in part by the literary theory of Harold Bloom,[48] but ultimately represents a translation of a hermeneutic trope named by Irenaeus who found this phenomenon to mark classical Valentinianism.[49] It denotes the phenomenon of a complex disfiguration-refiguration of biblical narrative, or any first-order interpretation of it. On the basis of this phenomenon being an ineluctable feature of classical Valentinian narratives, *Gnostic Return in Modernity* suggests hypothetically that it is operative in Boehme's and later narrative ontotheological discourses to the extent to which they replicate distinctive features of Boehme's discourse.

At the same time, metalepsis fills a lacuna in Baur's treatment, where the transformation of biblical narrative—what I somewhat hyperbolically call "narrative derangement"—so central to Irenaeus, is not made thematic, and this despite the fact that Baur champions the very difference of Boehme's and later Hegel's narrative articulation from pre-Reformation and post-Reformation orthodoxies. The systematic operation of metalepsis in Boehme and later narrative ontotheologies in modernity is crucial for understanding Gnostic return. For it seems idle to affirm that Valentinianism is defined by a narrative grammar if no notice is paid to the fact that everywhere this grammar is a grammar of derangement, or less provocatively, a grammar of transformation.

Recalling Irenaeus, however, serves to do much more than indicate intellectual honesty by confessing one's intellectual debts. While it is true that in one mood Irenaeus himself suggests something like a grammar of Valentinianism,[50] arguably, the clearest contribution that he makes with respect to the identification of Valentinianism is his insight that Valentinian texts represent a disfiguration-refiguration of biblical narrative. The Irenaean pedigree of the construct means that metalepsis functions at once analytically and evaluatively. It judges as well as describes. This means that as I side with Irenaeus's salvation history narrative over classical Valentinianism's narrative bravura. I side also with the narrative renditions of the mainline Christian traditions, and especially the mainline Protestant narrative traditions, over the pansophistic narrative of Boehme, and other narrative ontotheologies in the post-Reformation and post-Enlightenment periods that share its dynamic, developmental, and agonistic propensities.

In underscoring the importance of metalepsis, it is not going too far to say that Boehme's discourse is an instance of Valentinian narrative grammar only to the extent to which it displays the operation of metalepsis. Similarly, Boehme's discourse is an instance of rule-governed deformation of classical Valentinian genres only to the extent to which metalepsis is in operation. Metalepsis, then, even if it is not quite on the same level as the primary conceptual pair, both supports and helps specify their content. If Boehme is an originary site of Gnostic return he represents a paradigmatic case of the operation of metalepsis, whose operation in the modern context will lead to an erotic, kenotic, and agonistic anamorphosis of biblical narrative that is only gestured to in classical Valentinian narratives. Illustrating the systematic operation of metalepsis in Boehme's texts is one of the main burdens of the present work, and will occupy me particularly in Part II of the present work. Importantly, however, being a paradigmatic case of metalepsis does not necessarily mean that Boehme is an unsurpassable case. Later narrative ontotheologies in the Boehme tradition such as those of Blake, Hegel, and Altizer, for example, may turn out to have even greater metaleptic potency. On both logical as well as historical grounds a paradigmatic display of metalepsis is not inconsistent with biblical and orthodox residuals. But again this needs to be shown, and is in fact shown in Part II.

Metalepsis brings the theme of *haunting* into view in an especially acute way. In general, *haunting* signifies that an absence becomes a presence. That is to say, an absent discourse (such as Valentinianism) presumed dead (and thus an absence) becomes a presence. This presence, then, is both a surd and a challenge to scientific and philosophical discourses and both rational and orthodox forms of Christianity. Yet Valentinian haunting is not just any haunting; it has quite particular features. For even in its original state as a parasitic discourse, Valentinianism haunts modernity only to the extent to which it is attached to its host, a version of biblical narrative that sometimes also serves to disguise its presence. The second sense of haunting touches on a repetition that is a repetition of possession, that in the modern period demands the equivalent of the analytic and evaluative exorcism carried out by Irenaeus in *Against Heresies*.

Before I turn to give a brief description of the fourth and final construct, which together with the previous three form the conceptual core of the Gnostic return model, I should say a word concerning a feature of metalepsis about which I have remained silent until now. While it is true that the logic of Irenaeus's position implies that metalepsis is best interpreted as the disfiguration-refiguration of biblical narrative, at the most explicit level metalepsis refers to a picture or mosaic that is antithetical to the biblical depiction of the divine and its relations both to cosmos and to human beings and their history.[51] Thus, metalepsis functions poetically to point to an aesthetic that bears a contrastive relation to the aesthetic of the common Christian tradition, as this is normed by the reading of Scripture. It will be one of the tasks of this work to demonstrate the presence of this peculiar Valentinian aesthetic that places so much emphasis on vision and the iconic features of discourse, despite paying lip service to mystery and exploiting the full resources of the language of negative theology. Of course, my interest is genealogical as well as taxonomic. Demonstration of the operation of this peculiar aesthetic or counteraesthetic aids a proper description of Boehme's apparently idiosyncratic narrative discourse, but it also brings into play a genealogical category that can be deployed not only in the analysis of the literary discourses of Romanticism, but also the philosophical discourses of Hegel and Schelling, and the theological discourses of Altizer and Moltmann. I will have more to say about the contrastive theological aesthetic of Valentinianism in general, and modern Valentinianism in particular, when I discuss *Gnostic apocalypse*, which provides an essential part of the title of the present work.[52]

It is time now to turn to the fourth concept of the Gnostic return model—that is, the concept of *Valentinian enlisting of non-Valentinian narrative* genres. I suggest in *Gnostic Return in Modernity* that as classical Valentinian narratives show a capability of enlisting, and thus regulating apocalyptic and Neoplatonic narrative discourses, a narrative discourse on the cusp of modernity with Valentinian credentials such as Boehme's shows no less capability. Indeed, a discourse such as Boehme's, and in consequence, discourses broadly in the line of Boehme, illustrate the phenomenon of enlisting at an even higher power, since not only are apocalyptic and Neoplatonism enlisted and mastered, but also the Kabbalah. In making this argument I am conscious of turning an apparent taxonomic and genealogical disadvantage into an advantage. For the fundamental grain of Boehme's discourse has been variously assessed in commentary and criticism as 'apocalyptic,' 'Neoplatonic,' and 'Kabbalistic,' and thus, explicitly or by implication, Boehme's discourse has become the focus of a genealogical proposal that rivals my own. But speaking of Valentinian enlisting of non-Valentinian narrative genres is far from being opportunistic. It is not simply a way of disarming or outmaneuvering the taxonomic and genealogical opposition. Rather, Valentinian enlisting of non-Valentinian narrative genres reflects the judgment that the ontotheological narratives of Boehme and his successors look more like cables of multiple narrative discourses than a single discourse. And it reflects the judgment that the naming of these narrative strands in commentary and criticism as 'apocalyptic,' 'Neoplatonic,' 'Kabbalistic,' and 'Valentinian' is broadly speaking, correct. What remains to be done, however, is (a) to assess whether the narrative cable possesses any integrity of its own, or whether it is only a composite of its strands, and (b) if it does possess integrity, to assess the order of subordination-superodination between narrative discourses. I judge in this text that Boehme's discourse does display real narrative integrity, and that in the narrative cable, Valentinianism is superordinate, indeed, regulative of the other narrative discourses.

I would like to say a particular word about the Valentinian enlisting of apocalyptic. At one level the enlisting of apocalyptic discourse by Valentinian discourse is, I am arguing, just one of the three modes of enlisting performed by the governing Valentinian discourse in complex narrative discourses such as Boehme's, and which I suggest are essentially concurrent. At another level, however, with respect to Boehme's post-Reformation discourse, the enlisting of apocalyptic by Valentinianism has to be accorded a certain privilege. The

necessary condition for the enlisting of biblical apocalyptic, what I refer to as
apocalyptic inscription, in *Gnostic Return in Modernity* (chapters 2, 4, and 5), is
obviously the strong presence of biblical apocalyptic in a symbolically and narratively complex discourse.

This is the case with the discourse of Boehme. There is significant recall
of biblical apocalyptic's visionary aesthetic propensity, its peculiar hermeneutic
in which symbols are interpreted by other symbols, and in which it is difficult
to translate symbol without remainder. Likewise, its narrative focuses on the
struggle in history and the eschaton, and the savior figure who is at the center
of the struggle and who represents the guarantee of a successful resolution. The
sufficient, as opposed to the necessary, condition of *apocalyptic inscription*, however, is that the aesthetic, hermeneutic, and above all the narrative features of
biblical apocalyptic are dominated and regulated by a discourse with a different
aesthetic, hermeneutic, and narrative bias. Crucial is the containment of biblical apocalyptic's salvation history narrative by a more encompassing narrative
whose subject is divine becoming. This narrative containment is captured in
part by the metaphor of *inscription*, in which one narrative is in a spatial sense
contained by the more encompassing narrative.

In its containment by another form of narrative discourse, which I dare to
suggest is Valentinian, biblical apocalyptic comes to contribute to aesthetic,
hermeneutic, and narrative positions to which it does not typically subscribe.
At the same time, biblical apocalyptic exercises reflexive effect, even if this effect is not equivalent to the force exercised by the enlisting Gnostic or Valentinian discourse. Thus, there will remain in Valentinian discourses, and
especially those in the modern period, a leaven of symbolic excess, indeterminacy in interpretation, and above all a salvation history moment within a Valentinian narrative. Thus, put technically, one can expect to see in Boehme's
'modern' discourse, even more than is the case in the classical paradigms of
Valentinianism, the operation of *apocalyptic distention*, which centrally includes
this horizontal narrative extension, even if it not defined by it.[53]

Given this talk about the incorporation of biblical apocalyptic into a complex narrative discourse that is other than itself, the following question naturally
suggests itself: Given that the enlisting and enlisted narrative discourses have
relatively determinate identities, does this imply the denial of apocalypse ascription to Boehme's possibly Valentinian discourses? The answer to this question is no, and has to be no, and not simply for the reason that all visionary
discourse can be granted this title based on the etymology of *apokalypsis* as revelation or vision. In *Gnostic Return in Modernity*, I show that classical Valentinianism represents an apocalypse form distinct from that of biblical
apocalyptic, even as elements of biblical apocalyptic can be found within the
apocalypse discourse of Valentinianism. I suggest that hypothetically such will
also be the case in modern narrative ontotheologies that are live candidates for

Gnostic ascription. Here I will be more categorical as well as more concrete. I will show that Boehme's discourse represents a distinct apocalypse genre, thus the presence of *Gnostic apocalypse* in the title of this work on the seventeenth-century German speculative mystic.

As I move toward bringing this introduction to a conclusion, I wish to issue two interpretive imperatives with respect to Boehme that have genealogical value and that bring me into conversation not only with David Walsh and the Voegelin school of interpretation, but also with the radically different kind of genealogy of Michel Foucault.[54] The first imperative is that Boehme be submitted to a theologically dense analysis in which speculation on the symbols of the Trinity, grace and free will, creation, the nature of Christ and redemption, and the eschaton are all in play. Any analysis that pretends even to be relatively adequate will involve not only treating the relations between Boehme's discourse and late medieval mystical theology, the illuminist side of the Reformation,[55] and biblical apocalyptic discourse in general, especially the forms it took in Western thought after Joachim of Fiore, but also the relation between Luther and Boehme, which after all was the issue of Boehme's own day,[56] and which has been commented on influentially in this century by Heinrich Bornkamm and others.[57] Not to be disingenuous, however, this relation can be read at best as tensional, even if Lutheranism is understood to be open to mysticism and speculative bands of thought. To achieve an adequate understanding of Boehme it is crucial to grasp the ways his discourse fundamentally contests Lutheran thought on such key topics as Trinity, Christ, creation, and grace. Even more, it is necessary to grasp how Boehme's inclusive narrative of divine becoming transforms in a radical way the biblical narrative that norms Luther's entire theology. Not attending to the relation between Boehme's discourse and that of Luther leads to a detheologization and decontextualization of his discourse. In consequence there is the inability to see Boehme as more than a representative of an esoteric discourse whose most famous twentieth-century representatives include Rudoph Steiner and Madame Blavatsky. In addition, seeing the importance of the relation between Luther and Boehme, while failing to see that the relation is tensional both at the level of individual themes but even more importantly on the level of narrative structure, means that the interpreter is deprived of a central criterion for assessing the presence of Gnosticism or Valentinianism in modern discourses, especially Protestant discourses in the modern period.

Thus far, I have kept alchemy somewhat in the background in my discussion. Yet without a doubt Paracelus (1493–1541) and the Paracelsian tradition represent vital determinants of Boehme's discourse. Most interpreters of Boehme agree on this. Walsh is no exception, although his treatment is synoptic by comparison with that of Weeks. But there are two different kinds of danger that either assist in initiating or furthering a nontheological interpretation of Boehme. The first, which I have already broached, is the danger of so emphasizing this relation that not only the originality of Boehme but also other more explicitly theological stands in his texts are given short shrift. And second, there is the issue of how Paracelsus and the Paracelsian tradition themselves are construed, whether as a pure brand of *Naturphilosophie* that requires theological domestication in Boehme's texts, or as an already theologically adapted modality of alchemical discourse. The *Naturphilosophie* reading makes for a cleaner story, for then Boehme's theological adaptation is regarded unequivocally as a success or a failure; if the former, his originality is unequivocally demonstrated; if the latter, he is equally unequivocally reducible to a *Naturphilosophie*. The more complicated story is how Boehme reprises and surpasses an already theologized alchemical discourse, makes it an essential component of the history of effects of his discourse, and suggests a way in which this kind of post-Reformation alchemical discourse with its high incidence of metalepsis becomes itself a candidate for Gnostic ascription.

The unhappy genealogical consequences of the second line of interpretation of the Paracelsus-Boehme relation are put into relief when one looks at Foucault's *The Order of Things*, whose archeology unearths Paracelsian alchemy as the epitome of the episteme or mode of knowing exemplified in premodern discourse that is the 'other' of modern rational-instrumental discourse. The logic exemplified by Paracelsian alchemy is analogical, its semantic is a semantic committed to obscurity, its truth a sense of wholeness or pansophia, and its value that of illumination. By contrast modern thought is logical and inductive, its semantic committed to disclosure, its truth that of determinate outcomes based upon hypothesis and testing, and its value ultimately defined by power over the world of goods.

As I will suggest momentarily, there are problems with the structuralist way in which the opposition between premodern and the modern regimes of knowing is set up by Foucault, but the relevant point here is that Foucault defines Paracelsian alchemy exclusively as a *Naturphilosophie*, and reads Boehme as absolutely determined by this discourse. The theological dimension is, therefore, doubly excised, once from Boehme, who is nothing but Paracelsian, and again from Paracelsus—and ironically on the basis of texts that, as a commentator such as Weeks has underscored, are concerned with major theological themes such as the Trinity, creation, and evil.[58]

The second and interdependent imperative is that Boehme be regarded as a name for a discursive event on the threshold of modernity and not simply as a proper name. My objection here is no longer about the reduction of an author's discourse to the author's mental state or the experiential occasions of a discourse. That objection has been stated already. Rather the imperative is directed against a reading of Boehme's discourse as totally novel, and it has genealogical as well as taxonomic motives. The concern is not simply that an exclusive emphasis on originality makes the interpreter look away from the history of reception of Boehme's discourse which, on Gadamerian grounds at least, ought to be taken to be an important element of the very definition of the discourse. Rather Boehme's discourse is more than the discourse of Jacob Boehme, indeed, nothing less than a discursive event to the degree to which (a) it represents an amplification and correction of philosophical alchemy, (b) it creatively adapts traditions of narrative discourse that themselves have histories, discourses such as apocalyptic and the Kabbalah, which circulate without being synthesized in philosophical alchemy, and (c) it shows how apocalyptic, Neoplatonism, and the Kabbalah can live together in a master discourse that displays Valentinian transgressive properties.

In a sense, then, my method is formally closer to Foucault than to Walsh, while being materially closer to the latter. It is closer formally, since it values discourse over personality, and sees the challenge of Boehme's discourse to the practical and instrumental discourses of modernity to be the function of the challenge of a broader pattern of discourse such as alchemy, which has Boehme and Paracelsus as exemplary instances. But the formal overlaps between Foucault's type of genealogy and that prosecuted here ultimately do not cut deep. There is much that divides the two enterprises. In this text I reject the binary opposition of mentalities deployed by Foucault to suggest the impossible possibility of the operation in modernity of a premodern form of discourse that represents the 'other' of modern rational instrumental discourse. The structuralist way in which the opposition is made evades history, and particularly, the responsibility of seeing that discourses such as those of Boehme and Paracelsus are not totally banished from the precincts of modernity, but have effective histories not only to the side of the discourses of modernity but to a significant extent within them, particularly in the thought of Romanticism and Idealism and beyond.

Denying Foucault's binary opposition necessarily involves denying his view of the haunting of modern discourse by its other. From Foucault's point of view, modern thought illustrates an extraordinarily successful repression of premodern mentality, and thus the premodern discourse it supports and in which it finds expression. In the modern world the life of the premodern is difficult to access. It exists in the main as the negative condition of the modern mentality that defeats and displaces it, although its symptoms sometimes appear in modern discourses, and its regime is accessed by special individuals who adopt a transgressive stance with respect to modernity. In contrast, in the genealogy that my analysis of Boehme serves, the haunting is thicker, more historically embodied, and more mainline than Foucault would lead us to believe. In an important sense, it is less 'ghostly,' but, arguably, more 'ghastly.'

The book has three parts, with a short conclusion that reflects on the genealogical consequences of the analysis of the discourse of Boehme. The general movement is from description to explanation, though even the relatively descriptive part one is not devoid of explanatory moments. Part I consists of two chapters. In chapter 1, I provide a synoptic account of Boehme's visionary discourse whose central content is a six-stage narrative of the agonistic divine self-development. Chapter 2 continues the narrative line of reflection opened up in chapter 1 by first showing how Boehme's visionary narrative discourse inhabits the most radical form of Christian negative theology—that is, negative theology of the kind represented by Meister Eckhart, only to narratively deconstruct it by placing all perfection in the pole of the manifest God rather than the immanifest Godhead. Chapter 2 also shows how Boehme's visionary discourse, in both its content as well as its pansophistic ambition, has its background in alchemy of a Paracelsian vintage. This particular kind of alchemy, I argue, is systemically theological, and provides something like a basic frame for Boehme's narrative articulation. Against Foucault I want to suggest that Boehme's ontotheological discourse realizes the basic tendency of Paracelsian alchemy, rather than a nontheological or atheological form of alchemy setting the terms for Boehme's discourse.

Part II moves to a different explanatory level by asking whether, in what way, and to what extent Boehme's visionary discourse departs from the common theological tradition. The distinction between those departures or 'swerves' from the standard pre-Reformation and Reformation traditions that Boehme's discourse shares with minority pre-Reformation and post-Reformation traditions, and those that are distinctive to his discourse, serves as the organizing principle of this part. In chapter 3, I discuss the swerves that Boehme's discourse shares with pre-Reformation minority traditions (mainly mystical theology) and post-Reformation traditions (the Spiritual Reformers). These swerves are extensive and bear on the understanding of the intra-trinitarian divine, creation, incarnation, and redemption, and the nature of the self. In chapter 4, I discuss the swerves from the standard pre-Reformation and Reformation traditions that are unique to Boehme's discourse. The swerves are many and serious. They include the understanding of the intradivine Trinity, the understanding of divine nature and attributes, and the relation between judgment and mercy in God. But undergirding all the individual swerves, I argue, is a global narrative swerve. Specifically, I will argue that Boehme's visionary discourse constitutes a metalepsis of the biblical narrative, in that its six-stage narrative of divine becoming disfigures every single episode of the biblical narrative, as interpreted in and by the standard pre-Reformation and Reformation theological traditions, and it refigures them by including their altered form in his own narrative. Since it is not part of my brief to exaggerate the metaleptic ratio of Boehme's discourse, in chapter 5 I examine the ways in which Boehme's discourse still displays some orthodox reserves. Acknowledging and naming these reserves, however, does not imply, I argue, a withdrawal of a metaleptic characterization of Boehme's discourse.

While I believe that my analysis of Boehme in Parts I and II constitutes more than a repetition of what other commentators have written, Part III represents an original contribution to scholarship, since it bears the burden of explicitly arguing the taxonomic case. Calling on the conceptual framework generated in *Gnostic Return in Modernity*, I bring into play, in addition to metalepsis that is featured in Part II, the three other major concepts that pertain to Valentinian return in the modern period—that is, *Valentinian narrative grammar, rule-governed deformation of classical Valentinian genres*, and *Valentinian enlisting of non-Valentinian narrative genres*. Essentially, Part III deals with two different questions. The first question is whether a plausible case can be made that Boehme's visionary or apocalypse discourse is a Valentinian discourse, especially when measured against classical Valentinian genres such as *Ptolemy's System*, the *Tripartite Tractate*, and the *Gospel of Truth*. I try this question in chapter 6 and argue that Boehme's visionary discourse can be so regarded, provided we regard it not as an instance of something like a Valentinian *Urnarrative*, but rather, an instance of Valentinian narrative grammar. I also argue that its deviations from the classical Valentinian paradigms are (a) not such as to break with Valentinian grammar, and (b) are hinted at in one or more of these paradigms. In short, I argue that Boehme's visionary narrative discourse represents a rule-governed deformation of classical Valentinian genres.

The second question that is engaged is whether the Valentinian taxonomy can show its superiority to other possibilities of characterization—for example, that Boehme's discourse is an example of apocalyptic, or Neoplatonism, or even the Kabbalah. The answer to this question is extended over three chapters (7-9), where I examine each of the three rival taxonomic candidates in turn. I demonstrate the superiority of the Valentinian characterization over each of the rivals. More, availing of the concept of Valentinian enlisting of non-Valentinian narrative genres, I argue that Valentinianism represents not a partial but a total characterization of Boehme's discourse, since it can account for each of the three other main narrative strands in Boehme's discourse.

PART I

≈

Visionary Pansophism and the Narrativity of the Divine

Although, ultimately, there may be no difference between William Blake's and W. B. Yeats's common assessment of Boehme as a visionary and Hegel's assessment of Boehme as protophilosopher,[1] especially given Boehme's tying of vision to interpretive capability and intellectual capacity, still it is probably best to commence with Boehme's status as a visionary. For the visionary quality of Boehme's work, which makes possible articulation of the divine milieu, seems at once to be more basic than the undoubtedly tenacious, if not obsessive, return to the question Heidegger regards as basic to philosophy—that is, Why is there something rather than nothing? and to make more sense of Boehme's multiple lines of influence, in poetry, theology, and pace Heidegger, in philosophy. One might even suggest that vision provides a kind of 'meta-aesthetic' that gets parsed differently in distinct discursive genres, performatively and persuasively in poetry, intentionally and reflectively self-legitimatingly in philosophically tempered discourses, and as the aim of heuristic holism in theology, which can offer partial but not full justification for that which integrates the thematic regions of theology and its tasks. Whether this 'meta-aesthetic' view is sustainable or not depends, obviously, in significant part on how the as yet untreated relations between Boehme and Blake, and Boehme and the German Idealists, Hegel and Schelling get articulated. More than groundwork, however, can be provided in a treatment of Boehme that registers his rich comprehensiveness.

Visionary ascription, however, brings with it its own set of difficulties. One difficulty is that visionary ascription may encourage the view that the two documented experiences of Boehme's being overwhelmed by a reality of superabundant significance (1600, 1612) helps somehow to explain the complex, indeed inclusive or pansophistic, scope of Boehme's elucidation of reality.[2] Obviously, Boehme's personal and essentially private experiences have no such explanatory capability. On the one hand, Boehme's actual experiences of illumination are too indeterminate to offer the slightest clue with regard to the depiction of the superdeterminate encompassing divine reality, rendered in his texts. On the other hand, what amounts to an experiential reductionism devalues not only the processes of interpretation within experience and subsequent to it, but also the centrality of the processes of interpretation of Scripture and nature that drive Boehmian texts—and also, of course, drive the traditions of such interpretation.

Required, then, is precisely what I take one of Boehme's ablest commentators, Andrew Weeks,[3] to call for—that is, a hermeneutical historical qualification of vision that accompanies a shift of focus to Boehme's texts themselves. Vision or visionary functions not so much as an answer to the question of fundamental identity of Boehme's thought, so much as a pragmatic counter that has problemata on both subjective and objective sides. On the subjective side, it is clear that Boehme thinks of vision as an unexpected "glimpse into the center" (*Zentralschau*). It is an effect of a pregiven capacity for a form of knowing (*Verstand*) that transcends conceptual knowledge (*Vernunft*).[4] At the same time, Boehme not only suggests the accompanying ministrations of spirit (*Aurora*, preface, # 22–25; *Mysterium Magnum* [*MM*], preface) but in typical Reformation fashion suggests that Spirit is constitutive. In one of his letters Boehme makes the following profession: "I can write of myself no otherwise than a child that knows and understands nothing, neither has learned anything save what God has chosen to know in him" (Epistle 22).

And on the objective side, while vision is encompassing or pansophistic in scope, it also seems fundamentally tied to argumentative reason, for fundamental questions seem to drive a vision, whose presentation represents the answer. Boehme's famous setting forth of his program in the preface to his great hexameron, *Mysterium Magnum* (# 11) provides an eloquent example:

> 1. We will signify and declare what the center and ground of all essences is. 2. What the divine manifestation (though the speaking of the Word of God) is. 3. How evil and good have their original from one only ground, viz. light and darkness; life and death; joy and sorrow; and how it is in its ground; also whereunto every essence and source is profitable and unavoidable. 4. How all things have their beginning? from the great mystery, viz. from the spiration of the eternal One. 5. How the eternal One introduces itself into sensation, perception and division; to the knowledge of itself; and to the play of the divine power. 6. How human being may attain to the true knowledge of God, and to the knowledge of the eternal and temporal nature. 7. Also how human being may come into the real contemplation of the Being of all beings. 8. Also of the creation of the world and of all creatures. 9. And of the origin, fall, and restoration of human being; what human being is according to the first Adamic man in the kingdom of nature; and what human being is in the new regeneration in the kingdom of grace, and how the new birth comes to pass. 10. Also what the Old and New Testaments, are, each in its understanding.[5]

This coincidence of explanation and pansophism, which Will-Eric Peuckert (among others) thinks to be an indelible characteristic of Boehme's thought and argument,[6] mark off Boehme not only historically but also systematically from much of pre-Reformation and Reformation Christianity in general and the mystical traditions in particular. It is not that Boehme fails to appropriate seriously determinate strands of pre-Reformation and Reformation theology— I will provide detailed evidence of such appropriation in the next chapter—nor that he is absolutely eccentric with respect to pre-Reformation and Reformation mystical traditions by dint of the fact that the modality of his mysticism is more nearly objective than subjective, or to avail of the contrast used by Scholem to help characterize the Kabbalah, more nearly 'extrospective' than 'introspective.'[7] The pansophism, associated with the presumptive ability, and experiential fact, of seeing into the deep things of God (1 Corinthians 2.10), to recall a Pauline trope that Boehme recurs to,[8] has explanatory power, for the central question, the one that covers Why is there something rather than nothing?[9] and Why evil?[10] is, Why manifestation? Answering this question takes the form of articulating a myth that centrally involves the narrative enactment of the divine, the story of how the divine becomes personal.[11]

Offering a synoptic account of this metanarrative is one of the central tasks of Part I. I will prosecute it in chapter 1. There I will also reflect briefly on Boehme's interconnecting of dynamic metanarrative and the Trinity, which surprises, superficially at least, what would be expected in a Blumenbergian scheme of things, where Trinity represses or repels narrative,[12] especially narrative in its most radical form of ontotheological narrativity.

As important as this pansophistic-etiological and ultimately narrative specification of Boehme's mysticism is, one runs up against the danger once again that Boehme is defined not only as different, but also as sui generis. But to go down this interpretive road is to misunderstand Boehme; worse, it is to go outside understanding itself, which proceeds to identification on the basis of the perception of differences highlighted and given pertinence by commonness. Boehme belongs to multiple post-Reformation discursive traditions; indeed, he could be regarded as their intersection. Certainly from the historical point of view, a pansophistically specified tradition of philosophical alchemy, especially in its Paracelsian trajectory, is crucial. I will join my voice to the concert of other voices of commentary in exploring this relation in chapter 2.[13] This tradition, which freely blends *Naturphilosophie* and Christian faith, is an inheritance that Boehme honors throughout his work, and to which he demonstrates fealty in *De Signatura Rerum* (*SR*) (1622). It, arguably, recalls even more eloquently than Paracelsus, and in a decidedly accentuated theological form, the universe of sympathy and correspondence invoked by Foucault as the other of the specifically modern mentality.[14] But Boehme recalls more than the simple fact of correspondence; he recalls the fundamental Paracelsian esprit, which is to provide an explanatory account of signature, by charting the drive in invisible and ultimately divine reality towards expression in a form of a metanarrative. To avoid, therefore, the dehistoricization that is the nub and rub of Blumenberg's complaint, in chapter 2 Boehme's visionary metanarrative will be plotted against the backdrop of the mature Paracelsus and the Paracelsian tradition within Protestant Christianity in the sixteenth century. Boehme will be seen to carry on this tradition, while bringing it to new levels of philosophical finesse, theological depth, and narrative radicality.

But dealing with Boehme as representing the *Aufhebung* of philosophical alchemy also has its risks. It may tend to deemphasize the complex, multilingual nature of Boehme's narrative and fail to specify criteria of narrative radicality. Towards obviating a historicization that is not historicizing enough, and towards deepening the very broad gestures with respect to narrative radicality, I will attempt to further contextualize Boehme in chapter 2 by showing how Boehme situates his discourse within the horizon of an Eckhartian-style negative theology only to subvert it by reversing the relative priorities of mystery and manifestation with respect to the divine, and placing negative values on the unity and nondifferentiation that support a view of the archeological givenness of divine perfection. For Boehme, God defines godself as a project, indeed, *the* project.

CHAPTER 1

~

Narrative Trajectory of the Self-Manifesting Divine

In Boehme's mature work, which belongs to the incredibly fertile final five years of his life (1619–1624), what is articulated by pneumatically informed reason (*Verstand*), is nothing more nor less than the dynamics of the self-manifesting or self-revealing divine. As will be the case with Hegel and Schelling later, not only is divine revelation the condition for the possibility of theological insight, but the divine is the process of revelation. There is nothing accidental about this process. Revelation or manifestation is essential, and describes the path the divine takes towards full self-appropriation.

Six stages can be distinguished in the narrative enactment of divine manifestation that bear on divine self-constitution: (1) The radically transcendent divine, both mysterious and undifferentiated, gives way to divine self-manifestation and differentiation in eternal Wisdom (*die ewige Weisheit*) and the 'Immanent Trinity.'[1] (2) A teleologically engendered divine fall into a sphere of being radically other than the divine at once interrupts manifestation and makes it really possible, by serving as the refracting background of a form of divine light ultimately more real because of the tension between the refusal of manifestation and manifestation. (3) The fall of the dramatically realized divine world or community, provoked by Lucifer, leads to the creation of the temporal world (as an expression of the eternal tension) and human being (as the image of God). (4) Human being destroys the divine image (Adamic fall), due to a repetition of Lucifer's abortive exercise of freedom. (5) Christ appears both as the Second Adam and as the paradigm of rebirth, resignation, and wholeness, appropriatable by a sinful but unvitiated humanity. (6) History as salvation history, stretching from creation to apocalypse, is a movement of return to origins, proximally to Eden, but ultimately to the paradisiacal state lost in the Lucifernian fall. Descriptions of each of these six stages will be brief, and analyses will be kept at a minimum.

A relatively underdetermined account of Boehme's narrative sets the table for the interpretation of Boehme that begins in section two of this chapter, continues in Part II of my analysis of the comprehensive and radical nature of Boehme's departure from mainline Christian discourses, and concludes in Part III. There I make a taxonomic decision regarding the genre of Boehme's narrative discourse. I begin with the first stage of Boehme's narrative, which is as much prologue to narrative adventure as narrative adventure itself. The complexities of this preliminary stage are such, however, that with the exception of the second stage, I will tarry longer with it than with any of the other stages.

1.1. Boehme's Six-Stage Narrative

(1) *(An)archeology: Unground: Wisdom: 'Immanent Trinity'*

When Boehme considers the divine infinite outside any actual relation to determination and finitude, the most comprehensive symbol of which is the *Unground*,[2] he betrays the press of the negative theology tradition on his thought. In keeping with this tradition, Boehme does not eschew altogether kataphatic vocabulary when speaking of the transcendent divine. The divine is the being of beings (*Wesen des Wesens*) (*MM* 1, 2; 1, 6), the one and simple (*MM* 1, 2; 1, 6; 29, 1; *De Electione Gratiae* [*EG*] 1, 3), the eternal good (*MM* 3, 2; *Clavis* #2; [De Incarnatione Verbi (*IV*) bk 2. 5, 34), root (*MM* 1, 8; 60, 38), and light (*IV* bk 2. 3, 4). In the final analysis, however, apophatic vocabulary is the more predominant and powerful. The transcendent divine is nameless (*ohne Namen*) (*MM* 1, 8; 60, 38), ungraspable (*unbegreiflich*), inexpressible (*unaussprechlich*), beyond nature (*ausser der Natur*) (*MM* 60, 38), not an essence (*MM* 1, 6), hiddenness (*Verborgenheit*), and beyond beginning (*unanfängliche*) (*MM* 1, 8). Boehme is even willing to support the most extreme apophatic cipher countenanced by the German mystical tradition—that is, nothing (*Nichts*). But the language of "nothing" only makes explicit what is implicit in the language of oneness and undifferentiation—that is, the nonrelationality and immanifestation of the divine: "When I consider what God is, then I say: He is himself but one; with reference to the creature an eternal nothing" (*MM* 1, 3; also *MM* 1, 2; 1, 8; 29, 1; *EG* 1, 2-3; *SPT* 1. 1, 2; 1. 1, 4; 1.1, 7; *De Signatura Rerum* [*SR*] 2, 8–9).[3]

Obviously, as is typical in the negative theology tradition when applied to God, "nothing" is not absolute nothing. This point is made in a startlingly perceptive analysis of Boehme by Dionysius Andreas Freher, an eighteenth-century London emigré.[4] It is provided a precise technical expression when Berdyaev argues that Boehme's "nothing" bears more relation to Plato's *me on* than Parmenides's *ouk on*.[5]

Yet Boehme sees the possibility, even necessity, of movement from the Unground toward a ground, the movement from mystery to manifestation that will introduce differentiation and multiplicity into the divine. All the texts of Boehme's mature periods devote crucial chapters to this movement. They sometimes speak of it as something that happens to the Unground, sometimes as the very act of the Unground itself. In addition, without judging the value of the movement from Unground to ground, there appear to be distinct overall ways of characterizing the movement. One important line of characterization is *aesthetic*. Specifically, the movement is from a divine infinite, conceived as formless, even chaotic, to a divine that has form and definite limits, a divine, which, availing it of the metaphorics of space, is bounded.

Boehme writes:

> For the vast infinite space desires narrowness and enclosure wherein it may manifest itself, otherwise in the wide stillness there would be no manifesta-tion; therefore there must be attracting or enclosing, out of which manifesta-tion appears. (*De Triplici Vita Hominis* (*The Threefold Life* [*TL*] 1, 33; also *MM* 17, 23)

Another crucially important line of characterization is that of vision, which on Boehmian first principles is not a possibility of a unitary and simple divine. The vision of the Unground is a nonvision, its eye an eye that does not see, for vision and seeing are possible only if there is distinction between seer and seen, or subject and object (*MM* 1, 7; *EG* 1, 6; 1.8; *SPT* 1. 1, 7–8). The aes-thetic and visionary characterizations are mutually reinforcing. An anaesthetic, monistic, and apophatic divine is essentially a cyclopean divine; nonvision is the kind of vision appropriate to the formlessness and indeterminacy of the divine nothing. Contrariwise, a determinate divine infinite is a self-reflective infinite, while visionary self-reflection supposes the multiplicity of representation that limits the divine and provides it with determinacy.

Differentiation (*Schiedlichkeit*)[6] is, therefore, the means by which the Un-ground moves toward determinateness that has ontological, axiological, and ex-istential, as well, of course, as gnoseological dimensions (*Theosophic Fragments* [*TF*] 3. 6, 7). Boehme accounts for more than one register of differentiation. As it turns out, more than one register is required for a divine that is aesthetic and visionary. Boehme distinguishes between a preliminary nonagonic form and a fully developed *agonic* form, for which he coins the term the *contrarium* (*MM* 3, 4; 4, 19; *SR* 2, 2; *Theosopia* [Divine Intuition (*DI*)] 1, 8–11, 1, 19ff).[7] This preliminary register of differentiation itself takes two forms, the first of which is binary and involves the emergence of eternal Wisdom (*die ewige Weisheit*) as the projection (*Gegenwurf*) of the Unground (*DI* 3, 6).[8] This binary division is often spoken of in terms of the images of eye and mirror (*SPT* 1.1, 7; 1. 1, 11–12). The images are intended to render the split between seer and seen impossible on the level of the undifferentiated divine, and thus gesture toward divine consciousness and self-consciousness. In a secondary way, the images also render the possibility of multiplicity and totality, for upon the mirror of Wisdom are reflected archetypes of all things. Wisdom is the great mystery (*mysterium magnum*) as the repository of all things in their archetypal invisible form.[9] Boehme is quick to point out, however, that the archetypes lack stability and definition, and that their appearing and disappearing seem to suggest a dream state rather than a state of vision in which archetypes are the objective correlative of powerful divine seeing (*TF* 2, 13; *MM* 1, 6–7; *SPT* 1. 1, 8). As the eternal feminine, Wisdom does not appear to be what Novalis later wishes her to be—that is, a matrix or mother.[10] As Boehme suggests time and again, Wisdom or Sophia is a "virginlike matrix" (*SPT* 1. 1, 61-62; *IV* bk. 2. 5, 47).[11] Wisdom opens up the possibility of the real birth of difference and otherness, but does not accomplish it. Wisdom is not a gynecontotheological source, or Wisdom is only a pregynecontotheological source.

The second form of the first register of differentiation that trajects the divine beyond hiddenness, and in some respects overcomes its simplicity and agnosia, is trinitarian. Trinitarian differentiation is the exegetical result of a reading of John 1.1–3:

> For 'in the beginning' means the eternal beginning in the will of the Unground for a ground, that is, for a divine apprehension, since the will apprehends itself in a center for foundation. For the will apprehends itself in the one power, and breathes itself forth. . . . This amounts to saying the Word was in the beginning with God and was God himself. The will is the beginning and is called God the Father, and he apprehends himself in power and is called the Son. (*EG* 2, 7–11; also *MM* 2, 1)

As with Wisdom, the Word plays the role of providing the divine with a provisional ground of manifestation. Relative to the formless sublime of the Unground, the Word represents the introduction of an aesthetic horizon, and relative to the divine nothing, which is visionless, or at best cyclopean in vision, the Word is a site of some kind of reflexivity. Higher degrees of aesthetic or iconic configuration of the divine are hinted at, as are higher degrees of reflexivity. In the context of the Word's providing some kind of ground for manifestation, Spirit appears in the role of an adjunct—namely that of further articulating what is implicit in the ground.

Boehme's mode of expression is more declarative in *Mysterium Magnum* where he sets off trinitarian manifestation against the backdrop of the hiddenness of the Unground: "In the eternal generation there are three things: (1) an eternal will; (2) an eternal mind (*ein ewige Gemüthe*) of the will; and (3) an eternal emanation (*Ausgang*) from the will and mind" (*MM* 1, 3; also *MM* 2, 1; *EG* 1, 6).

And in the immediately following paragraph (*MM* 1, 4), Boehme identifies 1, 2, and 3 respectively with "Father, Son, and Spirit." For Boehme, it is
clear that it is the dynamic of differentiation-manifestation that is truly primary. The creedal language of "Father, Son, and Spirit" only approximately
register this dynamic of manifestation. It proves misleading to the extent to
which it signifies three persons, which, for Boehme, before Hegel and Rahner,[12] suggests three distinct centers of consciousness or self-consciousness
(*MM* 7, 5; 7, 11).

But if focus on the dynamic of manifestation tends to undermine a personal interpretation of Trinity, reflection on the stage of manifestation realized
at this level of differentiation makes the language of essence itself problematic.
Determining that essence (*Wesen*) implies life and energy, Boehme rules that
essence is an unhelpful category when applied to this incipient stage of divine
manifestation. An important passage in *Mysterium Magnum* expresses this
paradoxically by saying that the threefold Spirit (*dieser dreifache Geist*) is one
essence and thus no essence (*kein Wesen ist*) (*MM* 1, 5; also *MM* 1, 6; *SPT* 1. 1,
29). What Boehme offers by way of explanation—namely, that the matrix of
the 'Immanent Trinity' is a search for something (*Ichts*)—and to a considerable
extent also an 'I' (*Ich*)—does not seem enlightening on the surface, yet it is sufficiently informative to enable translation. What Boehme is saying is that while
one can call the trinitarian dynamic one essence insofar as it is a determinate
and determinable process of differentiation and manifestation, in an absolute
sense this trinitarian dynamic does not constitute an essence in that this dynamic does not bring about a determinate divine life. Simply put, the threefold
life is not the God that creates and preserves, judges and forgives, suffers and
redeems. The God of trinitarian process is still disengaged, while yet laying
down conditions of engagement.

I will return to make a final comment on the nonessential nature of the
'Immanent Trinity' shortly, but before I do so a few words need to be said about
the voluntarist contextualization of the Trinity and Wisdom and their relation.

The voluntarist dimension of the 'Immanent Trinity' is apparent in the
above-quoted passage from *De Electione Gratiae* (2.1), in which the Father is
identified as the will of the Unground for a ground and the Son is taken to be
the finding of a ground. But Wisdom also has a voluntarist context. Wisdom is
what is projected by the will of the Unground as the screen or mirror of possibilities—one might say with Leibniz in mind, the mirroring of possible worlds.
As suggested already, there are two patterns in which the extreme voluntarism of
Boehme's theosophical system gets registered. The first more nearly belongs to
the order of myth and privileges event (*IV* bk 2. 2, 2). The second is more nearly
philosophical and thinks of the process of manifestation as an explication of
what is already implied in the divine mystery. In the first case, will is conceived
as a breakthrough into the Unground as an absolutely quiescent eternity (*die*

stille Ewigkeit) (*SR* 2, 8; 2, 18). The second understands the Unground as still
and quiescent more subjunctively than indicatively, more as an object of thought
than as a real state of the divine, for the divine Unground is always already the
will for ground. Will, therefore, is both something that the superessential
Unground suffers and what it is. Arguably, it is the second of these two forms
that dominates. In any event, it is the second of these two forms that exercises
significant influence in the history of philosophy, in Schelling primarily, but
through Schelling, Schopenhauer, and through Schopenhauer even Nietzsche.[13]

Whether sophiological or trinitarian, Boehme's voluntarist rendering of a
divine that is relatively rather than absolutely transcendent, because incipiently
archeological, is theologically distinctive. Yet it is important not to dismiss the
noetic accompaniment of will and its gnoseological aim. In Wisdom and Word,
which Boehme declines to fuse as much of the Christian tradition had done, by
refusing to exegetically link Proverbs 8.22 with John 1.1-3, the divine finds
both a center and a modicum of self-reflection. Similarity in noetic specification of will raises the issue of the relation between the sophiological and trinitarian modes of differentiation. Boehme, it should be said, is anything but
decisive in determining which of the two modes is the more primitive.[14] Some
texts favor the sophiological mode, others the trinitarian. And in *Mysterium
Magnum* Boehme begins his text (chapter 1) favoring the trinitarian pattern,
only to reverse course in chapter 29, when he turns once again to the initial
move by the Unground toward a ground, mystery toward manifestation. At this
juncture the sophiological mode is given primacy. When Berdyaev claims in
'Unground and Freedom' that the two modes of differentiation are not contradictory, and that, ultimately, trinitarian articulation with divine Wisdom shapes
a Quaternity, he is undoubtedly correct. But his judgment can only be assigned
the status of a protocol, for in his Quaternity ruling he makes no attempt to
sort out the important issue of which of the two modes of differentiation is antecedent, which consequent.

Although Boehme risks incoherence, the short answer to the question of
anteriority-posteriority is that the sophiological and trinitarian modes of differentiation are in some respects both antecedent and consequent. The doubleness common to both trinitarian and sophiological modes of differentiation can
be illuminated by considering the role of Wisdom in the more complex quaternarian structure. Wisdom can be regarded as the hint of tear in the divine mystery that makes possible subsequent elaboration of manifestation. It opens a
space for meaning, which is then articulated by Word as the ground of manifestation and spirit as its differentiation. Regarded in this way, Wisdom is
archeological, because it connotes a beginning of manifestation, but still an
arche very much within the anarchic and meontological pull of the Unground.[15]
But Wisdom can also be regarded as the objectification of the Unground, now
understood dynamically as ungrounded will, and specified and differentiated by

a trinitarian dynamic. Though one might have preferred Boehme to have lexically marked off objectification both "before" and "after" trinitarian articulation by different terms, it is evident that Jung is correct in his insight, if not his formulation, when he suggests that Boehme supplements the Trinity by a fourth hypostasis. For finally what is important about Wisdom is that it offers an image of a possible world of integrated particulars, something that becomes clearer when Boehme moves beyond his treatment of this first level of divine manifestation and takes up the issue of the Kingdom of God.

It is obvious that Boehme puts the level of ontological, gnoseological, but also axiological and existential determinacy of the entire quaternarian sphere of divine self-manifestation into question. The Word or "Son" appears to be more a ground of the ground of manifestation than a ground proper, and Wisdom appears to be more a sketch of the totality than the totality itself. While in different ways both Word and Wisdom indicate representation and reflexivity, the incidence is, for better or worse, not particularly high, since differentiation is differentiation of the same, and does not involve true otherness. Correlatively, the mode of existence, or what might be called "sensibility,"[16] appropriate to a divine functioning at this ontological and gnoseological level is palpably without pathos of any kind. Goodness is what defines itself self-referentially—that is, without reference to evil, possible or actual.

Boehme determines that the quaternarian differentiation of the divine is limited because it lacks "essence" or "nature." For the divine to have different, and more significant, ontological, gnoseological, axiological, and existential values involves a move from a sphere of differentiation still beset by the superessential, haunted by monism and the specter of nothing, where reflection and language cannot receive even an adumbration, to a sphere of differentiation a second register—that involves real difference. The manifestation of the divine, as opposed to divine self-manifestation at the level of the Quaternity, supposes a "fall" into nature and essence.

(2) *Engendering a Divine Nature: The Configuration of Divine Attributes*:

For Boehme Eternal Nature (*die ewige Natur*) is not to be confused with material or temporal nature (*MM* 3, 20).[17] Eternal Nature is the nondivine other to the Unground and the quaternarian differentiation of divine self-manifestation. It is at once the antitype of Wisdom and a dramatic specification of will articulated by the Word—indeed, the Trinity as a whole. As an antitype to Wisdom, Eternal Nature is that virulent realm of antidivine reality that occludes representation and blocks reflection. It is a realm of nonknowledge, entirely different from the agnosia of the Unground, a sphere of nonbeing, yet a form of nonbeing different from the divine nothing. If both the Unground and Eternal Nature can be regarded as species of *me on*, the non-Parmenidean nothing of the Unground is that of possible, even potential, being, whereas that of

Eternal Nature represents the refusal of the relationality and spiritual completeness of being. By contrast with the "chaos" of Wisdom (*Clavis* #48–52), which
aesthetically circumscribes a horizon of archetypal being, Eternal Nature is an
anti-aesthetic chaos, a chaos that is aggressively formless.

I will return to Eternal Nature's status as antitype to Wisdom, but before
I do I should say something about Eternal Nature's relation to the axis of will
upon which the Quaternity in general, and the Trinity in particular, is plotted.
If the 'Immanent Trinity,' for instance, is constituted by will (*Wille*), Eternal
Nature is constituted by desire (*Sucht*) (*SPT* 1. 1, 37; 2.27; *IV* bk 2. 3, 13–18;
Mysterium Pansophicum [*MP*] 3, 4; *SR* 4, 5).[18] Desire is a form of counterwill
(*Wieder Wille*) (*TF* 4, 16), contractive rather than expansive.[19] Its direction is
centripetal rather than centrifugal. Desire represents, however, the emergence
of a force of will sufficiently substantial to create realities rather than schemas
that reflect an ontological force described as "thin" (*dun*) as a nothing (*TL* 1, 29;
SPT 1. 2, 24). One especially interesting way in which desire relates to the voluntarist sphere that "precedes" it gets focused in the discourse of imagination or
"magic" (*MP* 1 and 2; *IV* bk 2. 2, 19; 3, 20). As it functions in the quaternarian
sphere, imagination is the coincidence of the active will to manifestation and
the passive screen upon which will projects its schemas and possibilities. To the
extent to which the goal is the production of real otherness—and self-reflection
based on otherness—at this level of divine manifestation, imagination fails to
be creative. Required is that "self-darkening of will" (*die Selbstverfinsterung des
Willens*) referred to by Grunsky,[20] provided by desire, which transforms a divine
magic that lacks ontological correlatives into an imagination that has them.
One might say, having Coleridge in mind, that desire transforms fantasy into
imagination proper.[21]

Having its origin in desire, Eternal Nature introduces a ground of real difference and multiplicity into the divine of which both Word and Wisdom, in
the quaternarian sphere, are incapable. The contrast between Wisdom and
Eternal Nature is especially important, and is articulated in the distinction between the oxymoron of a "virgin matrix" and the real matrix. Eternal Nature is
a pregnant source of being from which a teeming multiplicity emerges. It is
precisely what Novalis's great aphorism suggests Nature is: the great womb of
revelation (*der Offenbarung mächtigen Schloss*).[22]

Introducing real multiplicity reflects the inauguration of a new sphere of
differentiation. In the quaternarian sphere differentiation is differentiation of
the same: a differentiation of a light or clarity that has no contrast. Eternal Nature sets in motion differentiation by contradiction: a differentiation between
sources of darkness and light, ignorance and knowledge, or as Boehme sometimes says, the conflict of *Ens* and *Mens*.[23] And while ultimately Eternal Nature
does prove instrumental in the issue of an ontological and gnoseological positive, in the short term it is a sphere of creative proliferation without rhyme or

reason, a sphere of ignorance and nonreflection (*MP* 3, 1; *SPT* 1.1, 49). As a sphere of essence (*Wesen*), it is a sphere of life (*Leben*) (*De Tribus Principiis* [*TP*] 2, 1; *TL* 1, 24), but as it turns out, it is a dark, poisonous (*giftige*), hellish life (*IV* bk 2. 3, 16; 2.2, 48; *SPT* 1. 2, 38). Eternal Nature brings into the divine the possibility of evil, if not evil itself, and existence as the restlessness for being rather than its realization.

The insight about the struggle at the heart of reality between the forces of dark and light, evil and good, is there already in *Aurora* (1612) (preface #8, 18).[24] It is however only in the context of Boehme's mature work that the struggle is explicated in terms of the problematic of divine manifestation and the conditions that must be satisfied if the divine is to be a divine involved with a world. Eternal Nature, however negatively characterizable, brings about essence without which nothing can exist (*ohne Wesen nicht bestehen mag*) (*TP* 1, 27), and without which manifestation cannot occur. But Eternal Nature is the necessary rather than sufficient condition of manifestation that leads to divine self-reflection (*TP* 2, 1; *IV* bk 2. 3, 16). Eternal Nature makes manifestation possible precisely by obstructing it and engendering a recoil (*MM* 25 [28 in English]; 26, 10, 36-38, 58). It can rightly be called a source (*Urkund*) or root (*Wurzel*) of manifestation, which truly occurs only when its darkness, substantiality, involution, compulsiveness, and even pain give way to light, spiritual being, eccentricity, freedom, and joy (*MM* 4, 17).

To underscore the agon between Eternal Nature and the space of manifestation proper—which is variously, concretely and abstractly, associated with Christ and Eternal Freedom—Boehme avails himself of the language of "Principle." He assigns to Eternal Nature the status of First Principle, and assigns to its contrary, which is grounded in it, the status of Second Principle. Despite the Manichaeanlike evocation in the language of principle, as well as the fact that the Second Principle is regarded as defeating the First Principle (*MM* 40, 8), the conflict between the Principles of Darkness and Light cannot be interpreted in a Manichaean fashion. First, in Boehme the two Principles are not absolutely originary. They have as their presupposition the Unground and the Quaternity. Second, they are not coeval despite occasional suggestions to the contrary such as the following: "The wrathfulness and the painful source is the root of joy, and the joy is the root of the enmity of the dark wrathfulness. So that there is a contrarium, whereby the good is manifest and made known that it is good" (*MM* 4, 17).[25]

In making each the "root" of the other, Boehme does seem to announce that dependence is a two-way street. Nevertheless, even in this passage, which is somewhat exceptional, there are hints of asymmetry. At the end of the citation it is evident that Boehme's focus is on the Good Principle being grounded or rooted in the "Evil" Principle (also *MM* 5, 7). A fairly easy way of making sense of the passage, however, is to suppose that Boehme understands "root" in two different ways. The First Principle is the root of the Second Principle as its narrative presupposition. The Second Principle is the root of the First Principle only in the order of finality. The First Principle is ordered toward the reality of the Second Principle, and plays a crucial role in bringing it about.[26]

I will return to the specifically agonistic features of the conflict between Principles momentarily, but first I will say a few words about Boehme's technical understanding of "Principle." A Principle represents a domain of essence (*Wesen*), thus a dimension of existence radically distinct from the Unground and the Quaternity. Crucially, however, Principle is a domain of life (*Leben*). Principles, then, are the sources of the living God of biblical depiction, rather than the God of the philosophers, characterized by aseity. As a thinker within the Lutheran tradition, perhaps not surprisingly Boehme characterizes the life of the First Principle by wrath (*Zorn*), fierceness (*Grimmigkeit*), and sternness (*Schwerigkeit*), and the life of the Second Principle by mercy (*Barmhertzigkeit*) and love (*Liebe*). But, importantly, Principles are Principles of life only in relation. This is obvious in the case of the Second Principle, which depends essentially on the First. But it is also true of the First Principle, which truly comes to life only in the transition to the Second Principle. Before this transition the First Principle is lifeless as well as entropic.

Transition is the fire that brings it to life—that introduces, one might say, genuine negativity into the divine. Or to use Boehme's own language: fire is the ignition of life (*die Anzundung des Lebens*) (*IV* bk 2. 3, 16; bk 2. 2, 36; bk 2. 2, 44). If fire is generated by the friction and internal contradictions of the First Principle, nevertheless, it qualifies the First Principle in the same way it qualifies the Second. If the Second Principle is a "light fire," the first is a "dark fire," where the matter of the fire is supplied by the chaos of Eternal Nature which needs to be purified. Though Boehme contrasts fire and light, and tends to think of this contrast as the contrast between the Father and the Son, the truly structural contrast is that of dark and light, or dark and light fire.

It is important to focus on what the transition says about the divine. The extraordinary reflection on the process of transition presented in *De Signatura Rerum* is illustrative. There Boehme imagines the transition as the movement from death to life, pain to joy, what Jung, meditating on alchemical traditions, calls *enantiodromia*.[27] As we will see shortly more clearly, pain is present at the level of Eternal Nature. It comes to light, however, in the transition. Transition itself is painful in a somewhat different way. Its pain is a little like the metaphysical pain Heidegger sees in Trakl—that is, pain as separation, cutting off, de-scission.[28] In chapter 5 of *De Signatura Rerum*, transition is thought of as a double movement of forward and up, and figured as a vertical line, representing the ascending movement from death to life, bisecting a horizontal line, representing the forward movement of manifestation. Thus, a Cross gets shaped that functions staurologically—that is, functions to block and separate a dimension of higher reality from a lower.[29] In fact, Boehme has no compunction about denying divine status to the First Principle, and insisting that God is God only in the Second Principle (*MM* 8, 14; *TP* 1, 2; 1, 8). Yet once again, as later assimilations of Boehme by Schelling and Berdyaev indicate,[30] Boehme's position is not Manichaean. True, the First Principle is antagonistic to the Second, and in that sense antidivine. But there is something pre about the anti, even if the activation of this sphere of existence necessarily introduces evil.

For Boehme, the two Principles differentiate into triads of divine qualities (*Qualitäten*), with a transition quality between them. Qualities play the role divine attributes do in most ontotheological systems, but as the best Boehme scholars have recognized, a quality in this system of divine expressiveness is more than an attribute. Along the dynamic, voluntarist axis qualities are dynamic expressions of divine life. Something of the difference between attribute and quality is graspable in the etymological roots of *Qualität*. One of these roots is *Quellen* or *Quell*, which points to a surging, pulsating force. Another is *Quall* or *Quahl*, which means "pain."[31] From *Aurora* (1612) on, Boehme thinks of qualities as the powers of expression in God that get manifested in the temporal-material world. Far from being a logical or conceptual entity with real or problematic reference, a quality is a surging power (*ein quellende Kraft*) (*Aurora* 1, 3) and the mobility, surge, and drive of things (*die Bewiglichkeit, Quellen und der Trieben eines Dinges*) (1, 3). And from the second part of the text (chapters 8ff.) the number is established as seven, largely, though not exclusively, predicated on the reading of Scripture,[32] with particular debts to *Revelation* (the seven lamps of chapter 1, the seven eyes or spirits sent forth of chapter 5) and *Genesis* (the seven days of creation).

What does represent a development in the mature work is the clarification of what might be called the narrative, but not necessarily temporal, order of the qualities. Boehme insists that the emergence of the qualities cannot be understood in the temporal manner of "before" and "after" (*Aurora* 23, 15ff.). At the same time, however, the qualities are not merely juxtaposed or simply structurally related. They constitute an indescerptible string arranged in an irreversible narrative order. This should come as no surprise: narrative irreversibility will be a property of the qualities as it is a property of the Principles the qualities articulate. The qualities also reinforce the tension within the divine between the negative and the positive, no and yes. Boehme avails himself of multiple vocabularies, including the not especially helpful vocabulary of sensation—"hot," "cold," "bitter," "sour," "sweet" (belonging to the undeveloped stratum of alchemy) (*Aurora* 8–11) as well as a vocabulary of "salt," "mercury," and "sulphur" (*MM* 10), (belonging to alchemy's more reflective stratum).[33] Linguistic impediments notwithstanding, it is clear that Boehme intends to name nonphysical forces instrumental in divine becoming that will eventually find expression in the visible world. The triads of qualities that articulate the

Principles seem to represent different parsings of form, mobility, and life, specifically imploding form (1), directionless movement (2), and angst (3), on the one hand, perfection of form (7), meaning-giving movement of word (6), and love (5), on the other. Between these two triads lies the transition quality of fire (4), which plays the role of chiasmus between the two sets, pairing 1 and 7, 2 and 6, 3 and 5.

In and through the qualities, the divine defines itself in terms of being, knowledge, value, and experience, or specifically as a divine that, as spirit, represents the unsurpassable realization of reality, unsurpassable self-consciousness premised on consciousness and its intentionality, the acme of a goodness that is tried and strengthened by evil, and a divine whose experience is ultimately determined by joy that could not be what it is without the background of suffering. Now, while all the properties of the Second Principle can be appropriated to Christ, this is especially true of the fifth quality, that of love. As Word and speech, the sixth quality also evokes the Son. However, the pneumatological resonance here is often loud, especially in *Mysterium Magnum* and *De Electione Gratiae*.[34]

Of all the qualities that articulate the Second Principle, it is the seventh, which corresponds to the first, that is the most interesting, for there is an obvious correlation with Wisdom whose archetypal world of possibility is deranged in the chaos introduced by Eternal Nature. The seventh quality is the "heavenly Eve," which has gone through the crucible of pain and alienation induced by Eternal Nature. And as the "heavenly Eve" and "New Jerusalem," the seventh quality is the complete world of harmonious divine expression.

(3) *The Emergence of the Temporal World and of Human Being*

The material temporal world is the outcome of a dramatic event of derangement, what Boehme refers to as the *turba* that disturbs the balance between two Principles expressed in the "heavenly Eve" or paradise (*EG* 8, 7–8; *TP* 1, 48).[35] Paradise is the matrix of the unity-in-multiplicity of divine expression, in which love, word, and joy dominate self-will, ignorance, and angst, but partake of their energy and power. Paradise is also the knowing of the divine by what has been "separated" from the divine, where knowing is humble and adorative, and involves a community rather than an individual context. For Boehme, then, paradise, as the angelic realm, is the really real realm of finite glorification of the divine. Human being represents a secondary layer in the doxological milieu, moreover, one predicated on the event of rupture in the order of eternity.

Like Augustine in the *City of God*, or Anselm in *Why God Became Man*, Boehme thinks of the temporal world and human being in particular as ingredients in a doxological replacement. The glorification of the divine in paradise, which in *Aurora* most clearly has Revelation as a background, is cut short by the act of self-assertion of Lucifer, "son of Light" (*Aurora* 13) who decides against doxological posture (*EG* 4, 29–32).[36] Lucifer's act is an act of counterwill or desire (*MM* 4, 9ff.; *EG* 4, 32) but also an act of imagination, which has as its basic stuff the center of nature as the nuclear force or power of God. The creative property of imagination guarantees that Lucifer becomes what he imagines.[37] This means that heaven and hell are at least as much internal states as objective places, a point that both Milton and Blake can capitalize on later.[38]

Considered as a reality, without the tempering or sublimation of the Second Principle, the First Principle is a chaos. Lucifer contaminates paradise, and his extrusion, which recalls Revelation's fall of the dragon (*MM* 12, 10–12), is the extrusion of the chaotic element. This extruded element is the *tohu va bohu* of Genesis 1 with which the spirit of God wrestles at the beginning of the creation of the material world (*IV* bk 1. 3, 21). At the base of temporal- material nature, therefore, is Lucifer's "no," which cannot fail to be urgent in the physical-material world, and which in *Aurora*, at least, Boehme seems to regard as responsible for all that is negative in nature (e.g., toads, snakes, bad weather, sickness, etc.).

Yet Lucifer's no is not the last word. The material world represents a prison for Lucifer and a defeat of his no, for it is primarily an expression of the divine will to manifestation, the divine yes that demands that light contain darkness and that the Word triumph over the refusal of communication. The visible material world is a signature of the invisible eternal world. It signs both Principles and their tension. Indeed, its meaning is this tension, and what makes it another, or Third Principle (*MM* 3, 20; 13, 9–11; *SR* 14, 8). As a signature of a complex invisible world, the Third Principle is both type and antitype—type in that it expresses the divine as a whole, but also in some respect the divine more narrowly defined by the Second Principle. But for the same reason it is antitype, and again in two different registers. It does not mirror the invisible world as a whole exactly, and it could be understood to mirror the paradisiacal realm so inexactly as to approach the condition of antithesis.

The basic elements of Boehme's reflection on the material world, which Boehme calls the "Spirit of the World" or in a language borrowed from alchemy, the *astrum* (*MM* 13, 10; 13, 16),[39] is contained in his anagogic exegesis of *Genesis*. Later texts like *Mysterium Magnum* (1623) and *De Electione Gratiae* (1623) are lucid in a way *Aurora* is not. The creative word of Genesis indicates a commitment to expressiveness, which is confirmed by the light of the first day of creation. The word is the word of formation through which divine imagination assembles a coherent whole from the confused mass of the beginning. And light represents a kind of fifth element, a *quinta essentia*, from which the elements of fire, air, water, and earth devolve. The Boehmian identification of light as the Principle of the cosmos is important in poetics (e.g., Milton), and, if Derrida is right, in philosophy also.[40] But, for Boehme, light is not only *arche*; it is also the pivot, since Boehme subscribes to the heliocentric theory of Copernicus that the planets revolve around the sun.[41] It is evident, however, that his reasoning is more metaphysical and theological than physical. The sun is the center because it is the sun that energizes the cosmos (*Aurora* 25, 65). Moreover, it is the sun that seems best to represent the expressiveness of invisible reality indicated by the light that banishes the darkness of chaos as the first act of formation.

Following Genesis, the creation of human being is regarded as the apex of the creative act in the Third Principle. As with much of the exegetical tradition, Boehme stresses the sovereignty of human being (*IV* bk 1, 3, 13; bk 1.4, 7) and its status as microcosm (Epistle 12.7). But Adam is in some respect distinct from temporal nature, since Adam is an image of God, specifically an image of divine will and wisdom (*EG* 1, 15 (*MM* 16, 17). Adam is an image of divine will in two different respects. He has the unconditioned or meontic power to confirm or disconfirm his intentional pattern of giving glory to the divine. He also partakes of the paradisiacal substantiality of the divine (*Sermons* 56, 52; 57, 9)—that is, Wisdom in her perfected aspect. Wisdom is a constitutive aspect of divine image, for it is only in relation to Wisdom—indeed a kind of spousal relation with it (*MM* 18, 17; 25, 14)—that image is divine.

Adam, then, enjoys a perfection of vision (*Blick*), for the perfection of vision is the consequence of participation in Wisdom that is pure noetic as well as pure ontological transparence. In Adam the eternal intersects the temporal, and paradise expresses itself in Eden (*MM* 36 and 39). In the Edenic situation the perfection of knowledge in Adam is a perfection of language, the language of nature.[42] In the Adamic situation language names in an essential fashion. There is no problem of linkup between language and reality, which problem is most forcibly seen in the tower of Babel (*MM* 35–36), but whose career is under way after the fall.

While Boehme is anxious to point to the connection between Adam and paradise as a force that obviates the Lucifernian fall, the image of God is firmly anchored in materiality. The second creation story of Genesis specifies the terrestrial stuff (*limbus*) that forms a basic constituent of Adam (*MM* 16, 7), into which spirit is breathed (*Clavis* #19). Adam is after all microcosm as well as microtheos. Nevertheless, any change in Adam's status has an effect on his material base. Were the image to be withdrawn or vitiated in some way, this would have repercussions on the level of corruptibility. As I will show shortly, Boehme does not disappoint this expectation.

But before I get to Boehme's account of the fall, a fuller description of the Adamic state is in order. Although recognizing the point to be controversial, Boehme believes a thick description of this state, or at least a thicker description than that provided by the mainline theological tradition, and especially his own Lutheran tradition, is possible (*MM* 18, 1). The Adamic state is a state characterized by incorruptibility (*SR* 2, 51), androgyny (*MM* 18, 17–18), angelic reproduction that proceeds by way of a kind of cloning (*Forty Questions Concerning the Soul* [*FQ*] 8, 2; *EG* 5, 34), and a form of nonphysical eating that avoids unsavory associative phenomena such as evacuation. All of these characteristics are important and obviously have nothing to do with the depiction of a historical Adam, who is recognizably like his successors in vulnerability and impurity.

Androgyny is especially interesting, since it suggests that Boehme is a link in the Western tradition of esoteric anthropology, but it also suggests that he is a practitioner of a certain kind of exegesis that downplays the historical nature of Adam: he reads the condition of Adam back from Pauline descriptions of the eschaton. In any event, sexual differentiation is not a primal characteristic of human being, but in itself it is a sign of the fall, a point hardly lost on William Blake, as we shall see in a subsequent volume.

(4) *Fall of Adam*

As Boehme depicts it, the fall of Adam has both abrupt and gradual features, a hermeneutic combination formally, if not materially, repeated by Kierkegaard in his *Concept of Anxiety*.[43] The abrupt aspect is the crystalization of counterwill, the self-involution (*Eigenwille*) that recapitulates the Lucifernian no to doxological eccentricity and receptivity. Recapitulated also is the *turba*—the opening up of the chaotic natural forces that split off from paradise as the concrete form of Wisdom. The *turba* certainly points to the exile of the sophiological element in human being, thus the occluding of the divine image. The *turba* has effects on both natural and moral levels that are catastrophic, but arguably less so than on the more absolute plane of eternity, where decision takes the form of a *nunc stans*. With sin, Adam's incorruptibility is withdrawn (*IV* bk 2. 6, 17; *TP* 17, 84), as is his knowledge or vision of divine things (*TP* 16, 22; *EG* 4, 2). Moreover, sin begets sin (*MP* 3, 16ff.). Boehme does not think, however, that human being is totally vitiated (*IV* bk 1.14, 19; *TL* 6, 68), nor that the vision of God thereby becomes impossible for corruptible human being. Rather vision becomes exceptional. The vision (*Blick*) that Adam enjoyed constantly is now possible only in glimpses (*Augenblick*). Real evidence for such glimpses are provided, as Boehme points out in *Mysterium Magnum*, by biblical history in figures such as Shem, Abraham, Moses, Enoch, and Ezekiel. In addition, Augustinian and Reformation views on original sin are denied. For however vitiated a state, the self is postlapsum; it is not the case that human being is incapable of not sinning. There continues to be a real but fragile freedom that can cooperate at least in the renovation of image.[44]

Importantly, however, and not the least from the point of view of Blakean mythopoesis that will be extraordinarily influenced by it, if the fall of Adam is in one sense all at once, in another it is gradual. Adam's act of saying no to God in choosing to eat from the tree of knowledge of good and evil has a prehistory in which Adam is robbed of an essential aspect of the divine image—that is, androgyny. Adam's dream in the garden (*TP* 32, 33; *FQ* 8, 3–5), during which God takes a rib and forms Eve, suggests that vision, as well as the wholeness that derives from the indwelling of Sophia as Adam's true spouse, is already in the process of being lost before the definitive refusal of God. The appearance of Eve represents the breakup of androgyny, the loss of innocence, and the appearance of eros and the illusions of its satisfactions (*TP* 13, 39–40; 46, 48).

(5) *Christ: The Savior as Exemplar*

This brings us to Boehme's Christology, with which his image theology bears the closest possible relation. For Boehme, Christ is the second Adam, which means that Christ represents the restoration of the divine image occluded in the fall (*MM* 19, 21). This implies, obviously, that Christ brings into the fallen world an illumination in which divine presence is a constant and a perfection of will in which will lets the Second Principle be an element of transformation and renewal in a broken life. As the second Adam, Christ also represents the perfection of discourse, the resumption of the power of language to render reality, especially divine reality, transparent. In this sense, Christ is the foundation of the "language of nature" that in another sense discloses Jesus as the merciful center of reality (*MM* 36, 50–53). The reemergence of an effective divine image in Christ involves the overcoming of the corruptibility of the flesh that is the result of the *turba* (*MM* 10, 56; *TP* 14, 48) and the irruption into history of the *soma pneumatikon* (*MM* 41, 11). Christ also represents the overcoming of sexual differentiation involved in the Adamic fall (*MM* 19, 7; 55, 20; 56, 20; 56, 46; *IV* bk 1. 8, 13) and the coincidence of fire and light that characterizes the androgynous state of Adam (*MM* 19, 17; 22, 43–44). Christ, then, represents the restoration of the *kairos* of Eden, where *kairos* is dependent on the presence of paradise and the expression of eternity in time (*MM* 36 and 39). At the same time, Christ points forward to the eschatological, communitarian realization of the divine image.

It is important to underscore here that the relation between Christ and Sophia is not simply inferential—that is, derivable from the Adam-Christ analogy. Far from it, the sophiological parameter of christological depiction is everywhere to the fore. Mary is not in any real sense the *theotokos*. In continuity with Eckhartian lines of exploration, Mary is the mother of the human Jesus.[45] The eternal Christ is given birth to only in the deepest recesses of Mary's soul, where Wisdom resides. Wisdom is the matrix of the birth of the Logos. Although Jesus is male, the Logos represents the coincidence of masculine will and feminine Wisdom, fire and light, or fire and water. Boehme's intentions are clearly anti-docetic. He wants to insist on the humanness of Mary and Jesus, and he operates in terms of the Alexandrian axiom that what Christ does not assume, he cannot save. When Boehme is hesitant regarding Christ's sharing the sinful human condition, he is simply at one with the Christian tradition in general, and his own Lutheran tradition in particular. But when he denies that Christ is literally corruptible, or exposed to death in anything that bears an analogy to our own postfall situation, then he definitely hugs the shore of Docetism. At the same time, he does everything he can to escape. The main strategy of escape is the hyperrealistic, apocalyptic focusing of Christ resisting the forces of evil. The dragon of Revelation and the principalities and powers of Colossians are obviously in the background, as is Luther's theology of *Christus Victor*. Christ, in any event, is involved in a transcosmic battle: "It is a battle between yes and no, between typical wrath and typical love, between the First and Second Principles" (*TF* 11, 14–15).

As such, Christ is the decision in the world between hell and heaven (*TF* 11, 15–20). Nevertheless, Boehme resolutely refuses to think of this agon in terms of sacrifice, or in terms of the conferring of merit. If Christ is the lamb, the lamb does not sacrifice himself for the sins of the world (*SR* 12, 3ff.). Vicarious atonement absolves human beings from responsibility for sin. And Boehme is dead set against forensic justification, for it is not only responsibility that is impugned, but also finite freedom. Not surprisingly, his antipredestination tract, *De Electione Gratiae*, is most eloquent on the topic: "For imputed grace from without is of no effect. . . . The imputed grace must be manifested in us, in the inward ground of the soul, and be one life. . . . If Christ is not in our soul, there is no grace nor forgiveness of sins" (*EG* 13, 7ff; also *IV* bk 3. 1, 2).

Christ, then, is the historically exemplary pattern of life that transforms no into yes, wrath into love, death into life. Christ is the real symbol of the pattern of *enantiodromia* at the level of eternity. The reality of the symbol is predicated on the Christ event integrating what had been sundered in the Adamic fall, and, in a sense, healing the wound of determinate eternal Wisdom, incurred in the Luciferian fall. Healing the wound involves a metamorphosis of matter, as well as fundamental changes on the level of will and knowing.

One can speak, then, literally, and not simply metaphorically, of a new heaven and a new earth (see Revelation 21), for there is a transfiguration into an eternal milieu that has shape and form, and is bodily in the sense that it is the receptacle and mirror of divine expressivity. On the level of spirituality, to live in Christ is to take on the pain of transformation, focused in repentance and conversion as critical stages on the way to perfection. As Boehme depicts it in *The Way to Christ* (*Christosophia*), for instance, there is a definite order of salvation *(ordo salutis)* in following the christic pattern from repentance to regeneration that affects will and knowledge, indeed the very basis of the self. The main point that should not be forgotten here, however, is that Christ redeems only if human beings open themselves up to grace by overcoming self-will

(*Eigenwille*), and on the basis of death of self come to function as agents in the imitation of Christ. Boehme is hardly being original here, and the death of self is perhaps the central motif of the fifteenth-century mystical text *German Theology*, appropriated by Luther and the other illuminists before him. Importantly, however, the trope is figured differently in Boehme and comes to acquire cosmogonic and eternal resonance that will be picked up later by authors as different as Blake and Hegel.

(6) *Eschatology and Narrative Circularity*

Boehme's most comprehensive reflection on the imitation of Christ—that is, *The Way to Christ*—is, obviously, a text of individual piety, a text of prayer, and a set of discourses evocative of the *Gelassenheit* or "letting be" that makes possible the restoration of image. In this respect, the text can be paired with the work of his contemporary, Johann Arndt.[46] But to identify Boehme's view of redemption with that found in Arndt would be to ignore Boehme's panoramic view of history and to insufficiently appreciate the communitarian and eschatological dimensions of Boehme's sophiological depiction of Christ. Christ is the pivot of human history. He is constitutive of the restoration of Eden, and via this restoration, Christ is constitutive of the restoration of the integrity of paradise disturbed in the Lucifernian fall. The wholeness of paradise as well as Eden is anticipated in Christ, a wholeness realized only in the eschaton when what can be transformed is transformed, and what cannot be transformed is sloughed off. In the meantime there is the stress of the agon between the Kingdom of God and the kingdom of the devil, or the battle between those who have given themselves to the Second Principle and those who have delivered themselves up to the First.

But as Boehme points out, this postincarnational battle is continuous with the agon that structures all of history. Cain and Abel figure history: the line of rejection and the line of promise (*MM* 26–28). The figuration is familiarly Augustinian, with the difference that the lines themselves are not the results of divine election to salvation or damnation, but rather the results of human choices. And, of course, there is at best no one-to-one correspondence between the Kingdom of God and the visible church or churches, the "stone houses" (*MM* 40, 98), as Boehme calls them, for the Kingdom may well be invisible throughout history and only visible eschatologically. And, at worst, there is flagrant contradiction between the invisible and visible Church, which latter is the "Babylonian whore" or "dragon" to be expelled by the lamb.[47]

Boehme's criticisms against the visible Churches are constant from *Aurora* on, and range from not unexpected lambastings of the Roman Church to general outrage at the rampant sectarian strife of his age, where politics and religion are confused, and religion is effectively reduced to particular beliefs that mark off one sect from another. For Boehme, Christianity is not a doctrinal religion, but a religion of internal transformation and, finally, a religion of speculative vision. True faith, which is neither historical knowledge nor subscription to articles (*IV* bk 3. 1, 2–4), issues in a vision not only of what the divine works in an individual human being, but what the divine works in history and in all of eternity.

Boehme's figuration of history is complex. The Cain-Abel figuration throws into relief what ultimately is at stake in a temporal existence destined to be sublated into eternity. Read from the vantage point of the eschaton, the Cain-Abel figuration, with Christ as the realization of Abel, has to be regarded as primary. But Boehme also articulates another figuration that takes the human world of venality more into account, as well as possibilities of vision repressed by the Cain-Abel pattern. This figuration, which finds its focus in the three Sons of Noah—Ham, Japhet, and Shem (*MM* 34)—with Ham and Shem oriented toward the First and Second Principles respectively, and with Japhet oriented toward the Third, is almost as fundamental. Of course, the orientation toward the flesh and the world that is typical of Japhet persists in postincarnational history, and it is only eschatologically revoked, for the eschaton is the moment of fundamental option for the First and Second Principles. The triadic pattern allows the visionary or prophetic element to stand out more clearly than the Cain-Abel contrast allows. For Shem, who is in Enoch's line (*MM* 30-31), and those visionaries in the line of Shem, live in the light of grace rather than nature[48]—a light which, however, comprehends and embraces the light of nature and enables an all-encompassing seeing (*MM* 34, 25; 34, 31).

The eschaton, with its circling back to Eden, abolishes the line of history. The eschaton also involves a circling back to eternity after an interval of posthistorical existence. The apocalyptic cast of Boehme's thought is here writ large: *Endzeit* repeats *Urzeit*, and recapitulated *Urzeit* folds into paradise, the mirror of determinate divine Wisdom shivered in the fall of Lucifer. Formally, at least, Boehme's great devotee and first biographer, Abraham von Franckenberg, is right when he insists on the importance of circularity in Boehme's thought.[49] But this raises the question of whether the circularity involves perfect parity between *Endzeit* and *Urzeit*, or whether there is some excess in *Endzeit* over *Urzeit*. There is some reason to favor the latter option, for the Christic pattern that articulates and shapes experience subsequent to the loss of innocence suggests nonsymmetry between *Endzeit* and *Urzeit*. It is only proper to point out, however, that the recapitulative notes are stronger in Boehme than they will be in thinkers like Hegel and Schelling.

This naturally leads back to the general issue of divine development on the plane of eternity. From the Unground to the divine milieu or paradise the divine enacts a story that is constitutive of divine self-identity. This story seems to be at once eventful and episodic, and an explication of the conditions of authentic divinity. Certainly, divine definition is always anticipated, and the teleological nexus always guarantees that whatever species of fall and alienation occur, the divine process of realizing maximal incidences of being, knowing, value, and existence will not be frustrated, indeed, is assured of a happy outcome. Boehme articulates, therefore, a divine comedy. If by and large the divine comedy is completed on the level of eternity, and specifically with the Second Principle, the temporal world or the Third Principle also plays a role insofar as it repairs the perforated wholeness of the mirror of divine expression in paradise.[50]

In as brief a compass as is possible, I have offered an outline of Boehme's circular yet developmental narrative ontotheology. Obviously, the asceticism exercised with respect to quotation and the trimming of detail has palpable effects on the communication of the flavor of Boehme's discourse. I confess that I am prepared to make this sacrifice in the service of revealing its underlying narrative commitment and structure, which I wager will help to show that Boehme's discourse is much more important, both systematically and historically, than most of his supporters have dared to entertain. The rest of this text, and especially Parts II and III represent a multifaceted investigation of the narrative structure that I have presented in outline.

Before I conclude this chapter, however, I wish to draw attention to two distinctive aspects of Boehme's ontotheological narrative. The first aspect is more or less lexical. As with the Bible and other religious texts, a number of symbolic oppositions move Boehme's narrative discourse along. What is different in Boehme's texts is how the symbolic oppositions get narratively coded by suggesting that one is the narrative presupposition of the other. The second is more substantive, and concerns the way in which Boehme's discourse tries to provide a trinitarian synopsis or configuration of a six-stage narrative ontotheology.

1.2. Narrative Teleology: Narrative Codes

Boehme's divine comedy, which flirts with tragedy, but is finally not so, is discursively moved by narrative codes, of which the ocular code, the codes of weight and nothing, the organic and speech codes, and the code of gender are the most salient. More specifically, the divine comedy is articulated by means of narratively coded binary contrasts of seeing and blindness, darkness and light, weight and airiness, nothing and something, life and death, naming and unnaming, and finally masculine and feminine, where the divine feminine is interpreted in the most negative as well as the most positive terms.

Concretely, this means that as Boehme plots the development of the divine, authentic divine seeing realized in Eternal Freedom presupposes the blindness of Eternal Nature, just as this blindness succeeds the empty seeing of the Unground and the Quaternity.[51] Still within the ocular parameter, Boehme opines that real divine light presupposes the darkness that succeeds the insufficient light of the Unground and the Quaternity, which, to mark off from the light (*Licht*) grounded in darkness (*SPT* 1.1, 32; 1.1, 38), Boehme refers to as "clarity" (*Klarheit*) (*SPT* 1.1, 10; also *SR* 14, 23). All manifestation, therefore, takes place against the tug of immanifestation. Similarly with the other narrative codes. The weightiness or substantiality (*MM* 3, 16; *SPT* 1. 1, 42) of Eternal Nature adds a gravitas to the divine not present at the level of the inessential or ethereal divine, and serves as a condition for the emergence of an ontologically "weighty" form of spiritual divine being in the Second Principle in general and the heavenly Eve of paradise in particular, which are intrinsically light and buoyant. At the same time, the "something" (*Ichts*) of Eternal Nature (*MM* 3, 5) obviates the regime of the nothing (*Nichts*) that is still showing signs of influence in the Quaternity. In turn, this something-nothing is negated and transcended by Eternal Freedom, which, as will, is a nothing having become determinate through the something (*Ichts*) of Eternal Nature.

Matters are not different with respect to the organic and speech codes. The entire divine movement is understood in terms of growth and birth (*Geburt*) (*MM* 1, 2; 1, 8; 2, 1). Life, for Boehme, is the ultimate specification of growth, and for life to be strong, it requires death (*SR* 3, 27; 8, 6–7). The death that belongs to Eternal Nature represents the overcoming of the lifelessness of the divine at the level of the Unground and the Quaternity, and serves as the condition for the elevation of life. Again, there are realized and unrealized forms of speech. For Boehme, the Johannine Logos is the ground of speaking, the Spirit is this speaking, and Wisdom is what is spoken (*MM* 2, 7). Yet, if this speech represents a transcendence of the silence and ineffability of the Unground, it is made truly effective only through the cacophony, deafness, and dumbness of Eternal Nature. True speech is uttered against the backdrop of a refusal of speech. Speech is always in some sense a victory.

This brings us to the last of the narrative codes—that of gender, and specifically the feminine. As observed already, Wisdom is the feminine pole in a primordial binary pair that has the Unground as Father as the other pole. Wisdom is also the feminine complement to a trinitarian process of differentiation, which if it revises the Father, Son, and Spirit language of the traditional Trinity, nevertheless, emphasizes the masculine activity of trinitarian differentiation over the feminine passivity of Wisdom as the completion of the Quaternity (*Clavis* #5, 15–19). Wisdom is also the feminine complement to Christ and Spirit in the domain of Eternal Freedom, where the divine has transcended the catastrophe of Eternal Nature. And, finally, as the eternal feminine or paradise, Wisdom is a fully realized presence in Christ (*Way to Christ* [*WC*], 154), a splendid presence in Adamic human being, an occasional presence in existences that must suffer the ambiguities of history (*WC*, 57, 61–62), and once again, a pleromatic presence in the eschatological situation. Enjoying a multitude of roles in the unfolding of an encompassing narrative of the divine, the divine feminine plays a role in theological reflection that it has not had since the early centuries of the Common Era.

Moreover, the divine feminine is complexly qualified. As the aboriginal mirror, Wisdom is positively interpreted, though Boehme, as I pointed out, adds caveats regarding her ability to be a real site of multiplicity and reflection. But as Eternal Nature, the eternal feminine is such a real source, but it is also a sphere of chaos and nonillumination. Eternal Nature is the antithesis to the Wisdom of the Quaternity. As the realization of a divine world or paradise, Wisdom, however, represents the other to Eternal Nature and its transmutation. Its manifestation in the world of Eden, in Christ, in visionaries, and in the eschaton are all superbly positive, such positives in fact helping to set the frame of reference for Russian sophiological thought at the end of the nineteenth and the beginning of the twentieth centuries. The realization of Wisdom is the realization of the "Kingdom of God" and the "body of God," the matrix of manifestation necessary for divine perfection.

1.3. Trinitarian Configuration of Ontotheological Narrative

As suggested by the nineteenth-century historian of dogma Ferdinand Christian Baur in *Die christliche Gnosis* (pp. 557-611), the texts of the mature Boehme attempt a trinitarian synopsis or configuration of a complex, absolutely comprehensive narrative of divine manifestation or self-manifestation. The specific form of trinitarian language that Boehme most commonly avails himself of is that of three Principles, though in line with *Aurora* (12ff.) Boehme continues to think of the three Principles as three Kingdoms, and often uses the language of kingdom to interpret the language of principle. Leaving in parenthesis for the moment the way in which the three principles actually cut up the six-stage narrative or metanarrative, there are any number of complexities in Boehmian use both with respect to coherence and Christian legitimation. It would be stretching things to call Boehme's synopsizing of ontotheological narrative by three Principles trinitarian unless there were some rough correspondence between the three Principles (or Kingdoms) and Father, Son, and Spirit. Some rough correspondence exists, but so also do difficulties in correlation. This difficulty is especially acute with respect to the correlation of the First Principle and the Father, for having essentially equated the First Principle with Eternal Nature, Boehme seems in turn to be in two minds: whether to associate or separate Eternal Nature from Luther's God of Wrath (*Zorngott*). No more need be said on this point for the moment, since this relation-separation of Eternal Nature and the *Zorngott* is best discussed in the context of an overall treatment of the massive transformation on the standard Christian picture enacted by Boehme's metanarrative. This will be the topic of Part II of the present text.

With traditional use serving as a touchstone, Boehme's trinitarian language shows some odd features. Though apparently the 'economic' correlative to the 'Immanent Trinity,' the three Principles or Kingdoms do not admit of an 'economic' appraisal—that is, unless 'economic' is read much more literally than it usually is in trinitarian theology. At the very minimum the First and Second Principles do not represent distinct missions of fully constituted persons. Not only are there no such fully constituted persons, or even a single person, before divine enactment in the First and Second Principles, but both Principles are the privileged domains of divine manifestation in eternity rather than in time. Indeed, it is questionable whether even the Third Principle, associated with the Spirit, is 'economic' without remainder. First, the temporal world is not so much defined as the domain of the activity of Spirit as identified with the Spirit (with the Spirit, however, being the "Spirit of the World"). Second, if the temporal world does provide the scene for salvation history, this salvation history seems to play some role with respect to divine self-definition, more conspicuously in operation in the case of the first two Principles. It does so to the extent to which it contributes to the reconstitution of the divine milieu, which itself is constitutive of divine self-definition.

All three Principles, then, seem to play a role in divine self-development, and thus they are noneconomic, whether 'economic' is given essentially an Augustinian or Joachimite reading. This noneconomic (in the sense of nonmissional) view of principle does, indeed, represent a sea change from Boehme's earliest use of the trinitarian language of Kingdom. In *Aurora* 12, spurred on by Revelation, with a possible assist from Colossians 1.16, Boehme speaks of the three Kingdoms, the Kingdom of Michael, Lucifer, and Uriel. The angelogical characterization of three Kingdoms, however, turns out to be relative, with the ultimate referents of the three Kingdoms being the Father, Son, and Spirit respectively. Leaving aside the tantalizing correlation between the Son and Lucifer enunciated in the text, and repeated by more than one Hegelian text,[52] it is clear that against the backdrop of a personalist rendition of the Trinity *in se*, Boehme's elaboration of the three Kingdoms here is more nearly economic and missional than his later work, though its economic mode of distribution is recognizably more Joachimite than Augustinian. Attributions made of Michael, Lucifer, and Uriel seem to be real rather than a matter of appropriation, and their activities discrete rather than mutually involving or perichoretic.

Nevertheless, it is still possible to say that traces of the economic or missional view continue to be recalled in Boehme's mature work to the extent to which the three Principles do not touch on the Unground, Wisdom, and especially on the trinitarian articulation of will. The trinitarian articulation does serve as condition for the emergence of the three Principles. But its anticipatory role does not redound to its credit. It too serves as a means for the realization of divine self-consciousness, only it does not perform the kind of ontotheological

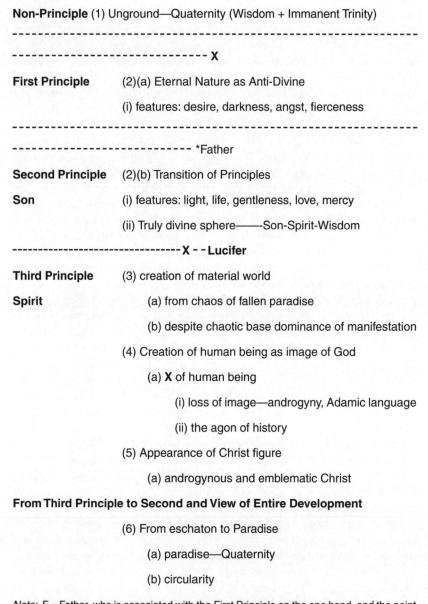

Non-Principle (1) Unground—Quaternity (Wisdom + Immanent Trinity)

----------------------------- X

First Principle   (2)(a) Eternal Nature as Anti-Divine

                          (i) features: desire, darkness, angst, fierceness

----

-------------------------- *Father

Second Principle   (2)(b) Transition of Principles

Son   (i) features: light, life, gentleness, love, mercy

                          (ii) Truly divine sphere———-Son-Spirit-Wisdom

-------------------------------X - -**Lucifer**

Third Principle   (3) creation of material world

Spirit   (a) from chaos of fallen paradise

                               (b) despite chaotic base dominance of manifestation

                          (4) Creation of human being as image of God

                               (a) **X** of human being

                                    (i) loss of image—androgyny, Adamic language

                                    (ii) the agon of history

                          (5) Appearance of Christ figure

                               (a) androgynous and emblematic Christ

From Third Principle to Second and View of Entire Development

                          (6) From eschaton to Paradise

                               (a) paradise—Quaternity

                               (b) circularity

Note: F = Father, who is associated with the First Principle on the one hand, and the point of transition between the First and Second Principles, on the other. Also the letter X is the symbol for fall.

Figure 1.1. Boehme's Trinitarian mapping of inclusive ontotheological narrative.

service offered by the three Principles, and especially the first two. As a means, the trinitarian articulation of will is not a foundation. But the trinitarian artic- ulation of Principles (as a means) does serve as a foundation of the divine self, who is maximal realization of being, knowing, value, and existence.

One of the ways of thinking of the relation between Boehme and Hegel, who according to Baur in *Die Christliche Gnosis* represents the apogee of theogonically-inclined trinitarian articulation of an encompassing ontotheo- logical narrative (pp. 665–735), is that all traces of immanent-economic trini- tarian distinction collapse, since nothing remains outside the trinitarian becoming of the divine itself. Thus there is the excision in Hegel of the divine nothing or the immanifest divine (what I called in *The Heterodox Hegel*, *apophatic erasure*[53]), for the divine is always *arche*, always the process of mani- festation. And thus also, there is in Hegel the interpretation of the trinitarian movement before the emergence of nature as a real source of multiplicity and dialectic. This trinitarian movement is for Hegel the first act of divine mani- festation rather than the rehearsal it is in Boehme. I will have more to say on this important topic in a later volume on Hegel, when the relation between Hegel and Boehme will be treated *in extenso*.

Before I move on, however, from Boehme's use of the language of the Trinity, perhaps it would be useful to provide a schematization of his trinitarian scaping of the encompassing narrative of divine self-constitution.

CHAPTER 2

≈

Discursive Contexts of Boehme's Visionary Narrative

In chapter 2 I attempt a partial contextualization of Boehme's discourse by presenting the alchemical and negative theology discourses that Boehme avails himself of to articulate his speculative vision. If this presentation makes a historical claim about influence, the real interest is the systematic one of assessing the degree to which these discourses assist Boehme's essentially theogonic program. As I make clear in section one, alchemy, especially Paracelsian alchemy, offers considerable assistance in this respect. Boehme's narrative ontotheology can be regarded as the sublation of Paracelsian alchemy, in which theogony, at the very least, is inchoate. The linking of Boehme with Paracelsian alchemical discourse, however, subserves more than a taxonomic interest. It points toward genealogy. For it is not simply the case that each of these discourses helps to define the other as germ and realization respectively, but that one discourse (alchemy) anticipates Boehme's discourse that completes it, but most importantly recollects it. To the degree to which Boehme's narrative discourse is repeated in the modern period, then the Paracelsian tradition, and even Paracelsus remains alive. Conversely, echos of the Paracelsian tradition or of Paracelsus in modern discourse point toward Boehme's discourse as their most ample context.

The situation with regard to the relation between Boehme's discourse and the tradition of negative theology—especially negative theology in its more speculative Eckhartian form—is more complicated, and consequently, my account of relation will be less straightforward. While Boehme most definitely inhabits this tradition in terms of vocabulary and image, I will show that fundamentally he subverts this discourse. This has the important consequence that it essentially rules out a genealogy that would yoke Eckhart and Boehme together, as Baur does in *Die christliche Lehre von der Dreieinigkeit* (pp. 880–98).[1] More, it means that to sustain the case that one of these speculative discourses, for example, Boehme's, is Gnostic, not only does not necessarily entail that speculative negative theology is, but it also makes it

57

antecedently unlikely that such a verdict will be brought in. Notwithstanding speculative negative theology's considerable deviancy from the standard Christian traditions, another label will have to be found for it. The conditional anticipates the categorical. In Parts II and III I substantiate the hypothesis that Boehme's discourse is Gnostic or Valentinian.

2.1. Alchemy as Discursive Context and its Sublation

Since alchemy has an extensive and varied career in Western thought from the Middle Ages onward, not a great deal of light is shed on Boehme's discourse by maintaining that it is influenced by alchemy. What is required is some notice of the identity of the specific brand of theology-friendly, but not necessarily Christianly-orthodox species of alchemy in circulation in the post-Reformation thought of the sixteenth and early seventeenth centuries. If overall this identity is reflective and speculative rather than practical, and absolutely encompassing or pansophistic in its ambition, its particular identity is bound up with the name of Paracelsus (1490–1543) rather than with the names of Raimond Lull (1235–1315), Marsilio Ficino (1433–1499), or Giovanni Pico della Mirandola (1463–1494).[2] This is not to deny, however, that the work of Paracelsus bears some relation to these speculative alchemical traditions, and particularly to that of Ficino and Mirandola, whose names are invoked by him, and whose thought is current in Paracelsus's teacher, Trithemius (1467–1516).[3] But the Paracelsian form of alchemy is itself a post-Reformation event in an ideational sense and not simply in a chronological one. Whatever the Renaissance ingredient, then, in Theophrastus Bombastus von Hohenheim (Paracelsus's real name), it is the brave new world opened up by the Reformation that best situates his work.[4]

At one level, Paracelsus's thought can be understood as the humanistic complement to Luther's exclusive concern with Scripture. Nature too is a book, and no less than Scripture its mysteries or arcana demand elucidation. Moreover, the task of elucidation is far from hopeless, for like Scripture, nature is perspicuous. Transparence, however, demands critique, and becomes a real possibility when the distorting lens of Galenic and Avincennan medicine and Aristotelian physics is exposed. Truly earning the sobriquet of "bombastus," for Paracelsus, transparence only becomes actual in his own works, which represent the reformation of physical and medical science. At another level, the book of nature is not Paracelsus's exclusive focus—although even in this area Paracelsus does everything possible to upset the received wisdom of his empiricism, as observations quickly fade into abstruse speculations about origins. Scripture too is a concern, as is theological reflection on creation, Christ, and even the Trinity.[5] Paracelsus produces commentaries on the Psalms and

Matthew.[6] Genesis, John's Gospel, and the letters of Paul are recurred to with some frequency. Ultimately what Paracelsus seeks is a kind of knowledge, theory, or wisdom that embraces physics (or metaphysics) and Scripture and theology, a wisdom in which *Naturphilosophie* is theologized, and a theology is, to an equal extent, naturalized. It is important to assert the inclusive and synthetic ambitions of Paracelsian thought against the background of earlier literature, which tended to ignore the biblical and theological dimensions,[7] and against some of the more recent literature which, though it acknowledges the presence of both *Naturphilosophie* and Scripture, seems to think of them as representing two hermetically sealed universes.[8] This is not to say, however, that the synthesis is realized in Paracelsus's own work, but rather, it animates the Paracelsian tradition. As Andrew Weeks points out, it still flourished in Gorlitz, Bohemia, at the end of the sixteenth century,[9] a town forever associated with Boehme, who is sometimes represented by the proper description of "the shoemaker from Gorlitz."

That there is considerable nonsense in Paracelsus, and an abundance of evidence that his abilities fall short of his aim, almost goes without saying. What he does succeed in doing is bequeathing to the following generations a comprehensive vision of reality in which the visible world as a whole is a sign or "signature" of the invisible dynamic reality, and individual entities signs or signatures of invisible microprocesses. The theory of signatures is at once closed and open-ended, mechanical and inferential: the correspondence of planets and metals is established, the influences of the stars on human life offered as a fact requiring explanation. There are in addition invisible forces beyond the astral level that get exemplified in nature and human beings. The theory of signature is central to Paracelsus's self-interpretation as a physician, who must go beyond the bodily manifestations or symptoms of a disease to its cause. And, obviously, it supplies an optics for the scaffolding of the world. Thus, Michel Foucault is not totally beside the point in underscoring its importance,[10] an importance only aided by its subsequent history in the sixteenth century in Weigel (1533–1588), and in the seventeenth century in Boehme, whose *De Signatura Rerum* (1622) represents an unsurpassed recapitulation of what is articulated in Paracelsus's *De Rerum Naturae* as well as in the *Opus Paramirum*, *Philosophia ad Athenienses*, and *Philosophia Sagax*, all of which belong to the second period of two decades of furious Paracelsian production (1530s). Yet the universe in general (human being in particular) is not only semiotic but iconic. The universe is an image (*bilt, biltnus*)[11] (as is human being) of the invisible, though the universe and human being also image each other as macrocosm and microcosm. As such, both universe and human being have form, shape, and figure. One might say that they have aesthetic definition. In one sense the universe and human being express divine crafting. In a more important sense, however, as image, they demonstrate the power of imagination that can be traced back to the root of reality, but whose functioning, for good or ill, is particularly evident in human being.

Scriptural warrant can be provided for the view of universe and human being as signature and picture. Paracelsus can appeal to the Psalms (esp. 63) and Romans (esp. 1.19–20), among other texts. It is important, however, to make two points about Paracelsian semiosis and iconism. First, the thing is the sign, and not simply its disposable vehicle, and the picture does not simply mimic, but in a sense renders its nonmaterial presupposition. Second, the semiotic and iconic universe is underwritten, Koyré suggests, by a vitalism and organicism that has few equals in the sixteenth century.[12] Sign and image have to do with the process of life that interprets, and in turn is interpreted by, the production of gold in the alchemical retort, on the one hand, and creation and redemption as re-creation, on the other. For Paracelsus, life is dramatic, involving a reversal to chaos, as evident in creation and redemption as in the alchemical process. But for a physician, signs and images are not always, or even generally, benevolent.

Signs and images indicate and represent the out-of-joint, life restricted and blocked, life in its negative or poisonous quality. Signs and images, then, show a complex reality with the problem of evil and salvation very much to the fore. The form of salvation for Paracelsus is obvious: on physical and moral levels salvation represents the triumph of the healthy over the poisonous, the positive in life over the negative. How salvation is to be enacted, and how the negative is mastered and "separated out," is the stuff of a theory that can no more avoid christological and eschatological ruminations than accounts of origin can avoid the discourse of the fall.

To think of the universe as signature and image, from an explanatory point of view, is to think of it as expressive of invisible forces or powers of dynamic life. But Paracelsus is not happy simply to trace the proximate arcana of the visible elements or their effects. His discourse concerns itself with the ultimate origins in the domain of the invisible. The descent into origins is an ascent along a chain or ladder of more and more refined invisible dimensions of existence. Moreover, the calibrated move *to* origin is matched by a description of move *from* origin, whether origin is defined in terms of the Trinity, *mysterium magnum*, or by means of the "ultimate matter" at the basis of "prime matter"—although, as I will show later, the discourses of *mysterium magnum* and ultimate and prime matter overlap. Essentially, therefore, the speculative thought of the mature Paracelsus charts something like a narrative of the expressivity and dynamism of reality. But Paracelsus neither can nor does avoid identifying reality with divine reality. In this sense, no less for Paracelsus than for Aristotle, who is the object of his invective, *to on* is *to theion*. Paracelsus is certainly no exception, therefore, to the so-called ontotheological illusion that Heidegger asserts haunts all of Western thought.

Until very recently there would have been resistance to this ontotheological claim, even in commentators such as Pagel and Koyré, who acknowledge the
religious or theological dimension in Paracelsus's thought. Aside from some
residual effect from the previous antitheological interpretive dispensation, the
main reasons are that while *mysterium magnum*, which is the ultimate origin or
"mother" of all things,[13] admits of theological reading, it does not demand it, and
that the three prime Paracelsian properties of sulphur, salt, and mercury are
metaphysical and cosmological properties that, at critical points in Paracelsus's
work, function independently of religion and theology.[14] To the degree, therefore, that *mysterium magnum*, other relative origins,[15] and the three prime properties are interpreted in this exhaustively metaphysical or naturalistic way, it has
an effect on how one construes the relation between Paracelsus and thinkers in
the Lutheran field like Weigel and Boehme who assimilate his work.

The reading becomes simple and simplified: Weigel and Boehme represent nothing more nor less than the biblical and theological cooption of purely
cosmological and metaphysical categories of speculative alchemy in the post-
Reformation situation. But Paracelsus's texts suggest a more complicated story.
Certainly, the narrative of ontological expressivity is more developed in him
than has hitherto been thought, to the point of anticipating the encompassing extent of Boehme's narrative. Most importantly, however, at its very
root the narrative of manifestation is theologically defined, for not only does
Paracelsus interpret the three Principles by means of the doctrine of the Trin-
ity and vice versa (as in Boehme), but again, as in the most speculative of the
Protestant mystics, more originary than *mysterium magnum* is the realm of the
Trinity and the divine feminine.

In his important early work on the Trinity, the *Liber de Sancta Trinitate*
(1524), Paracelsus reflects on the Trinity that overcomes the hiddenness and
unity of the divine. Either ignorant or sanguine about the deviance of his view
of the Trinity from that of the tradition, Paracelsus writes:

> God was in the beginning alone (*allein*), without any beginning (*ohn allen an-
> fang*) and not in three persons, alone one (*ein*) God, who is not called either
> God the Father, God the Son, [nor] God the Holy Spirit, or all three to-
> gether. But rather God, the Almighty Creator and Destroyer of all, was *one*
> God (*ein gott*), *one* being (*ein wesen*), one divinity (*ein gottheit*), one counte-
> nance (*ein gesicht*), one person, and no [was] one with him. And [he] remained
> so long alone until it pleased him to wed and increase himself and reveal him-
> self (*sich zu erzeigen*). (*SW* 11. 3, p. 238)[16]

Although somewhat incoherent in speaking of God both as one person and
three, the basic drift of Paracelsus's trinitarian thought is Sabellian. Important
as this typologization of the Trinity is, however, the obvious narratization
should not be ignored. Weeks is right in drawing attention to the folktalish or

mythic quality of "once upon a time" followed by an event in which the one undergoes multiplication into a three. One could say that what this Paracelsus text achieves (a few decades before Weigel, a century before Boehme, and almost three centuries before Hegel's *Lectures on the Philosophy of Religion*) is a remythicization of the divine, prosecuted ironically by the symbol of the Trinity, whose major function in the tradition, according to Hans Blumenberg,[17] is to repress myth. Moreover, a generic Sabellian trinitarian frame provides the basic coordinates for such remythicization. Before Boehme, one sees evidence of that kind of narrative mutation of Sabellianism that the nineteenth-century Catholic thinker Staudenmaier thought to be operative in the Reformation tradition, and which, according to him, achieved its apotheosis in Hegel.[18]

Arguably at a level that exceeds Jung's wildest assertions, Paracelsus elaborates a quaternarian rather than purely trinitarian view of the divine realm that overcomes oneness.[19] Coeternal with the Trinity of Father, Son, and Spirit is the "celestial queen," which forms the prototype of Eve and Mary (11.3, 244–46). The anticipation of Boehme is here remarkable. The celestial queen is sometimes associated with Sophia, construed as the passive complement to the more active Trinity, figured as a mirror that reflects the divine back into itself. Paracelsus insists on the latter point: "From the beginning of the number of the Trinity God has first become double (*selb ander*), that is, two persons in one person" (11.3, 244).

Paracelsus is no less incoherent here in his announcement of two persons in one person than in his announcement of three persons in one person. To be fair to Paracelsus, however, his real interest appears to be that of specifying the conditions of origin or revelation that precedes the emergence of a ground of differentiation and multiplicity that will be represented in the material world. Momentarily, I will speak to Paracelsus's shifting identification of the ground, which gets reflected in Boehme's discourse, but the obvious is, perhaps, worth stating. Discussion of trinitarian and sophiological differentiations of the divine provide a theological frame for Paracelsus's more nearly cosmological or cosmogonical discussion of *mysterium magnum, yliaster,* and *astrum* as the devolution of ever less refined invisibles, just as they do in the discourse of Boehme, and especially of *De Signatura Rerum* (1622), which represents the crescendo of Paracelsian influence.

As in Boehme later (for whom the concept and not simply the term is important) in Paracelsus, *mysterium magnum* is a matrix or "mother." Paracelsus is not sure, however, whether *mysterium magnum* is a real matrix, thus a real source of differentiation and multiplicity, or just its preformation, thus an anticipation of a true source of differentiation and multiplicity. These alternatives are hinted at in the association of both ultimate and prime matter with *mysterium magnum,*[20] where it is prime matter and not ultimate matter in which there is a power of differentiation (*archeus*).[21] The Paracelsian conundrum, and

Paracelsus's basic attempt at a solution, is recapitulated by Boehme, who, however, is never tempted in a way that Paracelsus is to think of *mysterium magnum* as a true gynecological source.

One obvious corollary of Paracelsus's account of the devolution from *mysterium magnum* of less refined (but ontologically more creative) matrices involves the overcoming of the traditional creation-from-nothing account of creation. Creation is understood to involve just what Augustine early on ruled as the contrary of the Christian view—that is, creation *from* God.[22] As Paracelsus puts it in the *Book of Minerals*, God is all in all (*alles in allen*); God is both the ultimate and prime matter of all things (1.3.34).

The trinitarian and sophiological framing of expressivity and manifestation also contextualizes Paracelsus's reflection on sulphur, salt, and mercury as the principles of transition, fixity, and mobility respectively. One of the clearest declarations of this is to be found in the tract *De Genealogia Christi* (1530), in which the triad of properties grounding the physical world is associated directly with the Trinity (11. 3.63).[23] Confident of the general correspondence, Paracelsus does not work out systematically specific correspondences between Father, Son, and Spirit and particular alchemical properties, as Boehme, with great ingenuity does later. Nor does Paracelsus speculate overmuch about the relation between the alchemical properties and Sophia, the fourth 'hypostasis,'[24] who, extraordinarily interesting from the perspective of Boehmian appropriation, is said to be not powerful (*gewaltig*) (11.3.246) from the point of view of creativity.[25]

These are issues, which if they engaged the Paracelsian and Weigelian traditions, were sorted out over time by Boehme, who associated sulphur with the Son, mercury with the Spirit, and salt with Sophia.[26] Paracelsus is also unclear (in a way that Boehme is not) about the relationship of the triad of properties to *mysterium magnum*, on one hand, and the *yliaster*, on the other. Whether these properties articulate the former or the latter will depend on whether or not the former is considered a real matrix or not, for these properties articulate a real matrix. Boehme, who ultimately identifies *mysterium magnum* and Sophia (e.g., *SPT* 1. 62; 6.1–4; *DI* 1, 23),[27] judges therefore that the real link between the alchemical properties and a cosmogonic Principle occurs at the level of the *yliaster* or Eternal Nature, though Boehme's configuration of the *yliaster* is considerably more complex than that of Paracelsus's, and considerably more theologically (and specifically christologically) developed.[28]

The theological emphasis is apparent also in Paracelsus's account of the emergence of the physical world. The proximate origin or matrix that goes under the name of the last invisible (that is, the *astrum*)[29] is associated with the abyss or chaos of Genesis 1 on which order is imposed. The correspondence depends, however, on a reading of the Genesis creation story that refuses to demythologize it, and, arguably, mythologizes it further by thinking of order as emerging rather than being imposed on chaos. What relation the chaoses of *mysterium magnum* and the *yliaster* have with the *astrum*, and in turn with the abyss of Genesis, is not elucidated. Its working out exercises the Paracelsian tradition, and finds its completion in Boehme. The emergence of human being is even more biblically and theologically specified. Like the physical universe, human being has its origin in the chaos that is the source or root of the physical universe. And as with the universe, human being is an image.

Yet Paracelsus agrees with the theological tradition that human being is an image in a way unlike any other entity in the universe, and the biblical distinction between likeness and image is intended to register the difference that flatters human being. That which precisely is the content of the difference is ciphered in the second creation story, where, made out of the stuff or *limbus* of the physical universe, human being is infused with the breath or spirit of the eternal and divine. Thus, human being transcends the cosmos, something absolutely essential to Paracelsus, who thinks of Aristotelian hylomorphism as providing a mundane and reductionistic anthropology.[30]

Despite the pneumatic differentiation of human being that constitutes likeness, the human condition is fraught. Though Paracelsus tends to judge all those who have disappointed him as being incarnations of evil, understandably, given the fact that he is a physician, the emphasis tends to fall on natural evil and especially diseases that ruin whole communities (e.g., plagues) as well as individuals. Disease is so rampant that life cannot be characterized as good; one must see life as the battle between poisonous and healthy life. But disease also demands an explanation. Since no rational explanation is forthcoming, Paracelsus recurs to the fall and the perturbation of nature—*turba*—that is its consequence. The *astrum* is to a large extent the *ca-gastrum*.[31] The myth of fall has its correlative in the overcoming of the poisonous life that finds its image in the alchemical retort. In the context of a description of human existence and the hoped-for cure, Christ is the image of the physician who heals, or, perhaps better, the image of the physician who gets healed. For Christ is the one who lives with the poison of life and goes down to death to emerge whole and entire. Christ is the process of transition, what Jung calls *enantiodromia* (*SR* 11, 6; 11, 11). This view is also present in Boehme, who borrows from non-Paracelsian alchemical sources in his figuring of Christ as androgynous.[32] But Christ is also an eschatological figure, for he is the promise of the separation of the poisonous from the healthy elements that cover psychic as well as physical life.

The rehearsal of the theologically framed Paracelsian narrative puts the issue of the relation between Paracelsus and Boehme on the proper footing. For failing to get the religious and theological measure of Paracelsus's science or wisdom means that one tends to frame the relation between Paracelsus and Boehme in terms of a Paracelsian *Naturphilosophie* that Boehme either fails or succeeds in domesticating. There is no denying that the latter way of construing the relation is at least relatively adequate. Though the theological dimension to Paracelsus's reflections on origins and the three alchemical properties are ineluctable, it is true that these constructs are still somewhat theologically underdetermined. If there is significant appropriation by Boehme of Paracelsus, then this, certainly, would involve ratcheting up the theological incidence. And there is, of course, significant appropriation of Paracelsus.

From my account of Paracelsian narrative, it is clear that Boehme endorses its basic drift and repeats many of its individual features. By contrast with what is found in Paracelsian narrative, Boehmian narrative represents a much higher level of synthesis between alchemical processes and cosmology, and between both of these and theology. Relations between *mysterium magnum*, *yliaster*, and the three alchemical properties are worked out much more methodically, and Boehme is able to achieve a much greater integration of alchemy, cosmology, and theology in his reflection on the eternal Christ who rises from the chaos of the Eternal Nature or the *yliaster* as the new being that is shining and splendid. And it is precisely in his agonic Christology that Boehme also looks squarely at evil as a nonaccidental force with which the divine has to reckon.

Any number of further illustrations of the greater synthetic power of Boehme could be provided. But two are especially worthy of comment: (1) the newfound role of imagination as a source of reality for evil as well as good and (2) the development of the narrativity dimension of Paracelsian narrative. I begin with Boehme's profound reflections on the imagination.

(1) If Paracelsus's reflection on the imagination ultimately represents something of a breakthrough,[33] this is not to deny that much of Paracelsus's reflection is disappointing. For the most part he operates within an anthropological frame, and his insights probably fall short of what is realized in the Renaissance.[34] His discourse is bedeviled with misogynist accounts of why the imagination of women pregnant or menstruating should be feared.[35] Whether for good or evil, one can say that for Paracelsus, as for Coleridge much later, imagination is a plastic power—that is, it impresses form and shape on a substance. Occasionally, however, Paracelsus thinks of imagination more globally as an invisible power of formation in the universe,[36] indeed a power that one can ultimately trace back to the divine itself, of which human being is the image. It is this later aspect that is capitalized on by Boehme, for whom imagination becomes associated in the first instance with the Trinity and Sophia. The Trinity is regarded as the projector of images, with Sophia understood to be the passive screen or mirror.

Yet another dimension of Paracelsus's understanding of imagination gets recapitulated and integrated into Boehme's speculations on Eternal Nature. If Paracelsus claims that imagination is a power that impresses an image on a substance, he also wants to claim that imagination impresses an image *as* substance (*Sämtliche Werke* [*SW*] 1. 7, p. 329). In fact, Paracelsus tries to underscore this point by reference to Hebrews 11.1, where faith is the substance of things unseen (*SW* 1. 7, p. 369). Here the creative dimension of imagination seems to be more to the fore. Boehme appropriates both senses of imagination, and assigns them to different narrative dimensions of divine expressivity and manifestation. For him, imagination as a bestower of forms characterizes the dimension of the Trinity and Sophia, whereas in the dimension of Eternal Nature that corresponds to the *yliaster*, imagination functions as providing substance.

Of course, the informing dimension is not absent from the second sense of imagination, since the giving of substance is ultimately also the giving of form. Moreover, as with Paracelsus (*SW* 1. 7, p. 369), in Boehme the second sense of imagination brings imagination into proximity with will or desire, even lust, though in Boehme's case the erotic dimension of imagination functions at a much more primordial level than that suggested by the writings of Paracelsus. In any event, it is only against the backdrop of this theological identification of imagination, which is an event in post-Reformation thought, that Boehme plots the episodes of concupiscent outbreak of imagination in Lucifer, which leads to the creation of the temporal world, and a similar outbreak in Adam, which leads to the loss of Eden and the agon of history that is only eschatologically overcome.

(2) This brings me to a second area in which Boehme's discourse goes beyond what is found in Paracelsus and his tradition. Boehme develops symbolically coded oppositions that, at best, are virtually narrativity-oriented in Paracelsus. By and large the Paracelsian narrative describes a circle, although it is unclear whether the circle has its origin-end in the Godhead or in the Quaternity. Three symbolically coded oppositions in Paracelsus, which are also found in the Boehmian narrative, put the circular pattern under pressure. The force of this pressure is worth examining. The first of these is the symbolically coded opposition of speech and silence. Anticipating a position that becomes central in all of Boehme's texts (and is particularly evident in *De Signatura Rerum*, e.g., 1.14–15), Paracelsus makes clear that in speaking of physical reality as signature he is thinking of it as a form of speech.[37] This means that the expressivity of reality can be regarded as a form of speaking, and narratively this speaking can be traced back to the Son as Word, and to a lesser extent Sophia, to the degree to which *sema* and *icon* overlap in Paracelsus. In a certain sense, as grounds of speech, *mysterium magnum* and the other origins are not themselves speech but eloquent forms of silence. And clearly the world disturbed by Adam's concupiscence is a world in which language is no longer transparent. Paracelsus does not draw the conclusion Boehme does—namely, that speech in its fully realized sense has as its condition a refusal of speech or communica-

tion, a conclusion that would make narratively later forms of speech superior to narratively earlier forms of speech, including the speech of the Quaternity.

Similarly, with the symbolically coded oppositions of light and darkness, blindness and seeing: the light of the Spirit operative in the physical universe (though ultimately not of it),[38] in Paracelsus can be retrojected back to the Quaternity in general, the Trinity in particular. The word involved in creation is the word of light, of visibility, where visibility and expression are as connected as speech and ocular codes tend to be. And again, Christ is connected with light (*SW* 1. 7, p. 271).[39] Of course, there is a relation between darkness and light, but the real issue is whether this relation pushes Paracelsian narrative in a narrativity or theogony direction or stops short. In most cases of relation covered by Paracelsus, the relation turns out to be of an anterior-posterior kind, rendered in more a descriptive than explanatory mode. The intratrinitarian Word has as its background the hiddenness of God, and as active in creation, the Word supposes a background of a dark chaos. Moreover, as the symbol of light, Christ has as his indispensable background the darkness of godforsakenness and death. It is, perhaps, on the christological plane that Paracelsus most nearly rises to asserting a relation of anteriority-posteriority between darkness and light of a more than descriptive kind. Along the Christology axis, therefore, there is a trace of narrativity momentum in the ocular narrative code.

I will be brief about the second of the two oppositional ocular pairs—that is, the pair of blindness and seeing, or blindness and insight. When Paracelsus thinks of the fourth hypostasis as a mirror, he is implying two things: (1) that the Trinity, or Quaternity in general, is a seeing or knowing, and (2) that the privilege or curse of the Godhead or unitary divine is that it is not a mirroring, seeing, or knowing. Mirroring or seeing are concretely approved of in Paracelsus, so that the question is raised at least whether affirming the blindness and unknowing of the Godhead would be consistent with this approval. Moreover, this mirroring or seeing, virtually there in the fourth 'hypostasis' and the Trinity, is also an eschatological realization, in which ignorance is banished. Sophia functions prominently in the eschatological realization of knowledge that represents the conspectus of the lineaments and forces of all reality. There is potential in Paracelsus for saying that Sophia functioning eschatologically has a wisdom superior to the mirroring and wisdom of Sophia of the Quaternity, which would decisively break the Paracelsian circle. Despite Paracelsus's emphasis on wisdom as a work, the so-called *labor sophia*, the texts do not necessarily oblige. Distinctions between the beginning and end of divine knowledge in general, and specifically between modalities of mirroring, await Boehme.

Finally, there are the symbolically coded oppositions that make up the organic code. At least on the level of observation, life has negative as well as positive aspects. Being a physician, Paracelsus often parses this as the conflict between the poisonous and the healthy life.[40] More importantly, there is a general sense in which, at the level of the cosmos, he is prepared to think of poison being a presupposition of what is healthy. It is only in the ability to deal with and extract the poisonous that health truly is possible. Here again there is a narrativity thrust, but connections are not made with more primal elements of narrative, nor does Paracelsus undertake an investigation into the *turba* with respect to whether the fall really represents a *felix culpa*. These connections would have radicalized Paracelsus's position. What might also have radicalized Paracelsian narrative is a generalization of the growth image by which Paracelsus characterizes life—that is, the image of 'seed' that perishes before it gives rise to the plant.[41] Such generalization would help to introduce the kind of global teleological incidence to metanarrative found in Boehme. By contrast with Paracelsus, Boehme will trace the poisonous life back to Eternal Nature, Paracelsus's *yliaster*, and argue that poisonous life is necessary for the healthy and elevated life of the Second Principle, which is often identified with Christ.

Taken together, therefore, while speech, ocular, and organic codes in Paracelsus put pressure on the circular pattern of the narrative, they do so fairly feebly. Ultimately, therefore, we are not dealing, as we are in Boehme, with a narrative pattern in which the articulation of expressivity and its conditions constitute a divine that is more in the end than in the beginning.

It is clear from the foregoing interpretation, then, that in the domain of a narrative of divine manifestation Boehme both repeats and surpasses Paracelsus. This, of course, implies that Paracelsus is a presence in Boehme's texts, whose significance is a function of the textual extent of recall and its exigence. While for scholarly reasons it is important to admit that Boehme's work up to and including *De Signatura Rerum* (1622) shows greater Paracelsian presence than later works like *Mysterium Magnum* (1623) and *De Electione Gratiae* (1623), the Paracelsian narrative is present in these later texts, albeit in more covert form. Moreover, it is important to point out that the presence of Paracelsus throughout Boehme's texts is exigent. Paracelsian alchemy or pansophism offers an incomplete sketch of an encompassing narrative of divine expressivity, and hints at least of the logic of narrativity. Paracelsian 'influence,' therefore, should not be underestimated. By the same token, the presence should not be overestimated. First, Boehme is not reducible to the sum of the discourses he presupposes, not to mention this single discourse. Second, however exigent Paracelsian discourse is in Boehmian texts, it cannot be assumed to be more important than the other discourses woven into Boehme's complex discursive web, especially the threads of Luther, mystical theology, and Kabbalah. But Paracelsian discourse may well be a more exigent presence than some others. The account of the deconstitution of negative theology enacted by Boehme's narrative predeliction will, I hope, suggest that Paracelsus is ultimately more of a force than the Eckhartian mystical theology tradition that is also an indelible part of Boehme's discursive inheritance. It is to this negative theology inheritance that I now turn.

2.2. Narrative Deconstitution of Negative Theology

In chapter 1, I provided an interpretively underdetermined sketch of Boehmian metanarrative, a metanarrative that horrified the nineteenth-century Catholic Staudenmaier as much as it pleased the Protestant Baur. The first section of this chapter focused on the role Paracelsian alchemy played in Boehme's metanarrative discourse both with a view to contributing to the historical contextualization of Boehmian discourse in the complex post-Reformation field, and suggesting that in its sublated Boehmian form alchemy continues to be a trace element in certain Romantic (e.g., Blake) and Idealist (e.g., Hegel) discourses. In the second section of this chapter, I wish to contribute further to the historical contextualization of Boehme's narrative discourse by considering its relation to the German negative theology tradition that in Boehme's mature texts is constantly recalled and also, I am suggesting, subverted.[42] The accent falls on the act of subversion of negative theology by radical narrative with a deep iconic predilection that repeats itself in the meta-aesthetic projects of Romanticism and Idealism. Placing the accent thus is in part determined by the suggestion made by Baur in *Die christliche Lehre von der Dreieinigkeit* (pp. 880–98) that Eckhart is really Boehme *avant la lettre*, who, of course, in turn is the anticipator of Hegel.

As Baur describes it, what is central to Boehme is also central to Eckhart—namely, the understanding of the divine as becoming (*Werden*), process (*Process*), and development (*Entwicklung*) (p. 889). This suggestion, no notice of which is given in *Die christliche Gnosis*, where Boehme is understood to be a post- Reformation thinker, is misleading on a number of counts. It fails to place Eckhart in his own largely Neoplatonic ideational context in which the "divine birth" (*Gottesgeburt*) has to be understood in the context of an antecedent privileging of divine unity.[43] Expressive dynamism cannot necessarily be equated with process and development, a narrative of divine manifestation with divine narrativity or theogony. Relatedly, Baur's account fails to pay attention to those elements structuring the dynamic of manifestation in Boehmian narrative that make it distinct from the narratives of negative theology, elements such as *eros*, *kenosis*, and the agonic pattern of development.

As we have seen already, in Boehme the Unground (*Ungrund*) is the most general cipher for the divine that is beyond being, or better, the divine that transcends God considered as personal, creative, and redemptive ground of reality. Articulated proximally within the horizon of the Eckhartian line in

German mysticism,[44] the ultimate horizon of such a cipher is the mystical theology of Pseudo-Dionysius, in which the superessential Godhead (*hyperousias thearchia*) serves as the critical limit to intellect's attempt to comprehend and language's power to name.[45] In Eckhart, the superessential Godhead (*Überwesentliche Gottheit*) transcends knowing, and is encountered only in unknowing. Or, given that this unknowing is yet an experience, one might say in the language of postmodernity, that the superessential Godhead is accessed only by "knowing otherwise."[46] Boehme's *Ungrund* recalls the *Urgrund* of Eckhart's Godhead (*Gottheit*),[47] whose reality is different from, and ultimately superior to, that of the personal God who is the object of faith, worship, and solicitation. But the *Urgrund* is also different from the Trinity as the interior manifestation or conversation of the divine. In recalling Eckhart's *Urgrund*, then, Boehme also recalls Eckhart's radicalization of Pseudo-Dionysius's position on the relation between the superessential Godhead and the Trinity.

Whereas in the case of Pseudo-Dionysius, at the very worst there exists occasional suggestions of a distinction between Godhead and Trinity,[48] in Eckhart's case the distinction is relatively systematic.[49] The Godhead is mystery not manifestation, "barren" and inexpressive rather than expressive, silence rather than word. To the degree, therefore, to which the Trinity introduces manifestation, expressivity, and expressibility, it belongs to the God side of the Godhead-God distinction. Boehme also recalls Eckhart's further radicalization of Pseudo-Dionysius's mystical theology by linking the Unground with the extreme apophatic cipher of nothing (*Nichts*).[50]

Recall of Eckhartian positions suggests that Boehme is occupying a form of Christian mysticism threatened at least by a Christianly undomesticated form of Neoplatonism. Nevertheless, the occupation is more nearly like a reoccupation, for while, unlike positive theology, Boehme continues to think that a radically transcendent divine (that is, a divine that is hidden, mysterious, inexpressive, and inexpressible) can and should be cited as the reality presupposed by all manifestation, thus anarchic (*an-arche*),[51] he completely reverses Eckhart's priorities and transvalues the ontotheological values operative in Eckhart's commentaries and sermons that circulate in the German mystical tradition, albeit most often in diluted form. The priority now is not the hidden God but the God of manifestation. Or put otherwise, the focus is not on the mystery on which no illumination can be shone, but on the mystery of divine manifestation and self-manifestation, divine expression and self-expression, and the establishment of relation between the divine and its other, constitutive of its very selfhood. The reversal has as its context, if not its explanation, Luther's focus on the revealed God, who is hidden in his very revelation and, arguably, is supported by Paul's own reversal of the definition of mystery in Acts 17, where mystery can no longer be identified with the Unknown God but with the divine communication that achieves unsurpassable form in Jesus Christ.

The transvaluation of Eckhartian values enacted in Boehmian texts is focused on the process whereby the supereminent estimations of unity (Sermons 2, 13, 22, 29, 65, 67), simplicity (Sermon 13), divine unknowing (Sermon 77), impersonality (Sermons 10, 67), a state of being beyond good and evil (Sermons 9, 23, 24, 40), and passionlessness (Sermons 6, 12, 13) devalue themselves in favor of difference, multiplicity, divine knowing of a subject-object sort, divine personality, effective divine goodness, and divine passion or feeling. The system of Eckhartian evaluation obviously has roots in Neoplatonism, but a Neoplatonism that, on the one hand, disturbs the equilibrium in classical Neoplatonism between inexpressive and expressive, and between kataphatic and apophatic tendencies, in favor of the first term of each of the pairs, and, on the other hand, a Neoplatonism that functions without the benefit of Christian expressive and kataphatic tempering, introduced by the commitment to God revealed in Jesus Christ and the Trinity. Boehme does more, however, than restore the equilibrium. Proceeding antithetically, he uncovers the movement of deconstitution whereby the divine Unground or "nothing" (*Nichts*) sheds itself of inexpressive and apophatic disvalues. Interesting also, in the light of Boehme's mature texts, is Eckhart's simultaneous denial of knowledge or self-knowledge in the divine nothing and his suggestion of the superiority of knowledge to being (Sermon 9). In the first case Eckhart seems to give priority to the ontological and puzzle over how knowledge is possible, if knowledge in the proper sense supposes a distinction between subject and object. The options are the classical ones of Neoplatonism, denial of knowledge altogether, or positing of a form of knowledge without subject-object differentiation.[52] Eckhart seems to articulate at different times one or other side of the Neoplatonic dilemma. In the second case, anxious to distinguish his position from that of Aquinas, Eckhart seems to prioritize the gnoseological. The beyond of being is knowing.[53] No contradiction exists here, however. To speak about knowing at the level of ultimate reality is necessarily to speak of it in ontological or meontological terms. And to speak about ultimate rather than relative reality is to speak of it in gnoseological terms. Nevertheless, it is clear that by granting the gnoseological parity with the ontological, Eckhart prepares the way for its dominance in Boehme texts like *Mysterium Pansophicum* and *Sex Puncta Theosophica*. For the question to be answered in Boehme is, as the great French commentator on Boehme, Alexandre Koyré has put it, "What are the conditions necessary for the divine to have or acquire self-consciousness or self-knowledge, of saying I?"[54] And answering that question also answers the question whether self-consciousness of the divine must necessarily proceed through a form of knowledge that is finite.[55]

The reversal of priorities and transvaluation of Eckhartian values has as its condition Boehme's underwriting of the narrativity of the divine. No less than

Pseudo-Dionysius, Eckhart's description of the divine had to take the Christ-ian metanarrative of trinitarian articulation, creative expression, the incarnation of Christ, and human divinization into account. But Eckhart's radicalization of Pseudo-Dionysius made him less inclined than even his apophatically inclined precursor to think that the Christian metanarrative implied the narrativity of the divine. This is precisely the move made by Boehme, and ironically made by him with the help of Tauler and the *German Theology* that mediated Eckhart-ian ideas while domesticating them.[56] Of course, Eckhart is an unwitting agent in his own subversion to the extent that he speaks so often and so eloquently on the "divine birth" (*Gottesgeburt*).[57] 'Divine birth' is the trinitarian generation of the Word, whereby the Godhead moves from hiddenness to manifestation, namelessness to name, and from divine unselfconsciousness to consciousness and self-consciousness. At one level Eckhart is articulating the neoplatonic principle of diffusion that is the complement of the unitary nature of reality, while on another level the divine birth is a demand of soteriology. Salvation consists in being given birth to in the Word, and to a large extent *as* the Word. To turn Eckhartian negative theology against itself, in Boehmian texts the dif-fusion tendency is maximized,[58] while the soteriological drive is repressed. Di-vine birth is assimilated to an ontotheology of divine manifestation in which the narrativity of the divine is indicated by the anticipative-recollective narra-tive form and aided and abetted by the narratively coded conceptual and sym-bolic oppositions discussed in chapter 1.

In Boehme the basic mechanism of transvaluation-devaluation of Eck-hartian ontotheology is will. Will executes this devaluation, first, by undoing the would-be complacency and stillness or repose of the Unground as the divine nothing—features promoted by Eckhart and sponsored by Pseudo-Dionysius and Plotinus before him—and, second, by launching the process of manifestation in and through which a determinate, self-reflexive divine comes to be. Will deconstitutes the discreative anarchy of the divine beyond, and in-augurates beginning, or the beginning of beginning, which, sensing the possi-bility of a misunderstanding, Boehme insists, is not an absolute beginning but the beginning of manifestation (*MM* 4, 7). In one sense, therefore, will is *arche*, but in another, will is anarchic, because it has no foundation and admits of no further explanation. Negative and positive aspects of will, however, are only an-alytically separable, since will defines the radically hidden depths of the divin-ity as insufficient, mere potential for perfection rather than its actuality.

Much more significant than his much touted prioritization of will over in-tellect in the divine—a prioritization that is the achievement of nominalism and Luther—is Boehme's interpretation of will as the actualization of divine potential, which implies that privation belongs to the divine, as does the rest-less, dynamic process of development. Neither within the Eckhartian tradition, which serves as a proximate backdrop, nor the mystical theology tradition in general, nor, of course, the general theological tradition, is a privative reading of the divine regarded as legitimate.[59] For Neoplatonists like Eckhart and Pseudo-Dionysius, potentiality is a property of the world of multiplicity, and becoming is a sublunar phenomenon. While one reserves the right to go beyond the language of being, which possibly ensnares the divine in finitude, the divine, nevertheless, is not less than being as the really real (*ontos on*), just as the really real is not less than fully self-sufficient. Aquinas sums up what he considers to be the consensus Christian stance on the issue of whether potentiality and becoming can be ascribed to the divine when he states that God is pure act (*actus purus*) without a trace of potentiality, pure being without a shadow of becoming, and, of course, a reality fully sufficient and self-contained in Principle.

The process by which will negates the privative nothing of the Unground, and inaugurates the meontological process of divine self-constitution, is not blind. If will articulates Wisdom and the Trinity, and especially the Word, it is in turn articulated by them and shares in their luminosity which, however, remains virtual rather than actual. Will, therefore, has divine perfection and self-sufficiency as its aim, and as its goal, a differentiated, reflexive, passionate, and effectively good divine self or person. Against the backdrop of privation, and within the horizon of aim or intention (as the mechanism of transvaluation), will can be classed as erotic. *Eros* does not name an affect, but rather an ecstatic movement in which the expropriated "self" at the beginning—the self as placeholder—moves toward equality with the fully adequate and normative self that it desires. Importantly, within the classical frame set down by the *Symposium*—though obviously the analysis of *eros* in that text was intended only to apply to human beings and not to the divine as such—ingredient in *eros* is lack (*penia*). In Boehme's treatment of divine self constitution this lack is most apparent at the sophiological and trinitarian stages, where divine *eros* shows itself insufficiently powerful to constitute a true other to the divine, which is necessary for divine self-reflection. In these stages, Boehme suggests, divine will is still the will of the nothing, sufficient perhaps for breaking with the barrenness, inexpressiveness, and inexpressibility of the divine depths but not sufficient, or not yet sufficient, for radical divine fertility, expressiveness, and expressibility. In the earliest stages of its development (which might perhaps be illuminated by Freud's discussion on wish-fulfullment) will at best provides an outline of duality, an adumbration of variety and multiplicity, an indeterminate form of self-knowledge riddled by the *aporia* of whether infinite comprehension of the divine is possible, or more importantly, worthily predicated of the divine. Will also presents a form of goodness untested, thus "unproved," by its contest with evil, and sketches a form of divine experience without pathos and depth. The divisions or differentiations engendered by will at the level of the 'Immanent Trinity' and Wisdom neither constitute the divine ground, nor the principle of divine self-reflexion: they constitute simply a rehearsal of another kind of division or differentiation more tensionally powerful and dramatic, and with demonstrably superior actualizing force.

The erotic definition of the divine clearly deconstructs the Eckhartian tradition of discourse it inhabits. Eckhart reads the prologue of John's Gospel, for instance, to authorize a conception of the divine as superabundant generosity.[60] Boehme reads it contrarily. The indeterminacy and indigence of the radically transcendent divine set the basic terms for divine movement. Will is the interest in and power of overcoming indeterminacy and insufficiency in the apophatic divine, a partial sign of which overcoming is the "mirror" (*Spiegel*) of Wisdom. A more than partial sign of the trinitarian articulation of will is the creation of the eternal world. Obviously, it is Boehme, and not Eckhart, who is eccentric on this point. Though Eckhart raises the stakes by suggesting that in the final analysis divine solitude trumps divine love (Sermons 45, 56, 62, 66), he is persuaded no less than Aquinas and Bonaventure that the Neoplatonic trope of *bonum diffusivum sui* provides a relatively adequate metaphysical representation or underpinning of the biblical witness of divine love, whether this love operates at the intratrinitarian level (Sermons 56, 61) or in the economic sphere (Sermons 45, 56, 61). A diffusive love is obviously an agapaic love and supposes the superabundant reality of the divine. Within the contours of mystical or negative theology, therefore, Boehme opposes an erotic understanding of the dynamic of divine expression and manifestation to an agapaic understanding.[61] Or better, Boehme shows how the latter is interpreted by the former.

It is important to say more about the mechanism of will—now defined as a mechanism of *eros*—in and through which the divine becomes divine. Specifically, it is important to point out the mutation in the order of will that constitutes will as an ontological as opposed to a meontological source, and thus the transformation in the nature of eros that brings the divine closer to its self-realization in which it becomes possible to express itself agapaically. The erotic constitution of the divine is consolidated with the eruption of desire (*Sucht*), which represents the transformation of will into an ontologically productive power. Desire, which is responsible for the introduction of essence and life into the divine, is productive, however, only dialectically. That is, desire serves as the ground of divine expressivity by violently negating it, and the ground of divine expressibility (or divine self-naming) only as dumb inexpressibility. Desire represents will as fallen, as overcompensated implosion in which the *eidos* governing the teleology of the divine appears to be lost. Yet this fall into desire turns out to be happy, since the unbearable weight of being can be elevated into buoyant divine spirit or freedom that actualizes a heavenly eternal world objectified in the mirror of Wisdom.

Desire represents both the limit of the pull of the superessential or inessential divine, and the threshold at which the schemas or predelineations of divine existence gives way to vital and dramatic life. Desire is the foundation of Eternal Nature or the First Principle, the necessarily excessive counter to the ontological, gnoseological, axiological, and existential ineffectuality of the divine on both the level of the Unground as such and the Quaternity. The function of Eternal Nature is to provide for a matrix of otherness in the divine that is at once the condition of independent existence and a domain of essential reality that can be "used up," literally serving as fuel in the realization of a divine life as a spiritual essence. In itself, Eternal Nature is just the opposite of the kind of divine unity-in-difference that is the goal of divine will for self, just as its ignorance is the opposite of divine consciousness and self-consciousness, its evil the opposite of divine goodness, and its chaotically irresolvable pathos the opposite of the divine joy (*Freude*) that represents the term for the replacement for and the transvaluation of divine apathy. For divine being, knowledge, goodness, and feeling to be realized, the compulsive eros of Eternal Nature must give way to the agapaic love of Eternal Freedom. Dark desire must give way to an illuminated will in which the divine intention with respect to manifestation and self-manifestation is realized.

More needs to be said about the point of transition, especially in the light of Romantic appropriations of Boehme. What is important to observe here, however, is that along the evolutionary path of *eros* not everything proceeds incrementally. Contradiction is required, and transition is abrupt, occurring in a lightning flash (*Schrack* or *Blick*). This abrupt, dialectical transition is central to the narrative coding of conceptual and symbolic oppositions, for transition is at once both the point of greatest tension between dark and light, nonseeing and seeing, silence and speech, death and life, as well as the threshold of resolution, the movement from negative to positive states of being, in short *enantiodromia*. Though Boehme's view of contradiction finds a starting point in Luther's reflections on the *sub contrario* and possibly also in his view of *Anfechtung* and the suddenness of divine grace, Luther is at best a point of departure for a form of speculation that he likely would have felt pried too much into the "deep things of God" (1 Corinthians 2.10), speculation which certainly the Lutheran orthodoxy of Boehme's day thought smacked of ungodly curiosity.

Boehme's powerful statements about contradiction or contrariety (*contrarium*) in the heart of the being of beings, or God, attracted Blake, Hegel, and Schelling, and resounded in their discourses. It even attracted Engels, as he attempted, against the contrary judgment of Marx, to articulate dialectical materialism as a kind of *Naturphilosophie*.[62] And despite attempts to neutralize the originality of Boehme on this score, especially by Croce, who sees no difference between Boehme and Nicholas of Cusa, on the one hand, and between Boehme and Heraclitus, on the other,[63] this originality cannot be gainsaid. In neither Cusa nor Heraclitus is contradiction development; in neither is movement erotic. In Cusa the coincidence of opposites in God, who is not a possible object of perception or conception, is more structural than narrative, and more contrastive than contradictory.[64] No more than any other Christian Neoplatonist does Cusa, in *De Docta Ignorantia*, or his other major works, think that the divine integrates good with evil, or that the supreme being literally coincides with what is a privation of being.[65] As an object of comparison, Heraclitus is superficially in a better position, for at least in his case contradiction, struggle (*polemos*) and difference (*diapheron*) are at the heart of all reality. But again contradiction is not erotic: it does not admit of resolution. Becoming, for Heraclitus, is process without development, just the sort of view attractive to Nietzsche and Heidegger, both of whom wish to break with the teleological and narrative commitments of Western metaphysics and theology.

Consolidated by desire, the erotic physiognomy of the divine is reinforced by the symbol of fire. Grounded in desire, and the First Principle in general, fire represents the breakthrough to a genuinely divine life—that is, a life defined as divine by the normative standards of the Christian tradition—where God is considered to be perfect being, knowledge, and goodness. Reacting reflexively on Eternal Nature and its structuring qualities or forces, it is fire that gives energy and life to a sphere of being manifesting clear signs of entropy and movement toward death. Fire stands, therefore, at the center of the divine, such that the First and Second Principles articulate it as a dark and light fire respectively, thus a dark and light life. As the crossover between two Principles and two sets of qualities, it is through fire that the excessive features of Eternal Nature (that is, features such as massive constriction, chaotic formlessness, and eternal death) are burnt off as it were, and the qualities are sublimated into their constructive properties of form, positive energy, and life. The goal, of course, is a determinate divine self and a divine world, reflective of the divine self, in which form is living and not undone either by excessive centripetal or centrifugal force.

Implicitly, this brings fire and imagination into relation, for fire is a means whereby the divine world anticipated in divine Wisdom concretely comes about in the constitution of a heavenly Jerusalem that is a harmonic whole transparent of the divine. A point worth making here (as it both picks up elements of discussion in the first section of this chapter and anticipates reflection on the relation between Blake and Boehme in a subsequent volume) is that the proximate discursive context of the symbol of fire is alchemy. From *Aurora* to *De Signatura Rerum* the alchemical location of fire is indicated by the use of the term "*flagrat*," the pivotal point of "flaring up" and melting down of the prime matter that has as its aim the philosopher's stone that in the Paracelsian tradition is associated with the *filius*,[66] the Son or Christ, who is more an emblem than a distinct historical figure. Fire, therefore, is the transformation from discreative blockage into creativity and expression, the vulcanism of the genesis of divine selfhood, constitutive of which is the finalization of a divine order that constitutes a true other to God as real, self-conscious, personal, and good. The eternal Jerusalem, as the body or corpus of the divine, is the complete realized expression of the imaginative sketches in divine Wisdom, which without will turning creative, remains phantasmagoric.

It is Boehme, therefore, who on the threshold of modernity sets the precedent for the general Romantic association of imagination with will and energy, and for Blake's specific association of imagination with the powerful vitality of Christ and the Heavenly Jerusalem, at once Christ's bride and the mystical body of which he is the head. It is also Boehme who sets the stage for confounding the planes of divine and creaturely production, whether angels or human beings—although, arguably, here he was preceded by Paracelsus who also, as we saw in the first section, linked imagination and will. The divine magic brings a glorious expressive world into being out of the inchoate nothing through the detour of Eternal Nature, which functions as a crucible of pain, death, and transformation for the divine. The poetics of the divine mirror exactly the poetics of creaturely self-constitution, with the difference that the sublimation of desire, chaos, and wrath is more fraught in the case of creatures, as the mythologems of the fall of Lucifer and Adam so eloquently show. The divine is always and already the victory over nondivine darkness and death. As the later Schelling will put it: chaos and darkness are always the "past" (*Wesen*) in God.[67]

The finalization of *eros* lies in the Second Principle, which represents a liberation from the compulsiveness of desire and the realization of the divine milieu of determinate freedom and will. The Second Principle is light to Eternal Nature's darkness, as well as light to the fire of transformation, associated with the energy and power of the Father. Identified with Luther's God of Mercy (*Barmhertziggott*), the Second Principle identifies God as such in contradistinction to Eternal Nature, which is not so much God as God's narrative presupposition, that without which God cannot be all that God can be. If sometimes identified unequivocally with Christ, the Second Principle is more nearly a christic principle, which includes in addition to an agonically marked divine love, a pneumatologically marked expressiveness, expressibility and power of naming, and a sophiologically marked paradise. It is in the Second Principle that the divine is the really real, that divine knowledge is a comprehensive vision of a totality independent of, but not estranged from, the divine. It is in the Second Principle that divine goodness is effective because resistant to evil, and that divine feeling does not so much exclude pathos as elevate it into joy (*Freude*) (*MM* 40, 8).

While overall it is true that Boehme's model of the divine is erotic rather than agapaic, one could say that in the context of the finalization of eros that *agape* gets reinscribed. Agapaic expression is possible for a fully real or perfect divine, and the heavenly Jerusalem is the first instance of such expression, which welds power and love, energy and form. Other expressions follow like the creation of the material and temporal world in response to the perturbation consequent on the evil imagining of Lucifer, and, of course, the incarnation of Jesus Christ, whose Cross is a parable of the Cross and the agony at the heart of eternity. Nevertheless, in the last instance, *agape* is conditioned by eros. Indeed, if in one sense the heavenly Jerusalem is an expression of a divine fecundity that is unsurpassable, and thus realizes the definition of *agape*, in another sense it is the realization of divine eros, for it is only in such a totality of expression or self-objectification that the divine fully appropriates itself and becomes capable of agapaic love. Of the episodes covered in Boehme's metanarrative, it is the creation of the material-temporal world and incarnation that stand out most nearly as agapaic. Notwithstanding the fact that the divine is now fundamentally constituted, and thus in a potentially agapaic condition, it is not clear, however, that any unequivocal agapaic characterization is possible. First, the divine that acts in creation and incarnation is a divine determined by erotic production. Eros, therefore, haunts the *agape* of divine expression responsive to the destruction of the eternal world brought about by Lucifer's glance into the chaos of Eternal Nature, whereby he becomes what he sees and wills. Second, the creation of the temporal world in response to the Luciferian fall, and also, the incarnation in response to Adamic fall, appear to serve roles in reconstituting the totality of expression, truncated and rendered opaque in the two falls. And the restoration of the totality of expression is in a sense the restoration of the divine perfection itself that is the aim of divine development. Thus, even here eros seems to be effectively present in acts of a superficially agapaic character.

I turn now to the function of the trope of kenosis in Boehme as it is underwritten by the divine erotics of self-development. Boehme's speculative interest determines that kenosis functions more comprehensively in his system than it does in mainstream Christian, and specifically Lutheran thought, where its locus is primarily christological, though with the prospect of analogical extension to creation.[68] In Boehme's mature works kenosis appears to be an iterable operation present from the beginning at the deepest level of the divine. As the "being of beings" (*Wesen des Wesens*), the Unground empties into Wisdom and the Trinity, which empties into Eternal Nature, which in turn empties into divine freedom. The operation of kenosis, however, appears to be not only comprehensive but also radical. That is, it seems to involve more than the replacement of a divine form by an apparently nondivine form. In its movement from the inessential plane of the Quaternity of Wisdom and the 'Immanent Trinity,' it seems in fact to involve the emptying of what is nominally a divine reality and the corresponding filling of a nondivine content, which in turn gives way to a divine content that sublates the nondivine. Structurally speaking, therefore, the kenotic horizon of Boehme is essentialist rather than morphological.

Which is not to say that kenosis has nothing to do with form. In fact, the movement of kenosis is a movement in the divine toward form, toward aesthetic wholeness that corresponds to the divine as imagination.

Ultimately, however, neither the comprehensiveness nor radicality of kenosis, nor their union, adequately identify the Boehmian mode of kenosis, which Altizer rightly suggests is a precursor of the kenotic theologies of Blake and Hegel.[69] What makes an adequate identification of the Boehmian mode of kenosis possible is the erotic movement of the divine development. The eros, which enables the divine to constitute itself, determines that kenosis operates ironically, at least until the creation of Paradise or heavenly Jerusalem, and, arguably, even beyond this into creation of the material world and the incarnation. Kenosis functions ironically because in its operation what is emptied is not the perfect but the imperfect, not the full but the empty. Kenosis empties itself only of nothing and its shadow, of divine complacent unity, divine nescience, ineffectual goodness and feeling and perception. Correlatively, kenosis empties the divine into greater being and life, true differentiated unity, a mode of divine self-consciousness that presupposes consciousness of a complexly articulated divine world independent of the divine, of a mode of divine goodness exercised over evil, and a mode of divine feeling marked by, though not dominated by, pathos. Because of the mechanism of eros, then, kenosis is a form of plerosis, a way to divine perfection and self-sufficiency.

As a form of divine self-actualization, kenosis involves contradiction and death. Agonistics are central to the operation of kenosis on the level of the divine anterior to its expression in the material-temporal world. The agon is, of course, focused in the descent of divine will to expression into Eternal Nature which, as the chaotic ground of the divine, is the nothing with weight, the darkness that excludes light, and its triumphant reemergence and consummation in the heavenly Jerusalem. It is Eternal Nature that serves as the ground for the equally eternal Cross, which is the symbol of transformation as well as suffering, and which serves also as the referent of the historical Cross. As Berdyaev suggests, the temporal Golgotha points to the eternal Golgotha as its prototype.[70]

Needless to say, nothing like this view of kenosis is to be found in the discourses of mystical theology. Though the Eckhartian tradition was more prepared than Eckhart himself to insist on the importance of divine manifestation,[71] when Eckhart does focus on manifestation, no less than in Tauler or the *German Theology*, manifestation implies the superabundance of the giver. Presupposing the Neoplatonic trope of *bonum diffusivum sui*, the gift of presence no more depletes than repletes the divine. If the divine is the rich man who, discovering that his lady has lost an eye, takes out one of his own, this supposes that divine integrity from the beginning (Sermon 53). By contrast, in Boehme, on the divine level, as iterative divine emptying, manifestation moves from the less to the more, and thus involves a subversion of the Neoplatonic diffusion trope or, at the very minimum, its erotic rereading.

The ironic, because erotic, function of kenosis can also be read against the backdrop of mystical theology's view of divine activity. While the German mystical theology tradition after him, and Pseudo-Dionysius before him, gave activity a place at least the equal of the repose or stillness of the Godhead that transcends activity and inactivity, in his most daring moods Eckhart was inclined to draw an absolute line of demarcation between the inactivity of the Godhead and the activity of the personal God. God acts, the Godhead does not. Boehme's prioritization of activity over inactivity presupposes Eckhart's antithesis, while reversing the value or sign. Boehme's valorization of activity, then, does not constitute the kind of restoring of balance to be found in Ruysbroeck's correction of Eckhart in which activity is accorded equal value with the inactivity of the divine nothing, but a radical reading in which the activity of divine manifestation is a condition of the establishment of the divine self that is only inchoate in the divine nothing.

In making his correction, Boehme is dependent on Luther's emphasis on the activity of God, and his correlative disdain for the divine nothing of the mystical tradition. But, for biblical rather than metaphysical or theological reasons, Luther could no more have countenanced Boehme's vision of divine poetics than the tradition or traditions of mystical theology. In any event, it is clear that the ironic operation of kenosis permits the kind of economic interpretation of Boehme's erotic-agonistic narrative of the divine to which Bataille submitted Hegelian dialectic.[72] Divine self-emptying is a form of work that reaps ontological, gnoseological, axiological, and existential dividends. Moreover, the divine starts almost as "nothing" and with "nothing," so that the laborious giving or sacrifice of the divine is the scene of infinite accumulations of wealth of self. When Bataille, therefore, challenges the economics of Hegelian dialectic, he could equally be challenging Boehmian agonistics in which the rule is the rule of production and self-production. What is especially interesting about Bataille's challenge is that it is made in the name of the negative theology of Eckhart disavowed by Hegel and, as I hoped to have shown, deconstituted by the Boehmian variety of mysticism, which represents a kataphatic trojan horse in the folds of apophatic discourse, of that speaking and thinking otherwise that a number of postmoderns wish to recover.

Concluding Remarks

Part I of this text set itself the limited goal of offering a "good enough" account of Boehme's pansophistic mysticism, as well as exposing the effective presence of two other discourses that condition his discourse, arguably, to the point of making it possible. Throughout its two chapters it is the notion of 'narrative' that functions as the unifying key. In chapter 1 I provided a synoptic account of the six-stage narrative that both defines the object of vision and includes the subjective act. If the basic form of this narrative is circular, nonetheless the narrative describes a divine that becomes and develops in and through what is other than it on the plane of eternity and, arguably, in and through what is other than it in the world and history. I noted how this developmental or narrativity dimension plays out in Boehme's use of symbolic oppositions to structure his discourse, and how Boehme uses the symbol of the Trinity to interpret and configure the six-stage theogonic narrative. Although the purpose of the chapter is basically descriptive, not only the speculative boldness but also the oddness of Boehme's narrative and his trinitarian figuration should have been apparent. In any event, this oddness provides the impulse for Part II which deals with Boehme's multifold departures from the hermeneutic and substantive theological positions of the pre-Reformation and Reformation traditions.

In chapter 2 I focused on two "Christian" discourses that both historically and textually condition Boehme's discourse. In section one I showed that Boehme not only borrows a considerable part of his vocabulary from the Paracelsian tradition, and continues the process of theologization, but that he also amplifies and radicalizes a narrative figuration of the divine that stresses agon. In my account of the relation between Boehme's discourse and that of Paracelsian alchemy the emphasis falls on continuity, although discontinuities get their due in my treatment of the different accounts of imagination and the different use of symbolic oppositional pairs. By contrast, the emphasis definitely falls on discontinuity in section two when I discuss the relation between Boehme's discourse and the negative theology tradition of Eckhart. I show not only that significant discontinuity exists between these discourses over a number of theological regions such as view of the Trinity, Christ, and human being, but that in his very borrowing of speculative negative theology Boehme deconstructs or, as I put it, "deconstitutes" it. More specifically, I show that Boehme's discourse represents a transvaluation of Eckhartian commitments to a divine characterized by aseity, immanifestation, undifferentiation, unity, inactivity, and apathy into their opposites. Articulating this deconstitution serves the positive purpose of marking off three distinctive features of Boehme's ontotheological narrative that separate it from the exit-return model deployed by Eckhart and whose basic lineage is Neoplatonism. These features I name as eros, kenosis, and agon.

Even as my treatment of the relation between Boehme's discourse and the discourses of Paracelsian alchemy, on the one hand, and speculative negative theology, on the other, contextualizes Boehme's narrative discourse, and by implication removes some of its strangeness, possibly, even probably, the net result is to increase the feeling of strangeness. For one thing Paracelsian alchemy is not a "normal" discourse, or with Foucault in mind, not a "normal" Christian discourse. For another, Boehme does not inhabit just any negative theology stream of discourse but its most speculative and radical Eckhartian version. Again, however, as with chapter 1, the appearance of the oddness of Boehme's discourse is productive, and points to the need for the kind of systematic exploration that will be conducted in Part II. But in addition, there are also gestures here to Part III, which adjudicates on the relative merits of rival taxons for Boehme's discourse. For we see how in his discourse Boehme departs from and even subverts Neoplatonic-style negative theology, and this clearly damages the case for a Neoplatonic labeling of Boehme's narrative discourse.

~

PART II

Metalepsis Unbounding

Even though up until now I have operated by and large in the descriptive mode, it should be fairly obvious from Part I that by whatever measure, whether pre-Reformation or Reformation, Boehme's systematic unfolding of an absolutely encompassing narrative of the divine is anything but standard. Swerves from the mainline construals are evident over a whole host of theologoumena, and with respect to some theologoumena, for example, the Trinity, Boehme's departure is self-conscious. If anything, Boehme's swerve from the common tradition is even more startling on the general narrative level. For there seems to be little in common between his erotic-agonistic narrative and what would pass in most pre-Reformation and Reformation discursive contexts for the biblical narrative. Nevertheless, the full extent of Boehme's swerves in both their breadth and their depth have not been explored. And absent such exploration it is not possible to justify attributing to Boehme's system the kind of total and systematic narrative disfiguration-refiguration to which I have assigned the technical term *metalepsis*, or better *strong metalepsis*. In this part, therefore, I treat in an explicit fashion the full gamut of Boehme's hermeneutical and substantive theological swerves from the pre-Reformation and Reformation traditions.

    I begin with an important distinction. Boehme's hermeneneutical and substantive theological swerves are both *nondistinctive* and *distinctive*. By nondistinctive I mean to suggest pre-Reformation and post-Reformation traditions of exegesis and substantive theological position recollected by Boehme, which themselves are in significant tension with the common tradition. In practice, the post-Reformation tradition will be focused in the work of the so-called Spiritual Reformers, Sebastian Franck (1499–1545), Caspar Schwenkfeld (1490-1561), and Valentin Weigel (1533-1586), which was rejected by emerging Lutheran orthodoxy. By distinctive hermeneutical and substantive theological swerves I mean those features of Boehme's exegesis and theological position that go beyond what he shares with pre-Reformation and post-Reformation minority traditions, and that actually identify the unique forms of Boehmian deviance.

Under distinctive is included the swerve of Boehme's discourse at the level of narrative itself. If Boehme's pansophism ultimately is to be read as articulating a paradigmatic metaleptic form of Christianity, then the primary responsibility is borne by the distinctive swerves, and above all by the peculiarity of a narrative structure and dynamic that unites and explains individual swerves. The nondistinctive swerving elements, however, also play a role, and facilitate metalepsis by supplying a general background of swerve in Protestant thought that supports and encourages further experimentation and improvisation on the hermeneutical and substantive theological level. Of course, the contrast between nondistinctive and distinctive swerves is purely analytic. Nothing in Boehme's texts marks where one ends and the other begins. The purpose of the contrast is to separate out the sufficient (distinctive) from the plausibly necessary, but insufficient (nondistinctive), conditions for a swerving modern Christian discourse to be admitted to Gnostic return candidacy.

Even as I explore Boehme's multivalent swerving, however, I will pay attention to features of his discourse that seem to be more continuous with the more mainline pre-Reformation and Reformation traditions. Since the object is not to hoist Boehme on a metaleptic petard, which renders automatic the Gnostic return attribution, I will serve notice of where in Boehme's discourse there is a refusal to fully recast the tradition. Baur, who sees so perspicuously Boehme's relation to both the Spiritual Reformers, who precede him,[1] and Hegel, who succeeds him, does not seem to bother with Boehme's orthodox latencies. Yet it is important to keep them in mind, and not simply for reasons of intellectual honesty. Rather, the presence of such latencies plausibly sets off its absence in two figures, whom Boehme puts in his debt—that is, Blake and Hegel—whose own contributions to Gnostic return in modernity will be treated in two volumes that immediately follow. The real issue, however, is whether the latencies are powerful or weak. If the sheer number and variety of Boehmian swerves prepare one for the conclusion that orthodoxy can at best be a residuum, then the depth of swerve indicated by the distinctive band of swerves, and especially the swerve on the level of narrative, allows a fairly conclusive verdict that the latencies are weak. Thus, if Boehme does not instantiate a fully realized form of metalepsis, he is well on his way. This is registered by the metaphor of "unbounding" in the title of this Part. Obviously, playing on the Promethean myth that Blumenberg thinks so defining of modernity,[2] metalepsis in Boehme is not as in some of Boehme's successors, totally "unbound." But neither is its transformation of pre-Reformation and Reformation Christianity greatly hindered by standard Christian commitments.

Part II has three chapters. The first of these, chapter 3, examines Boehme's nondistinctive swerving from the pre-Reformation and Lutheran Reformation tradition on both hermeneutical and substantive theological fronts. Here the emphasis falls heavily on the precedents for swerving within the post-Reformation Protestant tradition, even as this tradition connects with and avails itself of pre-Reformation contestations of traditional practices of exegesis and takes on doctrine. As is fairly standard in Boehme commentary I will highlight the contributions to Boehme's discourse made by the fairly heterogeneous band of thinkers commonly assumed under the rubric of "Spiritual Reformers." I deepen what otherwise might be a point of merely historical interest by outlining in systematic fashion (1) the ways in which Boehme's discourse repeats the contestation by these figures of such basic Lutheran hermeneutical principles as the priority of the literal sense of Scripture, Scripture's fundamental perspicuity, and the community locus of interpretation. (2) The ways in which Boehme's discourse repeats many of these figures theological counterassertions, which range over the understanding of God, creation, Christ, the nature of redemption, and human being.

Discussion of Boehme's nondistinctive deviations from the standard pre-Reformation and Reformation traditions sets the stage for the second, and most important chapter of Part II, that is, chapter 4. This chapter investigates Boehme's distinctive hermeneutical and substantive theological swerves. Although I will give priority in my discussion to the substantive theological features of Boehme's discourse that exceed the contestations of the post-Reformation tradition, as well as the pre-Reformation traditions they recollect, I will briefly discuss a band of interpretive moves that distinguish him from the interpretive scheme of the Religious Reformers, and especially from that of Franck and Schwenckfeld. In my discussion of distinctive substantive theological swerves, I will pay particular attention to Boehme's understanding of the relation between the intradivine Trinity and the Godhead, his understanding of divine nature or essence, his understanding of the struggle and the pain at the heart of eternity that is symbolized by the Cross, and finally his understanding of the Kingdom of God as the realization of Wisdom, and as the realization of the "body of God." The discussion of substantive theological swerves brings me to the heart of my argument: the hermeneutical and substantive theological swerves from the Reformation and common tradition is both tied together and undergirded by ontotheological narrative whose developmental dynamism is motored, as I suggested in Part I, by eros, kenosis, and agon. In the sense that I am using the term, I am suggesting that Boehme's discourse tends toward metalepsis. This means that Boehme's narrative not only disfigures the biblical narrative by changing the meaning of individual narrative episodes, but it refigures it—that is, it includes the disfigured episodes in a new and different encompassing narrative whole. It is in and through a discussion of metalepsis that the central claim of this book comes into view. For as argued in detail in *Gnostic Return in Modernity*, the fundamental criterion for Gnostic or Valentinian ascription is metalepsis. Making an explicit case for Gnostic or Valentinian ascription is, however, the task of Part III rather than Part II. In the third of the three chapters (chapter 5), I broach the question of what limits to swerving, if any, exist in Boehme's discourse and what consequence this might have with respect to the ascription of metalepsis. I will argue that there are limits to swerving in Boehme's discourse, and that it does not completely break from the common and Reformation traditions. There exist a number of what I refer to as *orthodox latencies* with varying strengths of resistance to disfiguration and refiguration. In the end, however, I judge that the level of resistance exhibited by the orthodox latencies in Boehme's discourse is not particularly high, and is unable to stem the metaleptic tide.

CHAPTER 3

~

Nondistinctive Swerves:
Boehme's Recapitulation of Minority Pre-Reformation
and Post-Reformation Traditions

Texts like Boehme's hexameron, *Mysterium Magnum*, presuppose a long tradition of allegorical interpretation in the Christian tradition. If Augustine himself hardly eschewed allegorical interpretation, as the anti-Manichaean tracts and the *Confessions* clearly show—and in this he was followed by much of the Western tradition up until the Reformation[1]—at least officially, allegoresis was not given free reign. As *De Doctrina Christiana* made perfectly clear,[2] allegorical interpretation was justified only on an ad hoc basis to resolve conundra that could not be resolved by appeal to the literal sense of a scriptural passage or by appeal to similar passages in Scripture whose meaning was clear. Allegorical interpretation could not be justified systematically for Augustine, since such a justification implied that Scripture was obscure, a supposition that directly contradicted the view that Scripture is the privileged means for unveiling God's purposes for humanity. Where, however, a systematic justification was proposed in patristic thought, as it was in Alexandrian Christianity, in which a Platonic split between the visible and invisible dimensions of reality supported a sometimes dualizing split between letter and spirit, in its major figures, Clement and Origen,[3] allegorical interpretation was intended as an aid to deepening faith and not, as was self-consciously the case in Valentinian Gnosticism, as a replacement of the Word, its persuasive power and authority.[4] Boehme clearly taps into this more systematically allegorical line, which supposes that Scripture is a secret to be revealed, a hieroglyph to be decoded, just as lying behind the visible surface of reality is an invisible depth. At the same time, Boehme recapitulates the anagogic supplement to allegory typical of Alexandrian exegesis.[5] Only privatively in Alexandrian exegesis is allegory a theoretical activity in which a hidden meaning is disclosed to be surveyed. Though the accent is contemplative, and contemplation is in a broad sense 'aesthetic,' it is also self-involving and ecstatic.[6] The supplement, therefore, is not something merely added on, for anagogy is the ultimate intention of allegory: interpreting Scripture implies participation in the divine truth, which at once is the goal of interpretation and that which is disclosed in the process of interpretation. To inhere in truth as a process means that interpretation is at once a transformative activity and an activity that supposes the transformation of the self in and by the Spirit.

As *Aurora* (1613) and his later texts (1619–1624) demonstrate, Boehme taps into a mode of exegesis related to and different from Alexandrian-style allegory. Allegory within the Alexandrian parameter is not visionary, nor does it demonstrate a principled preference for the visionary texts of the Bible, whether Ezekiel's chariot (*merkabah*), or apocalyptic texts of the canonic or noncanonic Scriptures.[7] While the visionary texts elicit interpretation, in moments when their role becomes central their symbols are called on as much to explain reality as to be explained. Indeed, the imperative behind their interpretation is that they themselves are interpretive. If the chariot had a life in the Jewish tradition it did not have one in the Christian,[8] at least before Boehme, apocalyptic texts in general and Revelation in particular had a checkered history. Perhaps more than anyone else in the tradition, it was Joachim of Fiore who prioritized Revelation as the text that both interprets the rest of Scripture and historical reality.[9] Thus, Revelation's symbolic irreducibility, the sense that it necessarily resists translation and remains superior to interpretation. Nevertheless, the obscurity of its symbols encourages interpretation, even demands it, and this opens up a space for allegory and anagogy as well as typology and tropology. Vision and symbol open up to allegorical interpretation, as allegory opens up to visionary completion. Perhaps more than any Christian exegete before him, Boehme grasped that allegory without vision is without content, and vision without allegory is blind. His discourse represents the union and transformation of two related but different modes of exegesis, one whose purview is more nearly the eternal, the other whose purview is more nearly the dynamic of history, marked by agon, defined by a crisis that holds the promise of a complete transformation of time and history.

Operating in terms of both these interpretive paradigms opens up a significant gap between Boehme and the historical Luther, and puts him at odds with a Lutheran orthodoxy vehement in its criticism of his failure to remain faithful to the literal sense of Scripture (Carlov, Frick).[10] Luther makes it perfectly clear time and again that he is as hostile to allegory as he is faithful to the literal sense.[11] Alexandrian style exegesis especially incurs his wrath. In his interpretation of *Genesis* he writes: "The bare allegories, which stand in no relation to the account and do not illuminate it, should simply be disapproved of as empty dreams. This is the kind which Origen and those which follow him employ" (*Works* 1, p. 233).[12]

But, as is well known, Luther also disbars the less systematic kind of allegorical exegesis practiced by Augustine, and brings Augustine to task for offering allegorical interpretations of the biblical account of creation (*Works* 1, pp. 4, 7, 69). Any and all versions of allegorical interpretation of Scripture are wrongheaded, since they suggest that the Word of God is less than perspicuous and less than reliable.

While Luther's unwavering commitment to the literal sense serves as the benchmark for the development of Lutheranism, there is no doubt that the illuminist tradition, which served as a proximate intellectual backdrop for Boehme, not only disobeyed declarative injunctions against any kind of allegorical kind of interpretation, but tended to recapitulate the stronger Alexandrian form of allegorical interpretation, rather than the weaker Augustinian form. Sebastian Franck distinguished between the inner and outer word, privileging the former. For Franck in *Paradoxa* (1534),[13] his most well-known text, there is nothing lucid or open about Scripture. In the famous preface to that text, Scripture is said to be enigmatic, indeed sealed by seven seals (*septem signaculis clausus*). Consistently, Scripture is regarded as an allegory requiring interpretation (pp. 3, 5; also 140, 203, 207, 220), which can only be carried out in the Spirit.[14] Moreover, wearing lightly his Reformation scruples with respect to allegory, for Franck, Augustine and Origen were on the right track (pp. 5, 7): they recognized what Franck's contemporaries apparently did not, that the letter kills (pp. 6, 216 alluding to 2 Corinthians 3.7). Yet it is clear that Franck wants to go even further in relativizing the external word. Certainly the New Testament surpasses the Old Testament, yet the real New Testament is the Holy Spirit and not a book (p. 305). Caspar Schwenckfeld also vigorously contested Luther's prioritization of the external word (*verbum externum*) and insisted on the greater importance of the inner word.[15] Though not as committed to allegory as Franck, in Schwenkfeld the outer word is at best a sign of the inner word, sometimes identified with the Spirit, but most often with Christ. And Valentin Weigel follows Franck in speaking of Scripture without spirit as a closed book and enigma.[16] Following the Pauline maxim, the letter kills, the spirit makes alive, Weigel suggests that bookish knowledge (*buchstabisch Wissen*) is transcended in the spirit of the divine Word that is infinite, invisible, and ineffable. Weigel not only authorizes searching for the meaning of the Word *behind* the biblical text, but also thinks that this meaning will be a Wisdom inclusive of the book of nature and Scripture.[17] With Weigel meaning becomes speculative rather than soteriological.

What is important to underscore here is that Boehme reprises the interpretive attitude, and even the language, of his illuminist predecessors. For instance, a text like *The Way to Christ* rails against the external word (5.6.12–18), repeats the Pauline opposition of spirit and letter (5.7.7), and thinks of interpretation as the taking on of Christ. At the same time, interpretation is the movement into the great mystery and the panopticon of the philosophical globe in which all is revealed.[18] In a real sense Boehme represents the end point of a process in which there is a shift away from the authority of Scripture to the authority of interpretation. At this end point, there is also a corresponding shift from interpretation normed by a community of believers to powerful individual interpretation that constitutes the norm for a community that is not yet, but that effectively calls it into being.

But Boehme's work also represents something of a *terminus* to the apocalyptic trajectory in Lutheranism. Luther's belated softening (1545) with respect to Revelation may as much reflect an accommodation to a Protestant sensibility—unprepared to give up Revelation's powerful symbols that seem to apply to strife-filled historical existence—as an essential retreat from an earlier judgment (1522) in which Revelation is thought to contain little that is specifically Christian. Luther's acceptance is, however, conditional. Luther can read his age and his own situation into the text. Specifically, he can think of the Reformation as a crisis, and himself as Elias, the prophetic angel of Revelation 14.6.[19] Typology rather than allegory, then, is the way to read the text, even if the visionary-symbolic manifold of the text tends to excite allegorization. In any event, as Robin Barnes has demonstrated, Lutheranism is a vehicle of apocalyptic resurgence in the sixteenth century, taking numerous forms, from high scholarly chronicles of the world that rushs toward conclusion to histrionic readings of the signs of the times. Revelation is a text of endtime (*Endzeit*) that admits of being interpreted only in endtime; it is a text of vision that requires seers to participate in and interpret the vision, for, minimally, it holds the key to unlock the secrets of history, divine judgment, and mercy. Ultimately, however, as *the* symbolic text, Revelation holds out the prospect of more. That is, Revelation comes to be regarded as providing the key to unlocking the secrets of nature, as open to, if not inclusive of, astrology or the new astronomy. The question whether this means that Revelation functions as symbolic code becomes pertinent in Weigel, for in his work Revelation provides the context for the interpretation of nature, which for the most part is conducted via an interpretation of Genesis.[20] Boehme's texts presuppose the apocalyptic exacerbation of the sixteenth century that was showing signs of calming down by the time he commenced his literary-theological career with *Aurora* (1613), whose very title is self-consciously apocalyptic.

In *Aurora*, apocalyptic texts in general, and Revelation in particular, are central. If this text, like Boehme's subsequent productions, avoids the prevailing chialism of the sixteenth century, nevertheless it is continuous with the apocalyptic trajectory in Lutheranism to the extent to which the vision of apocalyptic texts promises knowledge of the vicissitudes of history—and, by extension, of nature. For Boehme, however, it was not simply that an interpretation of Revelation would itself bring knowledge of nature, but also that Revelation provided the visionary code for interpreting other scriptural texts like Genesis, which might be in a superior position to unlock the secrets of nature. Revelation announces that the condition of disclosure is that of endtime, which, in line with the apocalyptic tradition of the sixteenth century, Boehme associated with Enoch (*MM* 31–36).[21] At the same time, Revelation announces that interpreting reality represents a breaking of the seals, which encourages the view that in principle Scripture is constituted by its sublime theophanous moments that escape paraphrase. Interpretation could not be other than allegorical if the meaning of creation, evil, and redemption is embodied in symbols overdetermined with meaning.

On the substantive theological front, Boehme recalls at least four important swerves of a nondistinctive kind from positions adopted by the common Christian tradition, accepted by Luther, and enthusiastically embraced by Lutheran orthodoxy. One important repetition of swerve from the common tradition is the separation of the mysteriously transcendent Godhead from the Trinitarian God, disposed toward creative, redemptive, and sanctifying relation to the world. As we saw in chapter 2, this is a basic Eckhartian tendency, although Eckhart seems to operate with the assurance that such a view has roots in the Dionysian tradition. Mediated plausibly by Weigel,[22] the split between Godhead and Trinity puts a Sabellianlike pressure on the personal interpretation of the Trinity, since by being rendered secondary or epiphenomenal with respect to an anterior divine (super)essence, Father, Son, and Spirit lose the ontological authority they enjoy as the ultimate ground of reality. The recall of Eckhart, however, goes deeper than repetition of the Godhead-Trinity split. In Eckhart's scheme Father, Son, and Spirit are not regarded as equally personal in the sense of equally grounding divine manifestation. The *Gottesgeburt* guarantees that the Son has priority. Without repeating the details of Eckhart's position, Boehme does believe that the personal candidacy of the Son, as Word or Logos, is superior to the Father or Spirit. Whether the Son or Word is personal in the strictest of possible senses depends on definition—specifically on Boehme's sorting out definitional criteria. Such sorting, it turns out, not only results in Boehme's coming to different conclusions than Eckhart about whether the Son at the level of the immanent divine, strictly speaking, is entitled to the attribution of person, but it also results in a relativization of the entire sphere of the immanent divine. I will deal with this point in some detail in chapter 4.

In departing from the creedal tradition, Boehme is also departing from the historical Luther, as well, of course, from Melanchthon and the tradition of Lutheran orthodoxy. If Luther inveighs against the scholastic treatment of the Trinity with its technical language and logic, this by no means suggests that he is prepared to abandon the trinitarian creed.[23] He certainly cannot concur with the Eckhartian tradition in supposing a divine reality beyond Father, Son, and Spirit, for hiddenness and revealedness do not name two distinct divine realities, but the self-same divine reality looked at in two different ways.[24] In addition, even if Luther's own focus is on the Son, no more than Melanchthon is he prepared to privilege ontologically the Son by affirming his personal status while denying it to Father and Spirit. If the Son is personal, so also is the Father and Spirit (*Works* 1, pp. 5-6). The Son is given preference in Luther's discourse for the obvious reason that it is the Son who becomes incarnate, and whose suffering and death brings about the redemption of the world. Luther goes beyond this relatively formal commitment to the personhood of Father, Son, and Spirit when he employs prosopographic exegesis to suggest that the Trinity is the space of conversation, in which the Father addresses the Son, the Son addresses the Father, and the Spirit is the listening between them. Performatively, then, as well as officially, Luther is against Sabellianism in either its ancient or medieval guise, just as he is against Arianism, which (not surprisingly given Luther's christological focus) bears the brunt of his criticism (*Works* 1, pp. 5–16)

Lutheran orthodoxy's attacks on Boehme on this front are hardly obtuse. Certainly, it is no accident that in seventeeth-century critiques of Boehme by Frick and Thummio,[25] Boehme and Weigel are associated. For there are signs in Weigel of what is accomplished in Boehme—namely the transformation of the soteriological primacy of the Word into an ontological primacy, consistent with the Word transcending the pure hiddenness (*Verborgenheit*) of the divine and its darkness (*Finsterniss*). As Logos, the Son illuminates the darkness of God and represents transcendence in its visible and effable form. In Weigel, the dynamic of the birth of the Son—which in Luther's exegetical works (e. g., *John*) and nonexegetical works shares time with the more structural appraisal of the equal divinity of each of the three terms Father, Son, and Spirit—is submitted to an Eckhartianlike accentuation. The result is a form of Sabellianism more dynamic, and more focused on Word and Wisdom than that in evidence in the first centuries of the Common Era.

Boehme's view of creation also swerves from the Christian standard. Boehme's seventeenth-century Lutheran orthodox detractors were in no doubt that the illuminist from Görlitz had violated the doctrine of creation from nothing that had come to be a basic tenet of Lutheran orthodoxy,[26] just as it had been in the pre-Reformation tradition. As with Irenaeus and Augustine (the two most powerful early proponents of creation from nothing), the developed Lutheran view of the relation of the divine to world both reflected a plain reading of Genesis and a defensive stance taken against establishing strong lines of continuity between the divine and the world that threaten the transcendence and sovereignty of the divine, writ large over the whole biblical text. One of Boehme's ablest, if most long-winded of Lutheran critics, Frick,[27] explicitly noted the link between Boehme's hermeneutic swerve and his view of creation. Since allegory points to a reality behind the biblical text, there exists no impediment for calling on nonbiblical views to account for the divine-world relation. No surprise, then, that the doctrine of creation from nothing, which accurately reflects Genesis and the biblical view in general, is passed over!

The first line of Lutheran orthodoxy's critical reflection on Boehme's discourse is the obvious one: its position on creation is errant. A second, subsidiary, and arguably more interesting line also exists. In light of Luther's articulation of the Word of God and his material position on creation passed on faithfully by Lutheran orthodoxy, Boehme's position also is judged to be anachronistic. There is something essentially right about the perception of Boehme's innovation being also a regression. For at a very general level Boehme's view of the God-world relation bears a family resemblance to both the Platonic prime matter view and the view produced by the line of Christian Neoplatonism that begins with Eriugena and proceeds through Eckhart to Cusa, in which the doctrine of creation from nothing is submitted to something like an emanation make-over.[28] That the Platonic view of creation, as the demiurgic activity enacted on a pregiven formless material, could not be blithely dismissed in Christian theology is shown by Augustine in the *Confessions* (bk 11), where this construal is thought to represent a plausible—although ultimately unsatisfying—way of interpreting Genesis. The view is plausible, since neither Genesis nor any other biblical text pronounces explicitly on the matter. Moreover, Augustine was not unaware that certain images in the Old Testament, like that of potter, may suggest something analogous to the demiurgic theory articulated in the *Timaeus*.

If the medieval Neoplatonic trajectory of Eriugena, Eckhart, and Cusa cannot be blamed for introducing the tension between emanation and the generally accepted—although little understood—view of creation from nothing, certainly there it achieves a highly exacerbated form. If all three thinkers officially acknowledge the distinction between uncreated and created, in none of the cases is the distinction upheld with any kind of energy or conceptual force. In Eriugena, the created natures abide in the uncreated theophanous expressions of divine life.[29] In Eckhart at his most extreme, creation in the strict sense does not exist, or exists only to the extent that it abides in the generation of the Word.[30] To that extent all existence is generated rather than created, intratrinitarian rather than extratrinitarian. And, finally, in Cusa, creation seems to be absolved by being implicated in the divine, or coimplicated (*complicare*) in the divine in which it is divine and thus uncreated.[31] Moreover, while there is certainly no wish to deceive, there is an element of conceit in construing the movement of creation as a movement from the divine, for whom "nothing" is an adequate descriptor, and thus providing *creatio ex nihilo* with a *creatio ex Deo* interpretation.

In the post-Reformation tradition, despite the creation from nothing hegemony, these two minority traditions continued to be recalled. Although with the exception of Weigel the Spiritual Reformers were not especially focused on creation, to the extent to which all three were major couriers of the medieval mystical traditions, and especially of Eckhart, they provided examples of the collapse of the distinction between the uncreated and the created orders.

Correlatively they exemplified the collapse of the distinction of the processes of generation and creation. Thus, through the Spiritual Reformers the emanationist-tending medieval Neoplatonic tradition continued to have some influence on the post-Reformation scene. Moreover, through Weigel and Paracelsus, the reading of the *tohu va bohu* of Genesis 1 as prime matter, and God as fundamentally a shaper, continues, even as the mythic configurations of Paracelsus and Weigel complicate matters, as does Boehme, by postulating a more ultimate matter (*yliaster*) behind the quasi-material matter (*limbus*).[32]

To a certain extent, it is the achievement of Paracelsus and Weigel to have begun combining the two countertraditions by placing the demiurgic activity in the context of a process that begins with the radically apophatic divine and the mirror of divine wisdom. Boehme completes this process, and transcends it, in part on the basis of extrapolations possible within the Paracelsian and Weigelian systems, and in part on the basis of a more than notional acquaintance with the Christian domestications of the Kabbalah. More will be said about the latter element in Part III, when taxonomic determination of Boehme's discourse becomes the explicit focus.

This brings me to the third nondistinctive swerve in Boehmian discourse—that is, his swerve from the christological tradition. Two Boehmian features in particular disturb traditional christological interpretation. First, while Boehme does not dispute the claim that Christ is the one who redeems, he most certainly contests the view that human being does not participate in his or her own redemption. Perhaps the clearest expressions of his departure are to be found in *The Way to Christ*: "it is not enough that we believe in Christ and confess that He is God's Son and paid for us. No externally imputed righteousness that we only believe has happened [has any value]; only an inborn childlike [righteousness] counts" (*WC* bk 5. 1, 9, pp. 139–40; also bk 5. 5, 8–11, p. 158).

Connected intrinsically to the avowal of participation, Boehme's christological exemplarism seems to go beyond that of the general tradition. And needless to say, this could only be read as a trespass by Lutheran orthodoxy, which from the time of the Confession of Augsburg (1530) and Melanchthon's *Loci* (1537) understood exemplarist Christologies as regressions to an inadequate theological state.

Second, and somewhat paradoxically, in the texts of Boehme there is a tendency toward Doceticism at the level of the incarnate Christ. Despite the agonic pattern of imitation, what is crucial about the incarnate Christ is that he represents the coincidence of opposites, the perfect balance of forces (*temperamentum*), of energy and knowledge, strength and compassion, and, as we have seen, even masculine and feminine. To the fore is a far from innocuous application of the Pauline Second Adam motif. As the Second Adam, Christ restores all the qualities surrendered by Adam in the fall introduced by evil imagination. But Adam exists in a dimension outside history, and the conditions of his exis-

tence transcend the materiality, mutability, generation, and mortality of historical existence, which is existence in the wake of the fall. The principle of analogy
dictates a similar description of Christ. Here Docetism is encouraged by what
might be called a prospective application of the Adam-Second Adam motif.
Also at play is a retrospective application, in which Paul's reflection on Christ's
resurrected body, the *soma pneumatikon*, is retrogressed back on the First Adam.
The retrospective view confirms the ahistorical reading of Adam, which functions as the prospective base for proper description of the incarnate Christ.

Having briefly described these two aspects of Boehme's nondistinctive
christological swerve, I would like to outline the way in which Boehme's views
are linked to patterns of christological assessment in pre-Reformation and post-
Reformation traditions. I begin with exemplarism everywhere transparent—
understandably more in the edifying *The Way to Christ* (4.2.29) than in a highly
speculative text such as *The Incarnation of the Word*.[33] Christological exemplarism has, of course, a long tradition in theology. It is an important trend in the
Alexandrian fathers, a significant note in the early Augustine, and a mainstay in
the monastic and mystical traditions. More importantly, and relevantly, it is a
major strain in the medieval ensemble of Tauler, the *German Theology*, and the
Imitation of Christ, which was the textual bread and butter of the early Luther
as well as his illuminist critics.[34] Although Luther's Reformation break did not
involve wholesale renunciation of these texts, reservations about their marginal-
ization of the Cross led to their eclipse. This is something regretted by Luther's
illuminist critics, who availed themselves of these texts at a rhetorical and substantive level against both Luther and evolving Lutheran orthodoxy.

As the Spiritual Reformers understand it, the critical nub was constituted
by the doctrine of justification. In that doctrine was condensed the soteriological extrinsicism of the Western tradition. In neither Franck, Schwenckfeld, nor
Weigel, however, is justification expressly denied. Rather, it is reinterpreted in
the light of exemplarism of the medieval textual ensemble referred to above. In
Franck, for instance, if Christ is our redeemer, this by no means lessens the importance of "putting on" Christ (*Paradoxa* #109–14, esp. p. 201). "Putting on
Christ" involves treating Christ's pattern of existence as exemplary, especially
the aspects of humility and resignation. Similarly, for Schwenckfeld justification has to be interpreted in such a way as to deny the forensic interpretation of
Melanchthon (XII, 196, 458). Such a view is external and rationalistic (II,
494–96), and allows insufficient scope for the internal transformation of self,
one of whose indispensable media is following the servant pattern of Christ's
existence.[35] No less for Weigel than for Franck and Schwenckfeld, there are
problems with Melanchthon's model of imputation (*imputativae justitiae*).[36]
Justification has to be interpreted in the light of regeneration (*Wiedergeburt*),
brought about by Christ or the Spirit. For Weigel, the real religious phenomenon is not "Christ for me," but "Christ in me." And it follows logically for

Weigel that the transformative presence of Christ or the Spirit requires a self for whom the exercise of free will is basic.[37]

Boehme is firmly in this tradition. Throughout a work such as *Mysterium Magnum*, Boehme recommends *Gelassenheit* as the opposite of the prideful self-will (*Eigenwille*) of both Lucifer and Adam. Less connected with the biblical narrative, and more in keeping with the medieval mystical tradition's general anatomy of the self, are Boehme's reflection on *Gelassenheit* in *The Way to Christ*. Human beings find themselves betwixt and between fundamentally different tendencies in the self, the one incurving, the other ecstatic. Boehme could not be clearer in this text that free will is a condition of the movement toward God. The assertion of the reality of free will in this text, as in *De Electione Gratiae*, is made typically with an eye to avoiding Pelagian-sounding notes about human autonomy. And finally, as I have already pointed out, Boehme is against a forensic interpretation of justification. Juridical notions of satisfaction are strenuously resisted as hypocritical and deceptive (*WC* bk 4. 2, 37, p. 133).

The second nondistinctive element of Boehme's swerve from the christological tradition is that of Docetism. This swerve is by far the more serious of the two. For in the christological tradition, exemplarism often peacefully, if not in necessarily full consistency, coexists with claims that redemption is solely and dramatically wrought through Christ. Indeed, cases of pure exemplarism are difficult to find. Even obvious candidates like Alexandrian Christianity and Pelagianism all have significant nonexemplarist elements. Docetism, however, is a more transparent, because more focal, swerve. It pronounces directly, as in the case of Apollinaris and Nestorius, on the person and nature of Christ. Moreover, Docetism offers explanations of Christ's person and nature that seem to be at odds with the soteriological requirement that only what Christ assumes is saved. Docetism in any form was abjured by Luther, and in the development of Lutheran doctrine, Apollinaris and Nestorius became catchwords for Christologies that do not take the self-emptying of Christ in the incarnation and the Cross sufficiently seriously.

Nonetheless, the Spiritual Reformers provide a significant tradition of critique of the standard Lutheran proposal, determined in significant part by its opposition to Doceticism. In Franck, revalorized Docetism has two distinct but related channels. The first is dictated by Franck's resolute spirit-flesh opposition that requires emphasizing the difference in Christ between flesh and spirit. Ontological union between spirit and flesh is as impossible in Christ as it is in us. Yet the flesh of Christ can function symbolically or anagogically for the spirit that is the Word. Secondly, as the Gospels depict Christ's progress and growth—although the theological lens is provided by Paul—Christ's flesh ultimately transcends the state of human flesh. Schwenckfeld's Docetism has a different source, but is no less real. Evolving out of the eucharistic controversies, Schwenckfeld's particular version involves a deemphasis on the Cross[38] (where the human dimension of God is most transparent) and a focus on Christ's glory. Using Hebrews 5.12 as the language of critique, the focus on the Cross and Jesus's humanity is the milk teaching of Christ (*die Milchlehre ihn Christi*), the latter "strong, bold food" (*die starche keche Speise*) (IX, 147–49). Avoiding Franck's distinction of spirit and flesh in Christ, which almost reaches the level of antinomy (*Paradoxa* #85, 254), Schwenckfeld insists that the flesh of Christ is spiritual and thus other than our flesh. Moreover, unlike Franck, Schwenckfeld asserts that Christ's flesh is spiritual from the beginning. The wide departure of the Christologies of Franck and Schwenckfeld from the theological tradition make it not the least surprising that their views were respectively charged as Nestorian and Apollinarian by their Lutheran detractors.

Doceticism is also transparent in Weigel, who of the three Spiritual Reformers exerts the greatest influence on Boehme. The issue of the flesh of Christ in Weigel occupies the same kind of prominent place it does in Schwenckfeld, although Weigel is dealing with a more settled Protestant orthodoxy, whose christological mainstays are the Chalcedonian two natures-one person Christology annotated and buttressed by *communicatio idiomatum*. In texts such as *Vom Leben Christi* (1578) and *Dialogus* (1584), in opposition to Lutheran orthodoxy, Weigel's emphasis falls on the unity of Christ. Granted unity in Christ, both spirit and flesh in Christ are heavenly, and heavenly from the beginning. This means that the glory of Christ is obscured by the humiliation of the Cross, and that the flesh of Christ from the very beginning is not subject to death or the other vicissitudes of human flesh. Boehme borrows whole-cloth the Weigelian view of the difference-relation between flesh and spirit, which he transforms into the internal relation between feminine and masculine in a unitary reality that is fundamentally androgynous.

This brings me to Boehme's fourth and final nondistinctive substantive theological swerve from the mainline pre-Reformation and Reformation theological traditions. This swerve is effected on the level of theological anthropology. Even if one were to ignore the mature Luther's reservations with regard to the divinization traditions of East and West, this still would not be sufficient to absolve Boehme from the charge that his theological anthropology, and particularly his theology of image, represents a swerve from the Christian tradition in general, and the Reformation view in particular. At issue is createdness, a determination of human being, arguably not imperilled by the divinization tradition, but put under extreme pressure by Boehme's theology of image and such related notions as son and child of God (*WC* bk 4. 2, 44–45, p. 134). Mediated by the *German Theology*, and there given a voluntarist turn, the Eckhartian symbol of 'spark' (*Fünklein* or *spinter*) plays an important role in Boehme's anthropology. It suggests that there is an element in human being that is not 'created,' and that belongs properly to the eternal rather than temporal dimension of reality. For Boehme, the spark is the spark of primordial divine will, before good and evil, and the spark is the power whereby the self constitutes or de-constitutes itself by deciding for good or for evil. Deciding for good involves a surrender of one's own will and an openness to the divine. In other words it involves *Gelassenheit*, which, paradoxically, is the only way in which the self gets formed as a self, maintains personal integrity, and succeeds in producing a determinate and viable form of freedom. Deciding for evil involves capitulating to the self-will (*Eigenwille*) that marks the demonic. The consequence is a deformation of self: the self becomes contracted and chaotic, compulsive and angst-ridden, a vicious circle of ever-unsatisfied desire for a more powerful and secure self that remains elusive.

The proximate background for Boehme's view of the uncreated or eternal dimension of the image is again provided by the Spiritual Reformers. As appropriators of Tauler and the *German Theology*, and in the case of Weigel also of Eckhart,[39] the Spiritual Reformers in varying degrees think of the human image as more than created. In the case of Franck, the inner word-outer word distinction correlates to the inner man-outer man distinction, in which the inner man is 'born' or is 'generated' not created (*Paradoxa* #79). In the case of Schwenckfeld's full-blown treatment of divinization (*Vergottung, Gottwerdung*), as the true image of God, human being transcends creaturehood (VII, 566). Peter 1.4 is especially important to Schwenckfeld, as he articulates a view of divinization more radical than that found in Tauler and the *German Theology*. And Weigel follows Eckhart in being unabashed about interpreting the divinization formula of God becoming human so that the human becomes divine in a radical ontological way in which the uncreated dimension of the self is rendered transparent.

Again, it is the Spiritual Reformers who serve as the proximate context for Boehme's appropriation of the Eckhartian trope of *Gelassenheit*. In the context of their use, *Gelassenheit* is tied to a process that seems to signify not only the overcoming of self-will or self-centeredness, but also a process of excavating the recessed image of God. If this remains somewhat inchoate in Franck, who refers to the new birth of the self as a "new creation," it is not so in either Schwenckfeld or Weigel. In Schwenckfeld, the discovered image is a self so turned away from the temporal and created order that it involves no licence to claim that the image is unequivocally the product of divine generation (VII, 202). And in Weigelian texts such as *Gnothi Seauton, Kurtzer Bericht und Anleitung zur Teutschen Theologey*, and *Zwei nützleiche Tractate*, the notion of *Gelassenheit* figures prominently. What is liberated in the attitudinal relation that transcends practical, contemplative, and affective relations to divine and mundane reality is an inner self that transcends createdness.

A reinforcing feature of the Eckhartian tradition's theology of image is also repeated in Boehme. The most famous passage in Eckhart—the one famously cited in Eckhart's condemnation and commented on enthusiastically by

Hegel—is ocular as well as oracular: "The eye with which I see is the same eye with which God sees himself. My eye and God's eye are one eye."[40]

The ocular metaphor reinforces the uncreated and eternal status of the self. While in the *German Theology*, the text's Augustinianism does not allow the "eye of eternity," which contrasts with the "eye of time," to connote a distinct spiritual eye that does not share in the materiality and boundedness of the physical eye, in Boehme, in line with the illuminist appropriation of the *German Theology*, vision is not simply the vision of eternity, at once human and temporally perspectival, but eternal vision. In Franck, to know God is not simply to hear in faith, but to see God as God eternally sees Godself (*Paradoxa* #7, 24, 115–18). In Weigel, the superior eye, in contrast with the eye of flesh (*das fleisch Aug*) and the middle eye (*das mittelste Aug*), sees God in a transsensual and transconceptual way that corresponds with divine vision. And Weigel makes it perfectly plain that the metaphors of eye and vision correlate with knowledge. If the eye of flesh corresponds to sense knowledge, and the middle eye to conceptual knowledge (*Vernunft, ratio*), the superior eye corresponds to transconceptual knowledge (*Verstand* or *intellectus* or *mens*).[41] The superior eye is divine, as is its mode of knowing, both *intensivé* and *extensivé*. It looks from the divine point of view at God's expression in nature, human being, and text. The vision of God, as God's vision, is thus panoptical and pansophistical. It is this specifically Weigelian extension, dependent in significant part on the assimilation of Paracelsus, that provides one of the basic frames for vision in Boehme. As I have suggested already, apocalyptic provides another.

A view of divinization conducted in the registers of uncreatedness, *Gelassenheit*, and vision put Reformation views of createdness, justification, and faith under extreme pressure. Again, Boehme is not simply unique. At one level, at least, he represents the term of a process in a particular trajectory of post-Reformation thought. Especially important is the way in which the emphasis on *Gelassenheit* contributes to a revisioning of the doctrine of justification and a defense of postlapsarian will. In Franck, Schwenckfeld, and Weigel, as I have already pointed out, justification is less denied than reinterpreted. In Franck righteousness is the new birth (*justitia est renascentia*) (*Paradoxa* #255, p. 426). Without regeneration, justification in the true and proper sense does not occur (*Paradoxa* #133). Similarly, in Schwenckfeld, justification is not other than sanctification. Rather, it is interpreted by it (XIV, 791; XIII, 867; XII, 196; II, 57). Weigel maintains that by contrast with the early Luther, who is influenced by Tauler and the *German Theology*, the later Luther represents a derailment. Playing on the rhetoric of Luther's theology of the Cross, in *Dialogus*, Weigel profers the view that the imputation of righteousness codified by Melanchthon is less a theology than a grammar—that is, a piece of Greek or Aristotelian rationalism. In addition, free will has to undergo something of a rehabilitation. While Franck does not wish to take Erasmus's side against

Luther, it is clear that he regards *De Servo Arbitrio* as too severe. If free will is to function as a condition of responsibility, it must be real (*Paradoxa* #126–31). Even more importantly, the acceptance of prevenient grace presupposes the freedom of the will (*Paradoxa* ##216–20). For Schwenckfeld, ethics is impossible unless one supposes the capacity for divine grace and the prospect that a way of life contributes to it. And Schwenckfeld abjures the doctrine of double predestination as misrepresenting Christianity (IV, 89ff.). And Weigel goes even further, regarding predestination as heretical. *Postille* 2, for example, argues consistently for the reality of free will. Generally, the point is made negatively: salvation of the human being cannot be prosecuted against human will.

Boehme's theological anthropology is wrought in opposition to a Lutheranism that insists on *sola gratia* and is seen as tending toward a Calvinist reading of predestination.[42] Boehme inveighs against the latter in *De Electione Gratiae*, arguing that predestination is a doctrinaire misconstrual of evangelical faith and an ethical abomination.[43] He argues for a place for human freedom, both postlapsarian as well as prelapsarian, without disregard for the real affects of the mercy of God in Jesus Christ, as he denounces interpretation of the biblical God as a God who does evil and good, and a God equally of justice and mercy. As we saw in chapter 1, for Boehme, God is God only in goodness and mercy. God does not predestine most, or even some, of the angels and human beings to damnation. God intends only the good; God only intends salvation. Yet, by manifesting Godself in what is other than Godself, God takes the risk of a reality that can turn hostile to God's intention, to its own detriment. Even in this case, God remains faithful, and Christ appears as the symbol of God's love and mercy in the fallen world that has not lost all traces of agency and freedom. As I hinted in my discussion of Boehme's Christology, Boehme does not so much deny justification by faith as reinterpret it in such a way that Christ is the real symbol of transformation (*enantiodromia*) that can be appropriated in human freedom. In a sense, then, justification is a dramatic figure of sanctification, even divinization. As such it disturbs the *ordo salutis* established by Lutheran orthodoxy.

To sum up my discussion of Boehme's swerve from the Reformation and common theological traditions thus far. In this chapter, I have focused on the hermeneutical and substantive theological contestation of the common and Reformation traditions that Boehme's discourse shares with a number of pre-Reformation traditions (e.g., medieval Neoplatonic Christianity, Meister Eckhart) and post-Reformation contestations that had as their specific target Luther's turn to Scripture and his articulation of a theology of the Cross. In my discussion of the latter I foreground the work of the Spiritual Reformers. My aim, however, was not simply to contextualize further Boehme's Christian discourse, but rather to expose the nondistinctive hermeneutical and substantive theological swerves as providing the necessary but not sufficient conditions for a contestation of the biblical narrative that would be metaleptic in the strict sense. The distinctive hermeneutical and substantive theological swerves, which provide the sufficient conditions for metalepsis, will be elucidated in the next chapter.

At this point it only remains to underscore the *Protestant* nature as well as context of the movement toward metalepsis. In the context of the movement, the Reformation event makes Catholicism anachronistic, given its institutional structures and respect for tradition that lessens the kind of authority Scripture rightly can be presumed to have. This is so even as thinkers of the pre-Reformation period such as Eckhart are evoked in Boehme's discourse, in addition to the post-Reformation Spiritual Reformers, to contest the Reformation traditions, especially that of Lutheran orthodoxy. At the same time the Reformation calls for interpretation. In the context of what amounts to a conflict of interpretation, what is inauthentic has to be distinguished from what is truly authentic. In this respect the kind of interpretation enacted in the Spiritual Reformers is crucial for setting the overall parameters of Boehme's view of the Reformation and even Luther himself. From this point of view, the entire trajectory of Lutheran orthodoxy is considered to be a deformation, including the theology of Melanchthon and the Confession of Augsburg. The Reformation has to be fully appropriated, speculatively and narratively. And in such an appropriation, Luther's thought itself is fully realized. It is interesting that the two centuries between the work of Boehme and Hegel does nothing to change the basic focus or ambition of speculative Christianity.

CHAPTER 4

~

Distinctive Swerves: Toward Metalepsis

In this chapter, I turn to an examination of those departures—or what I am calling "swerves"—from the theological tradition in excess of what is realized in general in the pre-Reformation tradition and more specifically in excess of what is realized in the post-Reformation tradition in the shape of the Spiritual Reformers (chapter 3). It is these swerves that define Boehme's discourse and that move it toward metalepsis—that is, move it toward a total disfiguration-refiguration of the biblical narrative as this narrative has been rendered in magisterial pre-Reformation and Reformation theological forms.

As is the case with nondistinctive swerves, distinctive swerves are both hermeneutical and substantive in kind. I will identify and discuss briefly five features of Boehme's interpretation of Scripture that makes his hermeneutic distinctive. These are (1) his heightened sense of the intertextuality of the biblical text, (2) his commitment to a divine, which however sublime is an object of vision—what I call the *visionary sublime*, (3) his commitment to a divine that is the subject as well as the object of seeing—what I call the *visionary supplement*, (4) his pansophism, and (5) his language of nature. I will spend considerably more time, however, on the distinctive substantive theological swerves. I will review in order Boehme's radicalization of Eckhart's Godhead-Trinity distinction, his reflections on the constitution of a divine nature or essence, his vision of the Cross at the heart of eternity, and finally his vision of the Kingdom as the realization of Wisdom and the "Body of God."

Discussion of these distinctive substantive theological swerves leads to a discussion of the more comprehensive and radical narrative swerve that defines metalepsis. On the basis of my discussion in Part I, it should not surprise that narrative form constitutes a decisive discrimen between Boehme and the standard pre-Reformation and Reformation traditions. Note particularly: (1) The comprehensive and radical swerve on the basis of narrative sums up and interprets the individual swerves, which involve transgressive interpretation of specific episodes of the Christian narrative (chapter 1). (2) Boehme's six-stage

103

narrative represents more than the sum of its disfiguration of individual episodes of the biblical narrative. It integrates the series of disfigurations into a narrative more encompassing than the biblical narrative. This refigured narrative in turn makes a claim to knowledge that is self-certifying. (3) Boehme's comprehensive and radical narrative swerve admits of a trinitarian synopsis that does little for the orthodoxy of Boehme's Trinity, already in question as the depiction of a divine life that is the ground of creation, redemption, and sanctification (chapter 1). (4) Boehme's comprehensive six-stage narrative shows an erotic-agonistic constitution that one would be hard pressed to find in a single thinker in the mainline theological tradition (chapter 2). It is also largely absent in those discourses that contest the common (e.g., Eckhart) (chapter 2) and the Reformation (e.g., Spiritual Reformers) (chapter 3) traditions.

4.1. Distinctive Individual Hermeneutic and Theological Swerves

I begin with the swerves of Boehme's discourse on the level of hermeneutics. One important aspect of the distinctiveness of Boehmian swerve has been hinted at in chapter 3—that is, Boehme's integration of the minority traditions of allegory and the visionary sublime in general and apocalyptic in particular. Boehme's integration of hermeneutic traditions is not totally without precedent, and a good case can be made that Weigel constitutes an antecedent. Nevertheless, the level of integration of allegorical interpretation and the visionary sublime in Boehme exceeds that of any and all precursors. Firstly, apocalyptic texts like Revelation, Enoch, and Fourth Esdra, and texts of theophany like Ezekiel's vision of the chariot, have a much more prominent place in Boehme than in Weigel or other Lutheran allegorists of the sixteenth century. Secondly, and correspondingly, for Boehme, these biblical texts reveal, directly or indirectly, meanings that, strictly speaking, are beyond the purview of Scripture as a soteriological document. That is, the texts of the visionary sublime help both to institute and to unfold a speculative or pansophistic matrix. A more specific account of the relatively unique realization of the synthesis of allegorical interpretation and visionary sublime is in order. There are at least *five* different aspects to this synthesis, not each aspect of which is unique, but whose synthesis is.

(1) A distinctive aspect of Boehmian synthesis is the high level of *intertextuality* it both presumes and enacts in the interpretation of Scripture. Neither apocalyptic texts, nor Ezekiel, function merely to suggest that the Bible in general is a symbolic code that must be cracked. Boehme does not disagree with this tropic reading. But as *Aurora* and *Mysterium Magnum* show clearly enough, Revelation, apocalyptic texts in general, and Ezekiel throw specific light on other biblical texts, especially Genesis. This light can be partly confirmatory, as it is with respect to the importance of the number seven. The seven

candlelights in Revelation highlight the importance of the seven days of creation, this confirmation in turn doubling the efforts to plumb the meaning of number symbolism which, we have seen, issues in reflection on the seven divine qualities. Although not without further textual mediation, the fall of the angel in Revelation sheds light on the *tohu va bohu* of Genesis 1, since the fall of the angels is now regarded as the narrative, and maybe even material, condition of the possibility of the physical universe and human being.[1] Similarly, the vision of the chariot in Ezekiel sheds light on the theophanies in Genesis and Exodus, which Luther shied away from in his exegesis, for fear of encouraging precisely the kind of speculation that Boehme's theophanically saturated Bible does in fact encourage.[2]

(2) The prominence of the texts of the *visionary sublime* in Boehme suggest not only that interpretation is completed in vision, but also, and more specifically, that the ultimately adequate reading of the divine and the divine milieu is *iconic*. That is, in however a sublime fashion, the divine, like human being, has form, shape, and circumscription that admits of representation. This is a crucially important consideration in a context in which, in texts such as *Mysterium Magnum*, *De Electione Gratiae*, and *Six Theosophic Points* the divine is framed by apophatic discourse and gestured to in the aniconic battery of "nothing," "ineffability," "invisibility," and so forth. The texts of the visionary sublime, therefore, encourage an aesthetic disposition that comes into play in the interpretation of other biblical texts, Genesis and the Gospel of John in particular, where Boehme tries to pierce the veil of the mysteries of creation and the trinitarian divine. A kataphatic divine is the predictable result of iconically motivated interpretation. Accepting the relative probity of apophatic language, as we saw in an earlier chapter (chapter 2), Boehme deconstitutes it in favor of a rigorous kataphaticism of a narrative kind.

For Boehme, the adequacy of iconic figuration bears a close relationship to the attribution of personhood or personality to God. As Boehme's deconstitution of apophatic language suggests a critique of the impersonality of the divine (privileged by Eckhart), conversely, a rejection of the impersonality of the divine represents a judgment against the apophatic and aniconic representation in favor of the kataphatic and iconic. The connection between an iconic biblical hermeneutic and a commitment to the divine as person proves extraordinarily fertile. As we shall see in later volumes in which I reflect on Gnostic return the connection is a deep one in Blake. At the same time forms of this connection get recapitulated in Hegel and Schelling. Via German Idealism and Blake, the connection is repeated in a number of important twentieth-century theologians such as Altizer, Tillich, and Moltmann.

(3) A distinctive Boehmian feature associated with iconic preference is what might be called the *visionary supplement*. If the theophanous and iconic divine is the object of revelation, then this reality is not only seen but also

supremely the reality of seeing. The eye (nonphysical) that sees God is beheld by the nonphysical divine eye that sees all, and whose seeing is a condition of ecstatic human sight. In a passage dealing with the mystery of divine manifestation, which is the central topic of Boehme's hexameron, Zechariah and Ezekiel are condensed, so that the wheels of the chariot are full of eyes:

> Thus the essence of the Deity is everywhere in the deep of the unground, like as a wheel or an eye, where the beginning has always the end; and there is no place found for it, for it is itself the place for all beings and the fullness of all things, and yet is apprehended or seen by nothing. For it is an eye in itself, as Ezekiel the prophet saw this in a figure at the introduction of the spirit of his will into God, when his spiritual figure was introduced into the wisdom of God by the Spirit of God, where he attained the vision. (*Sex Puncta Theosophica*, pt. 1, 19)

In addition, the Wisdom of Proverbs 8.22 and the Word of the Johannine prologue are conceived in visionary terms. If Wisdom is more nearly identified with the ideal object of divine vision, God's intended world, the Word is more nearly associated with the act of vision. As Wisdom and Word, however, God is seer and seen. On a somewhat more interpretive and philosophical level is Boehme's symbol of the philosophical globe in which the full conspectus of divine vision in its objective, as well as subjective dimensions, is compacted. What is seen now is not simply the ideal world of divine intention but also the physical world and its eternal presuppositions. The philosophical globe translates the Hermetic maxim that God's center is everywhere, circumference nowhere, into a visual idiom.[3] With the symbol of the philosophical globe we are bordering on another distinctive feature of Boehme's hermeneutic swerve from the tradition—that is, Boehme's pansophism, which is totally without reserve.

(4) Boehme's *pansophism* has proximate precedents in Paracelsus and Weigel, both of whom seek a wisdom that envelops the knowledge of nature and Scripture. But not even the bravest texts of these authors—for example, the former's *Philosophia Sagax* or *Philosophia ad Athenienses*, on the one hand, and the latter's *Vom Ort der Welt*, on the other—compares with the chutspah of Boehme in the preface to *Mysterium Magnum*. In a passage I cited at length in chapter 3, it would be difficult to imagine a more encompassing range of topics: the nature of the divine, angels, the physical world, and human beings, and the why of the fall of the angels and human being. But it is not only the comprehensiveness of Boehme's pansophism that sets him off from his predecessors, but also the level of integration of the elements. Pansophism suggests more than an inclusive aggregate of particulars; it points to something like a systematic arrangement that is more than regulative, in fact, a system, which in Kant's terms, would be classed as constitutive. This Foucault seems to under-

stand perfectly: in a universe of signatures each thing relates to everything else, both horizontally and vertically. For Boehme, the systematic character of reality is guaranteed by a narrative suggested by Scripture, but completed only in a pneumatic or sophiological state that transcends the letter of Scripture.

(5) The fifth and final distinctive swerve on the level of hermeneutics is focused in Boehme's *language of nature*. At one level, all of reality, nonverbal as well as verbal, is a form of manifestation, and thus analogically a form of speech. This is implied in Paracelsus's theory of signature, and developed considerably by Boehme, who also attends to the specifically linguistic aspects of revelation. As *Mysterium Magnum* (chapter 35) shows most clearly, Boehme is fascinated with the idea of an Adamic language in which naming constitutes the reality of the named. When Adam names the animals, their essence is revealed. If such naming is no longer a general prospect, nevertheless, in the fraught postlapsarian condition, fundamental aspects of naming are retrievable. For behind all languages, even behind the privileged language of Hebrew (*MM* 23), is a primordial language that interpretation can tap into to disclose reality and especially Scripture. Beyond the ordinary meanings of words and sentences of Scripture, there are nonobvious meanings, and, of course, Boehme has the resources of the allegorical and anagogical traditions to get at these nonliteral meanings. But, for Boehme, words and even syllables reveal meaning. Undoubtedly, here Boehme's views bear more than a family resemblance to interpretive currents in the Kabbalah that assign values to the letters of the alphabet.[4] What separates Boehme from Kabbalistic reflection, however, is that meaning is embodied in sound, understood as much in terms of how the sound is produced as the sound itself, whether euphonious or cacophonous.[5]

Enough has been said for the moment about Boehme's distinctive hermeneutic swerves. It is time to explore Boehme's distinctive substantive theological swerves. Individual substantive swerves from the pre-Reformation and Reformation traditions of a distinctive kind are numerous in Boehme, but four are especially important. The first concerns deepening the gap between his post-Reformation trinitarian theology and that of Nicene orthodoxy, which continued to be subscribed to by Luther, and enthusiastically endorsed by Lutheran orthodoxy. The others are, in order, Boehme's peculiar view of divine essence and attributes, his view of the agon at the heart of eternity, and finally his view of the body of God, also the "heavenly Eve" or Jerusalem. I begin with what in Boehme's trinitarian theology—understood in the broadest sense—adds: a further and, arguably, more radical dimension to the swerve from the Nicaean tradition than that which he shares with Eckhart and his heritage in the Spiritual Reformers, and especially in Weigel.

There are two interdependent aspects of Boehme's distinctive trinitarian swerve. The first of these is what might be referred to provisionally as the introduction of a fourth hypostasis into the divine. In texts such as *Mysterium*

Magnum and *De Electione Gratiae*, as we saw in the previous chapter, Boehme rows against the time-honored exegetical convention of conflating the Wisdom of Proverbs 8.22 with the Word of the Johannine prologue. Wisdom is granted a certain independence, and must be taken account of separately as the visionary interpreter tries to unravel the movement of the hidden divine into manifestation. In particular, it is in Wisdom, rather than in the Word, that the archetypes of things are found. And it is Wisdom, rather than the Word, that more nearly realizes the subject-object structure of reflection that is the condition of the possibility of divine self-consciousness that is absent at the level of the Unground. In multiplying entities, Boehme is involved in a decisive departure from the common tradition, and indeed a decisive departure from the background Eckhartian and Lutheran traditions of exegesis and trinitarian elaboration. Both Eckhart and Luther operate in terms of the exegetical conventions. Indeed, for Luther (in contrast to Eckhart, who is affected by the mirror possibilities of Wisdom,[6]) as a noncanonic text Proverbs cannot shed deep light on the divine plan, which, of course, is the divine plan of salvation.

The second aspect of Boehme's distinctive trinitarian swerve concerns the specific feature of depersonalization and dehypostatization of the Trinity. In chapter 2, I showed that Boehme is neither unique in his depersonalization or dehypostatization of the Trinity, nor in his providing a dynamic spin to a position for which modalism or Sabellianism has been the cover-term since the earliest centuries of the Common Era. Granted the considerable overlap between Eckhart and Boehme regarding their trinitarian swerve from the common tradition, nevertheless, one must resist the genealogical implications of Baur's reading in his monumental history of trinitarian thought, in which Boehme's trinitarian contribution is exhausted by its repetition of Eckhart's dynamic subversion of the classic hypostatic view, which is static and structural. Drawing on my account of the erotic figuration of Boehme's Trinity in chapter 2, it is clear that the discrimen between Boehme and Eckhart is that in the former the dynamic of trinitarian manifestation is developmental in a way it is not in the latter. Two genealogical consequences follow, which ironically can enlist the support of *Die christliche Gnosis* against what Baur asserts in his *Die christliche Lehre von der Dreieinigkeit*. (a) It is Boehme, not Eckhart (nor Eckhart *and* Boehme together) who provides the precedent for Hegel's determination of the 'Immanent Trinity.' (b) More specifically, it is Boehme who introduces the narrative or developmental type of modalism or Sabellianism, and not simply a dynamic type, that is realized in German Idealism, and in Hegel in particular. Later in the chapter, when I come to treat Boehme's infrastructural narrative swerve from the tradition, I will have more to say about Baur's genealogy of modern trinitarian thought, and his specific figuration of the relation between Eckhart's and Boehme's reflection.

In more immediate need of explication is the relation-difference between Eckhart and Boehme regarding the relatively privileged personal status of the Word vis-à-vis Father and Spirit. As I suggested already in my treatment of Boehme's nondistinctive trinitarian swerve, whether the Word or Son continues to admit of personal or hypostatic ascription depends on definitional criteria. One obvious criterion would be that of ultimacy. At the level of the 'Immanent Trinity,' the Word would admit of a hypostatic or personal interpretation to the extent to which it instantiates unsurpassable levels of ontological, gnoseological, axiological, and existential perfection. If this is plausibly true in the case of Eckhart,[7] it is certainly not so in Boehme. As I indicated in chapter 2, the immanent Word remains deficient on all four axes. Thus, despite its relatively superior personal credentials, and its relatively greater prospects for personal or hypostatic ascription at more evolved levels of ontotheological narrative, at the level of the immanent trinitarian divine, unqualified ascription of personhood or hypostatic status to the Word is ruled out of court in Boehme's discourse.

It is the same with Wisdom, whose relative independence from the Word was provisionally marked by fourth hypostasis status. Given the definitional criteria for the ascription of personhood and hypostatic status, operative in Boehme, at the level of the immanent divine, no more than Word does Wisdom have the required level of ultimacy. Wisdom too is deficient at the level of being, knowledge, existence, and value. Denying personal and hypostatic status to Wisdom at the level of the immanent divine, however, no more rules out ascribing personal or hypostatic status at more developed levels of divine evolution than it does in the case of the Word. As concretized in the milieu of divine attributes that structure divine essence, it becomes possible, if not necessary, to think of Wisdom as a hypostasis or, at least, as having hypostaticlike features.

Mention of divine essence and attributes brings me to the second distinctive substantive theological swerve of Boehme's discourse from the pre-Reformation and Reformation traditions. On the more general front of divine essence, it is easy to see that Boehme inhabits and radicalizes the problematic concerning the ascription of essence or nature to the divine, which in different ways was to the fore in negative theology, on the one hand, and Nominalism and Luther, on the other. In significant part the mainline theological tradition was relatively unanxious about using essence or nature language with respect to the divine, even though divine transcendence prohibited essence or nature being articulated in an absolutely positive fashion. If some anxiety did intrude into the mainline pre-Reformation theological traditions, it had to do with the issue of whether a divine nature or essence limited or restricted the divine, thus compromising the freedom that seemed implied in the transcendence that marked the biblical God, and to which theology was obliged to be faithful. If the tradition of negative theology put pressure on the assumption of a divine nature open to conceptualization, the traditions of Nominalism and Luther judged as evasive the scholastic identification of will and reason in the divine, where reason is a synecdoche for essence. These traditions also regarded as facile a squaring of will and reason—in which the impossibility of God contradicting Godself and engaging in actions that would be found vicious in human beings—is taken to be perfectly consistent with the priority of divine will or divine "good pleasure."[8]

Inhabiting this complex negative theology and Nominalist-Luther space of problematization, Boehme deepens the issue along both fronts. In the negative theology tradition in general, the superessential divine does not mean straightforwardly that the divine as such has *no* essence, but simply that no adequate concept of the divine can be formed, since all such concepts, which have essence as their objective correlatives, are forged within the order of the finite. It is likely that this is still the case in Eckhart, even if the frequency of language of "abyss," "nothing," "barrenness," and "purity" applied to the superessential divine (*überwessentliche Gottheit*) tends to encourage, if not licence, a reading of the absolute divine as being without essence, conceived as ontological, gnoseological, axiological, and existential restraint. To the extent that the relation between the superessential divine and the essential God and, therefore, more specifically, the movement from the former to the latter, was a concern of Eckhart's mystical discourse and of the German negative theology tradition, the relationship was open to being interpreted as a movement whereby the divine does not simply come into our conceptual sight, but also really takes on an essence for the first time. In describing the movement from the superessential, mysterious divine to God as manifest as a movement of essentialization, Boehme radicalizes and surpasses his proximate Eckhartian negative theology inheritance.

Boehme also radicalizes and surpasses the problematization of essence, vouchsafed in Nominalism and Luther, which was not carried through in Lutheran orthodoxy, as compromises were forged with the medieval tradition regarding the status of predication and the relation between will and reason. Boehme fundamentally agrees with Nominalism and Luther that in the divine, will or freedom is logically, and even ontologically, prior to reason or essence, but codes the distinction and order of priority in a language that blends Eckhart with Nominalism and Luther. As Boehme says again and again, prior to essence, the Unground is ungrounded will or freedom. Boehme agrees with Nominalism and Luther that essence restricts or limits the divine, and does so in a way disguised by the apparent inconsequentiality of the assertion of the impossibility of self-contradiction in God and ethical limitation.

However, these agreements between Boehme and the voluntarist perspective of Nominalism, especially as Nominalism is reflected in Luther and inflected by him, serve as the base for even more important disagreements.

Boehme breaks with the theological voluntarist view by refusing to think of the assertion of the logical or ontological priority of divine will or freedom as putting an end to the issue of the relation which, for Boehme, is ultimately that of a dynamic movement from freedom to essence.

The issue cannot be summarily dismissed for Boehme, since by contrast with the voluntarist tradition, essence is held to be real rather than nominal. Here Boehme leans on the negative theology tradition, which presumes the reality of essence only to inquire whether the divine as such is beyond essence. Moreover, the priority of divine will or freedom over essence itself becomes an object of a higher order evaluative discourse. While it is not inaccurate to claim ontological priority for divine will, it would be more accurate to claim a meontological priority, leaving open the question as to whether the divine beyond essence or the essential divine, or otherwise put, God in God's ineffable mystery or God in divine manifestation, is the more really real. As we saw in chapter 2, here Boehme's discourse functions like a Trojan horse. Within the confines of a radical form of negative theology that he inhabits, Boehme subversively articulates a very untraditional judgment of priority.

In addition, Boehme adopts a totally different stance toward the restriction of divine will or freedom. Even while exacerbating nominalist concerns about introducing necessity into the divine by construing necessity in terms that model fate or *ananke*, Boehme welcomes the restriction of divine will by essence. Without such restriction divine will is indeterminate, and indeterminacy in Boehme is always a negative. At issue, for Boehme, is the adequate rendering of the biblical divine that the antimetaphysical stances of Nominalism and Luther are designed to protect. For Boehme, however, this involves more than positing divine will *behind* God's essence. For this essence translates divine action, and thus can be said to be enacted in divine works of generosity, goodness, justice, benevolence, and mercy.

What is needed, therefore, is not a less positive, but a more positive depiction of divine essence in which the biblical tension between various manifestations of the divine is registered, even to the point of the divine contradicting itself, indeed, contradicting itself in more than a logical fashion. For as I pointed out in chapter 1, essence is a contrary scene (*contrarium*) between the negative and the positive, between divine judgment and mercy. The tension, however, is not interminable, and the negative is resolved into the positive, as God's judgment is sublated by God's mercy. For Boehme, then, the divine is limited by a real essence of a dipolar sort that can be read off from Scripture, although importantly, not from Scripture alone. At the same time, the resolvability of the tension in favor of the positive dictates that ontological restriction involves the restriction by ethos feared by Nominalism and Luther alike.[9]

Inherent in this particular swerve from the theological tradition is a rethinking of the nature of divine predicates or attributes. A number of features mark off Boehme's view of divine attributes from that typical in the more standard pre-Reformation traditions, the historical Luther, and especially Lutheran orthodoxy. (1) For Boehme, attributes are not only real, as they are in the common tradition, but also intrinsic in the sense that there is no measure of convention in ascription. (2) The number of attributes is definite in number, not simply finite. There are seven and only seven attributes. (3) For Boehme, attributes are divided into negative and positive, as these reflect distinct sides of divine manifestation. (4) Attributes are more than an aggregate; they constitute a bipolar system of two triads with another attribute functioning as a transition. (5) The systematic organization of attributes is underwritten by narrative in that the transition is unilinearly and unilaterally from negative to positive, and the positive triad of attributes incorporates or recollects structural elements of the negative qualities. (6) The above five features can be read off Scripture, but also nature, which bears the impress of these attributes that are invisible and divine. The set of individuating features underwrites Boehme's discourse about divine qualities (*Qualitäten*) as forces or dynamic powers of divine life (*Quellen*), energy, and even pain (*Quahl*). These qualities configure a divine essence that more fundamentally identifies the divine than the superessential God. The latter, Boehme determines, is ontologically, gnoseologically, axiologically, and existentially challenged.

Once again, however, the distinctiveness of Boehme's position need not entail that it is without discursive presupposition. In my presentation of Boehme's view of divine qualities in chapter 2, Boehme's debt to the Paracelsian triad of salt, mercury, and sulphur was evident. In Paracelsus the triad ultimately names not the physical entities salt, mercury, and sulphur, but dynamic, invisible forces or powers that express themselves in the visible material world. Nonetheless, while Boehme's position is not without precedent, its originality is not undermined. Boehme's analysis not only cuts metaphysically deeper by construing the alchemical triad much more loosely and metaphorically than Paracelsus had, but the analysis also represents a fundamental deepening on the level of the theological appropriation of alchemy which, as texts such as *Philosophia ad Athenienses* and *Philosophia Sagax* make clear, was already afoot in Paracelsus himself. Moreover, as I have had occasion to observe, this process is accelerated in Weigel. Although Paracelsus's discourse, despite its theological drift, has a high *Naturphilosophie* index, Weigel fails to integrate alchemical reflection on invisible divine forces into reflection on Scripture, and especially into Luther's theology of the Cross. This is Boehme's achievement.

Kabbalistic reflection on divine names or *sephiroth* also functions as a discursive presupposition. Although Boehme's first works show little evidence of Kabbalistic intrusion, the later works definitely do. If analogies exist between Boehme's elaboration of the trinitarian dynamic prior to essentialization in the two principles and the first three divine names of the Zoharic Kabbalistic system, Glory, Wisdom, Intelligence (*Kether*, *Hochmah*, *Binah*), the analogies between Boehme's seven essential qualities and the seven remaining Kabbalistic names are no less strong. In the Kabbalah, as with Boehme, the names of the divine are more than abstract attributes; they are real powers expressive of divine life.[10] In addition, Boehme's bipolar distribution of qualities into negative and positive, into those expressive of wrath (*Zorn*) and those expressive of mercy (*Barmhertigkeit*), mirrors the Kabbalistic bipolar division of names into those on the side of judgment (*Din*) and those on the side of mercy (*Hesed*).[11] Moreover, in both cases one quality mediates between the two poles, and the seventh and final quality, in Boehme the *Salitter*, in the Kabbalah *Malkuth*, represents the Kingdom of God as the plastic expression of divine life.

More specific similarities between individual Boehmian and Kabbalistic qualities cannot and should not be stretched too far. For one thing, the impact of alchemy on Boehme's thought in this respect, as in others, is both more longstanding and more urgent. For another, mining for more individual connections suggests less independence in Boehme's own conjugation than is in fact the case. I will have more to say about the Kabbalah in Part III where the taxonomic issue of Boehme's metanarrative is decided. What needs to be underscored for the moment is that whatever contribution the Kabbalah makes to Boehme's elaboration of divine qualities—and it does make a significant contribution—it is no more constitutive, and plausibly less so, than the contribution provided by a theologized alchemy.

Much has been said already about Boehme's agonistics, and discussion of divine essentialization once again brings it to the fore. Still more needs to be said about the swerve agonistics involves from the pre-Reformation and Reformation traditions. There is no reason to doubt that Boehme was deeply affected by Luther's reflection on the vulnerability of the biblical God and the dramatic figuration of *Christus Victor*. If the first emphasis in Luther put the apathetic axiom, which functioned in the patristic and medieval theological traditions, under considerable pressure, the second suggests a more narratized relation between the one who suffers and dies, and the one who is glorified than that apparent in Luther's basically Johannine allegiance to the glory of the Cross. But Moltmann notwithstanding,[12] Luther finally resists saying that the divine nature as such becomes passible in Christ. Indeed, according to some reputable scholars of the Reformer,[13] Luther's use of the communication of properties is intended to protect divine impassibility, at least in some restricted sense. Luther's scruples with respect to deipassionism, and the even greater scruples of Lutheran orthodoxy, are pushed aside by Boehme, who makes a move within Lutheranism that renders fundamental aspects of Hegel's reflection on 'the death of God' belated.[14] Suffering and death are now features of the process of divine becoming.

Although through his assertion that the First Principle, which is the proximate site of suffering and death, is precisely the nondivine, Boehme tries to protect the divine from a deipassionist reading; nonetheless such a reading is basically unpreventable for two reasons: (1) Unlike Manichaeism, the two principles have a single grammatical subject that they specify. (2) The First Principle, or Eternal Nature, is the indispensable condition of the Second Principle's plenitude of being, knowing, goodness, and existence. Suffering and death, therefore, are intrinsic to the divine conceived as a complex but ultimately unitive developmental process.

For Boehme, the *Christus Victor* motive, which in Luther was a dramatic soteriological symbol, becomes implicated in deipassionism when the narrative sequence of death and life is objectified, ontologized, and transferred onto the eternal plane.[15] What in principle was an encouragement offered by Christ defeating sin and death on our behalf, now becomes the movement of death to life in Christ, essential to the definition of the divine as a whole. When Boehme speaks of *Überwindung* (winning) (*MM* 40, 8), he is not simply recalling, therefore, a symbol in Luther that has its ancestry in patristic writers like Irenaeus. Nor is he invoking a resurrection complement to the focus on the Cross. Rather he is speaking to the necessary conditions of divine genesis, of which at best the biblical Cross-Resurrection sequence provides a symbol.

The final area of distinctive swerve from the pre-Reformation and Reformation traditions lies in Boehme's depiction of the "heavenly Eve," conceived as Wisdom in the form of a real objectification of a divine world of teeming multiplicity and variety projected by divine imagination.[16] Heavenly Eve is a mirroring in the ontologically fertile field of the Second Principle, which because of the First has gone beyond the meontological incapacities of the nonessential divine. Still, even here, Wisdom is the passive complement to the manifesting activity of the Son and the Spirit, which I indicated in Part I are associated with the fifth and sixth qualities respectively. It is undoubtedly the case that, as paradise, heavenly Eve is the Kingdom of God as the perfect expression of divine power and goodness, as well as the realization of the right kind of relation within the order of expression and between the expressing divine and the expressed.

Boehme does everything he can to underscore the organic relation of the Kingdom to divine manifestation. The Kingdom is the "Body of God." In making this connection, the analogy of the relation between body and soul is operative. Yet the *as* gets elided: the Kingdom *is* the Body or *corpus* of the divine, the truly divine matrix. For support Boehme reaches back into the alchemical traditions, and finds precedents in alchemy's insistence both on fixity (*Sal*) and the transmutation of base matter. And if Yates and Hirst are correct,[17] the Hermetic tradition provided a general ideological background that supported alchemy and philosophically developed it. In any event, both the corporalization and feminization of the divine depart in radical ways from pre-Reformation and Reformation standards. In Lutheran circles, such speculative reflections were with some justice experienced as an interruptive event, viewed in fact as the return of a mythology Christianity has surpassed.

Moreover, as a major player in the temporal physical world in general, and the human drama of salvation in particular, the heavenly Eve could be understood to compromise the role of Logos and Christ respectively. For it is the active presence of heavenly Eve in Eden, and not the Logos, that is constitutive of Eden's sublime status, as it is her presence, and not the presence of the Logos, that is constitutive of the image of God that upholds Adamic integrity. The fall leads to the occlusion of image and the loss of integrity rendered in what for Boehme, and for Blake later, is the blight of sexual differentiation. That sexual differentiation, as a sign of the fall, is at odds with the Western Augustinian tradition and the Lutheran tradition goes without saying. Neither support the myth of the androgynous Adam, nor its eschatological complement, despite the Pauline promises of there being neither male nor female in heaven. For Boehme, however, the loss of image is not total, and not simply for the reason that Christ restores it. The eternal feminine is not so much absent as episodically present as, for instance, in the biblical patriarchs and prophets, but also in those after Christ who remain open to the gifts of the divine. And Christ is the restorer of the image of God only to the extent that he is the *mysterium coniuctionis* of an openness of spirit and the heavenly Eve. Christ is constituted by the heavenly Eve; he does not constitute her. In a sense he provides the real symbol of her eschatological realization, which brings about nothing less than the reintegration of the divine image in finite being, first wounded in Lucifer and again in Adam.

4. 2. Narrative Swerve: Metalepsis

Against the background of nondistinctive swerves from pre-Reformation and Reformation traditions, however, the distinctive swerves indicate a general swerve that is as comprehensive as it is deep. While in itself such a general swerve need not imply that it operates at the level of narrative, suggestions that this is in fact the case are provided by Boehme's reflection on the Trinity, divine essence and attributes, agon within the divine essence, and the constitution of the Kingdom. In all these cases it is emphasis on a unitive process and development that ultimately functions to unhinge Boehme from the standard pre-Reformation and Reformation theological traditions. In this specific sense, Boehme represents a remythologization that standard, more epistemically humble theological accounts of the biblical narrative are intended to forestall, and in the event of breakout, intended to curtail. In a fertile interpretation of the Trinity, the antitheological Blumenberg suggests that a singular function of the doctrine of the Trinity is the repression of the plurality and becoming necessarily insinuated by the Trinity in its principled opposition to monotheism, a monotheism that is more easily alignable with metaphysics, indeed, a metaphysics of the One. Blumenberg writes:

> The Trinitarian hypostases remain processes of pure inwardness, and on account of the identical nature of the three Persons—that is, their equal eternity—no story can be told, either of what led to this generation or spiration. Dogma, having awakened a need for myth, ultimately summons it back to *raison* [reason].[18]

There are two important implications of this view. One implication is that where trinitarian hypostases are in fact submitted to a developmental reading, other theologoumena, formed through community interpretation of particular episodes of the biblical narrative, such as creation, incarnation, and the Kingdom of God will tend to be submitted to a similar rereading, for what has been unleashed is narrativity, which renders all aspects of the divine as ingredients in the divine story at the deepest level of reality. Another implication is that the commitment to a story or developmental view is reflective, and that consequently rereading the standard theological presentations of the biblical narrative suggests that mythic description is of secondary rather than primary order. Specifically, critique of the theological tradition's reading of each component of the biblical narrative is presupposed in the rendition of the metanarrative presented not only as adequate but as true, indeed, as the unsurpasable truth.

Here, of course, one is not simply talking about second-order myth in general, but a second-order theogonic myth in which the divine, as the one that becomes, is tracked in its movement from mystery to manifestation, darkness to light, absence to presence. Moreover, as with the first-order theogonic myths of the Western tradition, for example, the Babylonian creation hymn, *Enuma Elish*, the becoming of God involves the genesis of the world. Or more technically put, in Boehme's discourse theogony involves cosmogony. A point sensed by Blumenberg—although admittedly only inchoately—is that theogony allows two patterns, one agonistic in which the divine becomes only by a form of self-opposition, and the other more evolutionist. If Blumenberg's primary identification of these patterns with Goethe, on the one hand, and Bruno on the other, is not especially helpful for our purposes, his secondary identifications are more pertinent. Without explicitly making the connection between Gnosticism and Boehme, he cites both as instantiating the agonistic pattern.[19] In both of its patterns, however, theogony represents a critique of the God of the philosophers—that is, Aristotle's unmoved mover—and also of the supremely actual God of the Bible, who apparently does not share our virtuality.

Tillich, Berdyaev, and Altizer, each in their different ways, would un-doubtedly agree with the main drift of Blumenberg's assessment. They would, however, probably want to qualify his judgment somewhat by suggesting that the actualist interpretation of the God of Judaism and Christianity may do an injustice to the biblical God and underestimate the measure of divine self-development involved in creation, incarnation, redemption, and Kingdom.[20] For these thinkers, it is still possible to contend that it is Boehme, and not the orthodox tradition—and certainly not Boehme's Lutheran orthodox contem-poraries—who gets it right with respect to the biblical God.

Most biblical theologians (and not simply those of Barthian persuasion) would tend to agree, however, with Blumenberg's assessment, and thus rule against Boehme's own perception of fidelity to the living God of the Bible. In any event, although Boehme thinks of his ontotheology as exhibiting and elu-cidating the biblical narrative, it is clear that, as presented in the work of clas-sical narrative theologians such as Irenaeus and Luther, the biblical narrative is subjected to disfiguration and refiguration. Refiguration is the key. For it is not only that Boehme's visionary or apocalyptic discourses indicate a multitude of disfigurations of the biblical narrative, but that these disfigurations are narra-tively integrated into a narrative or metanarrative that is put forward as knowl-edge or *Verstand*. In this disfiguration-refiguration the biblical narrative comes to be understood not as the drama between the divine and the world, and more specifically the divine and the community of finite beings, but as the agony of divine self-constitution as subject and person in and through the world and community.

To the extent to which such disfiguration-refiguration of narrative is in-volved, then what I am calling metalepsis, or strong metalepsis, is indicated. But this raises the question of what actually effects a transformation from a narrative of action and encounter between agential subjects to a narrative of di-vine becoming and development. As I suggested in Part I both material and formal elements play a role in metalepsis. Considered as agonistically, even thanatologically specified, the three most important material elements are, in order (1) will, (2) eros, and (3) kenosis. The relevant formal features are the maximal presence of narrative anticipation (*prolepsis*)-narrative recollection (*analepsis*), as well as the narrative, even narrativity coding, of common binary symbolic pairs used in stories of fall and redemption that have religious signif-icance.[21] Given my relatively substantial treatment of these material and formal elements in Part I, I can be brief here. I begin with the material elements of narrative transformation.

(1) If divine will plays a role in Boehme's visionary narrative that it does not play in the mainline theological tradition, this is not because Boehme makes fashionable divine "good pleasure" in the way of the later Augustine, Nominalism, and Luther. It is rather because divine will is the divine will for a

self that is a project rather than a given. The clue as to why will is typically a narrativity or theogony agent is offered by Blumenberg when he contrasts this commitment to will explicitly with the complacency of Aristotle's divine of *noesis noeseos noesis*, and implicitly with the actualist God of the Bible.[22] The will of the divine for the divine symptoms the rupture of noetically protected divine self-satisfaction. As indicative of the noncoincidence of the self with itself, will creates, however, only the possibility of purpose and teleology, and thus at once promises and puts in jeopardy the intelligibility of God-talk. Without some noetic element, one could not rule out the possibility of purposeless process. This possibility, however, is in fact ruled out in Boehme, for Wisdom resides at the most archeological level of the divine.

As illuminated by Wisdom, will is imagination. The converse, however, is also true: as energized by will, Wisdom is imagination. In any event, divine imagination is the power of the constitution of Eternal Nature as the other than God. And precisely as such, imagination is also the power of divine self-constitution, for divine integrity is founded on the divine's integration of the other than divine.

Boehme's view of imagination as constitutive of the divine, as well as his view of imagination as the mutual interpenetration of will and intellect, had a significant career in Romanticism and German Idealism. His view that imagination constitutes the divine is highlighted in Blake, Coleridge, and the early Schelling. His view that imagination is constituted by an interpenetration of will and intellect is to the forefront in Blake and the later Schelling. But it is apposite to draw attention again to the alchemical presuppositions. As I pointed out in chapter 2, Boehme finds a willful view of divine imagination or creativity already at hand in Paracelsus, who himself can call upon a Renaissance rhetoric of creativity, irreducible to reason in either its instrumental or contemplative deployment. Still, once more Boehme exceeds his discursive presuppositions.

While imagination in Paracelsus sometimes functions in a full-blown theological way, it does not usually so function. Most often its domain is anthropological, with Paracelsus commenting on the power of imagination to "impress" itself on a plastic reality. Of course, Boehme's proximate Christianly heterodox discursive web includes prior theologizations of alchemy by Weigel and the pseudo-Weigelian tradition,[23] which made the creativity of the divine an issue, and which figured the divine as imaginative artificer. Nevertheless, nothing is as worked through as Boehme's account. And nothing in his predecessors justifies granting to them, rather than Boehme, credit for providing imagination with an ontotheological status by emphasizing not only its cosmogonic power but its power to constitute the divine as such. Mutatis mutandis, this is the case with respect to the role of will in general. When Schelling unfolds his account of the primordial nature of will in *Essay on Human Freedom*,[24] neither the level of reflection in Paracelsus nor Weigel justifies displacing Boehme as Schelling's main precursor in the tradition. This brings me to the second material element at the basis of Boehme's disfiguration-refiguration of the biblical narrative.

(2) The purposeful nature of a divine will for self suggests that, contrary to the mainline pre-Reformation and Reformation traditions, the relation of the divine to the other than divine is erotic rather than agapaic. As outlined in chapter 2, the erotic dimension of Boehmian narrative, lexically indicated by words such as *Sucht* and *Begierde*, is a function of the fact that the archeological divine, also apophatic divine, is neither perfect nor full. In this sense, as Schelling recognizes later,[25] the eros of a theogonic narrative represents a coincidence of *penia* and *poros*, indigence as well as plenty.

Of course, this erotic interpretation of the divine movement of manifestation at the inner trinitarian and subsequent narrative levels does not represent merely the subversion of the Eckhartian negative theology tradition. It also represents a major departure from standard pre-Reformation and post-Reformation theological traditions. For Thomas, for example, the manifestations of the divine in creation, incarnation, and redemption are gratuitous, and finally, therefore, expressions of God's self-giving and expending love. Indeed, in their common commitment to the Dionysian model of *bonum diffusivum sui* there is little difference between Thomas and Eckhart. Boehme's departure from the apophatic and heterodox Eckhart implies his departure from the more kataphatic and orthodox Thomas.

Boehme's erotic interpretation of the divine movement of manifestation also represents a subversion of the Lutheran tradition in which the embargo on the interpretation of grace and salvation as somehow dependent on human eros for the divine is,[26] arguably, surpassed by its embargo on the erotic interpretation of the divine as such. While the metaphysical language of divine self-sufficiency and superabundance of being was not congenial to the Reformer, neither Luther nor subsequent Lutheran orthodoxy broke with the tradition by conceding that God is other than gift and giver. As love, the giver is perfect. Structurally, the prerogatives of *agape* are resolutely affirmed, albeit under the biblical restriction and with the theological proviso that love be interpreted in the light of the Cross.[27] With this I come to the third of the three material elements of transformation of Christian narrative or its first-order interpretation in the pre-Reformation and Reformation traditions.

(3) The primitive neediness of the divine leads to a transvaluation of the symbol of kenosis as this symbol operates in standard pre-Reformation and Reformation discourses. First, kenosis comes to function tropically: kenosis names any process of emptying or leaving behind. Thus what applies in the standard pre-Reformation and Reformations traditions specifically to the incarnation as realized in the Cross is generalized to other sites in the Christian narrative, for example, Trinity, creation, Kingdom of God. Second, kenosis

functions essentialistically rather than morphologically. Kenosis in Boehme's discourse is an emptying that involves a change in the underlying substance or subject, and not simply a change of form that leaves this substance or subject intact. Given the unity of the subject undergoing process, the emptying of the divine Trinity and Wisdom into the eternal essence involves, as we have seen already, genuine pathos. Thus kenosis, as it operates in Boehme's discourse, represents a fundamental challenge to the apathetic axiom that played an important role in the pre-Reformation theological traditions. Such an axiom serves a vital function in both Irenaeus's and Augustine's rejection of mythic systems—although, as Thomas shows,[28] the principle of divine impassibility could be defended outside the context of polemic against myth.

Boehme's view of kenosis also represents a challenge to how kenosis functions in Luther's discourse, and thereafter throughout Lutheran orthodoxy. While Luther's *theologia crucis* evidences a completely different sensibility to that of Thomas, even in his case the analytic tool of communication of properties was intended to prevent the conclusion that God as such suffers.[29] As Luther scholars have pointed out,[30] in Luther, as with the early Church Fathers, the communication of properties functions essentially as a rule of interpretation and proper Christian speech. The divine and human attributes, apparent in the Gospel narratives, are both predicable of Christ the subject. It is, therefore, the same subject who is almighty and suffers, who is omniscient and grows in wisdom. At once, because of this unity and a means hyperbolically to evoke it, it is permissible under the rule of Christian grammar to speak of God as suffering and human nature as omnipotent. But this does not involve the conclusion that metaphysically speaking God as such suffers. If the Lutheran hymn of 'God is dead' faithfully represents Luther, its meaning should not be determined by Hegel's deipassionist appropriation.[31] This was even more true in the case of Lutheran orthodoxy, which, putting the doctrine of the communication of properties at the center, and ignoring the sometime monophysite tendency in Luther, could affirm with the rigor of the Church Fathers that God does not suffer, and be appalled by Boehme's flouting of this rule for the Christian reading of narrative.

Third, against the backdrop of a univocal and essentialist tendency in reading kenosis, the indivisible erotic logic of Boehme's rendition of the Christian narrative ensures that kenosis can only function ironically. Emptying from Unground to 'Immanent Trinity' and Wisdom, from 'Immanent Trinity' and Wisdom to First Principle, from First Principle to Second Principle, involves a movement from less to more. Indeed, in the case of the movement from the Unground to Wisdom and the 'Immanent Trinity,' the point of departure is a reality so inchoate and incipient that it justifies the attribution of "nothing." Thus, in a real sense kenosis is plerosis, supposing perfection as a goal, rather than presupposing perfection as a given. Once again, Boehme goes beyond the

historical Luther and is resolutely opposed to the tradition of Lutheran orthodoxy. If Nygren is right about Luther,[32] then kenosis is without need or possible gain. All the more so is a plerotic interpretation of kenosis ruled out in
Lutheran orthodoxy, as the orthodox critics of Weigel and Boehme make abun-
dantly clear.

Related to this erotic and kenotic destabilization of the Christian narrative
is a redeployment of the trope of *felix culpa*. For the theological tradition in
general, *felix culpa* had as its domain the Adamic fall, and in parameters variously doxological (as in the case of Augustine,[33] for instance) or focused on the
stability of human attunement to the divine (as in the Cappadocians)[34] the
trope reflected the view that however horrible the fall, the believer could
nonetheless envision it as involving a net gain. When Luther felt inclined in the
felix culpa direction, it was to the more Augustinian pattern that he inclined.
And Boehme himself operates in terms of this Augustinian pattern to the extent to which he sees God's glory heightened in the drama of history.

Even more importantly, Boehme adds the Augustinian wrinkle of the fall
of the angels, which complicates the *felix culpa* trope that works best in the anthropological field. But in the final analysis the *felix culpa* trope has more comprehensive work to do in Boehme than in Augustine or the Cappadocians,
since the movement from the First to the Second Principle involves a fall, and
a fall is insinuated in the case of the movement from the Quaternity to Eternal
Nature. To valorize these falls, as Boehme does, is to introduce a qualitatively
different *felix culpa*. This is what can be called narrative or theogonic *felix culpa*,
for the simple reason that all falls in the divine are narratively recuperable and
contribute to the realization of divine personhood perfect in being, knowing,
value, and existence.

To round out my account of the material features of Boehme's metalepsis
of the Christian narrative, I will say something about the agonistic, even thana-
tological, specification of the entire Boehmian narrative. Since I have commented on this aspect of Boehme's thought more than once already, my
remarks will be brief. I recur again to Blumenberg's distinction between agonistic and nonagonistic forms of divine expressiveness and, relatedly, divine
self-constitution. That Boehme's works instantiate the former type has been established, albeit with the caveat that Boehme's mythic reflection operates on
the second level rather than the first.

This implies among other things that even in the event of massive paral-
lelism between first-order agonistic myths like *Enuma Elish* and Boehme's
second-order myth, defined by its self- consciousness, the second-order nature
of Boehme's myth would count decisively against identity. Moreover, while par-
allels can be made between the gradual differentiation of the divine realm and
its consummation in Marduk and divine self-differentiation and the realization
of self-reflective selfhood in Boehme, and between the agon of Marduk and

Tiamat and Boehme's agon of principles, there are differences. Marduk is fully personalized before the agon with the primaeval force of nature, and Marduk does not die in the nondivine to emerge from death to life. On the first-order plane, a plausible primary facsimile of the Boehmian myth would have to supplement *Enuma Elish* with the Near Eastern myth of the dying and resurrecting gods like Dionysus, Dumuzi, and Osiris. In any event, Boehme's myth is second order, and the proper comparisons are with second-order theogonic myths in which there is a unitive basis of reality that guarantees that nature is not simply other than spirit but a condition for its appearance. But, of course, Boehme's second-order myth is a Christian myth, and thus an interpretation of Christian narrative. This suggests Gnosticism or Valentinianism at least as a comparandum, since, as Ricoeur points out,Gnosticism is the exemplary second-order theogonic myth.[35]

I will postpone until Part III trying the question as to whether Boehme's myth is best identified as 'Gnostic' or as 'Neoplatonic,' 'Kabbalistic,' 'apocalyptic.' At this point, it is important to point out precursors who not only read the Christian narrative theogonically but also agonistically. As I have pointed out already, theologically reflected alchemy views Christ as the luminous or golden body (i.e., the *lapis philosophorum*) that emerges from the blackening (*nigredo*) of nature. Christ is the Son as the Sun (*Sol*), or the coincidence of the heavenly masculine (*Sol*) and feminine (*Luna*). Boehme presupposes this pattern right down to the *Kreuzrad*, the retort as wheel of pain in which nature gets crucified and spirit gets elevated. Adopting this pattern from alchemy, Boehme can only take his prompt from Luther, and not his rule, as he interprets the Cross not as a sign of God's love for finite beings (angels and humans), but rather as an indication of divine acceptance of the price of perfection. Contradiction, agony, and death, then, provide the horizon for divine will, eros and kenosis, and inflect them. Altizer could not be more right, then, in making the connection between Boehme and Blake and Hegel[36] although, as we shall see in Part III, Altizer's corresponding denial that this connection functions as a sign of Gnostic return will be challenged.

Also not without consequence for German Idealism and a number of modern theologians is that the agonistic narrative is in Boehme trinitarianly framed. Although, as I have already pointed out, Boehme does distinguish between a trinitarian moment beyond the triad of principles that bear the burden of divine becoming and its struggles, the fact that agon enters, however inchoately, a trinitarianly structured narrative discourse, implies a major departure and has consequences with respect to standard pre-Reformation and Reformation theological traditions. If agonic construal of the Trinity can be insinuated in the discourses of the mainline theological tradition, for example, Luther, it finally has to be rejected. More than Moltmann, then, Baur recognizes the role Boehme plays in subverting a trinitarian tradition that bases itself on divine aseity. And it is Baur, and even more Staudenmaier, who recognize that the introduction of agonistics into a trinitarian frame is an introduction that has as its conditions a Sabellianlike loss of hypostatic substance.[37] Staudenmaier recognizes that this modern variety of Sabellianism differs from the ancient versions. The new species proceeds according to a dynamic developmental logic absent from earlier varieties.

I have said all I want to say about the material effects Boehme's narrative ontotheology wrecks upon the biblical narrative. At the more formal level changes are also rung on the Christian narrative. In most of its standard pre-Reformation forms (e.g., Irenaeus, Augustine, Thomas), and in the form it takes in Luther, the Christian narrative proceeds on the condition of divine openness to the adventure of creation and redemption that manifests who God is. At the same time, in standard pre-Reformation and Reformation forms, while the adventure is ongoing, the narrative, in principle at least, has a "sense of an ending."[38] That is, narrative closure is presumed to be brought about eschatologically in which the divine brings its work to completion and is glorified.

Narratologically stated then, standard pre-Reformation accounts as well as the account of Luther suggest the operation of narrative openness (*anaclasis*) and narrative closure (*synclasis*). Now the disposition of the biblical narrative is fundamentally altered when, in addition to this narrative pair, biblical narrative is also articulated by *prolepsis* (anticipation) and *analepsis* (recollection), functioning not simply as guaranteeing the basic coherence of the plot, but rather as productive of the persona of the divine. In standard pre-Reformation renditions of the Christian narrative, and similarly in Luther, however the divine anticipates or recollects (obviously eternally) the adventure of creation and redemption, anticipation and recollection do not furnish the divine with an ontological identity. The most the narrative can do is to illustrate such an ontological identity accessible to knowledge. It is part of the definition of the divine that by contrast with human being this identity is given from the beginning. The fully fledged operation of *prolepsis* and *analepsis*, then, homogenizes a narrative field by mediating the inalienable difference between the divine and the nondivine, and the drama that has its basis in this difference. The level of *prolepsis* and *analepsis* in Boehme is such that everything preindicated from the beginning and recollected in the end has to do with divine self-formation. Thus, while drama is abolished, paradoxically agon is preserved. For divine self-definition involves travail and birth pains; the Cross is a principle of divine becoming.

A second formal feature of the transformation of the biblical narrative, as the narrative is rendered in its standard pre-Reformation and Lutheran forms, is a new weaving of symbolic oppositions that provide the biblical narrative with some of its depth. Five symbolic oppositional pairings are subjected to a different narrative coding, in effect a *narrativity* coding.[39] A few words can be said in order about each of these codes: the ocular code, the codes of weight, nothing, speech, and the organic code.

Influenced by a biblical reflection that joins Genesis to John's Gospel and that does not forget prophetic asseverations about the divine, the standard pre-Reformation narrative theologies typically maintain that God is the light that excludes the darkness, the vision that is other than blindness. The exclusion is absolute, such that relations between light and darkness, and vision and blindness, are nonreciprocal and certainly nonnarratively determined. In Boehme, however, divine light and vision become completely relationally implicated with darkness and blindness, so that light in the proper sense depends upon darkness just as vision depends upon blindness. The relation, then, is not only reciprocal but narratively determined. Light is, for Boehme, in some sense an archeological reality in the divine. As Boehme is prepared to suggest that the mysterious divine can be referred to as dark, he equally suggests that the Unground, and even more so the 'Immanent Trinity' and Wisdom, is invested with light. Perhaps, one could say that at the level of the divine that precedes the emergence of a darkness, one is neither talking about light nor dark, vision nor blindness, but their coincidence. What succeeds this at best indeterminate light and unfocused vision, and what proceeds from it, is darkness that is the withholding of light and a blindness that is the withholding of vision. This darkness and blindness—what might be called the tain in the mirror of divine self-reflection[40]— in turn set the stage for the dramatic emergence of light and vision. These, however, remain internally related to darkness and blindness as their transformation or metamorphosis. Against the background of Boehme's Copernican-like option for the sun as the center of the cosmos, and Derridian surmises about the structural importance of light in the Western ontotheological tradition, Boehme's articulation of light amounts to a narratively based heliocentrism that gets rearticulated, particularly in Blake and Hegel, and about which I will have a considerable amount to say in subsequent volumes.

Boehme's use of the codes of weight and nothing point to a similar process of transformation. Especially in its pre-Reformation instantiations, the contrast of the lightness of God with the heaviness of the world (which is a function of the contrast of spirit and matter) and the contrast of the being of God with the nothingness of the world, function nonrelationally and nonnarratively. That is, in relatively first-order theological renditions of the biblical narrative, these oppositions mark off the divine from the nondivine. This function determines, therefore, the possibility of inversion: the material heaviness of the world might indicate an ontological lightness, and correlatively, the lightness of the divine as spirit might indicate an ontological heaviness. Similarly, since the nothingness of the world is yet something, the superdeterminate reality of the divine, as in the apophatic tradition, might be thought to be more adequately nominated by the term 'nothing' than 'being.'

The transformation of coding in Boehme's narrative rings major changes on the binary symbolic pairing of 'light' and 'heavy.' In the Boehmian narrative there exist not one but two locations of contrast between light and heavy. The first is that between the nonmassive divine will and knowing in the Unground, the 'Immanent Trinity' and Wisdom, and the heaviness of divine will—that is, *desire* in Eternal Nature. The second is that between the massiveness of Eternal Nature (First Principle) and the lightness of Eternal Freedom (Second Principle). The lightness of the divine narratively prior to Eternal Nature is qualified by the latter's massiveness and density, only to have this massiveness and density relieved in the lightness of determinate spirit or Eternal Freedom. As there are two relations of narrative dependence, there are two forms of lightness, with Eternal Freedom being the form of lightness that is not unbearable because, paradoxically, it has weight. Availing oneself of a Heideggerian contrast, one might say that Eternal Freedom is ontically light and ontologically heavy, just the inverse of Eternal Nature.

Of course, it is evident throughout Boehme's mature work that his major concern is ontological. Specifically, Boehme is concerned with the conditions of production of a perfect being, an *ens perfectissimum*, none greater than which can be thought.[41] What really matters for Boehme in his metaphorics of weight is whether the divine is ontologically substantial, and this relativizes contrasts of density and lightness on the ontic level. For instance, on the surface level the light-weight contrast between the immanent divine realm and the *centrum naturae* is in favor of the former. Ontologically, however, the latter introduces real being, or its possibility, into the divine, and accordingly it must be valued over the immanent divine realm that bathes in lightness and purity. Only in the Second Principle, where divine perfection is realized, do we have a real coincidence of ontic lightness and ontological substantiality.

The ontological concern is even more evident in the case of the transformation of the code of nothing (*Nichts*). This code is transformed in both its primary and secondary manifestations. The contrast of the superlative being of the Unground (and Quaternity) with the nothing of Eternal Nature is not left intact when the nothing of Eternal Nature becomes essential to defining the perfection of divine being actual only in an Eternal Freedom that elevates rather than annihilates Eternal Nature. Similarly, with regard to the intention behind the reversal: the nothing of the Unground, by contrast with the something of Eternal Nature, does not enjoy the superlative kind of transcendence that the theological tradition ascribes to the divine. For Boehme, such transcendence which, indeed, is a superlative form of nothingness, is only realized in an Eternal Freedom that selectively recollects properties of the somethingness (*Ichts*) or determinacy of Eternal Nature.

The code of speech and the organic code as they function in Scripture, or in relatively first-order renditions of the Christian narrative, are also radicalized. In standard pre-Reformation theological renditions of the biblical narrative, God, as Word, is the other to the wordlessness and unintelligibility of that which is without God. Even, or especially, in the overcoming of wordlessness by the Word, wordlessness and the Word cannot be mediated. This is not the case in texts such as *Mysterium Magnum* and *De Electione Gratiae*. The incipient Word of the 'Immanent Trinity' and also Wisdom are mediated by the wordlessness of Eternal Nature to constitute an eschatological Word superior to the archeological word. In Boehme, this narrative rereading affects all dimensions of the Word-wordlessness contrast. On the one hand, the Word as Name must be lost in the namelessness of Eternal Nature to be refound—or found for the first time—as Eternal Freedom (Mercurius). On the other hand, as a form of divine speech or elocution, both the form and sweetness of language must be given up to the formlessness of prelinguistic rattle, cacophony and sourness to reemerge as real elocution.

There is no difference with respect to the last code, the organic code. It too is narratively radicalized in Boehme's discourse. In standard pre-Reformation renditions, and also in Luther, God is dynamic generation or birth (*Geburt*) that has no analogy on the finite plane. God is the life that contrasts with death. For Boehme, by contrast, divine generation is accessible, since in Boehme's signatural universe it is understood to bear an analogy to birth on the physical plane. This means that analogy is so much in force that generation implies the growth in divine being that grammatically is excluded in the pre-Reformation and Reformation traditions. And, as we have seen already, for Boehme death is not simply a narrative interruption. It is an event and reality that is a condition of the true form of life that narratively incorporates it. Death, then, is something that not only does happen to God, but must happen to God, if God is to be absolutely all-embracing reality. Before the emergence of Eternal Nature, therefore, the divine is not living, for the divine has not encountered and consummated its victory over death. As Boehme put it, "*In die Überwindung ist die Freude*" (*MM* 40, 8). *Freude* or joy is nothing less than the existential marker of the perfection of divine being that has integrated pain and death.

As I bring my discussion of Boehme's swerve on the level of narrative to a close, I would like to remark on one important general consequence. The coincidence of these formal and material elements of transformation of more standard versions of the biblical narrative bring about a significant change in the theodicy genre. There were a number of viable options in the post-Reformation period. The most common one is the Augustinian and Reformation strategy of subverting the need for theodicy by questioning the theological coherence of making the divine accountable to human standards, denying the accuracy of the complaint regarding the universality and depth of suffering and evil, and finally, suggesting human responsibility for what is awry because of sin. Despite the power of the Book of Job, the etiology of sin as rendered in Genesis 1.3 continued to be the answer of choice, even when the issue was more that of natural evil. What happens in the Boehmian frame of reference is that while the problem of the origin and nature of evil is, if anything, exacerbated, this is accompanied by the presentation of a divine whose very identity is predicated both on articulating chaos and on emerging triumphant from death. The divine is justified by a narrative presentation that suggests that no alternative to divine realization can be imagined. Versimilitude in presentation gives way to an account of narrative necessity.

CHAPTER 5

∾

Boehme's Visionary Discourse
and the Limits of Metalepsis

The adjective "unbounding" that qualifies metalepsis in the heading to Part II is not decorative. It intends to suggest, albeit in a metaphoric way, at once the tendency in Boehme's texts toward an unrestricted metamorphosis of biblical narrative, and the de facto restriction of this tendency. Up until now in Part II my concern has been to elucidate the very real tendency toward unrestricted metalepsis. It is time, however, to ask the question whether there are any elements in Boehme's discourse that help to impede its full realization.

A number of factors force this question. First, and most obviously, my interpretation focused selectively on the moves Boehme made beyond the standard pre-Reformation and Reformations forms of Christianity, without commenting on whether his discourse in any way meshes with these traditions. Intellectual honesty means that this question has squarely to be faced, and requires the features he does share with the standard pre-Reformation and Reformation tradition be elucidated.

An equally important reason, however, concerns the genealogical implications of not raising the question of overlap between Boehme's discourse and that of the common theological tradition, and more specifically not bringing forward what there exists in his discourse that resists metalepsis. Failure here encourages, or supports, the perceptual fallacy that Boehme is everything that Hegel's and Schelling's philosophical discourses are, on the one hand, and what Blake's mythopoetic discourse is, on the other. And this affects the interpretation of development that genealogists posit as occurring between Boehme and Romanticism and Idealism. Throwing out Boehme's *orthodox reserve* dehistoricizes discourses of the modern period, and especially narrative discourses of the modern period. More specifically, it evacuates the specific contexts of both the post-Reformation and post-Enlightenment periods that function as the *terminus a quo* and the *terminus ad quem* respectively of the career of a particular kind of agonistic ontotheological narrative. Reflection on this issue is instigated in particular by the work of Baur, who labors mightily in linking Boehme with nonliterary Romanticism (e.g., Schleiermacher) and German Idealism as part of his explanation of Gnostic return. Engagement with, and contestation of Baur's undramatic view of development, is necessary if the movement from post-Reformation to post-Enlightenment narrative ontotheology is to be correctly understood. And resolution of this issue contributes, as we will see in Part III, to a more viable rendition of the Gnostic return hypothesis.

Baur's case about the Gnostic character of significant modern discourses ultimately turns on the relation between Boehme and Hegel. In both *Die christliche Gnosis* (pp. 555ff.) and *Die christliche Lehre von der Dreieinigkeit* (3, pp. 261–97), Baur suggests that Boehme and Hegel share a common theogonic narrative that has an essentially triadic form. Development from Boehme to Hegel—such as it is—is a reality merely of the symbolizing medium. The reason why Hegel can be regarded properly as the apex of religious philosophy (or ontotheology) is that his conceptual apparatus allows him to demonstrate and justify what can only be asserted in the representational discourse of Boehme. This particular way of framing development is basically borrowed wholesale from Hegel, whose generous treatment of Boehme in his *History of Philosophy* glosses his borrowings from Boehme in *Lectures on the Philosophy of Religion* (vol. 3, 1827, Lectures, p. 289), the *Phenomenology* (e.g., #774, 776–77), and the *Encyclopaedia* (e.g., #247 zu; #248 zu). Precisely because Hegel's account concerns form, it is peculiarly undialectical. Certainly it is undramatic, since in the articulation of ontotheological content no account is given of losses and gains that are the stuff of historical development. The Hegelian-Baurian reading, then, puts in *epoché* facets of Boehme's particularity and historical-discursive situation, which, ironically, Baur is more capable of appreciating than most other historians of dogma of the nineteenth century.

An essential element of resistance to Hegelian-Baurian reading involves emphasizing Boehme's Reformation context, even as one qualifies this by drawing attention to Paracelsus and the Spiritual Reformers as providing discourses that Boehme articulates, extends, and transforms. More than this is required, however, for as Baur's own work indicates, providing historical context for a particular form of thought may not alter in a fundamental way the interpretation of its relation to broader patterns of Christian thought and discourse. In *Die christliche Lehre von der Dreieinigkeit* (2, pp. 217–95), Boehme is, in fact, associated with Franck, Schwenckfeld, and Weigel. Yet this neither effects nor guarantees any distanciation between Boehme and Hegel. The Spiritual Reformers are read with an eye toward their completion in Boehme's discourse. To the degree to which the discourses of the Spiritual Reformers are taken up in Boehme's discourse, they too become contemporaries of Hegel, as Hegel's discourse masters and sublates Boehme's visionary, trinitarian narrative. Beyond the specificity of Boehme's post-Reformation context, what needs to be acknowledged is the fundamental exacerbation in the shift in discursive authority instituted by the Enlightenment. Boehme is simply more rooted in the Christian tradition, and specifically the Protestant tradition, than post-Enlightenment thinkers such as Hegel. If the Bible is not self-interpreting, for Boehme, and demands the intervention of interpretation, it is still not the "wax nose" of Hegel's *Lectures on the Philosophy of Religion*.[1] Relatedly, if Boehme's speculative narrative substitutes for the biblical narrative, it does so unconsciously, whereas the substitution is programmatic in Hegel and Blake and in contemporary theologians such as Altizer. In addition, even if there is less emphasis on divine transcendence in Boehme's discourse than in mainline Lutheranism, the level of transcendence is higher than that found in Hegel or Blake. It is indicated in and by the continued currency of the language of negative theology and the insistence on the objective reality of the Holy Spirit that inspires.

Yet a recognition of Boehme's greater embeddedness in mainline Christian discourse ought not to be a mere piety; it should do some interpretive work. In particular, it is not sufficient to point out that in Boehme's nondistinctive swerves from the common tradition there are also overlaps with it, especially in the area of theological anthropology, where Boehme is engaged in a massive repetition of the mystical tradition. Nor is it sufficient to recall, after Coleridge,[2] the relative orthodoxy of Boehme's first text, *Aurora*, or point to Boehme's apocalyptic discourse as a disturbing, but not necessarily disreputable, Christian discursive option within and without the Protestant field. It is not evident, for instance, that those features of the mystical theology tradition actually recalled in Boehme's discourse function in a pivotal way, and thus constitute a serious obstacle to unrestricted metalepsis. Pointing to the manifest orthodox features of *Aurora* will not do on hermeneutic grounds. As his earliest, and by his own admission poorest text—a text that he says was written in a childlike and magical spirit[3]—*Aurora* cannot function as the interpretive key to his work. Finally, conceding a significant presence of apocalyptic in Boehme's discourse—this was conceded in Part I—does not Christianly domesticate Boehme's discourse in a decisive way. It has yet to be considered whether apocalyptic functions, as it usually does within the pre-Reformation and Reformation traditions, as a dramatic intensifier of the biblical narrative or as its subversive substitute. I will argue in Part III that the apocalyptic elements in Boehme's discourse do not align him with the apocalyptic tradition, but as controlled by another narrative form, they suggest the presence of a nonapocalyptic form of apocalypse, or more specifically, a Valentinian form of apocalypse.

Required, then, to mark Boehme's difference from his more radical post-Enlightenment successors are notes of orthodoxy present at some of the more important sites of the Boehmian narrative. Only such notes would constitute real resistance to metaleptic tendency, bringing it up short, as it were, so that one could affirm real development from Boehme to Romanticism and Idealism. I would like to suggest that a set of five such notes can be found in Boehme's texts, which relate variously to the depiction of the Unground, the creation of Temporal Nature, the fall of angels and human beings, the God of Wrath (*Zorngott*)-God of Mercy (*Barmhertziggott*) relation-distinction, and the status of knowledge. In what follows I will examine each of these traditional notes with respect to how they contribute to stem the metaleptic tide.

This examination fulfils the most important task of the present chapter, which is to show that Boehme is more traditional than some of his successors. A second task complements and supplements the primary task. Here the focus is on the power of resistance inhering in the set of orthodox notes, understood individually and together. This task is important from a genealogical point of view. For were it decided that resistance is not only real but truly strong, then Baur, Staudenmaier, and their genealogical successors would not simply be deficient with respect to the clarity and comprehensiveness of their reading of development from Boehme on; they would be fundamentally wrong. The discontinuity between Boehme and Romanticism and Hegel would be of such a kind so as to jeopardize Boehme's pivotal role in a genealogy of Gnostic discourses. If, on the other hand, the judgment is brought in that in Boehme's discourse the set of features, which constitute the orthodox reserve, function weakly, then Boehme's difference from his Romantic and Idealist successors would be guaranteed, while his place in the genealogical chain of modern ontotheological narrative discourses would be assured. As will shortly become clear, I support the second of the two options.

The set of five resisting features can be envisaged as constituted by a center of two, around which the other three orbit. On most accounts, Boehme's depiction of Temporal Nature and his understanding of the fall of Lucifer and Adam represent the two main areas of traditional theological or narrative repetition.[4] The manifestation of Temporal Nature seems to occur under a different regime than the manifestation of Eternal Nature, since, overtly at least, the latter is integral in divine definition in a way the former is not. In contrast to Hegel, in Boehme the becoming of the divine seems to have been completed on the nontemporal level, and thus divine personal identity to have been established prior to divine manifestation in Temporal Nature. In principle, then, Temporal Nature is not the means of divine becoming, but rather the illustration of the divine as the unsurpassable realization of being, mind, value, and existence. Neither the self-referentiality of divine will, nor the eros that structures the entire movement from ungrounded will to the paradisiacal body of God, nor, finally, the ironic operation of kenosis, apply here. Temporal nature seems to indicate a divine will for the other as other, a genuinely agapaic view of divine love, and a real, as opposed to an ironic, emptying of a subject who is superdeterminate rather than indeterminate. The challenges posed by the vision of Temporal Nature to a judgment of unrestricted metalepsis with respect to his discourse are clear. Recalling in a relatively unaltered form a theologoumenon of the pre-Reformation and Reformation theological traditions removes an important element of the biblical narrative from theogonic cooption. By doing so, it deals a blow to an unqualified metaleptic reading of Boehme's discourse.

The importance of the above act of resistance has been recognized even by a commentator like Walsh, who argues for the closest possible connection between Boehme and Hegel. At the same time, Boehme's insistence that the fall of the angels and human beings is attributable not to the divine but to creaturely will and the wrong exercise of imagination has encouraged more than a few commentators to retreat from the construct of an absolutely heterodox Boehme.[5] The latter is prevented by the ascription of agency to beings other than God, whose choices inaugurate a drama between Lucifer and the Son, and Satan and Adam. Although there are mythic notes to Boehme's depiction of the perturbation or excitation of the chaotic forces of Eternal Nature that occur when the creaturely self (whether angel or human) decides for self instead of God, the traditional credentials of Boehme are relatively impeccable. Choosing inadvisedly involves what Augustine called *amor sui*, and what the medieval mystical tradition, to which the early Luther and Boehme are both indebted, called *Eigenwille*. This kind of decision is judged against the backdrop of the prescriptive contrary—the eccentric movement of the will toward the divine as mystery, or, more determinately, toward the divine as merciful and loving in whom wholeness, peace, and joy, as essential forms of doxological existence, are realized. Boehme's position once again is redolent of Augustine, this time Augustine's *amor Dei*, as mediated by Luther, and filtered through the medieval mystical tradition's emphasis on *Gelassenheit*.

As Boehme sees it, the myths of fall are, among other things, myths of the constitutive power of the imagination. Imagination, as eidetically informed will, brings about 'magically' what is desired, form or formlessness, definition or chaos. Imagination constructs or deconstructs the self, makes the self possible or impossible. Obviously, Lucifer's and Adam's acts of imagination are acts of deconstruction. Yet even these are read against the backdrop of the divine imagination that integrates the unruly chaotic powers of will. Schelling's *Essay on Human Freedom* provides a gloss for the way in which infinite and finite freedom and imagination are related in Boehme. In divine imagination the negative is always already integrated into the positive. In Lucifer and Adam, however, the bond is not indissoluble in the way it is in the divine.[6] Finite being exists under the shadow of the possibility of nonintegration and the setting free of the demonic.

Free will, however, not only operates archeologically, but in the case of human being, at least, postlapsarianly. Conversion is a possibility. If grace is a necessity, human agency, at the very least, must cooperate. Boehme is here clearly on the side of the Spiritual Reformers rather than Luther and Lutheran orthodoxy. Structurally, human existence is a being in time demanding a decision between darkness and light, Lucifer and Christ. Phenomenologically, however, human existence and history is threefold insofar as individuals conform themselves to the First or Second Principle, but also to the principle of this world. As *Mysterium Magnum* presents it, the structural pattern is biblically captured in Cain and Abel; the phenomenological pattern is captured in the triad of Shem, Japhet, and Ham. Boehme at once recalls Luther's dramatic figuration of existence (structural and eschatological), while indicating a humanist patience with venality not typical of the Reformer.

One can be a bit more perfunctory about the other three features, which, if nontrivial, do appear to be somewhat secondary. On one level at least, the Unground, as radical divine mystery, appears to represent the divine in its absolute transcendence. Though not as religiously relevant as the God of manifestation,[7] referring to the Unground by means of a vocabulary of "One," "All," and "Nothing," suggests a certain ontological preeminence, since typically in negative theology, (which provides the context of attribution) the terms are unequivocally terms of the highest praise. Moreover, as the "Beyond," the Unground does not appear to be involved in the process of self-constitution that is on its way with Wisdom and the 'Immanent Trinity' and that reaches a new and defining level in the First and Second Principles. Otherwise put, Boehme encourages the view that the Unground is outside the divine dynamic of divine will for self, divine eros, the ironic operation of kenosis, and also, it is not subject to narrative operations like *prolepsis* and *analepsis*, which aid and abet narrative self-constitution. In suggesting in some texts at least—and perhaps more than suggesting in a few—that the Unground remains outside the process of divine self-differentiation, dynamic development, and agonistic self-constitution, Boehme sets limits to an exclusively theogonic or narrativity reading of the divine. By doing so, he obviously restricts metalepsis in a way not found, as I will argue, in later volumes, within the radically iconic regime of Blake and the radically antiapophatic regime of Hegel.[8]

The final two features in Boehme's work, which set bounds to metalepsis, are the reluctance witnessed there to identify Luther's *Zorngott* with the First Principle, on the one hand, and the various strategies he follows to relativize the claim made on behalf of knowledge, on the other. I will say a brief word about each of these in turn.

Boehme, certainly, shows some concern to uncouple the wrath of the Father from the First Principle, the principle of darkness, chaos, and death. Boehme attempts to effect this uncoupling on the symbolic plane by identifying God the Father with fire, which, if it emerges from the friction of Eternal Nature, nevertheless gives it life, and at the same time serves as the energic base of the light and gentleness of the Son. As we shall see in a later volume on Romanticism, Blake is responsive to the uncoupling of the Father from the forces of contraction, chaos, and death, and the corresponding nearing of the Father and Son in a complex apocalyptic figure combining wrath and gentleness.[9]

The second of the two features—that is, Boehme's tendency to relativize claims made on behalf of knowledge—is arguably, more important. Certainly, here Boehme shows greater consistency and less tendency to backslide. The strategies pursued by Boehme in limiting the claims for knowledge are multiple. They range from assertion of the Christianly trivial truth that faith and love are soteriologically more pertinent than book knowledge and notional assent to *credenda*, to celebration of finite existence as doxological. And between these lower and upper limits one finds Boehme's elaboration of the positive nature of spiritual baptism in which one dies in and with Christ (*WC*, pp. 38–41) and the necessity of good works as indicators of rebirth (*WC*, pp. 78, 133). There is a definite tendency in Boehme that avoids, and even rejects, claiming that vision is paradigmatic for finite existence, human existence in particular (*MM* 51, 39–44). Vision, he admits, is a prophetic mark. Yet the medium is not to be confused with the message. Although extraordinary, vision is not normative. Again, here there seems to be some limiting or bounding of metalepsis and of the narrativity and theogony that are consolidated, if not legitimated, by vision regarded as a normative form of knowing.

These two groups of features, summing to five, function to bound metalepsis. Thus they establish a difference between Boehme and later metaleptic outbreaks in Romanticism and Idealism. In speaking in this way, I am aware that I appear to put at risk precisely what I most mean to assert—that is the radicality of Boehme's departure from the mainline Christian traditions, and his privileged place in the remythologization process that links post-Reformation and post-Enlightenment thought. Toward validating the difference between Boehme and his successors, while protecting his pivotal role in the process of remythologization, I now raise the question of the precise strength of resistance to metalepsis of these five features. Given my prior differentiation into two groups of features of *orthodox reserve*, it is antecedently likely that resistance will be stronger in the first than in the second.

I begin, however, with the second group to find out whether my hypothesis is correct. If each of the three members of the second group of features effect some measure of restriction to metalepsis, it is equally evident that their power of resistance is itself limited. In the case of the Unground, the transcendence that is posited is relativized in two different ways. One of these involves a shift in evaluation of the Unground, the other a shift in perception concerning its independence. A shift in the order of evaluation of the Unground as transcendent occurs when, having gestured to the Unground by means of the battery of negative theology, whose rhetorical function is to indicate preeminence, Boehme effectively withdraws the deposit of credits. One witnesses the transformation of a hyperbolic modality of negative theology ascription into a

privative mirror-image. The most general form this takes in Boehme is the
evoking of the *super*essential Godhead of Eckhart and the Dionysian tradition,
while interpreting superessential as *in*essential. The more specific forms of this
transformation have been commented on at length in chapter 2. They involve
Boehme's denial that the Unground is the supreme realization of being, knowing, goodness, and existence. The second shift involves a critical assessment of
the identity of the Unground itself and particularly, its putative standing outside the process of divine self-constitution. Here the distinction between a will-
less, unerotic, and nonkenotic Unground and a divine moved and constituted
by these forces is undermined by thinking of the "crisis" or "breakthrough" of
the will to manifestation as always already having occurred. The Unground,
therefore, and the will to manifestation are not ultimately different moments:
the Unground identifies itself as the "ungrounded will to manifestation."

The measure of metaleptic resistance provided by the other two members
of the subsidiary group is similarly nonsterling. With all due respect to
Boehme's interest in uncoupling Luther's *Zorngott-Barmhertziggott* pair from
the two principles, as Bornkamm rightly sees,[10] the pressure toward their identification, with the concomitant ontologization and narratization of Luther's
existential couple, is almost irresistible. Moreover, Boehme's favorite strategy
of identifying God the Father with fire as transition satisfies the Christian
need of not making the divine evil, but only at the risk of incoherence. The Father is now both consequent and ground of the First Principle. And Boehme's
other associations of the Son with the Second Principle and the Spirit with
the Third puts some pressure on Boehme's uncoupling maneuver, for it is difficult, given these two other identifications, to deny it in the case of the Father
and the First Principle.

Again, while Boehme's caveats with respect to knowledge are real, there
is a strong sense in which faith, which involves "rebirth," is inchoately vision.
This is certainly a trend in the Spiritual Reformers, and the medieval mystical
tradition repeated there. In Boehme's discourse this trend is not only repeated,
but is augmented by pansophistic ambition. Faith, then, is never really average.
Open to, and being opened by, Spirit, it is already *Verstand* or transconceptual
knowledge. At an express level denied as a norm, at another level vision and
knowledge take on something of the character of norm that prevents the principled equality of salvation opportunity between unreflective and reflective
pneumatological orientation having the kind of critical leverage it might otherwise have. One of the ways in which Romanticism and Idealism could be said
to develop Boehme is by making explicit this implicit visionary norm, one of
whose most salient effects is the dismantling of the distinction between the
preeschatological and eschatological states.

Having considered the second, I now turn to the first group of the two
groups of features, with the understanding that their level of resistance to total

metalepsis is higher than the second. The question can be asked even here, however, whether the level of resistance is of that kind that it exposes the appropriations of Boehme by Hegel and Schelling as not simply facile, but illegitimate, or, on the contrary, whether the level is such that it not only makes Hegelian and Schellingian appropriations intelligible, but to a certain extent justified.

That Temporal Nature reinscribes *agape* into the manifestation of the divine is not to be denied, and this reinscription forever separates Boehme from Hegel. Yet even here resistance to metalepsis is subject to undertows. The imperialism of theogonic construal asserts itself in the granting of "principle" status to Temporal Nature, since "principle" suggests a modality of the divine life. Nor is the antitheogony cause helped when Temporal Nature is associated with the Spirit. The latter identification makes Boehme susceptible to two different kinds of charges. The first, found in Boehme's Lutheran orthodox critics, maintains that Boehme has temporalized the Holy Spirit, thereby evacuating it of the kind of personal existence that goes hand in hand with its eternity. The second criticism is the converse of the first. Associating Temporal Nature with the Holy Spirit essentially involves the apotheosis of the finite.[11] In either case, however, the distance between time and eternity is lessened, and the gap between eros and *agape* narrowed. The resistance to theogony is still real, and the distinction between time and eternity still intact. Boehme is not yet Hegel. But as Walsh observes, there is not enough distinction in Boehme's discourse between the eternal and the temporal, not enough distinction between the divine and nondivine to resist a Hegelian and non-Hegelian appropriation in the post-Enlightenment period.[12]

The other main hinge of resistance to metalepsis—that is, the Lucifernian and Adamic falls that excite the chaos at the basis of all form—is effective only up to a point. Certainly, falls on both the angelic and human planes of existence presuppose freedom, and eloquently declare that the origin of evil is in the finite rather than the infinite. In a sense, therefore, these falls and resulting (per)turbations suggest that Boehme not unequivocally supports a theogonic view of evil, which Ricoeur, for instance, maintains is intrinsically opposed to the mainline construal of finite origin that explicates the biblical view based predominantly, but not exclusively, on Genesis 3.[13]

Nevertheless, many of the features of the theogonic view are there: form rises from chaos, consciousness from unconsciousness, freedom from necessity, and in general the positive from the negative. Moreover, the dramatic pattern of specifically divine experience provides the template for both Lucifer and Adam, thus restraining the difference in agency. There is a tendency in Boehme's discourse to enfold the agency of Lucifer and Adam into the negative agency of Eternal Nature. Or conversely, there is a tendency in Boehme's, discourse to depict the agency of Eternal Nature unfolding itself in the evil imaginations of Lucifer and Adam. Of course, there are different results in the order of agency, and the different results matter. In the divine, considered as complete narrative movement, the chaos of the First Principle remains implicit, or rather, past and overcome. In the case of Lucifer and Adam, there is an actual outbreak of chaos, and it is the reality of this outbreak that Boehme takes to define evil in the full and proper sense. Chaos is the possibility of evil, and the divine is the narrative movement that depotentiates this possibility. Boehme, therefore, definitely stops short of the kind of fully-fledged theogonic account of the origin and end of evil that will be subscribed to by Hegel.[14] And to the extent to which Boehme stops short, there is genuine resistance to comprehensive metalepsis. At the same time, however, theogony exercises a massive undertow throughout all episodes of the six-stage narrative.

Another way of getting at Boehme's proximity—and his distance—to a theogonic view is to deploy the Hegelian categories of "drama" and "epic" in the way von Balthasar deploys them in the second part of his great trilogy.[15] On von Balthasar's account, which has Gnosticism and Hegel particularly in its sight, epic accounts of reality tend to construe the divine as an inclusive process of development that requires a real chaos, angst, and evil as necessary presuppositions.[16] By contrast, the standard Christian narrative account is dramatic, where drama requires both the irreducibility of infinite and finite freedom, and also, the clear sense that the site of the outbreak of evil is finite freedom (which outbreak, nevertheless, is such as to provoke divine judgment, but even more, divine love). Without absolutely declaring it, Balthasar suggests that 'aesthetic' thinkers of the Boehmian sort offer epical narrative renditions of reality. Certainly, even given dramatic notes, one can only be skeptical about their strength to resist the epical tide.

On the account I have offered here, the dramatic notes are basically recessive, and everywhere are limited by the theogonic undertow of Boehme's discourse. This is true even in the case of the two features that put up the most resistance to the powerful metaleptic current of Boehme's narrative that gropes toward the kind of theodicy that will mark Hegelian and Schellingian philosophy, and especially the former—that is, a theodicy that offers a self-authenticating account of divine self-constitution. If Boehme's discourse is not purely or fully metaleptic, it is sufficiently so for this discourse to function as "origin" for post-Enlightenment discourses that are metaleptic without remainder.

Concluding Remarks

Given the case that I am prosecuting, unsurprisingly, the central focus of Part II has been on Boehme's narrative ontotheology as it moves toward a complete disfiguration-refiguration of the biblical narrative. Thus the hub of Part II is my account of the metaleptic disposition of Boehme's discourse and the distinctive hermeneutical and substantive theological swerves from standard pre-Reformation and Reformation traditions that it both articulates and undergirds.

As I have said on a number of occasions already, identifying the operation of metalepsis is a necessary step in bringing in a Gnostic or Valentinian verdict with respect to Boehme's discourse. Here I understand myself to be in line with Irenaeus as he points (in the opening books of *Against Heresies)* to the narrative operation of *metharmottein* that expresses itself in Gnostic, and specifically Valentinian alteration of theologoumena, which correspond to distinct episodes of the communally adopted and adapted biblical narrative (Books 2-5). These theologoumena include the view of a perfect trinitarian divine immune to fall, a view of creation that reflects the absolute sovereignty and goodness of God, a view of fall that places the onus on finite creatures, a view of Christ focused on the redemption that he achieves on our behalf, and an eschatology that supposes an embodied form of redeemed life that is not yet ours and is God's to give. I have discussed the Irenaean aspect of my interpretive program in considerable detail in *Gnostic Return in Modernity* (chapter 4.1). I will return to it in Part III.

Chapters 3 and 5 frame chapter 4. Chapter 3 shows how many of Boehme's hermeneutic and substantive theological departures from the mainline pre-Reformation and Reformation traditions repeat departures found in minority pre-Reformation and post-Reformation traditions. Getting a sense of this repetition is important both historically and systematically. It is important historically in that it helps to reinforce the point that Boehme's discourse presupposes the tradition of negative theology, and more particularly, the radical speculative form it takes in Meister Eckhart. It is important historically also in that it helps to underscore the dependence of Boehme's discourse on post-Reformation contestations of Luther's theology and that of emerging Lutheran orthodoxy. At the same time, a description of what Boehme's discourse shares with the negative theology tradition and the post-Reformation traditions that offered alternatives to Luther's thought is important systematically, since it establishes baselines from which and by which we can measure those hermeneutical and substantive theological contestations of the tradition that are original. Finally, I submit that a description of this repetition is important genealogically—if only indirectly. For it is by distinguishing the nondistinctive Boehmian swerves (from the standard pre-Reformation and Reformation traditions) from the distinctive Boehmian swerves that the interpreter becomes clear as to what kind of departure from the theological tradition is required to bring in a Gnostic or Valentinian verdict. On the basis of the presentation I offered in chapter 3, by contrast with Boehme's discourse, neither Eckhartian negative theology nor the Spiritual Reformers depart from the tradition at a level requisite to label either as Gnostic or Valentinian.

Given the general thrust of my interpretation, it is clear that I do not seriously entertain an orthodox reading of Boehme's discourse. Still, an orthodox reading cannot be dismissed out of hand. Chapter 5, then, offered something like a best-case scenario for the orthodox interpretation as it sketches the positive connections between Boehme's discourse and the discourses of the standard pre-Reformation and Reformation traditions. Two interests are served by such an account. If fairness in interpretation is one, the other is genealogical pertinence. A Gnostic or Valentinian genealogy, I judge, is only apparently well served by repressing the orthodox or traditional elements in Boehme's discourse. For repressing such elements encourages the view that no differences exist between Boehme's post-Reformation visionary discourse and the speculative discourses of the post-Enlightenment period. But this would essentially mean that no development exists. Such an ahistorical view cannot be justified either on exegetical or theoretical grounds.

It makes sense to presume that a basic difference exists between Boehme's post-Reformation discourse and the speculative discourses of the post-Enlightenment period. The former show more hesitation in departing from the theological traditions and illustrate more clearly orthodox reserves. I discuss five features that signal some resistance to the powerful metaleptic tendency in Boehme's discourse. I argue, however, that while the resistance is real in all cases, its level is not particularly high. I conclude that Boehme's discourse points the way toward complete metalepsis that is accomplished only in the post-Enlightenment period.

PART III

~

Valentinianism and Valentinian Enlisting of Non-Valentinian Narrative Discourses

In Part I I presented Boehme's metanarrative, and traced it against the back-drop of alchemy and negative theology. In Part II I showed how its extensive and intensive swerve from the pre-Reformation and Reformation theological tradition is ultimately focused in a metalepsis of the biblical narrative or first-order interpretation of the kind found, for example, in Irenaeus, Augustine, Aquinas, and Luther. I am now in a position to raise the question of whether Boehme's discourse represents a return of Valentinian Gnosticism, and thus a possible first link in a chain of narrative ontotheological discourses in the modern period that show signs of Valentinian haunting. This question of the return of Valentinianism in Boehme, and thus Valentinian ascription of his discourse will occupy me throughout Part III.

As I argued in *Gnostic Return in Modernity*, however, this question can be posed only on the basis of a grammatical understanding of Valentinian narrative. Forged in conversation with contemporary theological and philosophical readings of tradition as well as analytic studies of Valentinian texts and their relations, as used here *Valentinian narrative grammar* implies five things. (1) It refers to distinctive rules of formation for a six-stage plot that tracks the fall of the divine from perfection and its recovery. These rules can be extrapolated from classical Valentinian texts, and can account for the variety as well as the unity of these texts or discourses. (2) This six-stage plot, which is an object of vision and has soteriological capacity, represents both a shift of authority from Scripture to interpretation and a thoroughgoing metalepsis of biblical narrative. (3) This six-stage plot can be contracted into a synoptic triadic form. (4) Neither this six-stage plot, nor its synoptic triadic form, is exhausted by classical Valentinian discourses, as these are rendered in the writings of Nag Hammadi and the presentations of the heresiologists, especially the presentation of Irenaeus. More positively stated, a new strain of Valentinianism (and thus a new chain of Valentinian narrative forms) is a logical possibility even after a hiatus of over a millenium. (5) In this context, "Jacob Boehme" names a metaleptic discourse (with the caveats presented in Part II) that suggests itself as a point of departure for a chain of ontotheological discourses in essential continuity with the Valentinian narratives of the Hellenistic period.

Now the possibility, even necessity, of discontinuity in Valentinian narrative formations between the ancient and modern periods is registered in the construct correlative to—although not necessarily coordinate with—"Valentinian narrative grammar"—that is, *rule-governed deformation of classical Valentinian genres*. I generated this construct in *Gnostic Return in Modernity* in conversation with Ricoeur's reflection on the continuity and discontinuity of narrative form in the literary tradition. It implies the following: (1) Should we discover modern narrative ontotheologies of a metaleptic kind that obey Valentinian rules of formation, we should expect that these modern narratives deviate in important ways from genres of the classical Valentinian tradition. The obvious reason is that history matters. These discourses are separated by over a millennium and have quite different ideational contexts. (2) Major differences between the modern—that is, post-Reformation and post-Enlightenment—genres of Valentinianism and classical genres such as *Ptolemy's Sytem* (*PSY*), *The Gospel of Truth* (*Gospel*), and *The Tripartite Tractate* (*Tractate*) would include (a) the more theogonic and agonistic complexion of the narrative that results from a more *teleological view* of the six-stage drama of the fall from and of divine perfection and its recovery and (b) a more *positive view* of creation and history as the exegesis of a tragedy that from a higher order point of view can be seen as divine comedy. (3) The characteristics that distinguish the modern genres of Valentinianism from its classical genres would not be unanticipated in the classical forms, but would be present in a recessed and undeveloped form.

In *Gnostic Return in Modernity*, finding a construct that would accent discontinuity as well as continuity between ancient and modern genres of Valentinianism turned out to be a conceptual need in light of the serious downplaying of discontinuity in the two nineteenth-century genealogists who braved a Gnostic return hypothesis with narrative structure as the fundamental criterion. They thought of Boehme's discourse as the origin of a Gnostic form of thought that received its apogee in the Hegelian system. I am speaking, of course, of Baur and Staudenmaier. I argued in that programmatic text that the suggestion in both of a kind of Gnostic narrative invariant in the Hellenistic period and between the Hellenistic and the modern period has to be rejected on hermeneutic and methodological grounds. In addition, I rejected a univocal theogonic characterization of Valentinian narrative in general. Classical Valentinian genres such as *PSY*, the *Gospel*, and even the *Tractate* are not explicitly theogonic in the way that Boehme's and Hegel's narrative are. I should note, however, my observation in the same text that there were recessed teleological features in the classical Valentinian genres—particularly evident in the *Trac-*

tate—that suggested a developmental revision of a narrative whose surface seems to support a model of pure circularity. I drew the conclusion in that text that a theogonic Valentinian narrative was a logical possibility, or as I preferred to put it, a possibility of Valentinian narrative grammar.

Concretely, I wish to argue here that as Boehme's six-stage metaleptic narrative is a splendid example of Valentinian narrative grammar, it is an equally splendid, indeed originary, example of rule-governed deformation of classical Valentinian genres by ontotheological narrative discourses in the modern period. I will bring Boehme's discourse into conversation with all three classical Valentinian genres, with a particular focus, however, on the six-stage narratives of *PSY* and the *Tractate*. If from the point of view of access and level of lexical recall the conversation with *PSY* enjoys a certain privilege, from the point of view of narrative overlap the conversation with the *Tractate* is more fruitful. This is so, since it is in this classical Valentinian genre that the latent teleological drift of classical Valentinian genres most clearly can be seen.

In arguing for a kind of continuity respectful of discontinuity, I begin by adducing positive correlations between Boehme's narrative ontotheology and the classical Valentinian genres. These connections, it turns out, are thoroughly nontrivial at both the level of individual narrative episodes (such as the configuration of the divine realm, the fall of the divine, creation, the appearance of Christ as savior figure, and eschatology) and narrative structure as a whole, which, if it has a six-stage form, has a triadic rhythm. Unless theogonic disposition, however, is at least a trace element in classical Valentinian genres, then Boehme's narrative represents a *metabasis eis allos genos*. Granting the demonstration of such a trace element, however, one can speak of Boehme's teleological narrative being an instance of a Valentinian narrative grammar that covers both ancient and modern fields. Hence, one would be talking about a form of continuity between classical and modern forms of Valentinian narrative that takes account of teleological exacerbation of Valentinian narrative in the modern forms, in which (1) perfection is attributed to the divine at the end rather than at the beginning, (2) fall from perfection is a necessary feature of a divine that is what it is only in its recovery from fall, and (3) suffering of the fallen form of the divine is ingredient in the development of a fully realized form of divine perfection.

Looked at from the point of view of the correlative interpretive construct of rule-governed deformation of classical Valentinian genres, Boehme's ontotheological narrative would be a splendid example of such deformation, establishing a precedent for later encompassing narrative discourses in the Romantic and Idealist fields and beyond. Of course, in speaking of Valentinian narrative grammar it is assumed that it is a metaleptic grammar with specific reference to biblical narrative grammar. This was an important result of my investigation in *Gnostic Return in Modernity* (4.1) in which I gave Irenaeus credit for being less a proponent of a particular rendition of the biblical narrative, which is taken to be absolute, than a proponent of a specifically Christian narrative grammar. If one adds Irenaeus's insight into the metaleptic nature of Valentinianism that is captured in his figure of *methormottein* or *transfiguro*,[1] it is possible to think of Irenaeus as suggesting the argument that Gnosticism in general—Valentinianism in particular—represents a metaleptic grammar. In any event, I believe that the lens in and through which I read Boehme's discourse, and other poetic, philosophical, and theological discourses that hark back to Boehme as a point of origin, have been shaped by Irenaeus's original analysis of Valentinianism as he responded to what he regarded as a haunting of biblically informed Christian discourse by its other.

The argument that Boehme's narrative discourse can be read as an instance of Valentinian narrative grammar, which is the task of chapter 6 is not, of course, the same as testing its validity claims. Such testing belongs to a different explanatory level. Testing its validity claims requires demonstrating the explanatory superiority of the 'Valentinian' hypothesis against taxonomic rivals such as 'apocalyptic,' 'Neoplatonism,' and 'Kabbalah,' all of which have had their advocates. This demonstration, prosecuted in chapters 7–9, obviously involves showing that Valentinianism does a better job accounting for what is distinctive in Boehme's visionary metaleptic narrative. Given, however, that Boehme's narrative discourse does in fact clearly show the presence of all three narrative discourses, a viable 'Valentinian' hypothesis has to take account of their presence, and in a sense, give an account of their presence. There are weaker and stronger forms of taking and giving account. Paying considerable attention to the discursive complexity of Boehme's texts, the weaker form of the 'Valentinian' hypothesis suggests that Valentinianism is a presence that is first among equals, accounting for more elements—or more important elements—of Boehme's narrative discourse than its taxonomic rivals. In principle, and not simply in fact, therefore, 'apocalyptic,' 'Neoplatonism,' and 'Kabbalah' complement or supplement a 'Valentinian' taxonomy. By contrast, the stronger form of the 'Valentinian' hypothesis suggests that Valentinianism can account for all elements of Boehme's narrative discourse, even those elements that bear the stamp of apocalyptic, Neoplatonism, and Kabbalah. It is the stronger form of the 'Valentinian' hypothesis that I will support throughout Part III.

From an explanatory point of view 'apocalyptic,' 'Neoplatonism,' and 'Kabbalah' can be regarded as complementing or supplementing the Valentinian taxon in fact rather than in principle. By the locution 'supplementation in fact' I mean to suggest that it is possible for us to invoke one of these three rival taxonomic discourses for particular purposes of explanation. We might want to draw attention, as de Lubac does, for example, to the apocalyptic element in Boehme's discourse to mark an important point in the trajectory of apocalyptic in discourses at the dawn of the modern period. Since apocalyptic is an important strand in Boehme's discourse, there would be nothing fundamentally wrong with this attribution of apocalyptic, as long as we are aware that apocalyptic would not necessarily define Boehme's discourse as such. Similar reasons for emphasizing either the Neoplatonic or Kabbalistic narrative strands may apply. Indeed, elsewhere I have spoken of Boehme's role in the Kabbalistic trajectory in German thought.[2] And again, this is not misleading as long as no claim is being made that 'Kabbalah' essentially designates Boehme's narrative discourse.

A sustainable view of Boehme's discourse being an instance of Valentinian narrative grammar allows, therefore, only that form of *taxonomic supplementarity* that does not compromise the ability of Valentinianism to be completely explanatory of Boehme's discourse. As I showed in *Gnostic Return in Modernity* (chapter 4) the example of classical Valentinian genres prepare us to see how different discourses can become embedded in Valentinian discourse without making it anything other than Valentinian. Apocalyptic and Neoplatonism are two of the discourses that become embedded. Extrapolating such power of assimilation, or what I refer to as *enlisting* to Valentinian narrative grammar as a whole, it is not going too far to imagine that other narrative discourses also can be enlisted in addition to these two. In a sense, showing remarkable consistency between the modern and the ancient genres, I want to claim that with Boehme's post-Reformation discourse, a third narrative discourse is added to the two narrative discourses already shown to be Valentinianly enlistable—that is, apocalyptic and Neoplatonism. This third discourse is the discourse of the Kabbalah, which brings into focus in a way the other two narrative discourses do not, the relationship between speculative forms of Christianity of the Boehmian type and Judaism.

In arguing the case for *Valentinian enlisting of non-Valentinian narrative discourses* from chapters 7 through 9, I will make specific proposals concerning the enlisting (or inscription) of apocalyptic in a nonapocalyptic form of revelatory discourse (chapter 7), concerning the enlisting of a Neoplatonic discourse for narrative ends that it does not serve throughout its long tradition (chapter 8), and finally, concerning the enlisting of the Kabbalah for a metaleptic function it does not have in its original Jewish setting. By *enlisting* I mean that apocalyptic, Neoplatonism, and Kabbalah are all regulated by the basic Valentinianism of Boehme's narrative discourse and serve an erotic, kenotic, and agonistic version of a six-stage Valentinian narrative. As so regulated, each of these narrative discourses, I will argue, serves narrative ends that they do not serve in their primary contexts.

It would be wrong not to point out, however, that in being enlisted, each of these narrative discourses exercises some reflexive effect upon the enlisting discourse. I will detail this effect in all three cases throughout chapters 7–9. I speak to visionary, hermeneutic, but above all narrative modifications effected by the enlisted discourse. This reflexive effect, however, I take to have a much lower degree of power than the power demonstrated in Valentinian enlisting. It is important to acknowledge his reflexive effect both from the point of view of intellectual honesty and explanation. From an explanatory point of view taking account of this reflexive effect enables the interpreter to come to a better understanding of how Boehme's narrative discourse looks so different from the classical genres of Valentinianism, and helps to supplement the historical considerations as to why Boehme's narrative has the erotic, kenotic, and agonistic complexion that it has, and why it valorizes the cosmos, time, and history in the way it does.

Neither in my reflections on Valentinian enlisting in chapters 7–9, nor in my general argument concerning the probity of a Valentinian ascription of Boehme's metaleptic narrative discourse in chapter 6, do I drop the trinitarian concern of Parts I and II. In chapter 6 I draw attention to the overlaps between Boehme's articulation of the intradivine Trinity and the lean articulation of the realm of divine perfection that characterizes both the *Tractate* and the *Gospel*. I also observe the way in which Boehme's triadic synopsis of the six-stage narrative of the divine recalls at least the triadic rhythm of the *Gospel*. In chapter 7 I show that Boehme's articulation of the intradivine Trinity and the trinitarian matrix as a whole differs considerably from that of the intradivine Trinity and its economic relations as articulated in and by Joachim's second-order form of apocalyptic. While Boehme's discourse includes more than a trace of Joachim's trinitarianism, its own trinitarian scheme surpasses it, swerves from the Nicene tradition in a way that Joachim's discourse does not, and totally dismantles the immanent Trinity-economic Trinity distinction that Joachim presupposes. Similarly, I show how Boehme's complex trinitarianism engages both more and less standard versions articulated by Neoplatonism, while availing itself of the latter in particular, to show the way to a fully theogonic rendering of the Trinity.

Throughout these chapters, while I pursue the question of whether Boehme's discourse represents a form of Valentinianism on the threshold of the modern period, I do not hide my genealogical interest. I am particularly explicit on this matter in chapter 6. Nevertheless, it is not made thematic. The basic reason is that unless one can demonstrate that Boehme's supposed originary discourse is a form of Valentinianism, it is simply idle to talk about lines of Gnostic or Valentinian discourse in modernity. Taxonomy, therefore, takes priority over genealogy, even if genealogical considerations provide the basic motivation for taxonomic analysis. My conclusion will focus on genealogical consequences that follow a demonstration of the Valentinianism of Boehme's discourse for which no genealogist of Gnosticism has, up until now, provided even a relatively plausible case.

CHAPTER 6

∾

Boehme's Discourse and Valentinian Narrative Grammar

Although the inspiration behind the present project is genealogical, and genealogists such as Baur have shown the way with respect to the possibility of a Gnostic reading of Boehme's narrative discourse, in the order of demonstration, a Gnostic genealogical account of narrative ontotheological discourses, which has Boehme as the proximate point of origin, depends on establishing the prima facie credentials of a Gnostic taxonomy of Boehme's discourse. Baur's own reading of Boehme in *Die christliche Gnosis* shows that interpretive shortcomings with respect to the details of Boehme's narrative system, and lack of clarity with respect to its relation to both mainline and marginal post-Reformation discourse, undermine the taxonomic case. I have tried to obviate these deficiencies in the two previous parts. Yet it would be idle to read Boehme more multidimensionally and yet to fail (1) to bring forward the clarification of Gnostic, carried out in chapter 1, in which Gnostic was given hard edges by being identified with Valentinianism and (2) above all, to fail to take account of the grammatical reformulation of Valentinianism carried out in *Gnostic Return in Modernity*.

In due course I will have much more to say about Valentinian narrative grammar, and the way it allows for significant discontinuities between classical Valentinian narratives and the modern candidates for Valentinian ascription. It is important, however, not to consider the grammatical reformulation of Valentinianism as involving an end run around actually engaging Boehme's narrative ontotheology in conversation with the distinct and distinctive classical Valentinian genres. Without the Valentinian narratives of the Hellenistic period, we would not be able to extrapolate a Valentinian narrative grammar. And a Valentinian narrative grammar that demanded no actual correspondences between putative modern representatives and classical Valentinian texts would be a purely fictive entity.

On the antecedent presumption that there is more than an insignificant amount of overlap between Boehme's narrative and the narratives of classical Valentinian genres, here I begin to test the measure of overlap both with respect to individual narrative episodes and narrative figuration as a whole. Of the three Valentinian genres that came in for sustained attention in *Gnostic Return in Modernity*, *PSY* (as presented by Irenaeus in *Against Heresies* [bk 1 1–8]), and the *Tractate*, the longest text in the Nag Hammadi cache, will bear the burden of comparison with Boehme's ontotheological narrative. Evidence of positive overlap between Boehme's narrative and these two Valentinian narrative genres must necessarily be purely internal to the texts themselves, given that Boehme neither cites Gnostic nor Valentinian sources in his texts, nor mentions them in his letters. Nor again do we possess third-person accounts that Boehme had actually read heresiological accounts of Gnosticism. Needless to say, the only representative of the three classical genres with which he could have been in contact is *PSY*. Although this text becomes generally available through Gottfried Arnold at the end of the seventeenth century,[1] its accessibility at the beginning of the century is unclear.

Nevertheless, it would make sense to start with this text for a number of reasons. First and foremost, it is logically possible that Boehme had some knowledge of the text, if not directly, then indirectly as the heresiological account of Irenaeus was filtered through the Paracelsian or Weigelian traditions. Second, it is with this particular text that there exists the most obvious overlaps of a lexical kind between Boehmian and Valentinian discourse. Commencing with *PSY* as the comparandum, however, does not imply that it enjoys principled advantages over the other two Valentinian genres. Either the *Tractate* or the *Gospel* could prove more illuminating with respect to the erotic, kenotic, and agonistic constitution of Boehme's ontotheological narrative. Of these two Valentinian genres the focus will be on the *Tractate*. For in the *Tractate*, it is possible to see an erotic figuration of narrative (of the fall from divine perfection and its recovery) stirring beneath and struggling against the narrative surface that seems to support the pure repetition of the perfection of origin perforated and degraded by fall.

The repristination of *PSY* by Boehme's discourse can be divided into recall of more general and more specific features of this particular Valentinian narrative genre. On the more general front, Boehme's discourse recalls an encompassing metaleptic narrative, whose end points are the immanifest divine—abyss (*Bythos*) and silence (*Sige*) in *PSY*, the Unground beyond name and definition in Boehme[2]—and the reintegrated and stable divine milieu, in which the divine is the effable (yet perfect) domain of divine expressivity and divine expression. The recall of these end points is the recall of the divine in its aboriginal and eschatological orders of integrity, which supposes the faulting of aboriginal perfection and the emergence of a violent order of otherness that must be overcome.

The recall of *PSY*, however, does not operate solely on this general level. In Boehme's narrative, aspects of each of the six episodes, which I determined in *Gnostic Return in Modernity* (chapter 3) to constitute the narrative of *PSY*, are recalled. Working backwards from the soteriological and eschatological end point (stage six) in which enlightened human being achieves real participation in the sphere of divine perfection, Boehme's threefold distinction between human beings bears an analogy to *PSY*'s differentiation between three different kinds of human being—that is, pneumatic, psychic, and hylic—although the analogy here between discourses is structurally limited by Boehme's assertion of free will rather than nature being the basis of the distinction.[3] As in *PSY*, in Boehme's discourse something less than visionary perfection is required for salvation. In the terms of *Mysterium Magnum* not everyone is Shem, Enoch, or Abraham. At the same time there is still in Boehme's discourse, as in *PSY*, the suggestion that the visionary or pneumatic enjoys at least a relative advantage of quality of participation in divine perfection.

Similarly, there is significant overlap between Boehme's and *PSY*'s figuration of Christ, which constituted the fifth episode of Valentinian narrative (stage five). While Boehme's rendition of the incarnation and Cross is not Docetic in the way *PSY*'s (*Against Heresies* bk 1. 7, 2) is, his depiction of Christ as the perfect androgynous being, who has not undergone the disgrace of sexual differentiation, and his sense that the suffering of Christ is symbolic of a pathos anterior to the emergence of the temporal-material world, bear more than a superficial analogy to what is recounted in the classical Valentinian text where suffering and distress is attributed to *Physis* or Nature as the fallen form of Wisdom.

Correspondences also exist with respect to the figuration of the fall of human being (stage four). While aspects of Boehme's account of the fall of human being, especially in *Mysterium Magnum*, show allegiances to orthodox readings of the biblical narrative, nonetheless, as in *PSY*, the creation and the fall of human being get linked to the extent to which Adamic existence is regarded as being from the beginning a kind of dreamlike state, one aspect of whose fragility is the differentiation of male and female. The correspondence between these discourses separated by a period of approximately fourteen hundred years, continues in a depiction of creation that does nothing to honor the account in Genesis (stage three). While Boehme will not claim, after *PSY*, that the creation of the physical world is the work of an incompetent semi-divine being who has an origin in a fallen aspect of the divine—and who is prone to botching—he does assert, as we saw in chapter 1, a close relation between Lucifer and the chaos of Eternal Nature, on the one hand, and between Lucifer and the emergence of the physical world, on the other.

The core feature of *PSY* recalled in *Mysterium Magnum* and other texts of Boehme, however, is undoubtedly the faulting of the divine milieu of expressivity and expression, and the emergence of an antithetical force (stages one and two). After *PSY*, Boehme's texts not only seem to implicate Sophia in this interruption of divine perfection and divine self-reflection, but also seem to

(1) connect Sophia antithetically with Nature, (2) establish an intrinsic connection between Nature and desire (*Against Heresies* bk 1. 2, 2–4), and (3) link the movement from Nature back to Sophia to a staurological reading of the Cross, specifically to the Cross marking off the realm of deficiency from that of perfection (*Against Heresies* bk 1. 4, 1) and determining once and for all the finite nature of even divine knowledge of the divine.

Each of these three aspects of the debacle of ontotheological fall merits further comment. The first, the sophiological identity of the agent of debacle, admits of fairly quick dispatch. Even though Boehme indicates that he is distributing responsibility of the fall over the entire Quaternity, imagining the fallen divine as feminine (moreover, as a feminine reality, whose pregnancy and prolific womb represents the opposite of the virginity of Sophia, and whose negativity is obviated only by the reconstitution of a sophiological dimension of being) suggests that in the final analysis Sophia bears the burden of responsibility for the fall in and of divine being. Second, as in *PSY*, in Boehme's narrative Nature is represented as dark, as a realm of unintelligibility, as massive, as an aggressive kind of nothingness, as a withdrawal of communication and expression, and as a feverish kind of expressivity that indicates an abortive rather than truly viable kind of life. Above all, in his focus on the mechanism(s) of *Sucht* (desire) or *Begierde* (hunger), Boehme recalls the connection between Nature and desire (*enthumesis*) that so conspicuously marks *PSY*. Third, and lastly, in many of his texts, but especially in *De Signatura Rerum* (chapters 5, 13–15), Boehme offers a staurological interpretation of the Cross, in which, as in *PSY*, the Cross guarantees the separation of spirit from nature, perfection from deficiency, and sets ontological and gnoseological limits to spirit that provide it with form and shape, and specify the mode of knowledge appropriate to representation of the divine.

It is around this repetition of narrative stages one and two of *PSY* in Boehme's discourse that the other recalls in Boehme's discourse constellate. Needless to say, however, there are both numerous differences, and different kinds of difference. Some of the more specific differences have come to light already in discussion of overlaps in narrative episodes three to six, and some others can be read off the diagram, whose presentation closes our discussion of the first section of this chapter. Yet, arguably, it is the more general features of narrative figuration that mark off Boehme's narrative discourse most decisively from *PSY*. They in turn account for important different emphases in the area of greatest overlap—that is, the faulting of the perfect divine milieu of expressivity and expression. The three crucial features, as I see them, are the reflective level of mythic representation, the level of metalepsis, and the level of teleological incidence.

First, whatever about subsequent complaints in the German tradition about Boehme's lack of critical reflection,[4] Boehme's economic configuration of the divine milieu, together with his obvious ability to ask highly abstract questions such as, Why manifestation? suggest that Boehmian myth functions on a higher reflective level than *PSY*. More specifically, they suggest that his narrative discourse has a critical element absent in this particular Valentinian genre. Second, it is clear that *PSY* and Boehme's narrative evince somewhat different levels of metalepsis. As I tried to show in Part II in general, and chapter 5 in particular, in Boehme's narrative discourse the biblical narrative exercises some counterpull to metalepsis, which results in something like an orthodox residuum with respect to creation and fall. Nevertheless, although this counterpull might suggest that a verdict of a comparatively lower level metaleptic ratio has to be brought in for Boehme, Boehme's more intensive engagement with the biblical narrative possibly leads to correspondingly deeper forms of metalepsis that, minimally, compensate at least for the orthodox recalls.

Third, there exists a huge gap in teleological incidence between Boehme's narratives and that of *PSY*. The teleological incidence in Boehme's narrative is as conspicuous as it is inconspicuous in *PSY*. Even if one reads *PSY* with an eye on the *Tractate*, *PSY* seems wholeheartedly to endorse perfect symmetry between narrative alpha and omega, the purely accidental character of fall, and the emergency nature of repair of deficiency. By contrast, in Boehme's narrative, it is fundamental that this symmetry between narrative alpha and omega is upset, and that fall and its overcoming have teleological design. This will mean that (among other things) as a symbol of transformation, the Cross is as much a transformation *of* nature as a transformation *from* nature.

This brings me to the relation between Boehme's narrative discourse and the narrative discourse of the *Tractate*. Granting the historical privilege of *PSY*, arguably the *Tractate* provides a more illuminating Valentinian comparandum for Boehmian narrative.[5] With regard to individual narrative episodes, the level of correspondence is simply broader and deeper. Working back once again from the end of the encompassing ontotheological narrative, the advantages of the *Tractate* as a Valentinian comparandum for Boehmian narrative are obvious. With regard to eschatology (stage six) the *Tractate* (122ff.) corresponds more closely to Boehme's views than *PSY* by (1) deessentializing the scholastic Valentinian view of three kinds of human being and (2) by validating a language of election (123, 25-124, 25), but (3) ultimately insisting that the soteriological state is dependent on free choice and (4) extending the availability of salvation beyond those who have vision, and thus who are capable of scanning or narrating the ontotheological narrative of the fall from perfection and perfection's reconstitution. The figuration of Christ (stage five) of the *Tractate* also evidences a greater degree of correspondence with Boehme's figuration than *PSY*. Keeping the Gospel texts more clearly in view, it unembarrassedly elaborates a non-Docetic view of the incarnation and the suffering of Jesus, and on this basis supports an interpretation of the suffering of Jesus as symbolic of a deeper suffering and distress of the extrapleromatic Logos (114, 3–118, 14).[6]

The correspondence between the *Tractate*'s view of the fall of human being and that of Boehme's discourse is, arguably, in excess of that which pertains between the reading of *PSY* (stage four) and Boehme's interpretation of the Adamic fall in his hexameron, *Mysterium Magnum*.[7] Indeed, the very complexity of the *Tractate*'s account in which the voluntarist appraisal is offset by an involuntary succumbing to self-forgetfulness, one of whose signs is sexual differentiation and desire, seems to find a repetition in Boehme, who thinks of the act of creaturely assertion as subsequent to the sleep from which human being emerges as less than whole—that is, less than androgynous. Similarly, the correspondence between the *Tractate* (100–105) and Boehme's narrative with respect to the construal of creation (stage three) is also greater than the correlation of Boehme's narrative with *PSY*. Clearly the *Tractate* lessens the demonic features of the generation of the physical world and human being, even if it does not officially support, in the way Boehme's narrative does, the biblical view of a good creation by a good God. At the very least, there is no evil intention in the Logos, who is responsible for the original fall, that through the aegis of an inferior demiurgic power, evil ultimately issues in the material physical world (100, 19–105, 19). At the same time, it should be said that recognizing the chaos at its basis (80–81),[8] Boehme's interpretation of the seven days of creation manages to strike a celebratory note not found in the *Tractate* (78–81), where the physical world is shadowy, without root, and nothing (78–79).

Still, by far the deepest correspondences between the *Tractate* and Boehmian narrative belong to the first two narrative episodes, with these correspondences in turn having an effect on the level of correspondence between narrative episodes three through six. As in Boehme's narrative, the *Tractate* makes both apophatic and kataphatic attributions with respect to the immanifest divine.[9] Nevertheless, kataphasis, ultimately, seems privileged in the language of "Father and Son," where the latter seems to completely express the former who is the ultimate mystery of origin (56, 25; 57, 18–21; 58, 19). Again within the ordinance of the first narrative episode, the correspondence between the *Tractate*'s configuration of the divine before the fall into nature and that of Boehme is remarkable. As in Boehme's narrative, in the *Tractate* the realm of pure divinity is articulated by a Quaternity, a Trinity plus a hypostatic actor proximally responsible for fall.[10] While some of the terms are different, with the *Tractate* having Logos (75ff.) instead of Sophia for the fourth hypostasis, and Church instead of Spirit for the third (58ff.), these differences do not affect the level of correspondence that becomes even more significant at the second stage of the encompassing ontotheological narrative. The fall of the Logos in the *Tractate* recalls the fall of Sophia in *PSY* and models the fall of Sophia into Eternal Nature[11] that is central in Boehme's account. As such the perfect falls into the imperfect. Symbolically expressed, light gives way to dark, seeing to nonseeing, knowledge to ignorance, etheriality to massiveness, eloquence to speechlessness, appropriate fertility to inappropriate fertility, and life to death.

The truly radical correspondence between the *Tractate* and Boehme's narrative, however, concerns not so much the homology of symbols that describe the fall (into nature and its attendant angst and suffering) but its interpretation. In the case of both the *Tractate* and Boehme's texts, the primal fall has more or less a teleological design. If Boehme thinks that Eternal Nature, as a fallen form of the divine, is productive of the plurality and variety necessary for perfection, the *Tractate* thinks that such production realizes a good that otherwise would not be realized. In an extraordinary revision of the position adopted, for example, in *PSY* the writer of this third-century Valentinian text advises: "It is not fitting the movement which is the Logos, but it is fitting that we should say about the movement of the Logos, that it is the cause of a system, which has been destined to come about" (77, 5ff.).

Thus, divine fall from perfection in the *Tractate* has—at least implicitly— the same pattern of an ontotheological *felix culpa* it has in Boehme's texts, as it undermines both (1) the would-be Valentinian verities about the perfection of origin being unsurpassable and (2) the noninvolvement of the deeper depths of the divine in transgression against aboriginal purity. For the *Tractate* suggests (71, 14–19) what Boehme's texts make clear—that is, that the negation of perfection is willed by the divine from the very beginning with a view to noetic as well as ontological increase. In addition, the teleological design shakes, in a way similar to Boehme's *De Signatura Rerum*, the view that the relation between suffering and the divine is always external and accidental. Implicit in the *Tractate* is an anticipation of the rigorous deipassionism of Boehme's discourse which, nonetheless, forbids the entrance of suffering into the trinitarian and sophiological inner sanctum. The *felix culpa* interpretation of the fall of the divine into nature has also in both cases a prospective positive effect on the negative figuration of the demiurge, the universe he brings into being, the status of the human beings he creates, and the fall of human being—although, as one would expect, Boehme's correction of *PSY*, it must be granted, is more thoroughgoing than the *Tractate*'s. And finally, the teleological pattern in both cases tightens the symbolic relation between Christ and the fallen aspect of the divine, making Christ the real symbol of a suffering that exists on the transcendental plane.

In the context of the *Tractate,* this means giving the construct of kenosis much wider scope than it enjoys in *PSY*, but also much wider scope than the construct enjoys in classical renditions of the biblical narrative provided by such figures as Irenaeus, Augustine, and Luther. For the kenosis is dechristologized in its being transferred to the pain or suffering of the aspect of fallen divine responsible for the emergence of physical and temporal nature.[12] The *felix culpa* reading of fall and suffering in fact suggests nothing short of a thoroughgoing teleologization of

the entire ontotheological narrative such that the eschatological perfection recollects not only the aboriginal perfection of beginning, but also the entire narrative movement (*analepsis*). Indeed, this recollection is correlative to the
anticipation (*prolepsis*) of perfection that is inherent in the aboriginal perfection.

This is not to claim, however, that the *Tractate* appropriates fully its own
teleological suggestion, and explicitly draws the kinds of conclusions with respect to individual narrative episodes and ontotheological narrative as a whole
drawn by Boehme. These conclusions function implicitly in a text that subscribes to what might be called the 'official' Valentinian line concerning the in-
explicability of fall, the questionability of the creator and the negativity of
creation, the inessentiality of suffering to the divine, and above all the assertion that the narrative end point is the reassertion of aboriginal perfection. The
Tractate then is a text that paradigmatically realizes the division between surface and depth narrative dimensions suggested by Jonas and von Balthasar as
underlying Valentinian discourse as a whole.[13] As such, it is a text that belongs
to its time in that it is unable to transcend the narrative constraints of the sedimented Valentinian tradition. It is also a text that opens up a possible future of
theogonic radicalization in which the reflective level of mythic representation,
level of metalepsis, and teleological attitude are augmented. Above all, their
level of integration is heightened. Not only does the evidence suggest that no
such radicalization occurs within the Hellenistic field, but also there are good
grounds for believing that, Jonas notwithstanding, a thoroughgoing endorse-
ment of *kenosis* is not possible in the Hellenistic sphere, and that it must necessarily remain an "unfulfilled intention"—to avail of Husserl's language—in
classical Valentinianism.

If I am correct, radicalization awaits precisely the post-Reformation narrative of Boehme to completely liberate the teleological dimension from and
for a metaleptic encompassing narrative. The Boehmian narrative of divine
manifestation represents precisely the *novum* that Baur at once asserts and
undermines in *Die christliche Gnosis*. It releases the erotic potential from the
narrative constraints that bear on the classical Valentinian genres. The actualization of this erotic potential has an especially intense effect with respect
to the charting of the first two narrative episodes of an encompassing narrative of a metaleptic kind. The radicalization removes all support for construing the "unfallen" divine as truly perfect. Moreover, it has effects with respect
to what I have called the aporetics of representation, the conundrum of
whether infinite reflection is possible only through the detour of finite representation. The *Tractate* continues to hold the incoherent view that the mystery of the divine, whether father or forefather, can be completely known
(Son) (55, 3–4; 66), and not completely known (Logos), indeed, ought
not to be completely known (71.14–19). In erotic radicalization of the kind
witnessed in Boehmian texts, the givenness of this knowing or reflection is

Table 6.1. Relation of Boehme's Ontotheological Narrative to Classical Valentinian Paradigms.

This table schematizes the narrative relations between Boehme's narrative and the narratives of *PSY* and the *Tractate*. The numbers 1–6 in brackets each correspond to a specific narrative episode. The numbers 1–3 in square brackets correspond to a trinitarian or triadic synopsis of what is essentially a six-stage narrative.

Narrative			*PSY*	Boehme	*Tractate*
[1]	(1)	Pler -mc	complex, 30 hyp	trinitrian -quaternarian	trinitarian -quaternarian
		-bc	dyadic, natural procreation	monadic-eternal generation	monadic-eternal generation
		-nq	not conspicuous	conspicuous	conspicuous
		-prol	not obvious	real, determining	real
[2]	(2)	Fault-origin	failure of pler self-reflexion	ditto	ditto
		actor	Sophia	Sophia	Logos
		rationale	happenstance	design	design
		consequence	evil as fallen e of pler—Nature engender demiurge	ditto Eternal Nature Lucifer	ditto Logos as Nature engender-demiurge
		judgment	negative unqualified	negative qualified	negative qualified
	(3)	Cos - anth	separate but extension emergence of evil	not separate not complete continuous emergence of evil	not separate but extension of emergence of evil
	(4)	FPN-origin	forgetfulness, self-will	ditto	ditto
		rationale	happenstance	teleological	teleological
		judgment	negative	negative positive twist *felix culpa*	negative positive twist *felix culpa*
[3]	(5)	Saviour	Teacher of Gnosis	Redeemer	Teacher of Gnosis
		xtology	Docetic	non-docetic	non-docetic
		passion reference	suffering of fallen e-pler	suffering of fallen e-pler	suffering of fallen e-pler
		identity	Sophia as Nature	Sophia as Nature	Logos as Nature

(*continued*)

Table 6.1. (*Continued*)

Narrative	*PSY*	Boehme	*Tractate*
(6) Eschaton	pns and psys diff order of salvation	pns and psys same order of salvation	pns and psys same order of salvation
eschaton now	no	suggestion	suggestion
nc	recaps pler of origin	goes beyond pler of origin	goes beyond pler of origin
analepsis	not obvious	obvious	present
register	mythological–ontological	mythological–ontological epist. twist	mythological–ontological epist. twist
demyth	not obvious	obvious	obvious

Key to Abbreviations: anth = anthropogony; bc = basis of configuration; cos = cosmogony; demyth = demythologization; e = element; FPN = fall of pneumatic being; hyp = hypostasis; nc = narrative closure; nq = narrative quality; pler = pleroma; pns = pneumatics; prol = prolepsis; psys = psychic; mc = mode of configuration.

suspended, as the search for infinite reflection is valorized and finite representation validated. Divine mystery is known only through the detour of representation which in the end amounts to a perfectly adequate divine self-reflection.

6.1. Toward Genealogy

Were the kind of significant, but differential, correspondences I have adduced between classical Valentinian genres and Boehme's narrative discourse lacking, then any ascription of Valentinianism to Boehme would be vacuous, since it would lack historical anchorage and textual and conceptual determinacy. Clearly, however, these correspondences supply the necessary rather than sufficient conditions for Valentinian ascription of Boehme's discourse. Justified ascription requires the ability to account for differences in rendition of narrative episodes, narrative configuration as a whole, metaleptic disposition, and surrounding ideational complexes.[14]

As is obvious at this stage, this becomes possible only on the basis of the grammatical turn, in which Valentinianism is not identified by an invariant narrative pattern, but by a particular grammar of divine perfection-fall-reconstitution of perfection across a complex six-stage narrative that represents a metalepsis of the biblical narrative. A thoroughgoing theogonic (because erotic) rendition of a complex metaleptic narrative, such as Boehme's, is a possibility of Valentinian narrative grammar, even if it is neither instantiated, nor instantiatable, in the Hellenistic field. Relative to the sedimentation of the Valentinian tradition, Boehme's narrative must be regarded as deviant. Crucially, however, it is deviant in ways suggested by the classical Valentinian paradigms themselves, and especially the *Tractate*. Thus, Boehme's theogonic narrative can be thought of as constituting a rule-governed deformation of classical Valentinian genres, in which the hithertofore unrealized potential for erotic and agonistic construal of encompassing metaleptic narrative is realized, and where the implicit aporetics of representation gets thematized.

Under the rule of grammar, one can sustain the contention of Baur that Boehme's trinitarian narrative discourse represents a continuation of Gnosticism, without making the blatantly false claim that classical Gnostic, or specifically Valentinian, narratives are theogonic. Sustaining a taxonomic Gnostic or Valentinian case for Boehme's narrative is a condition for making the claim that Boehme's narrative is the privileged site of Gnostic return in modernity, and the proximate origin for the Gnostic discourses of the modern period. It was, of course, this genealogical claim that was to the fore in *Die christliche Gnosis*, as Baur charted the discursive trajectory from Luther to Hegel. As already outlined in considerable detail in *Gnostic Return in Modernity*, Baur's genealogy must undergo amplification and correction.[15] More important to stress at this juncture, however, is that the originary nature of Boehme's ontotheological narrative must be demonstrated by elaborating the actual affinities between these later narrative discourses and Boehme's metaleptic narrative, both in part and whole. This point is almost so obvious as to be not worth making were it not for the fact that Baur himself tends to substitute assertion for demonstration. Of course, if Boehme's position as source can be demonstrated, then it follows that he is entitled to a much more prominent place in the history of modern Christian thought than he is usually accorded.

Sustaining a Gnostic, or specifically Valentinian reading of Boehmian narrative discourse puts one in a situation to assess the second and, arguably, secondary claim of Baur—namely, that Boehme's visionary narrative discourse represents an explicitation of the Reformation. Of course, without reformulation this claim cannot be sustained. A straight line cannot be drawn between Luther and Boehme. In Part II, I provided considerable evidence of the extent and depth of Boehme's swerve from the Reformer, and especially from the assimilation of Luther by Lutheran orthodoxy. Having disposed of the illusion of direct development, however, the way is open to support a highly qualified version of Baur's view of Boehme's continuity with, or at least not total discontinuity from, the Lutheran tradition. There are three interdependent aspects to this highly qualified version. First, the Reformation sets the ineluctable baseline of focusing religious authority away from the theological tradition and making it reside within the biblical text and the narrative it renders. Although Luther will attempt to set constraints on idiosyncratic interpretation, and will insist on the communal nature of a text that is self-interpreting rather than interpretively provocative, these moves can, with some justification, be regarded as extrinsic to the mandate given to interpretation of God's speech to human beings, which it would make sense to presume is not absolutely clear.

Even in its adherents, the essential Reformation message will be a matter of dispute. Among other things it will be read exclusively in terms of what it rejects, or in light of its more positive statements, which do not so much depart from the common interpretive and theological tradition as put them once again securely on a sound—that is, on a biblical basis. The Reformation then sets at least a negative condition of the possibility of a metaleptic discourse (such as Boehme's) that involves outrightly transgressive interpretation.

There are two further more proximate and more positive factors. The first of these—and thus the second factor overall—involves viewing Boehme's discourse as continuous with the discourses of the Spiritual Reformers, who are themselves at odds with Luther. I have discussed this relation in some detail in chapter 3 in which I dealt with those hermeneutic and substantive theological departures from the Reformation tradition that Boehme shares with this heterogeneous group of post-Reformation thinkers. The second—and thus the third factor overall—involves acknowledging the continuity between Boehmian and Paracelsian discourses whose swerves from Reformation as well as pre-Reformation traditions are in excess of the level of the swerves realized in Franck and Schwenckfeld. If the point with respect to both recalls is more than historical, this is especially so in the second case. For the fact that Boehme's narrative discourse is not unanticipated, and that the alchemical discourse of Paracelus (and also Weigel) is an embedded element in Boehme's discourse, makes Boehme's discourse all the more powerful genealogically. For as representing a condensing of alchemical discourse and its theological elevation beyond the vulnerability of refutation by scientific discovery, the alchemical recalls in modern discourse, for example, Romanticism (e.g., Goethe, Blake), which otherwise might be without narrative lineage, can be traced back to a unitive, if complex discursive origin. A conspicuous example of how this works will be proposed in my volume on Romanticism. Alchemical features of Blake's discourse, especially those related to the movement from dark to light, heaviness to lightness, or death to life, or in other words what I refer to as the *enantiodromia* complex, will come in for discussion.

As an instance of Valentinian narrative grammar, which at the same time represents a rule-governed deformation of classical Valentinian genres, Boehme's theogonic narrative functions as an original site of Valentinian return. As originary, Boehme's narrative is at once a repetition and a novum. One has a right to expect, therefore, that narrative discourses claimed to be in line with

Boehme's narrative display erotic and agonistic features, as they too disfigure and crucially refigure in a more encompassing narrative frame the biblical narrative or its first-order interpretation. Needless to say, to be considered instances of Valentinian narrative grammar it is not necessary that these metaleptic narrative discourses repeat Boehme's narrative in every detail. The different ideational contexts of Romantic, Idealist, and post-Idealist thought will dictate certain systemic differences in narrative formation, though no complete plotting of the range of differences is possible.[16] I suggest, however, that the epistemic and demythologizing features of the *Gospel*[17]—to which I drew so much attention in *Gnostic Return in Modernity*—which are somewhat recessed in Boehme's narrative, would in an age dominated by epistemology, whether in its empiricist, transcendental, or Idealist forms, feature more prominently as a Valentinian touchstone. This will be borne out in my discussion of Blake, Hegel, and Schelling, and of modern theologians in subsequent volumes on the theme of Gnostic return in modernity. At the same time, the epistemological index of Boehme's discourse should not be underestimated. It is extremely high, and it is reflected in Boehme's positing a mode of knowledge (*Verstand*) that transcends ratiocination (*Vernunft*) and functioning as the equivalent of the Holy Spirit. It is reflected in Boehme's having the vicissitude of knowledge as an essential subject matter of his discourse. For if the subject matter of his discourse is divine self-development in and through manifestation, how the divine comes to know itself in and through the finite is a fundamental inflection of this subject matter that also necessarily includes the vision in which it is held up to view.

Yet the recessiveness of the *Gospel*'s parsing of ontotheological narrative should not mislead one into thinking that this Valentinian genre finds no evocation within Boehme's complex ontotheological narrative. Two features of the *Gospel* that seem clearly evoked are both trinitarian, with the first referring to the configuration of the milieu of divine perfection and the second referring to what could be construed as a triadic simplification of an essentially six-stage narrative.[18] Even more brazenly than the *Tractate*, the *Gospel* depicts a kenotic movement from Father to Son that makes the emphatically kataphatic Son all that the Father is.[19] It is just this radical kenotic view that is embraced in Boehme's view of the Son as ground and center. The *Gospel* also streamlines the complex narrative pattern into a triadic rhythm of perfection-loss-perfection regained.[20] In a sense, this is what Boehme does both more explicitly, and somewhat less successfully, in his attempt to impose a trinitarian pattern on the complex narrative—less successfully, insofar, as the Unground, Trinity, and Sophia remain outside the trinitarian schematization. From a genealogical point of view, one can read some of Boehme's successors as appropriating both Boehme's radical kenotic view and finding ways in which the complex metaleptic narrative submits without remainder to a trinitarian figuration. That such is paradigmatically the case in Hegel, I will argue in a later text.

CHAPTER 7

~

Apocalyptic in Boehme's Discourse
and its Valentinian Enlisting

In a noncontesting taxonomic and genealogical environment, the argument in chapter 6 to the effect that Boehme's discourse represents an instance of Valentinian narrative grammar, while also representing a rule-governed deformation of classical Valentinian genres, might well explanatorily suffice. But the taxonomic status of Boehme's discourse is contested, and this obviously has consequences with respect to any genealogical account of narrative discourses that harks back in some fundamental way to Boehme's visionary narrative. If *apocalyptic* ascription has had a certain primacy, *Neoplatonic*, and even *Kabbalistic* ascriptions, have not been lacking.

Thus, the *Valentinian* reading of Boehme's narrative discourse, both in itself, and regarded as the point of departure for later narrative discourses, must be demonstrated against rival possible or actual accounts. The demonstration of the explanatory power of Valentinianism vis-à-vis apocalyptic, Neoplatonism, and Kabbalah has two analytically separable elements. (1) It involves showing that neither apocalyptic, Neoplatonism, nor Kabbalah account for the basic structures of Boehme's narrative. (2) More positively, it involves showing that those elements of apocalyptic, Neoplatonism, or Kabbalah that can be discerned in Boehme's pansophism are explicable in terms of a Valentinian taxon, provided the grammatical understanding of Valentinianism is kept to the fore.

I begin this crucial task of demonstrating the explanatory power of the Valentinian taxon with a discussion of the taxonomic challenge presented by apocalyptic. Later chapters will deal with the taxonomic challenges posed by Neoplatonism and Kabbalah, and thus indirectly with their genealogical challenge.

Boehme's texts provide plenty of encouragement to construe his narrative as articulating apocalyptic. Evidence of the importance in Boehme's texts not only of visionary tropes, for example, Ezekiel's chariot, but also of apocalyptic texts in general, and above all Revelation, has already been adduced (chapter 2).

Boehme's texts continue a sixteenth-century tradition of Reformation, specifically Lutheran, Revelation interpretation, especially along its Melanchthon axis. If for the most part in this tradition interpretation involved an application of the biblical text to the contemporary situation of perceived crisis and promise, such that Revelation enacted perfectly an "absorption of the world,"[1] in a few cases, and above all in Weigel, there is a speculative interest that transcends the vision of the eschaton and the enervating conditions that are its signs. Boehme taps into the upper registers of post-Reformation apocalyptic interpretation, and especially its speculative forms, that leave behind the chronicles of salvation history, the diatribes against the contemporary situation of fallenness and apostasy, and the obsession with signs and prognostications of the end. What this speculative interest is, how it betrays itself in discourse, and in what way it modifies classical apocalyptic will be dealt with in due course. What needs to be explicated first, however, is the array of apocalyptic features in Boehme's texts. For practical purposes it is helpful to sort out this array into those features that more nearly concern apocalyptic as literary genre,[2] and those features that more nearly can be thought to belong to the level of the content of apocalyptic.

On the level of Boehme's recapitulation of apocalyptic as literary genre, one can include the emphasis in his texts on vision, and specifically on its suddenness and its overwhelmingly luminous quality, its pneumatic horizon, the numinousness of constitutive symbols such as the apocalyptic Christ and Jerusalem, and the authority of the immediacy of vision that, on the one hand, suspends interpretation, and, on the other, provokes it. Each of these genre elements is important and helps to reinforce, and in turn be reinforced by, Boehme's appropriations of apocalyptic on the level of content. Especially interesting is Boehme's reprise of the doubleness of the iconic matrix of Revelation. Symbols at once certify truth, and point beyond themselves. This endemic doubleness of Revelation also regulates its subsequent interpretation. This is especially the case in sixteenth-century Lutheran interpretation. Interpretation responds to Revelation's iconic matrix as both luminous and obscure, as disclosing and withholding. Both the text itself and its sixteenth-century interpretation forbid regarding the symbols as perspicuous in a straightforward way. Perspicuity is a possibility only in and through interpretation whose task is to fathom the symbols and remove their obscurity. Boehme understands the necessity of interpretation with respect to Scripture in general as much as any of the Spiritual Reformers, and understands that Revelation is the text that excites this recognition and encourages allegorical interpretive practice.

As I have already suggested in chapter 2, Boehme's discourse's assimilation of apocalyptic on the level of content is considerable. If his minor texts tend to figure history as the site of a battle between the mythic forces of good and evil, in major texts such as *Aurora* (1612) and *Mysterium Magnum* (1623), this mythic agon gets historicized in the tension between institutional and pneumatic church, the church visible and the church invisible. The pneumatic church is persecuted throughout history, but especially so in the last days. The objective condition of any pneumatic church is, of course, Christ as the one who submits to sacrifice even to the point of death.[3] Although Christ emerges victorious in Boehme's scheme of things, interestingly omitted are the celebration of the wrathful, judgmental aspects of Revelation's figuration of Christ. If the pivot of history is the paschal mystery of Christ—though the emphasis falls on the appropriation of sacrifice more than sacrifice itself—for Boehme, the real focus is eschatological. It is so in two different ways. (1) Endtime represents an essential breach of or transformation of time. (2) Endtime refers to the construction of a heavenly Jerusalem, which is the doxological milieu par excellence. Both of these aspects contribute to the conferring of meaning on history, for the transformation of time implies a solution to fallenness, and the realization of Jerusalem is the bringing into being of a world commensurate to the saving gesture of Christ and a world that corresponds to the world of divine intention.

If Boehme's discourse engages biblical apocalyptic texts in general, and Revelation in particular, along both genre and content fronts, this is hardly the limit of apocalyptic appropriation. In addition, one would, certainly, have to include the theology of history of Joachim of Fiore, which though sometimes denied apocalyptic characterization,[4] is justified in being construed as a second-order form of apocalyptic—a form, that is, that elicits truths about the divine, history, and their relation by means of interpreting apocalyptic texts in general (and especially Revelation) in a way that moderates the catastrophic character of the end and that insinuates a teleological pattern in history, such that the supposed break-in of Spirit is more nearly the plenitude of its explicitation.[5] The status of the question of Boehme's access to Joachim's texts remains open, although it is likely that Boehme depends for his knowledge on the Lutheran mediation of the sixteenth century.[6] Still, whether the line is indirect or direct, there does appear to be a significant recall of Joachim in Boehme's discourse. To the extent to which Boehme thinks that Scripture is a scene of ultimate perspicuity (but penultimate obscurity) that can only be dissolved through allegorical interpretation, he is recalling the hermeneutics of Joachim's *Concordia* and Joachim's commentary on Revelation *Expositio in Apocalypsim*.

Boehme's recall of Joachim on the level of content is equally significant. As with Joachim, in Boehme's major texts history is genuinely dynamic, tensional, and ordered toward a plenitude of knowledge and freedom, where freedom is provided a positive and normative interpretation, rather than merely negative interpretation of freedom from. Moreover, even if the favored periodization in *Aurora* and *Mysterium Magnum* is sevenfold rather than trinitarian,[7] nonetheless, trinitarian periodization is not absent. De Lubac, for instance, suggests that the triads of stars-dawn-midday and orsies-roses-lilies that mark Joachim's *Concordia* are especially to the fore. *Aurora* features both the symbols of transformation such as dawn and rose, and the eschatological symbols, with a particular emphasis on the lily. While the Latin title of Boehme's first text, *Aurora*, directly invokes dawn, the German title, *Morgenröte*, invokes the rose. In addition, the eschaton is called the time of the lily (*Lilienzeit*),[8] which is the time of the realization of vision, specifically, vision's communal and nonepisodic noonday. While in keeping with the authority of the Enoch figure in the sixteenth-century trajectory of apocalyptic,[9] "Enoch" comes to identify endtime in Boehme's *magnum opus*, the figure of the lily is never fully lost, indeed, being recapitulated in contexts that have "Enochian-time" (*Enochenzeit*) as their signature (*MM* 30, 34). Thus, the lily symbolically interprets the figure of Enoch, as Enoch figurally interprets the Joachimite symbol of the lily.

The measure of Joachimite recall in Boehme's discourse is sufficiently nontrivial to incite the question whether a Joachimite characterization of his discourse is at least relatively adequate. I will in due course try the question, as I will try the question as to the relative adequacy of an apocalyptic ascription in general. The point I wish to make at the moment is the very obvious one that recognizing the taxonomic importance of Joachim's second-order apocalyptic facilitates a genealogical case that would have Boehme as the proximate post-Reformation site for a form of apocalyptic discourse that flourishes in the context of German Pietism, especially in Bengel,[10] and survives in Lessing's periodization of history and his announcement of the "eternal Gospel"[11] only to be given new life in Hegel and Schelling.[12] Of course, Boehme's discourse need not simply be regarded as the proximate source of a trajectory of second-order apocalyptic, as de Lubac would have it, he could also be the proximate post-Reformation source for the mediation of biblical apocalyptic with its self-certifying vision and its vocation of iconically registering of all reality's secrets. This implies that Boehme could be thought to set in motion another order of visionary discourse that finds major representatives in Swedenborg and Blake, rather than Hegel and Schelling, although, of course, aspects of both orders of apocalypse discourse can be found in all these discourses.

I have tried hard to make as strong a case as possible on behalf of an apocalyptic ascription of Boehme's discourse. Nevertheless, persuasive as the apocalyptic taxon might appear to be, especially if one takes into account apocalyptic's double register, I want to suggest that crucial elements of Boehme's visionary narrative discourse do not admit of apocalyptic description, and thus suggest the inadequacy of an apocalyptic ascription. For instance, while Boehme can, and often does in fact, speak of his encompassing vision of the whole of reality as an event predicated on the agency of a divine reality distinct from and superior to human being, just as often the work of the Spirit seems to get incorporated in an epistemic structure of the self (*Verstand*), which contrasts with discursive knowledge (*Vernunft*).

Again, while interpretation of Scripture in general, and of apocalyptic texts in particular, follows in Boehme's texts the Joachimite pattern of moving toward illumination through allegorical and anagogical interpretation, arguably, there is an aim for interpretive closure not found in Joachim. One way in which the aim for closure gets expressed in Boehme's texts is that allegory moves the reader to an extrabiblical vantage point that expresses itself in an extrabiblical metadiscourse that accounts for the regional languages of Scripture and nature. The condition of the possibility of this metadiscourse is that allegory in Boehme has a more Alexandrian commitment to the eternal than it has in Joachim, where its primary function is disclosure of the future.[13]

But, perhaps, it is on the level of narrative content that one senses the greatest gap. One difference is, undoubtedly, the much greater focus in Boehme's narrative discourse on the eternal, especially in its archeological ambit. All of Boehme's mature texts pay an extraordinary amount of attention to the Unground as the divine nothing and all, the 'Immanent Trinity' and Wisdom, and the agon between negative and positive eternal Principles. Another difference is that in Boehme's pansophistic vision the narrative is not a narrative of engagement of a sovereign divine with a humanity that, even if abject, always remains a dialogue partner. It is rather a narrative of the divine in which the emphasis falls on the nondivine other being a means of divine self-realization. In neither biblical apocalyptic, nor its second-order reflection in Joachim, is the narrative of the divine fundamentally theogonic. Nothing in apocalyptic narrative of the first- or second-order kind reveals even a trace of the mechanisms of eros, kenosis, and ontotheological *felix culpa* that characterize Boehme's theogonic narrative, which are especially urgent, as we saw in chapters 1, 5, and 6 on the plane of eternity. For this reason, nothing in apocalyptic of the first- or second-order kind is implicated fundamentally in a theodicy program in the way that Boehme's visionary narrative is.

The ways in which the narratives are symbolically configured reflect the basic narrative differences touched on above. To the extent to which the narrative movement in apocalyptic texts is figured by the codes that structure Boehme's narrative, especially the ocular, speech, and organic codes, it is clear that they do not get narrativized in the way they do in Boehme's ontotheology. Light and dark, seeing and blindness, remain oppositional in Revelation, and encourage structural rather than narrative readings. The same can be said of the contrast between word (voice, book, scroll) (Revelation 1.9ff.; 4; 5.2–7; 10.2ff.; 22.7, etc.) and silence (nonbook, nonscroll), and above all life and death. In Boehme's case—and here he is in excess of classical Valentinian genres—every symbolic opposition is developmentally coded. Such coding reinforces the erotic and kenotic thrust of a six-stage ontotheological narrative that in the *Tractate* (the classical Valentinian genre) at least suggests a developmental reading.

Not unimportant in all of this is the way in which Boehme's narrative is fundamentally metaleptic with respect to first-order renditions of the biblical narrative in a way Joachimite apocalyptic is not. Although Joachim was perceived to have attacked the consensus view on the eternal Trinity[14] and to have compromised the christological omega of history,[15] still his theology as a whole did not involve the subversion of consensus first-order renditions of the biblical narrative, and thus constitute a metalepsis of it. Joachim, for instance, does not fundamentally contradict the common tradition in thinking of the divine as a Trinity of persons (Nicea), nor in thinking of Christ as a person, both human and divine (Chalcedon), nor the Augustinian *creatio ex nihilo* tradition in thinking of creation's dependence on the eternal Trinity.[16]

In contrast, Boehme's speculative narrative is wildly deviant with respect to the Reformation tradition to which it claims to be faithful. In the context of Luther's work as a whole, the articulation of the biblical narrative is arguably more implied than explicit. Nevertheless, the *Small* and the *Great Cathecism*, and the commentaries on Genesis and John, suggest that it is not far from the surface. For the basic dynamic is the movement from the trinitarian God back to the trinitarian God through creation, redemption, and judgment. And it is precisely this implied articulation of biblical narrative, whose ultimate horizon is provided by the conversation between the distinct trinitarian persons, and whose focus is provided by the redemptive activity of Christ on the Cross,[17] that is subjected to disfiguration-refiguration in Boehme's speculative discourse.

As I suggested earlier, the biblical narrative, as rendered in Luther, is already undergoing something like a metaleptic attack in Paracelsus and Weigel. Nothing in the post-Reformation period, however, is comparable to Boehme's narrative onslaught. In the redescribed Christian narrative, the intradivine Trinity is not a Trinity of persons, but rather a triadic process that comes to term well short of the realization of the divine aim for productive selfhood. More, Wisdom is not one of the names of the Son but rather a distinct moment of immanent divine articulation, referred to the possibility of divine self-reflection that provides one of the marks of divine completeness. Boehme denies what would be unthinkable in Luther, and most certainly was so in the tradition of Lutheran orthodoxy—that is, that the intradivine Trinity is unsurpassable reality, goodness, and existence, as well as knowledge.

In addition, if the battle between the dark and light Principles does not in every respect substitute for the tension between the wrath and mercy of God, in a very real sense the agon between the two Principles represents an analytic separation and ontologization of Luther's complex figuration of the God of Wrath (*Zorngott*) and the God of Mercy (*Barmhertziggott*). Other changes are also wrought. In Luther, "paradise" functions straightfowardly as the state of being lost through sin and regained through Christ's redemptive activity on the Cross. In Boehme's discourse, however, "paradise" is not only foregrounded much more, but in an almost literal sense, it comes to function speculatively. Paradise is Wisdom considered as the objectification (*Gegenwurf*) of divine will made concrete and real. It is constitutive of actual divine self-representation, a self-representation put in jeopardy directly by the fall of Lucifer, and indirectly by the fall of Adam. While at one level creation of the cosmos and human being are acts of gratuitous generosity, at another level, they are acts of divine self-interest in that such acts repair the divine milieu necessary for divine self-glorification and the self-reflection that attends it.

Arguably, what encapsulates the huge jump in the level of narrative deviance between Boehme and Joachim is what I referred to in *The Heterodox Hegel* as the difference between their respective *trinitarian semantics of kingdom*.[18] Whereas in Joachim the trinitarian succession of Kingdoms refers to the missions of the Trinity in salvation history, in Boehme the three Kingdoms or Principles are not missional in any straightforward way. Granted that Boehme, in line with Joachim and the mainline theological tradition, speaks of a Trinity that transcends the creation, redemption, and sanctification of finite and dependent reality, nonetheless, (1) the terrain the trinitarian Kingdoms cover, (2) their relation to the 'Immanent Trinity,' and (3) their essential purpose, all differ from that found in Joachim, whose placement alongside Boehme brings out his relative traditionality.

A brief word about each of these differences. I begin with (1). In contrast to the terrain of Kingdoms in Joachim, where all are temporal, the terrain of the first two of the three Kingdoms in Boehme's narrative is eternal rather than temporal. True, one can talk even in the case of the first two Kingdoms or Principles of creation, redemption, and sanctification. One can do so, however, only under the provisos that creation is the creation of a paradisaical other to divine will, that redemption is redemption from eternal death, and that sanctification is eternal self-glorification of the divine in and by the eternal divine milieu. In Boehme's semantics of kingdom only the third Kingdom is in any real sense temporal. In this third Kingdom or Principle, variously called the Kingdom or Principle of the Spirit or the world, Boehme compresses the entire prospectus of salvation history from creation to eschaton that in Joachim is extended over the three Kingdoms or Periods of Father, Son, and Spirit.

(2) In Boehme's visionary narrative, the foundational role enjoyed by the eternal Trinity in Joachim is withdrawn. There are two interrelated elements in this withdrawal. First, the 'Immanent Trinity' lacks the hypostatic density it enjoys in Joachim. Second, the 'Immanent Trinity' in Boehme's narrative does not represent the perfection of being, knowledge, goodness, and existence that Joachim, in concert with the mainline Christian tradition, assumes it does. The 'Immanent Trinity' is on the way toward full divine self-realization, yet barely

so, since it falls short of the adventure of death and life that is the condition of such realization. Thus, while the 'Immanent Trinity' is narratively anterior to the articulation of the three Kingdoms, it is the Kingdoms, especially the two eternal Kingdoms, that are foundational with respect to it, although obviously in a teleological rather than archeological sense.

(3) The pivotal difference, ultimately, however, lies in the purpose of the trinitarian Kingdoms in the different narrative regimes. If in the case of Joachim the Kingdoms refer to distinct arenas of divine activity in which dialogue with humanity occurs, and the essentially pedagogic conditions of freedom and knowledge that make for dialogue are set down, in the case of Boehme Kingdoms refer to specific sites of the process of divine self-constitution. This makes Boehme's semantics of kingdom 'economic,' but obviously in the post-Marxist sense of 'economic' used by Bataille and Derrida,[19] rather than in the classical missional sense applicable to Joachim. For in and through the succession of Kingdoms, and especially the first two, falling and agon reap dividends, make a profit in the order of being, knowing, goodness, and existence. And such economic gain cannot be otherwise, given the erotic, kenotic, and *felix culpa* mechanisms that drive Boehme's encompassing metaleptic narrative. No trace of these mechanisms can be found in Joachim's trinitarianism despite his determination to forge a view of Trinity that renders a divine more open to the world.[20]

Related to this economic reading is Boehme's emphasis on the divine object of vision being essentially a subject (grammatical) of vision that sets down the conditions of adequate self-reflection. Self-reflection is the aim of a divine articulation that achieves its realization in a heavenly paradise that functions as a mirror reflecting divine creativity and imagination back to it. Boehme's trinitarian narrative is thus focused (in a way that Joachim's trinitarian thought is not) on what I have referred to as the *aporetics of reflection*, on the conundrum of how the divine knows itself, whether infinite self-reflexion is regarded either as a contradiction in terms or as providing a form of thought that is imperfect rather than perfect. At the same time, in contrast to Joachim, but in continuity with classical genres of Valentinian narrative, and especially the *Gospel*, Boehme's discourse forges a much closer connection between the act of vision and its object. For the act of vision not only has the divine as its content or noema, but is itself also is a form of divine self-representation or noesis.

To sum up our discussion thus far. The features of Boehme's visionary narrative that cannot be accounted for by apocalyptic of the first- or second-order are sufficiently important to justify refusing an apocalyptic taxon to Boehme's visionary narrative. This taxonomic inadequacy in turn is the basis of the genealogical inadequacy of positing Boehme as the point of origin for apocalyptic modern discourses. Still, as I acknowledged from the beginning, apocalyptic in both its first- and second-order forms is a real presence in Boehme's visionary narrative. So the issue becomes how one can honor this recognition while continuing to maintain the validity of a Valentinian taxon. It is to this issue that I now turn.

In what follows I hope to show that the presence of apocalyptic elements in Boehme's should not be thought to limit the taxonomic capability of Valentinianism. This would only be the case if the apocalyptic elements remained independent and thoroughly unassimilated into a more encompassing visionary and narrative form. I will suggest that this is not the case, that in fact, in Boehme's speculative discourse apocalyptic of both a first- and second-order kind is pressed into Valentinian service.

7.1. Apocalyptic Inscription and Distention

As one observes the ways in which in Boehme's discourse, vision, mode of scriptural interpretation, rendering of episodes of the biblical narrative, and overall narrative structure depart from apocalyptic, it would not be unreasonable, if not necessarily justified, to extrapolate that in Boehme apocalyptic has undergone something of a mutation. The affinities, however, of Boehme's visionary metanarrative with classical Valentinian genres, and the possibility of discontinuity between Boehme's metanarrative and the classical Valentinian genres being explicable on a grammatical basis, suggest that an alternative explanatory avenue be opened up. A clue as to what this explanatory vista would look like is provided by my account in *Gnostic Return in Modernity* (chapter 3) of the neighborliness of different apocalypse genres in the Hellenistic field, and especially the ability of Valentinian revelation discourses to introduce elements that appear to belong to biblical apocalyptic. Of course, one is talking in this post-Reformation environment about much more than fluidity. One is in fact talking about the possibility of apocalyptic migrating into what is essentially a Valentinian form of apocalypse of much greater narrative differentiation, which essentially masters apocalyptic vision, its mode of interpretation, as well as its narrative schematization. The technical construct I coined to mark this phenomenon in the above text was *apocalyptic inscription*.

In Boehme's discourse the presentative aspect of apocalyptic is mastered when apocalypse is not simply satisfied to present divine secrets, but operates on the assumption that these secrets can be explained, and are in fact explained. Relatedly, Boehme's discourse corresponds to general apocalyptic interpretation in viewing the wrestling of interpretation with the biblical text as issuing in a modality of perspicuity not possible on the first level. Boehme's discourse departs from apocalyptic, however, in its aim, which is nothing less than an exhaustive and final illumination of reality. The deep things of God—the Great Mystery (*mysterium magnum*) that is the root of all things, the 'being of beings' (*Wesen des Wesens*)—are revealable. And this is so even with respect to the Unground, which if it is in one sense the limit of intelligibility and discourse, in another sense it is their condition, at least to the extent to which Boehme sees already in the Unground the thrust toward manifestation.

Crucially, on the level of narrative content and structure, Boehme's revelatory discourse masters first- and second-order apocalyptic. Boehme's metaleptic narrative dictates the terms for the interpretation of the agon between good and evil so important to first-order apocalyptic by determining its appropriate site and meaning. Boehme's metaleptic narrative also sets the terms for the figuration of the Lamb and Jerusalem, as well as the relation between providence and eschatology. In short texts such as *Mysterium Pansophicum*, and long texts such as the *De Electione Gratiae*, the ultimate site of agon is not cosmic, but truly eternal.

Moreover, the vertical spacing of Boehme's apocalypse discourse radicalizes the split between the mythic and historical dimensions of agon, making the latter the mere symbol of the former. Within the dynamics of Boehme's narrative Revelation's complex figuration of the Lamb is simplified with the intention of holding on to the numinous quality of Christ without commitment to apocalyptic wrath and judgment (Revelation 14.10–12; 16.7). While, as we have seen in Part II, both the Spiritual Reformers and the late medieval mystical traditions may very well have played a role in this deemphasis, narratively it is the distributing of harshness to the First Principle and mercy to the Second that is responsible for trimming wrath from Christ, who is associated exclusively with the Second Principle, the Principle of Mercy. The figuration of the Lamb is also, of course, central to Boehme's perception of the agon at the level of eternity in which the divine goes down to death only to appropriate it as fuel for life. What is the victory of the Lamb over the forces of iniquity in Revelation in Boehme's narrative discourse becomes the death of death and the depotentiation of chaotic energy that is the basis of divine form and life.

In Boehme's narrative the alteration of the figuration of Jerusalem is more subtle, if no less definite. Boehme's form of apocalypse preserves apocalyptic's sense of Jerusalem being a doxological community. Yet the alterity of this doxological community, indicated in Revelation by bridal imagery (Revelation 19.7–10; 21.9ff.) is undercut in a number of different ways. The realization of a heavenly paradise is closely, even intrinsically, tied to Sophia and her vicissitudes throughout the dramatic and traumatic development of the first two Principles. Jerusalem—a symbol of hope and of divine gratuitousness in Revelation—is transformed into a symbol of divine reintegration of fullness that is truly fullness for the first time. Moreover, the heavenly Jerusalem does not simply reflect gloriously on the divine in terms of power and intention, but establishes an authentic condition of divine self-representation. For the heavenly Jerusalem is the transparent mirror of the totality of divine imaging that reflects the divine to itself.

Finally, as assimilated into Boehme's apocalypse discourse, relations be-tween divine providence and eschatology that pertain in apocalyptic undergo some fundamental changes. While in biblical apocalyptic, and its second-order Joachimite interpretation, there is a correlation between divine intention before the foundation of the world and the eschatological realization of Jerusalem, these are wondrous facts that cannot be admitted into an explanatory circuit. In apocalyptic the construction of Jerusalem, predicated on the paschal mystery, is not teleological; rather, the construction is founded on the irruption or inter-ruption of the ordinary dynamics of history from the divine outside of history.[21] By contrast, within Boehme's metanarrative divine intention and the constitu-tion of the "heavenly Eve" are teleological through and through. The perfect correspondence between divine intention and heavenly community is actual-ized by a teleological narrative that has one of its indispensable way stations the suffering and death of Christ.

But it is not simply the case that first-order apocalyptic gets inscribed in a distinctly different apocalypse milieu, such is also the case with second-order Joachimite apocalyptic. Since I have spoken in some detail already on the dif-ference between Boehmian and Joachimite forms of apocalypse, it simply remains to indicate in a shorthand fashion the ways in which the former mas-ters the latter in terms of (1) vision, (2) mode of interpretation of Scripture, and (3) narrative content and structure.

(1) The vision of the Boehmian genre of apocalypse masters that of Joachim to the extent that both (a) the exteriority and exceptionality of pneu-matic vision is mastered by *Verstand* as a transconceptual form of knowing and (b) the soteriological focus of Joachim is displaced by a speculative focus that thinks of the subject of redemption as at least as much the divine as an alien humanity. One important result of this—and one with particular conse-quences for German Idealism—is that speculative thought and theodicy are inextricably linked.

(2) The interpretive scheme of the Boehmian genre of apocalypse mas-ters the openness-closure dialectic of Joachimite apocalyptic to the extent that in loosening the fit between intratextuality and allegorical interpretation it prioritizes the latter to the point of generating a master discourse of which Scripture and *Naturphilosophie* are regional specifications. Allegory functions, therefore, invidiously with respect to the authority of Scripture in a way it does not in the works of Joachim. Indeed, one can see clearly that despite the en-gagement with the biblical text its authority is in the process of being sy-phoned off into the explanatory text that articulates the narrative truth to which the biblical text only gestured.

(3) Finally, and most importantly, the Boehmian genre of apocalypse mas-ters Joachimite apocalyptic on the level of narrative content and structure. It does the former by adding an eschatological theology of history to a massive

narrative program that focuses on divine archeology and the eternal to an extent not even hinted at in Joachim. The eschatological theology of history functions like a giant parenthesis within a narrative that privileges the eternal alpha and omega. Needless to say, the critical hinge of the inscribing of second-order Joachimite apocalyptic by a distinctive apocalypse form is the mastering of Joachimite narrative, focused in a trinitarian elaboration of Kingdoms, by a non-Joachimite narrative form, also trinitarianly elaborated. Stretching across a terrain that includes eternity as well as time, Boehme's trinitarian narrative elaboration includes Joachim's theology of history as a trace in the third of the three Kingdoms. At the same time, Boehme's trinitarian proposal manages to fundamentally subvert the immanent Trinity-economic Trinity distinction that serves as the presumptive background for Joachim,[22] even as it emends the traditional view of the coinherence of divine persons in the acts of creation, redemption, and sanctification. In this massive departure from the tradition, Joachim's own emendation is localized and relativized.

I see, then, a double inscription of apocalyptic in operation in Boehme's discourse to the extent that this discourse gives evidence of inclusion and mastery of both first- and second-order apocalyptic. *Inscription* refers in the main to the way in which apocalyptic discourse is written into and incised on a more inclusive nonapocalyptic form of apocalypse. As inscribed into a host nonapocalyptic apocalypse form, apocalyptic's general view of vision, its understanding of interpretation, and its narrative emphasis can come to serve purposes they do not serve within their own contexts. But the question might be asked whether the inscribed apocalyptic discourses have any effect on the inscribing apocalypse discourse. Here I recall the construct, correlative to apocalyptic inscription, of which I spoke at some length in *Gnostic Return in Modernity*—that is, the construct of *apocalyptic distention*. With the Neoplatonic cipher of *distentio* very much to the fore,[23] apocalyptic distention refers to the complex operation in which the aesthetic or iconic horizon of nonapocalyptic vision is reinforced by apocalyptic, and in which interpretation is once again opened up in practice, if not in principle. But above all it refers to the extension of the narrative line of the inscribing apocalypse form along the lowest of its levels—that is, the level of cosmos, time, and history, with the consequence of modifying implied negative judgments with respect to them.

All three elements of apocalyptic distention I spoke of in *Gnostic Return in Modernity* appear to be in operation in Boehme's apocalypse discourse. Of the three it is the horizontalization of narrative that is the most important and conspicuous element of distention. Accordingly, it will receive the bulk of my attention. Still, I should not undersell the aesthetic and interpretive distention of Boehmian apocalypse by apocalyptic. Here combining, for the sake of dispatch first- and second-order apocalyptic, it is evident that the iconic horizon of apocalyptic helps considerably in articulating a commitment to a divine of form that is the correlative of vision.[24] One might even say that the inscribed apocalyptic facilitates opposition to anti-aesthetic renditions of the divine as immanifest, inexpressive as well as inexpressible, and aids in the deconstitution of apophatic theology that I discussed in some detail in chapter 2.

Again, running together first- and second-order apocalyptic, it could be said that apocalyptic's dialectic of closure and openendedness in interpretation exercises influence on the inscribing apocalypse form despite Boehme's pansophistic ambitions to bring all of reality to perfect illumination. For on the basis of treating again and again the same conundra of origin of manifestation and evil in successive texts, and even in the same text, for example, *Mysterium Magnum*, Boehme appears to recognize that in fact, if again not in principle, second-level perspicuity is neither exhaustive nor final.

Centrally, however, as it operates in Boehme's discourse, apocalyptic distention refers to the extension of a nonapocalyptic narrative along its lowest—that is, noneternal axis. The very expansiveness of Boehme's treatment of cosmos, time and history, and eschaton moderates what is clearly the major structural emphasis of Boehme's narrative—that is, divine self-constitution at the level of eternity. The very expansiveness of the treatment of world, time and history suggests that their status might be more than that of mere parenthesis. Focusing for the moment on the relation between the trinitarian forms of apocalypse in Joachim and Boehme, one could say that if Joachim's trinitarian theology of history is inscribed in Boehme's narrative trinitarian figuration, and so is marked by its theogonic drift, the inscribed trinitarianism of Joachim exercises a reflexive effect. Specifically, it affects, and maybe even, effects the validating of history, that accompanies the valorization of the eternal.

In addition, to the extent that in Boehme's narrative the cosmos is permitted to serve as the backdrop of a dramatic history whose outcome is about to be revealed, the inscription of Joachim's second-order apocalyptic serves to modify a view of the cosmos as fall. The revaluation of time, history, and cosmos, is, of course, not without ambiguity. One can construe the limitation on negative evaluation exercised by apocalyptic as suggesting, as Hegel will later, that cosmos, time, and history are good to the extent that they contribute to the erotic constitution of the divine.[25] Or one can construe the limitation as reintroducing an agapaic dimension to ontotheological narrative that seemed to be ruled out by the account of divine constitution on the level of eternity. On the reading I have offered of Boehme, there are good reasons for thinking that his narrative is the tension between both, with erotic constitution being decisive in the final analysis.

In passing, it could be said that the discursive phenomenon of apocalyptic distention of a nonapocalyptic metanarrative may go some way toward answering the question, What is it about Boehme's visionary narrative that would encourage an apocalyptic labeling provided by such intelligent readers of Boehme as de Lubac and Altizer? One could hypothesize that while the presence of second-order apocalyptic is rightly noted, it is not seen properly as merely distending a nonapocalyptic narrative that serves as the inscribing, and thus regulative, narrative form.

For systematic reasons it is important to keep in mind that apocalyptic distention is correlative to apocalyptic inscription rather than the other way around. It is by being introduced into, and being mastered by, a nonapocalyptic visionary narrative discourse that inscribed apocalyptic can distend, talk back as it were, and have a measure of influence on the inscribing apocalypse discourse. The proper name of the inscribing apocalypse discourse is Valentinianism, although in the modern field we have to think of a form of Valentinianism much more open to apocalyptic than the classical genres were. That apocalyptic inscription is a possibility of Valentinian narrative grammar is an inference made on the basis of my discovery in *Gnostic Return in Modernity* (chapters 3 and 4) of a surprising lack of exclusion of apocalyptic from the classical Valentinian narrative genres. To the extent, therefore, that Boehme is viewed as the point of departure in the modern field for the articulation of Valentinian narratives, he is also the point of origin of a phenomenon of apocalyptic inscription that at once validates apocalyptic and intradiscursively demonstrates Valentinianism's power over it. In later volumes on Gnostic return in Romanticism and German Idealism, I will show how this phenomenon is at play in Blake, Hegel, and Schelling, all of whom hark back to Boehme as precursor.

To sum up, I have made it clear that the presence of apocalyptic elements both of the first- and second-order kind are real. Any rendering of Boehme's discourse that claims to be explanatory must take account of them. At the same time, I showed how crucial elements of Boehme's discourse were not explained by apocalyptic, and that apocalyptic does not provide the most adequate taxon for Boehme's discourse. This did not, however, disqualify apocalyptic from playing the role of taxonomic supplement to Valentinianism. Apocalyptic functions as such a supplement to the extent that it points to elements in Boehme's discourse that have migrated from apocalyptic and are exercising some measure of effect on a narrative discourse whose grammar seems different from that of apocalyptic. Put theoretically, apocalyptic functions as a taxonomic supplement to the extent that Boehme's discourse shows evidence of apocalyptic inscription and apocalyptic distention. Of course, this means that to some extent at least, apocalyptic—and such will also be the case with Neoplatonism and Kabbalah—plays a role in establishing the specific difference between Boehme's narrative discourse and classical Valentinian genres—in fact, plays a role in Boehme's rule-governed deformation of classical Valentinian genres.

Needless to say, to the extent that Boehme is viewed as a plausible candidate for Gnostic or Valentinian return, this analysis has genealogical implications. The interpreter becomes primed to think that the other discourses in the ontotheological narrative line opened up by Boehme, and that display a similar metaleptic relation to biblical narrative, may also exhibit this feature of enlisting a non-Valentinian narrative discourse for a Valentinian purpose. As a matter of fact, I will make such a claim in later volumes where I will consider the discourses of Hegel, Schelling, Blake, Altizer, and others. But, of course, matters might be even more complicated. For it could be the case in Boehme's discourse that apocalyptic is not the only non-Valentinian discourse enlisted. There might be others. In the next two chapters (which fill out the narrative complexity of Boehme's discourse), I will deal with two other non-Valentinian narrative discourses enlisted in and by a narrative that is basically Valentinian in orientation. I am referring to Neoplatonism and the Kabbalah. The complexity of Boehme's narrative discourse, and the complications of the relation between enlisting and enlisted narrative again are both genealogically relevant. They provide a prototype of what we might expect in later Romantic, Idealist, and post-Romantic and post-Idealist discourses, which we have no reason to expect are simpler in complexion and operation than that exhibited by the simple shoemaker from Gorlitz, Jacob Boehme.

CHAPTER 8

❦

Neoplatonism in Boehme's Discourse
and its Valentinian Enlisting

Despite the lack of strong Neoplatonic readings of Boehme, and the absence of
anything like Neoplatonic self-ascription in his texts, Neoplatonism ought to
be taken seriously as a plausible taxon of Boehme's ontotheological narrative
discourse. It is implied in the genealogical suggestions of Baur and Staudenmaier,[1] suggested in the strong Neoplatonic readings proposed with respect to
Paracelsian alchemy,[2] which provides, as I showed in chapter 2, one of the main
discursive conditions for Boehme's thought, and is indicated by Boehme's texts
inhabiting the discourse of negative theology with its deeply Neoplatonic assumptions. In addition, and more importantly, there is strong textual evidence
of association with Neoplatonic patterns of thought. Thematically, the rendering in Boehme's texts of the split between the divine as mystery and the divine
as manifest, the positive view of the movement from one to the other, the differentiation of planes of manifestation, transcosmic and eternal, on the one
hand, and cosmic and temporal, on the other, their mimetic relation, and the
understanding of the circuit of manifestation as completed by the divine re-
turning to the point of origin, appear on the surface to be Neoplatonic recalls.
    Such is also the case with Boehme's view that the entire ontotheological
narrative is the object of vision, which is nonratiocinatively intellectual, his view
that the object of vision is itself an intellectual reality,[3] and his view that evil
somehow is a function of the system of manifestation. Reinforcing these material continuities are continuities of a linguistic and hermeneutical kind.
Boehme's discourse proceeds by referring to the absolute divine "before" manifestation by means of apophatic and kataphatic terms that recall Neoplatonism.
The language of "superessentiality," "being of beings," and "nothing" belong to a
common Neoplatonic repetoire, as does "root," "ground," "unity," and "coincidence of opposites." And hermeneutically, one can think of Boehme's commitment to allegory as having a Neoplatonic precedent, for allegory is the
interpretive means of choice in both classical and Christian Neoplatonism.[4]

Despite the scholarly intimations of affinity between Boehme and Neoplatonism, and the real presence of Neoplatonic features in Boehme's texts, however, I want to suggest that Neoplatonism can be sustained neither as an exclusive nor primary taxon of Boehme's visionary narrative discourse. I say this with the proviso, however, that no more than in the case of apocalyptic do these denials disbar Neoplatonism from playing a supplemental taxonomic role. As will become clear, however, it matters significantly whether the claim is that Neoplatonism is required as a taxonomic supplement simply because the primary taxon—that is, Valentinianism—explains most but not all elements of Boehme's discourse, or whether the claim is that Neoplatonism picks out an identifiable strand in Boehme's discourse that is dominated and regulated by Valentinianism in the final analysis. My shorthand way of making this distinction is that in the first case Neoplatonism functions as a principled taxonomic supplement, in the second case Neoplatonism functions as a merely factual or pragmatic supplement.

One final procedural point before I begin my construction of the best possible case for—and defeat of—a Neoplatonic reading of Boehme's discourse and a Neoplatonic taxonomic supplement of a principled kind. In order to avoid Neoplatonism functioning as ahistorical abstraction, I will specify it by marking three distinct types that get mentioned for comparison purposes when either Boehme's discourse or discourses putatively in his line come in for discussion. As outlined in *Gnostic Return in Modernity* these three types, which correspond roughly to ancient, medieval, and protomodern species respectively, are (1) classical Neoplatonism as exemplified in the works of Plotinus and Proclus, (2) Christian Neoplatonism, especially of the Dionysian line through Eriugena to Eckhart, and (3) Renaissance Neoplatonism intimated in Nicholas of Cusa and realized in Bruno. With these various procedural points in place, I can now commence my analysis.

I believe Boehme's deconstitution of negative theology, which I outlined in chapter 2, represents a departure of his discourse from that of Neoplatonism of such significance so as essentially to disqualify Neoplatonic ascription. A number of swerves from the negative theology tradition touch centrally on Neoplatonism that is its primary discursive vehicle and support. Boehme's discourse, as we saw, problematizes the perfection of the immanifest, inexpressive, and inexpressible divine, and articulates an alternative that finds neither a correlative in the classical Neoplatonism of Plotinus or Proclus, nor the Christian Neoplatonism of classical negative theologians such as Pseudo-Dionysius and Eriugena.

If classical Neoplatonism can be relatively unabashed by the superlatives ascribed to the immanifest first principle, while taking care to affirm theophany, Christian Neoplatonism's eulogy of the superessential Godhead permits only as much superlative as is consistent with divine manifestation that is a keynote of the biblical narrative. Therefore, in the case of classical Neoplatonism and the Christian Neoplatonic tradition until the thirteenth century, there are constraints on *apophasis*. Arguably, these constraints are put out of action, for instance, in Eckhart's discourse, which seems to provide the version of negative theology that is most urgently recalled in Boehme's discourse, albeit recalled only to be resisted and subverted.

Importantly, the constraints in place in classical Neoplatonism and Christian Neoplatonism to prevent vitiating manifestation do not reflect negatively on the incorrigible perfection of the transcendent divine in terms of being, knowledge, existence, and value. The anarchic perfection of the apophatic divine is not disturbed by the theophany exigence. A perfect example of the functional complementarity of apophasis and kataphasis is provided by a Christian Neoplatonist such as Eriugena who, after exhausting the entire battery of apophatic superlatives with respect to the Godhead including that of "nothing," insists in Book 1 of *De Divisione Naturae* on the theophanic component: manifestation is essential to the definition of the divine on the grounds that one of the roots of the word *theos* is *theo* meaning "to flow." An equally good example of the functional complementarity is provided by the Renaissance Neoplatonist Bruno, who gets associated in Blumenberg's mind in positive and negative ways with Boehme.[5] Bruno does not hesitate to avail himself of the apophatic cornucopia of Neoplatonism,[6] yet the kataphatic complement is splendidly in evidence. Bruno insists, even more than Eriugena, that the divine declares its divinity in its manifestation, which has its focus in the material world that Bruno refuses to derogate with the adjective "finite."

In questioning the perfection of the anarchic divine, Boehme is denying an attribution that in Neoplatonism is omnidimensional in principle, and multidimensional in fact. For classical Neoplatonism the immanifest divine unity is the really real (*ontos on*). It is also the normative form of knowing that operates outside the subject-object split. The immanifest divine unity is also the true good,[7] and a zone of beatific experience that once again is unsurpassable,[8] yet normative for all reality subsequent to—and consequent to—divine unity. Boehme's discourse should be understood essentially to question, therefore, Neoplatonic attribution of perfection in its ontological, gnoseological, axiological, and existential registers. The articulation of Boehme's narrative makes it clear, as we saw in Parts I and II, that (1) the immanifest, inexpressive, and inexpressible divine is not the really real, that (2) the noetic undifferentiation of the divine is a form of knowing inferior to the form of knowing that supposes differentiation (*Schiedlichkeit*), that (3) the goodness of the immanifest divine is inadequate by dint of not displaying its power against evil, and that (4) divine beatitude is less than the greatest that can be thought by not breaking through the circle of self-reference.

Questioning Neoplatonic estimation of the immanifest divine also implies a questioning of the Neoplatonic understanding of manifestation or theophany. In Boehme's discourse, manifestation (*Offenbarung*) is affirmed in a way that disturbs the balance of affirmation between mystery and manifestation that is a mark of almost all species of Neoplatonic discourse with the possible exception of its Eckhartian form. The cause of manifestation is taken up at the expense of the mystery of the divine that is hidden (*Verborgenheit*), nameless (*ohne Namen*), and inexpressible (*unaussprechlich*). This in turn involves revising the meaning of the superlative German *über* (equivalent to the Greek, *hyper*) from a positive to a negative, and relocating perfection in the milieu of manifestation, which no longer functions as the sign of a given perfection, but as an anticipation and participation in a perfection that is to be gained.

Another way of getting at the difference in the understanding of the relation between the immanifest and manifest aspects of the divine between texts of Boehme such as *Mysterium Magnum* and Neoplatonic texts such as Plotinus's *Enneads* and Eriugena's *De Divisione Naturae*, for example, is to think of differences in the fundamentally 'aesthetic' representation of the movement of manifestation. Both Boehmian and Neoplatonic texts provide aesthetic representations in the sense that they offer holistic accounts of the relation between the systematic order of divine appearance and its Ground or Unground. A crucial difference, however, sets them apart. In Neoplatonic texts, the presentation of the *Gestalt*, or systematic order of divine manifestation, pushes to the border of explanation without fully entering its domain. This is the case, for example, with Eriugena,[9] whom Staudenmaier thought to represent a cure for Hegel and the theogonic trajectory of modern thought. In contrast, in Boehme's texts the presentation of *Gestalt* has a decidedly explanatory edge. Boehme's discourse tries to offer answers to such questions as, Why something rather than nothing? Why evil? Why manifestation?

Two fundamental structures of resistance to explanation in the above varieties of Neoplatonism are dismantled within Boehme's discourse. First, in every variety of Neoplatonism, the metaphor of diffusion—which is a metaphor of metaphors—despite its naturalistic suggestion, underscores, if not underwrites, the noncompulsiveness of divine manifestation. In Boehme's discourse, by contrast, the dynamic of manifestation has, as I have shown, more than a few notes of compulsion. Second, in describing the move from mystery to manifestation, the language of necessity in Neoplatonism is not only supplemented by the language of will,[10] but also the type of necessity is more nearly the aesthetic necessity of verisimilitude than logical or ontological. In the case of Boehme's narrative, however, the movement from mystery to manifestation not only seems to be more compulsive, but also necessary in a way that has ontological and possibly even logical notes.[11]

Ultimately, as I indicated in chapter 2, what is afoot in Boehme's narrative is the displacement-replacement of Neoplatonic agapaics by erotics, which I am arguing is a possibility of Valentinian narrative grammar. It is not, of course, that eros plays no role in Neoplatonism. Historically speaking classical Neo-

platonism, most varieties of Christian Neoplatonism, and the belated Neoplatonism of the Renaissance (and particularly that of Bruno) evince a commitment to eros. But typically eros in Neoplatonism responds to the *agape* of
origin. The "fury" for transcendence within the milieu of manifestation in
Bruno, for example, responds to a divine manifestation that is total gift. This is
the position adopted by Bruno, for example, in a text such as *Eroici Furiori*,[12]
which follows the great tradition of Plotinus and Christian Neoplatonism in
this respect. Admittedly, there are moments in Neoplatonism in which eros
seems to be predicated of the absolute divine and not simply of the responsive
relative reality. In the *Divine Names* (*DN*), for example, Pseudo-Dionysius, one
of the most consistently agapaic of all Christian Neoplatonists, seems to insert
desire into the superessential divine:

> The divine longing (*eros*) is God seeking good for the sake of the Good. That
> longing which creates all the goodness of the world pre-exists superabun-
> dantly within the Good and did not allow it to remain without issue. It stirred
> him to use the abundance of his power to the production of the world (*DN* 4,
> 9, 708a–b; see also *DN* 2, 10, 648a–d).

But this would-be exception in fact proves the rule. What this passage
suggests is that divine love and goodness have an element of inclination. There
is, however, no sense of the divine being anything other than the fullness of
perfection. Certainly, there is not a hint that the divine goodness *lacks* something. Thus eros is agapaically contextualized in an absolutely fundamental way.
This contextualization of eros by *agape*, arguably, can be traced back to Proclus.
In any event it has a career in Christian Neoplatonism, is conspicuous in Eriugena, and continues to play a role in Bruno. By contrast, as described in the
texts of the mature Boehme, from the very beginning manifestation has as its
aim the realization of a merely virtual divine that is riddled with lack. The differences, then, between Boehme's discourse and that of classical and Christian
Neoplatonism, and even between Boehme's discourse and that of a Neoplatonism of a Brunan type, are elucidatable in part, at least, by Balthasar's distinction
between a "theological aesthetic" and an "aesthetic theology." That is, the differences between Boehme's discourse and that of Neoplatonism is illuminated
by the contrast between (1) a holistic view of the relation between divine mystery and manifestation, in which faithful description rather than explanation is
dominant, and in which narrative movement is interpreted in terms of *agape*
(Neoplatonism) and (2) a holistic view of relation between divine mystery and
manifestation that gets parsed in an explanatory manner and in which the
movement of manifestation is understood as a movement of eros (Boehme).

Thinking of Bruno in particular as a Neoplatonic comparandum for
Boehme's narrative leads naturally to reflection on the different function of

kenosis in both Neoplatonic and Boehmian narrative schemes. In the case of Bruno's Neoplatonic discourse, the *principle of plenitude*[13] works so unrestrictedly that the divine manifests itself totally without reserve.[14] In a passage in *De l'infinito universo e mundi*, the principle, which is nothing less than the radicalization of the Platonic trope of 'God is not envious,' finds classic expression:

> Why should we, or could we, imagine that divine power were otiose? Divine goodness can indeed be communicated to infinite things and be infinitely diffused; why then should we wish to assert that it should choose to be scarce—and to reduce itself to nought—why do you desire that it should remain grudgingly sterile? Why should you prefer that it should be less, or by no means communicated, rather than that it should fulfill the scheme of its glorious power and being?[15]

The divine empties itself completely into the world *as* the world. As is well known, such a kenotic view was deemed dangerous to Christianity in a context in which reserve in manifestation is understood to be a condition of divine transcendence. But from a narrative point of view, Brunan kenosis is fundamentally dangerous to Christianity, if and only if kenosis implies an ontological rather than an aesthetic mode of necessity. And while Bruno certainly heads in the former direction, the mode of necessity of kenosis embraced is finally, I would argue, more nearly aesthetic. By contrast, in Boehme kenosis is unequivocally ontological. What is more (as I suggested in chapter 2), kenosis proceeds ironically. For the emptying of the Unground into the Quaternity, and its emptying into the two Principles is an emptying that is in the process of gaining the very sufficiency presupposed of the operation of kenosis within a Neoplatonic environment.

Kenosis in the Brunan form of Neoplatonism, no less than in classical and Christian Neoplatonism, supposes a given pleromatic divine. It is not itself the process of overcoming the lack of perfection. More technically put, kenosis in Bruno's texts is not ultimately the process of plerosis, as is clearly the case in Boehme's texts. Together with the dominance of eros, the peculiarity of kenosis in Boehme's narrative determines that this form of post-Reformation ontotheological narrative does not instantiate an ontotheological narrative of pure return to origin typical of Neoplatonism. Eros and the operation of kenosis dictate that there is an excess of end over origin.

Differences between Boehme and Neoplatonism in the understanding of kenosis relate to differences in envisaging the modality of differentiation presupposed in manifestation. Bruno, for instance, is typically Neoplatonic in thinking that the emptying of the divine brings about an order of reality different from, but nonetheless similar to, its origin. Differentiation, then, operates in terms of likeness. And while Bruno's scheme of differentiation is in general

considerably more simple than that found in Proclus, for example, it is continuous with classical Neoplatonism and medieval varieties of Christian Neoplatonism, at least to the extent that radical dissimilarity appears only at the limit
of the narrative of divine manifestation.[16] In Boehme's discourse, on the contrary, only at initial levels of manifestation that pertain to the Quaternity does
differentiation function by similitude. At the truly real level of the eternal principles, there is contradiction between manifesting source and manifesting
medium. This means that Boehme sets down very different conditions for differentiation than Neoplatonism. For him, in contrast to all three narrative
species of Neoplatonism under discussion, and not simply the belated Renaissance variety of Bruno, manifestation cannot proceed without the opening up
of radical difference that functions to block manifestation.

In divine self-manifestation or communication, therefore, the emergence
of dissimilarity serves as the means to the realization of the greatest likeness between the divine and its expression. Put most simply, theophany in Boehme's
discourse is *dramatic* in a way that it is not in the Neoplatonic scheme of things.
Indeed, one could say that in Boehme's discourse theophany is *hysterical* (Greek
hysteria) insofar as it suggests the tear in manifestation that is necessary if manifestation is to occur. As I suggested in chapter 1, in Boehme 'doubling' is the
necessary condition of manifestation, but contrariety (*contrarium*) is the sufficient condition for fully-wrought divine self-manifestation.

Interesting consequences follow from the difference in the order of differentiation. Boehme's dramatic and hysterical view of manifestation places the
focus of divine manifestation in a different place than Neoplatonic narratives. If
the focus in Christian Neoplatonism is on the intradivine Trinity as the presupposition of expression, in Boehme manifestation has a real center and pivot in
the struggle of the two Principles that is subsequent to divine self-manifestation
in the Trinity and in Wisdom. The Principles in which differentiation is focused
are, however, indissolubly related. In particular, the Second Principle narratively
depends on the First. This, of course, involves, as suggested in our discussion of
the relation between Boehme and Eckhart, that common binary oppositions of
symbols such as dark and light, blindness and insight, aphasia and speech, etheriality and massiveness, nothing and something, death and life, and so forth, that
are structural in Neoplatonic narrative are narrativized in Boehme.

One could say that in a certain sense, Boehme superimposes on the Neoplatonic focus on manifestation (*proodos*) the Neoplatonic focus of conversion
(*epistrophe*) from time to eternity that comes much later in Neoplatonic narrative. What facilitates the dramatic centering of narrative, and to an extent the
superimposition of conversion on manifestation dynamics is, obviously,
Boehme's Christianity, and above all his subscription to Luther's theology of
the Cross. That a dramatic, agonistic view of manifestation is not a feature in
Neoplatonism, even in Christian Neoplatonism, is made perfectly evident in

Eriugena's *De Divisione Naturae* (Book 4), whose narrative in common with classical Neoplatonism has different centers for manifestation and return, with Christ functioning in the second and not in the first center. As an agent of conversion, Christ confirms the difference in the pattern of differentiation underlying Neoplatonic and Boehmian discourse. For Christ is the one who moves us from the limit of unlikeness, which is associated with matter and time, into the order of likeness, which is hierarchical, calibrated, and ultimately without gaps. In Boehme, by contrast, Christ is the pivot of manifestation and return. Even more relevantly, Christ is the hiatus, the tear in manifestation necessary for its real possibility, the tear that is death and the death of death.

Differences between Boehmian and Neoplatonic narrative in their respective understandings of eros, kenosis, and now in the modality of differentiation underlying manifestation, speak to a difference in theodicy configuration. Typically, the aesthetic holism of Neoplatonism encourages the perception that what might not be justified in the case of the particular is justified in terms of the whole.[17] In the *Enneads* this has something of the force of a prescription (8.2). Aesthetic holism is, of course, classical Neoplatonism's specific rendition of enjoining us to view the world *sub specie aeternitatis*, which is common to a host of Hellenistic discourses and especially prominent in Stoicism. This general contribution toward exonerating the divine from blame with respect to what is perceived as evil in the cosmos is supported by a metaphysics in which what is evil is understood as nonbeing, precisely to the extent that it represents the limit of manifestation. Of course, the derogation of the particular, which is a consequence of aesthetic holism in Neoplatonism, is modified almost from the beginning. Already in Plotinus, and exemplarily in Proclus,[18] providence affords some validation of the particular as such. The qualification is even more urgent in Christian Neoplatonism, where pressure is felt from the side of Scripture to think of the divine as with us in such an excess of love that our mean particularity is no objection to God's unique concern. Among other Christian Neoplatonists, Eriugena tries to articulate a view of providence that reaches down to the particular, thereby helping to remove accusations against the divine. And if one can cut through his feverish rhetoric, so does Bruno at the dawn of the modern age. The following example from *The Expulsion of the Triumphant Beast* (*Spaccio de la bestia trionfante*) could be multiplied from Bruno's texts: "Jove provides for all things in all places, just as being and unity are necessarily found in all numbers, in all places and all times and atoms of time, and the only principle of being is in infinite individuals who were, are, and will be."[19]

While it shares some important features with Neoplatonism, Boehme's theodicy program ultimately differs from it. Although Boehme's pansophism also elaborates a form of aesthetic holism, Boehme does not marginalize evil by making it only a limit or liminal reality. For him, evil, or better its possibility, is a pivotal divine reality. At the center there is a cleft, a "fell," a fall in manifestation.[20] And if in one sense, as the First Principle or Eternal Nature, evil is nothing or *meon*, in another sense evil is an exigent and virulent something (*Ichts*). Boehme, therefore, refuses the strategy of meontological exculpation that is typical of Neoplatonic narratives. Indeed, to the extent that the First Principle or Eternal Nature is a form of will, the divine gets meontologically implicated in the generation of evil, at least with respect to its Ground.

For Boehme, however, the distinction between the Ground of Evil and its actualization is important, for it enables him to say that God as such is good, because God is not only other than the Ground, but is the process of development whereby the (me)ontological exigence of the Ground is assimilated without actualizing it. Boehme attempts to square his view of the generation of the Ground of Evil and its depotentiation with the biblical narrative by insisting that it is only finite beings (e.g., Lucifer, Adam, Cain) who actualize evil potency. While it might be thought that this squaring is a nonunique feature of Boehme's thought, given that Christian Neoplatonism, as Ricoeur has pointed out, also consistently tries to square the meontological constitution of evil and the biblical narrative,[21] at best there is only an analogy between the two schemes. In Christian Neoplatonism the issue is that of relating the exercise of an originary freedom to a metaphysical result, which is thought to be privative with respect to the normative order of reality. In the case of Boehme, however, the issue is that of relating finite acts of freedom to a Ground of Evil that is originary.

Ultimately, of course, all differences in theodicy orientation reside in an infrastructural narrative difference. In Neoplatonism, the narrative, which is the object of vision, does not require evil as the explanation for the divine manifestation but for its limits. By contrast, in Boehme's ontotheological narrative, evil, or its ground, is required as an explanation for divine manifestation. Evil, or its ground, is, therefore, speculatively justified by presenting the ineluctable narrative conditions of the divine. And here speculative has to be understood more or less literally—that is, as suggesting that if the divine is to have authentic self-reflection, evil is in a sense the tain in the mirror that makes reflection, and thus divine self-presence, possible.

A final important differential between Boehmian and Neoplatonic narratives centers on their respective metaleptic potency. Since metalepsis is defined as a disfiguration-refiguration of biblical narrative, or any first-order rendition of it, obviously only Christian Neoplatonism is a proper object of comparison. Again while the level of swerve in a Christian Neoplatonist like Eriugena from the Christian tradition normed by the biblical narrative has been, and continues to be, a point in dispute, there can be little doubt that the great orchestration of theophany in *De Divisione Naturae* puts more standard theological renditions of the biblical narrative under stress. Certainly, traces remain of the Dionysian ambiguity about whether a unitary superessential

Godhead is ultimate or whether the sublime mystery of the Trinity is foundational for all finite existence. Again, if Eriugena insists, after Genesis, on the created status of the physical world and its fundamental goodness, created being, nevertheless, bears such a close relation to the uncreated archetypes (Book 2) that it puts under pressure the more stringent interpretation of creation as marking the unbridgeable difference between the divine and the nondivine. In addition, as Book 4 of *De Divisione Naturae* shows clearly, Eriugena's Christology is quintessentially exemplarist and docetic. And finally, Eriugena's theological anthropology is exceptionally high. Human being is archeologically and eschatologically *microtheos* as well as *microcosmos* (Book 5), and the divinization of human being is at the same time the divinization of the world.

It should be granted, therefore, that the level of swerve from standard Christian construal is significant in Eriugena's particular rendition of the Neoplatonic exit-return model. But in light of our discussion in Part II of both nondistinctive and distinctive swerves in Boehme's discourse, as well as the connection between the latter and metalepsis in the strict sense, it is evident that the level of swerve does not come up to the level displayed in Boehme's discourse. Indeed, it could be said that it falls well below the level of Eckhart, and barely comes up the level of the Spiritual Reformers, who were Boehme's post-Reformation predecessors. Certainly, there is nothing like the systematic rereading of the biblical narrative, which I demonstrated in Part II to be the hallmark of Boehme's pansophistic project, and which affects not only all episodes of the biblical narrative, but their relations to each other, and crucially, of course, the narrative dynamism that determines in significant part the meaning of the narrative whole.

Arguably, it is Bruno's belated form of Neoplatonism that provides an example in Neoplatonism of a level of swerve that suggests that metalepsis might be in operation. Bruno thinks of the Trinity as a secondary construction.[22] He considers the physical universe to be not only an expression of the divine, but also an expression essentially of the same order as the Son. In addition, in his texts the role of Christ is impoverished even by comparison with the exemplarist schemes of Eriugena and Cusa[23] of *De Docta Ignorantia* (Part III) and *De Visione Dei*. Christ is but one of a number of religious heros[24] not the real and ultimate symbol of participation in the divine. And finally, Bruno's anthropology demonstrates a predilection toward blurring the differences between the divine and the human, and marks, as both Blumenberg and von Balthasar underscore, a promethean escalation.[25]

The swerves from the common tradition evident in Bruno's texts are, obviously, both multiple and deep. Yet this does not necessarily mean that we are dealing with metalepsis in the strict sense. The issue rests on whether Bruno's narrative, with its exaggerated emphasis on manifestation thrust, nonsystematically interferes with the biblical narrative or represents its intentioned systematic disfiguration-refiguration. The evidence suggests that it is the former rather than the latter that more accurately characterizes Bruno's position.

Bruno is cavalier with the biblical narrative, but supports it when he can. This suggests a lack of deep interest in the claims of the biblical narrative that is a feature of the metaleptic attitude, for a powerful subversion is coordinate to powerful recall. This is not to say that his subversion of the biblical narrative is less interesting than that enacted in Boehme's discourse, nor even to deny that this discourse has its own important history of effects that are worth tracing. It is to say, however, that if we think of classical Valentinianism as providing the template for metalepsis, then it is Boehme's narrative discourse with its particular kinds of swerve, and its total refiguration of the biblical narrative on a erotic, kenotic, and agonistic axis that constitutes the example of metalepsis at the dawn of the modern period. To the extent that Boehme's discourse does provide the example, I have argued that the erotic, kenotic, and agonistic complexion of his narrative does not disqualify his discourse from Valentinian attribution, even if classical Valentinian genres do not display these narrative features, or at least do not display these narrative features on their lexical surface.

8.1. Valentinian Enlisting of Neoplatonic Narrative

In this chapter I have argued the negative thesis that despite the presence of Neoplatonic elements in Boehme's metaleptic discourse, Neoplatonism does not provide an adequate taxon. This, obviously, strengthens the case for Valentinian ascription, provided one works with a grammatical understanding of Valentinianism that permits one to take account of exacerbations of the erotic, kenotic, and agonistic levels of the classical Valentinian narrative genres. But this still does not amount to a full demonstration of the validity of Valentinianism, as a taxon. For such a demonstration would necessarily involve explaining the presence of Neoplatonic as well as apocalyptic elements in the Boehme's narrative. It is possible to read the Neoplatonic elements as being relatively autonomous in Boehme's discourse. In which case Neoplatonism would function as a bone fide explanatory supplement to Valentinianism. Consequently, Valentinianism would simply account for more facets or more important facets of Boehme's complex narrative discourse than Neoplatonism.

At issue is whether Valentinianism or Valentinian narrative can account for those Neoplatonic features themselves, thus allowing a unitary characterization of Boehme's discourse, while at the same time allowing Neoplatonism to play a supplemental explanatory role of a noncompetitive type. But if one is to show that the kind of taxonomic supplementarity in question is what I called in the introduction to Part III factual supplementarity rather than supplementarity in principle, I am obliged to show that the Neoplatonic features found in

Boehme's discourse support something other than a Neoplatonic narrative program, indeed, support a Valentinian narrative program, if I am allowed my grammatical interpretation of Valentinian narrative.

Fulfilling the above obligation will occupy me throughout the rest of this chapter. As a gateway to the discussion that will show how Neoplatonic elements are used, or *enlisted*, to serve non-Neoplatonic purposes, perhaps it is worth rehearsing once again the reasons why the erotic, kenotic, and agonistic physiognomy of Boehme's metaleptic narrative is not a possibility within Neoplatonism. In line with Plotinus's fundamental act of resistance to Gnosticism in *Enneads* bk 1. 8 and bk 2. 9, the subsequent Neoplatonic tradition up to the Renaissance displayed a massive level of consistency in rejecting an erotic and agonistic construal of the divine, even as it availed itself of the language of eros to both dynamize the love of the divine and to set the condition of response. In turn, the level of consistency suggests that these features are not grammatical possibilities of Neoplatonism and specifically that any emendation of the agapaic reading of manifestation would constitute something of an interpretive *salto mortale* for Neoplatonism.

In any event, none of the prima facie Neoplatonic elements, conspicuous in Boehme's texts, are anti-Valentinian in the sense that such features cannot be found in the classical Valentinian texts. The mixture of apophatic and kataphatic language to name the divine is every bit as much a feature of the *Gospel* and the *Tractate*, as it is of the *Enneads* and *De Divisione Naturae*. And mimesis of the divine paradigms recalled in Boehme's texts is a feature of classical Valentinian texts as it is of Neoplatonic texts in general, even if the emphasis in classical Valentinian texts often falls on antimimesis or countermimesis. And the noetic or gnoseological spin on narrative, where the object as well as subject of vision is the divine as a self-reflecting reality, is not unique to Neoplatonism. It is most definitely a feature of classical Valentinian texts. The point I am making here is that to faithfully recall these features, prominent in the Neoplatonic tradition, does not necessarily force a taxonomic choice between Neoplatonism and Valentinianism.

One can go further, however, and claim that in Boehme's discourse features of the Neoplatonic dynamic of manifestation are enlisted to support a different narrative regime. In all three varieties of Neoplatonism to which I have referred, the thrust toward manifestation is urgent. Equally, in all three varieties, manifestation has an agapaic origin: manifestation is manifestation of and from a divine perfect in being, knowledge, goodness, and existence. As I indicated in my discussion of the relation between Boehme's narrative and negative theology in chapter 2, Boehme's narrative can capitalize on the Neoplatonically affirmed drive toward manifestation while underwriting the dynamic by eros. As origin, the divine, for Boehme, is not perfect in any of the parameters that classical, Christian, and Renaissance Neoplatonism insisted on. On the contrary, the divine is the process of self-perfection.

This has the obvious consequence that changes are rung on the Neoplatonic meaning of kenosis. Under the shadow of eros, kenosis is as much a filling as an emptying. In addition, within the horizon of eros kenosis functions as an agent of metalepsis with respect to the biblical narrative. While Christian Neoplatonism in its more radical emanationist forms stresses the Christian narrative, its agapaic mechanism of manifestation and communication could be counted to limit theological damage. As the dynamism of eros enlists the dynamics of diffusion, emendation of the Christian narrative becomes total. The view, for example, of the divine as trinitarian ceases to be supportable. The Trinity becomes a field of divine self-manifestation in which the movement toward perfection is rehearsed but not realized. The result is a subversion of the Trinity's foundational status and, thus, of most of the superlative claims made on its behalf, with a specific casualty being the prospect of a hypostatic interpretation of the Trinity. Hypostatic density relates to a mode of realized reality that Boehme clearly suggests is not possible at such an incipient level of divine reality. The lack that fundamentally regulates eros also effects standard Christian estimations of creation, Christ, and human being, which in Christian Neoplatonism are realities of gift and thus divine self-sufficiency. In Boehme's ontotheological narrative all these realities are fundamentally satisfactions of divine need.

At the same time, the continuity of manifestation, promoted by Neoplatonism, is also enlisted. If in Boehme's narrative manifestation proceeds discontinuously and by leaps, there is a way in which despite discontinuity and tear in the fabric of manifestation, continuity in the movement toward the kind of complete divine disclosure, supported by Neoplatonism, is preserved. Eros dictates that continuity has the last word, and this, of course, is a teleological word.

Another potentially enlistable feature—and I am suggesting actually enlisted feature—of Neoplatonic narrative is Neoplatonism's reflection on providence. In classical, medieval Christian, and Renaissance forms of Neoplatonism, providence refers to the immanence of the divine in the world and the temporal unfolding of divine presence. It is providence that confers and guarantees integrity, value, and meaning in the face of the apparent formlessness, worthlessness, and unintelligibility of a world apparently remote from the divine. In no wise, however, does providence directly confer and guarantee the integrity, value, and meaning of the divine itself, although, of course, it does so indirectly or reflexively by indicating the divine's gratuitous presence in the finite. In the context, however, of a discourse committed to an erotic figuration of narrative of divine manifestation such as Boehme's, providence becomes self-referentially tied to the systematic explication of the archeoteleological conditions of divine selfhood. Meaning, value, and intelligibility of the whole of manifestation is not only sustained despite limits to manifestation, but precisely because of them. This archeoteleological enlisting of providence, I noted in chapter 6, is a feature of the classical Valentinian text, the *Tractate*, and thus a possible feature of belated Valentinian narratives, if such exist. It is, of course, my contention that such belated Valentinian genres do exist and that Boehme's discourse represents one such genre, indeed, the originary Valentinian genre in the modern period.

But I must necessarily repeat a point I made in connection with my examination of the taxonomic credentials of apocalyptic in the previous chapter. In the context of speaking of a non-Valentinian narrative discourse being enlisted by a Valentinian narrative discourse, it is necessary to ask the question whether the enlisted non-Valentinian narrative discourse exercises what I called reflexive—but not reciprocal[26]—effect on the enlisting Valentinian discourse. Given the determination in chapter 6 that such was the case, it is antecedently likely that such also will be the case here. I want explicitly to affirm this presumption.

There are certain moments in Boehme's metaleptic discourse where there is a suggestion that eros does not triumph over *agape*, and manifestation over hiddenness. For instance, as I suggested in my discussion of orthodox latencies in Boehme's discourse in chapter 5, Temporal Nature is described as an expression of divine love that is without need. Here Neoplatonism aids and abets a position that is typical in pre-Reformation and Reformation discourses, whatever the opinion about the legitimacy of Neoplatonic discourse. And to the extent that the Unground is considered as beyond the level of divine self-manifestation that defines the intradivine Trinity and Wisdom, the movement to manifestation could also be considered as having some note of agape. In addition, to the degree that the Unground is affirmed in the typical negative theology way, hiddenness is granted something of a priority over manifestation. As in the case of apocalyptic, however, even if the reflexive effect is real, its power is not such that it seriously challenges what I am referring to as an erotic form of Valentinian narrative grammar. As I have shown in this chapter and in chapter 2, by and large eros rules agape—this is certainly true of the Unground—and manifestation triumphs over hiddenness.

To sum up then, from a taxonomic point of view, Valentinianism demonstrates its power over Neoplatonism when it is shown that the former not only accounts for more (or more important) elements of a modern ontotheological narrative, but also, one sees clearly (1) the operation by which the Neoplatonic elements of a complex discourse are assimilated into a narrative of a Valentinian complexion and (2) how Neoplatonic narrative dynamics can be made hostage to the narrative mechanism of eros. As I understand it, I have demonstrated this with respect to Boehme's metaleptic discourse. This means that in the case of Boehme's narrative, at least, Neoplatonism can play the role of factual but not principled taxonomic supplement.

This factual supplemenarity must necessarily be integrated into the revised Baurian genealogical hypothesis. If Boehme plays the pivotal role in a particular trajectory of modern narrative ontotheological discourses, as Baur and Staudenmaier, suggest he does, and if his narrative discourse has a bone fide Neoplatonic aspect, then this might help to alert us not only to the complexity of modern narrative discourses, but also provide us a clue as to their hierarchical organization. In ontotheological narrative discourses in the post-Reformation and post-Enlightenment fields that have a metaleptic bent, we might hypothesize that Neoplatonism as well as apocalyptic belong to a less basic narrative level than Valentinianism, which functions as the hegemonic narrative discourse. But even as ruled by Valentinianism, these discourses exercise effects that aid in separating these discourses from the sedimented tradition of Valentinian narratives. To make the point in another way, complex narrative discourses that appeal (directly or indirectly) to Boehme's narrative as an ancestral discourse aid and abet the process of rule-governed deformation of classical Valentinian genres, while staying within the ordinance of a Valentinian narrative grammar.

CHAPTER 9

~

Kabbalah in Boehme's Discourse and its Valentinian Enlisting

From the very beginning I have insisted that Boehme's discourse is complex. It is complex symbolically in that symbols from a multitude of pre-Reformation, Reformation, and post-Reformation sources animate it. More, it is complex in terms of a narrative structure that aligns symbols and gives them their meaning. Thus far, I have identified three major narrative strains. First among equals is obviously what I am calling the Valentinian strain. But as I have indicated, apocalyptic and Neoplatonic narrative strains are also present in Boehme's discourse. As yet, however, I have not touched on the full level of the narrative complexity of Boehme's discourse. This is not, as one might think, because I have not as yet explicitly invoked Paracelsian alchemy. For I have made clear that Boehme's discourse is the realization of Paracelsian alchemy and its Weigelian theologization. Thus Paracelsian alchemy does not name so much an element of Boehme's discourse as represent this discourse in its theologically underdeveloped form. There is one other narrative strand to be taken account of—that is, the narrative strand of the Kabbalah, whose presence is palpable in Boehme's texts, as I will demonstrate shortly.

Of course, the task I have set myself is far more complicated than drawing attention to this further narrative strand and thus filling out the picture of the narrative complexity of Boehme's discourse. Given my taxomic focus, I am compelled to ask the question whether the presence of Kabbalistic elements is so extensive and intensive that it effectively challenges the Valentinian taxon for primacy. Or failing to do this, I am compelled to ask whether it accounts for elements of Boehme's complex narrative discourse that are not, and cannot be, covered by Valentinianism.

In short, I am putting the same question to the Kabbalah that I put to apocalyptic and Neoplatonism in the two previous chapters. As it operates in Boehme's discourse, Does the Kabbalah function as a principled taxonomic supplement to the Valentinian taxon, or simply as a factual taxonomic supplement?

193

Needless to say, analysis of a narrative discourse as complex as Boehme's is itself complex, and the pursuit of a viable taxon is itself taxing. I grant that my analysis would lose much of its point if I believed that Boehme's discourse was idiosyncratic and did not prepare us to see in a different way ontotheological narratives in the modern field in Romanticism, German Idealism, and beyond. But it has been my conviction throughout that Boehme's discourse is not idiosyncratic, and that he represents nothing less than the origin of a line of narrative discourses, expressed in philosophical, theological, and literary idioms, that itself represents the return of Gnosticism or Valentinianism in modernity. But if I am right about Boehme, the Valentinian verdict can only be rendered when one has taken full account of the narrative complexity, and shown why the non-Valentinian strands not only do not involve giving up Valentinian ascription, but help us to understand better its new form, what I have been calling its rule-governed deformed form in the post-Reformation and post-Enlightenment fields. I now turn to an analysis of the presence of the Kabbalah in Boehme's complex narrative discourse and to an adjudication of its taxonomic status.

A number of factors prompt investigation of the possibility of a Kabbalistic taxonomy. There is solid historical evidence of Boehme's contact with admirers like Balthasar Walther and Abraham von Frankenberg,[1] who were familiar with the Kabbalah. Moreover, Boehme does not disdain to use the word (*TF*, 3, 34; 6, 11), although admittedly the use is tropic in the way it is in the texts of Paracelsus, where it denotes an invisible expressive form or power. In addition, there is a long interpretive tradition of asserting a strong connection. While his comments are brief in *Unparteiische Kirchen- und Ketzerhistorie* (pp. 1130–55), the Pietist Gottfried Arnold represents one of the earliest mainstream associations of Boehmian and Kabbalistic discourse. Oetinger, of course, represents the classical expression of eighteenth-century avowal, with his *Die Lehrtafel der Prinzessin Antonia* being just one of the many texts in which the connection between Boehme and the Kabbalah is argued and recommended.[2] In the early nineteenth-century Franz von Baader assumed the connection to be more or less obvious. And the tradition of interpretation lives on in the twentieth century in the work of some of the foremost commentators of Boehme, like, Benz, Koyré, Stoudt, and most recently and perhaps comprehensively, John Schulitz.[3]

While these considerations do nothing to legitimate a Kabbalistic taxonomy for a whole or significant part of Boehme's discourse, they suggest certain possibilities that should not be summarily dismissed. What I will attempt to do over the following pages is to offer the best possible case for a Kabbalistic taxon of Boehme's discourse. While, as advertised, I will eventually judge that the Kabbalah cannot function either as an exclusive taxon of Boehme's discourse, nor as a principled supplementary taxon, I hope to bring out the extent and depth of the congruence between Boehme's discourse and that of the Kabbalah by focusing on key formal and material elements of overlap. More specifically, I will focus on the formal elements of vision and interpretation as well as the more substantive material elements of overlap that concern the narrative elaboration of the divine. I begin with a brief rehearsal of the more formal elements of connection.

First, typologically, both Boehme and the Kabbalah exemplify visionary or extrospective, rather than experiential or introspective kinds of mysticism. Concretely, both Boehmian and Kabbalistic discourse are concerned with presenting the dynamic flow of a divine that moves from hiddenness to manifestation, and whose media of manifestation—that is, qualities or names—provide both the contours for a pulsating divine life as well the means of its expression. These qualities or names have an organic relation to the degree to which they are regarded as emerging from each other and have a systematic arrangement. And, finally, it is these divine media of manifestation that are at the basis of the vitality of worldly and human reality. Vision, then, has as its conspectus a dynamics of manifestation that has various levels, from a divine level as such down to the level of the physical and human world.[4]

Second, both Boehmian and Kabbalistic discourse are hermeneutical as well as visionary. Indeed, both discourses are defined by the relation between vision and hermeneutics. In both cases, vision is the goal of the interpretation of sacred texts, and interpretation is regulated by the inchoate vision of a divine spectacularly different from the divine figured by theological rationalism as serenely aloft and above the fray of finite existence. The primary form of interpretation availed of and justified is the anagogical interpretation of biblical texts (*raza-de- mehemanutha* in Kabbalah).[5] This form of interpretation transcends the literal-historical and moral interpretations of the biblical text. But it also transcends allegory, at least to the extent that allegory generates meanings equal to the rational intellect. The interpretive commitments of both discourses also support ancillary beliefs about interpretive techniques, whereby hidden symbolic meanings are released. One such vehicle is the breaking down of scriptural passages into atomic elements, letters of the Hebrew alphabet in the case of the Kabbalah (*gematria*), German phonological units in the case of Boehme. The mystical meaning of biblical phrases is determined by conjugating the value of letters or the configuration of sounds. Moreover, the level of interpretation and its esoteric techniques are related to the depths of the questions that drive exegesis. The Kabbalist seems as aware as Boehme is in *Aurora* (1612) that the problems of creation and evil are addressed in the interpretation of Scripture and, to some extent at least, they are clarified.

More important are the material or substantive theological connections between Boehmian and Kabbalistic discourse on the level of the narrative of divine manifestation. Connections have been asserted by Boehme commentators over the whole range of Boehme's metanarrative. As early as the late seventeenth century, Gottfried Arnold pointed to both the androgynous nature of Adam and the presence in the prelapsarian Adam of Sophia in Boehme's texts as indicating an especially close link between Boehmian and Kabbalistic discourse. This is a connection also made by Ernst Benz,[6] who posits anthropology in general as an important area of substantive overlap. Boehme's understanding of the fallen world of nature and finite spirit as the departure of the feminine presence of the divine has been viewed as bearing a close relationship to the exile of the *Shekinah*. Scholars have noted remarkable overlaps between Boehme's interpretation of the chaos *(tohu va bohu)* of Genesis 1.1 and the interpretation prosecuted by Kabbalistic authors in general, the author of the *Zohar* in particular.[7] Understandably, however, much of the focus (from Oetinger in the eighteenth century to Benz and Schulitz in recent years) has been on the extraordinary overlaps between Boehme and the Kabbalah with respect to the depiction of the initial move from the depths of divine mystery to manifestation and the constitutive matrix of divine manifestation. Within this manifold, which concerns the first two episodes of Boehme's ontotheological narrative, there are three specific foci that seem to be especially important: (1) the relation between Boehme's Unground and the *En Sof* of the Kabbalah, (2) the relation between Boehme's articulation of the trinitarian or quaternarian divine and the first three divine names or *sephirot* of the Kabbalah, and (3) the relationship between Boehme's articulation of the pluralty of qualities that define the divine nature and its principle of organization and the Kabbalah's articulation of the plurality of the *sephirot* and its principle of organization.

(1) I begin with the correspondence between Boehme and the Kabbalah with respect to their depiction of the immanifest divine that is without name, and its upsurge into manifestation and nameability. The correspondence between the Kabbalistic *En Sof* and Boehme's Unground has two distinct aspects that reflect two different parameters for assessing the immanifest divine. The first aspect considers the immanifest divine within a contrastive parameter, within which the hiddenness, indeterminacy, impersonality, and disrelationality of the divine is set off against the divine as revealed, determinate, personal, and relational. Within this contrastive parameter both the Unground and the *En Sof* encourage apophatic attribution to the point of the most extreme apophatic attribution of all—that is, "nothing." I spoke in chapter 2 of the prominence of this apophatic parsing of the Unground in Boehme's texts. "Nothing" or *Ayin*, however, enjoys a similar prominence in the *Zohar*, where it is connected with the Tetragrammaton (bk 2. 64).[8] In fact, this Zohoric connection between 'nothing' and the Tetragrammaton itself is repeated in *Mysterium Magnum* (11, 34).

Needless to say, no more than in the case of Boehme is the immanifest divine in the *Zohar* unqualifiedly "nothing." First, as a cipher of radical transcendence, "nothing" *(Ayin)* must be understood in a relative rather than absolute sense. Second, in the *Zohar* the *En Sof* is designated by the term "all" as well as "nothing." And "all" is not simply another designation but one that is coupled with "nothing," and thus qualifies it, just as "nothing" qualifies "all" in return. This pattern is very much on the surface in Boehme's text, *Mysterium Magnum* (1, 8; 2, 3), which provides just one of the many examples of the mutual qualification of apophatic and kataphatic attribution. In fact, the kataphatic qualification of "nothing" does not stop here in either the Kabbalah or Boehme. If "nothing" is qualified by the "all," it is also qualified by oneness or unity. This could not be more emphatic in Boehme, for whom the "one" functions on the same level as "all" and "nothing" (e.g., *MM* 1, 2; 1, 6; 29, 1). At the same time it is hardly recessed in the Kabbalah. Within the contrastive parameter of mystery and manifestation, the *En Sof* is the 'one' that is other than the multiplicity of divine names.[9]

In the second parameter, the immanifest divine in the Kabbalah and in Boehme is considered in its aspect as the ultimate ground of the process of the constitution of a manifest, determinate, personal, and relational divine. The images of source and root are as central to the parsing of the grounding activity of the Unground in Boehme's discourse as they are of the *En Sof* in Kabbalistic discourse,[10] although both Boehme and the Kabbalah think of these images as only approximately applying to the transcendent divine nothing. As with the Unground, in texts such as *Mysterium Magnum*, the *En Sof* is considered under the auspices of act rather than substance. Indeed, it is considered as a project rather than a reality given once and for all.

In the Kabbalah, as in Boehme's discourse in general, theogony is not only validated philosophically, but exegetically. For both Boehme and the Kabbalah, Genesis 1.1 is a crucially important text, although obviously in the context of the Kabbalah it will not be read from the point of view of the Johannine prologue, as is the case with Boehme. One of the key texts in the *Zohar* for describing the reality of the movement of the divine away from the darkness and silence of the *En Sof* is Psalm 130, and specifically the phrase "out of the depths I have called to thee" (verse 1). The reading is anagogical. While what is disclosed in interpretation has meaning for the interpreter, bypassed completely is the standard existential reading in which the depths are the depths of an individual or community in despair, and also, the call the human cry for comfort and help. Instead, the *Zohar* favors an ontological reading in which the depths are identified as the hiddenness of the divine and the call is a form of divine solicitation or elicitation.[11]

The other locus classicus is the interpretation of Genesis 1.1 *Bereshith bara Elohim*, which is read "(in) the beginning created God." In this rendering Elohim is interpreted as the grammatical object rather than subject of the sentence, and substantively as a personal self-conscious divine in a way that the *En Sof* is not. The *Zohar* goes on to suggest that Elohim represents the conjunction of the hidden subject *Mi* with the hidden object *Eleh*.[12] As underscored by scholars from the Jewish as well as Christian side, arguably the most remarkable correspondence of all within the second parameter of reflection on the movement from mystery to manifestation is that the transcendence of the apophatic regime is predicated in both Boehmian and Kabbalistic discourse on the breakthrough of will, which is, of course, the will to manifestation and determination.[13] Will retrospectively specifies the nothing of the immanifest divine. Considered as act, the divine in both cases is more meontic will than *meon* proper. This brings us to the second major area of overlap.

(2) The association of Boehme's elaboration of the 'Immanent Trinity' and Sophia with the first three names or *sephirot* of the Kabbalistic tree, *Kether* (Crown), *Chochmah* (Wisdom), and *Binah* (Intelligence), has a distinguished history in both commentary and actual appropriation of Boehme. It is central to Oetinger's eighteenth-century linkup of Boehme and the Kabbalah as resources to attack a theological rationalism that threatens to undermine evangelical faith.[14] It is announced and supported, once again, by Franz von Baader in the early nineteenth century, who thinks of the conjunction as providing a plausible means of supporting a new vision of the distinction-relation between the inner and outer Trinity. Most recently Schulitz has reminded us not only of this history, but he also has drawn attention to the condition of correspondence. The basic condition of correspondence is that, in an important respect, the first three *sephirot* are not only prior to the other seven but also different, in that they do not serve as cosmogonic grounds in the way the other divine names do.[15] Whether this is a fully adequate reading of the first three *sephirot* in their specifically Jewish context is open to debate. Still it is certainly the case that Schulitz is accurately reflecting the history of the Christian linkup of Boehme's Quaternity and the three most exalted of the divine names in the Kabbalistic system.

In the tradition of Christian interpretation and appropriation, Boehme's Quaternity and the first three divine names of the Zoharic Kabbalah are understood to overlap in both general and specific ways. On the general level, Boehme's Quaternity and the first thee divine names of the Zoharic Kabbalah overlap to the degree that they are understood to articulate both divine will and knowledge, or divine will to knowledge. As I indicated in chapter 1, passages where the 'Immanent Trinity' specifies will are everywhere in Boehme. They can be found in his magisterial (*Mysterium Magnum* 1, 2–4; *Electione Gratiae* 1, 6) as well as nonmagisterial texts (*SPT* 5, 5). Sophia, of course, is also a reflection of will (*SPT* 5, 4). At the same time, albeit in different respects, the Son (*MM* 1, 4), Spirit (*MM* 1, 2; *SPT* 5, 5) and Wisdom are regarded as modes of divine self-reflection. More specific correspondences also appear to be present. On the specific level, the more interesting correlations are between Wisdom, Son, and Spirit on the Boehmian side and *Chochmah* and *Binah* on the side of the Kabbalah. The relation between the Father and *Kether* is fairly formal with both serving as proximate origins of divine manifestation and as specifications of will. Boehme's Sophia and the Kabbalah's *Chochmah* are more than lexical equivalents. They both point to a privileged site of divine self-reflection, and both get symbolized by mirror and eye (*MM* 1, 4).[16] At the same time the Son is not without relation to *Chochmah* in that both represent incipient stages of determinacy and shape in the movement away from the indeterminate divine nothing. There is also a nontrivial correspondence between the Spirit of the 'Immanent Trinity' and *Binah*. Not only are both agents of reflection, but also, their relation to Wisdom appears to be quite similar. If Boehme understands the relation between Spirit and Sophia to be that between seer and seen, so in the Kabbalah is the relation between *Binah* and *Chochmah* viewed as the relation between active and passive moments of reflection.[17]

(3) Granting the correlation between Boehme's Quaternity and the first three divine names, this leaves the issue of the general relation between Boehme's configuration of qualities and the Kabbalistic configuration of names. Again, there are general and more specific correlations, with the former, arguably, being ultimately more compelling than the latter. First, there is the simple fact that in both Boehmian and Kabbalistic discourse the basic forms of divine manifestation themselves constitute the divine as shape and form. If this form is organic in both cases, in the Kabbalah the form or *Gestalt* takes on the shape of the human figure—that is, *Adam Kadmon*. This specific parsing of organic form will obviously be important in my projected volume on the return of Gnosticism and especially in my treatment of Blake's metaleptic narrative that features the "human form divine." Second, the organization of forms of divine manifestation are in both cases essentially dipolar, with qualities or names banding into both a stern or wrathful side (in Boehme a side of *Zorn* or *Schwerigkeit*, in the Kabbalah a side of *Din*) and a merciful side (in Boehme a side of *Barmhertzig*, in the Kabbalah a side of *Chesed)*. Some specific correspondences also exist. As a particular name rather than representing a band of names, *Din* finds a close analogy in the first of the three harsh qualities depicted by Boehme, which like *Din*, is symbolized as a dark consuming fire. Similarly, *Chesed*, considered as a specific name, rather than representing a band of names, finds a close analogy with the first of the three qualities of the Second Principle, which like *Chesed*, is symbolized as a mild and light fire. The final significant correlation is that between *Malkuth* (Kingdom), the last of the ten *sephirot* and the last of Boehme's seven qualities, which is the "Kingdom" or "Body" of God. Both Boehme's seventh quality after the Quaternity and the tenth Kabbalistic name are identified with paradise.

The visionary, hermeneutic, and especially narrative overlaps between Boehme's discourse and that of the Kabbalah are such that the Kabbalah should be regarded as a bone fide taxonomic candidate. Its taxonomic credentials stack up reasonably well against both apocalyptic and Neoplatonism. One could make a case that its higher level of abstraction, shown in its vision and the fact that the content of vision is the movement of manifestation from an erstwhile immanifest divine, provides the Kabbalah with some taxonomic advantages over apocalyptic. At the same time, by comparison with Neoplatonism, one could make an equally good case that both its theogonic parsing of manifestation and its understanding of divine attributes as a configuration of expressive forces provide the Kabbalah with taxonomic advantages. I don't want to press these advantages. Still it should be clear that indeed, its prima facie credentials as a taxon look good enough to constitute a serious challenge to the Valentinian hypothesis.

Ultimately, of course, I continue to maintain that a Valentinian taxon is more adequate. This still allows me to allot to the Kabbalah the role of a taxonomic supplement, a courtesy that I have extended already to two other narrative discourses—that is, apocalyptic and Neoplatonism. I will postpone for the moment dealing with the issue of the kind of taxonomic supplementarity; rather, I limit myself to making the point that a high level of correspondence between Boehme's discourse and the Kabbalah is a condition for attributing any form supplementary taxonomic status, whether strong or weak. It is apposite to put on the table the reasons that disqualify it from enjoying primary taxonomic status. The argument that the Kabbalah cannot function as the primary taxon of Boehmian narrative involves heterogenous kinds of considerations: (1) It involves attention to breakdowns in correspondence between Boehmian and Kabbalistic narrative, precisely at those places where there seems to be the greatest overlap. (2) It involves reflection on the historical constitution of Boehme's narrative, specifically, on how much of Boehme's narrative is in place before his narrative elaboration comes to be in conversation with the Kabbalah. (3) It involves exploring the question, How Kabbalistic can the Kabbalah be in a Christian situation in general, and a post-Reformation tradition in particular? By far the most important of these considerations is the first. Accordingly, it will receive most of my attention.

(1) The simple presence of elements in Boehmian and Kabbalistic narrative that do not overlap does not count against a Kabbalistic taxonomy of Boehme's discourse, any more than the lack of correspondence in particular areas between Boehme's narrative and classical Valentinian narratives count against a Valentinian ascription of Boehme's discourse. What is crucial is whether the noncorrespondences are significant or not. Given that the significance of departures of Boehme from the Kabbalah are a function of the context of these departures as much as their intent and extent, I will begin my examination with the zone of narrative articulation in Boehme's discourse that bears the closest resemblance to the Kabbalah—that is, its articulation of the divine powers, their organization, and their immediate conditions in the immanent

divine. Despite general congruence between Boehme's articulation of the immanent divine sphere and the first three *sephirot*, it must be admitted, the match is far from perfect. Boehme's "Father" and the Kabbalah's *Kether* correspond merely to the degree that they both represent the first kataphatic specification of an erstwhile apophatically symbolized divine and can both be interpreted under the designation of will. In Boehme's quaternarian articulation, both the Son and Sophia correspond to *Chochmah*, with the level of correspondence between Son and *Chochmah* being much lower than in the case of Sophia and *Chochmah*. With respect to Sophia and *Chochmah* in the Zoharic Kabbalah, *Chochmah* does not bear the same narrative freight Wisdom does in Boehme's narrative. *Chochmah* is neither the matrix of the archetypes of concrete existence nor a zone of manifestation, essentially limited and fragile, and implicated in a fall into divine alienation and evil.

Turning to Boehme's general articulation of the configuration of divine qualities, one can say that if Boehme's scheme recalls the Kabbalistic differentiation into two bands of divine names, one representing the judgmental and wrathful side of the divine, the other the side of mercy, there are at least four important differences: (a) A first important difference is that Boehme does not think of the 'Immanent Trinity' and Wisdom as belonging to the same plane as the seven qualities of the two Principles. They are conditions of manifestation rather than forces of manifestation, conditions of divine naming rather than its enactment. By contrast, if the first three *sephirot* of the Kabbalah enjoy some special prerogatives, they too are divine names and as such they are not absolutely separable from the other seven divine names in the way Boehme's Quaternity is separable from the seven divine qualities. Even in *Mysterium Magnum* (11, 34), where Boehme speaks of three qualities in addition to the seven qualities of the two Principles, he does not name the Trinity, which narratively precedes the Principles, but rather, he names features that articulate a divine constituted as "Kingdom." He names fire, tincture, and finally Cross, which is on the apophatic border of the Unground or Jehovah. In fact, the appearance of the Cross in such proximity to the apophatic divine strongly suggests the kind of staurological view of the Cross that marks the Valentinian narrative genre, *PSY*, with which Boehme's narrative overlaps most extensively.

I will be more brief with the three remaining differences. (b) Scholars like Schulitz, notwithstanding, only quite general rather than highly specific correlations can be argued for between the Boehmian qualities of the two principles and divine names on either the wrathful or merciful side of the Kabbalistic tree. For instance, despite great ingenuity, no convincing correlations between Boehmian qualities and the names of *Tifereth* (Beauty), *Hod* (Majesty), *Nesach* (Endurance), and *Yesod* (Foundation) have been proposed. (c) As we saw in Part I, if Boehme associates the harsh life of the First Principle with divine judgment and wrath, he more nearly associates it with Eternal Nature as a fallen and antithetical form of divine Wisdom. The negativity of Eternal Nature is both more freestanding and excessive than that of the "left-hand" side of divine manifestation in the Kabbalah. (d) Finally, and relatedly, while in both cases depiction of the harsh side of divine manifestation plays a role in the account of the origin and nature of evil, which at the very least theogonically qualifies the anthropological account that is officially supported in both discourses, Boehme's depiction of the "poisonous" life of the divine has implications that are not there in the Kabbalah. These implications in fact cut in precisely opposite directions. On the one hand, Boehme's depiction more deeply implicates the divine in evil, for the Source or Ground of Being in the divine is chaotic in a way divine judgment in principle is not.[18] On the other, and arguably more conspicuously, Boehme's depiction disimplicates the divine, for it proposes an ontological separation between the harsh and merciful sides of the manifesting divine that cannot be found in the Zoharic scheme of things.

A final difference within the field of correspondence worth commenting on concerns the level of eros asserted within both narrative frameworks. As I said earlier, the assertion that eros, mediated by will, operates at the archeological level of the divine, gives the Kabbalah a major advantage over Neoplatonism when it comes to a taxonomy of Boehme's discourse. The issue that arises is whether any significant differences with respect to either the limitation or figuration of *eros* exists between Boehme's narrative and that of the Kabbalah. The basic drift of Kabbalistic interpretation is to think of the movement from the nothing (*Ayin*) of the *En Sof* to its determination as *Kether* as a production of will, and at least in a restricted sense, as a production of eros. I mentioned earlier the *Zohar*'s interpretation of Psalm 130.1, and especially its theogonic interpretation of the first verse of Genesis, *Bereshith bara Elohim*. While it would not be going too far to extrapolate that the sephirotic tree also is a production and representation of divine will, there is almost no warrant to think of it as an erotic production in our technical sense of eros. Despite the theogonic rehearsal at the ultimate archeological level in which the personal divine comes to be, one does not get the impression from the *Zohar* that the divine names express anything less than a divine mystery that is a plenitude. We are not led to believe in the case of *Malkuth* that it represents, as Boehme's final quality does, not only a summary of divine manifestation (its englobing *Gestalt*) but also the ontological, gnoseological, axiological, and existential integration of the divine. Thus, even if one wished to associate eros with a drive to manifestation that could be conceived unilaterally as voluntarist, one would still be obliged to hedge it with the qualifier that eros, as it functions in the Kabbalah, is agapaically constrained or qualified. In the case of Boehme, however, as we have seen already, eros is productive across the entire range of divine qualities, down to the very last quality of "Kingdom." Boehmian narrative suffers no agapaic restraint of eros.

(2) It is these departures that bear the primary burden of disqualifying the Kabbalah as the primary taxon. Nevertheless, historical considerations confirm and strengthen the appearance of secondariness by pointing to the prior constitution and thus relative independence of Boehme's narrative from the Kabbalah. It is important to underscore that Boehme's engagement with the Kabbalah begins circa 1622, which is late in Boehme's development, although admittedly early enough for it to be a force in *Mysterium Magnum* (1623). By 1622, however, one could argue that through his dealings with the negative theology tradition Neoplatonism had provided Boehme with an outline of the problematic of the movement from mystery to manifestation, even if it had not offered a satisfying interpretation, and that the tradition of Paracelsian alchemy had set the basic contours for reflection on divine qualities. On the basis of these givens, the Kabbalah contributed to Boehme's theosophy by offering a model of visionary-interpretive discourse of encompassing narrative breadth and suggesting refinements to his elaboration of the immanent divine and the field of divine attributes.

Quite a different type of historical confirmation of the secondariness of the Kabbalah for Boehme's discourse is provided by Oetinger, who in the middle of the eighteenth century champions the causes of both Boehme and the Kabbalah as resources in the construction of an evangelical theology that avoids the pitfalls of rationalism and fideism. Oetinger's essential task is to provide a synthesis of Boehme and the Kabbalah. Of course, the very attempt to provide a synthesis is a confession of nonidentity. To be fair to Oetinger, however, he has the added problem of squaring Boehme not simply with the *Zohar*, with which through Balthasar Walther and Abraham von Frankenberg Boehme plausibly had contact, but also with the Lurianic Kabbalah,[19] for which there is no evidence of transmission, but whose dramatic figuration of manifestation sets up other lines of comparative approach with Boehme. When Oetinger advocates a reading of divine attributes that leaves behind all traces of philosophical (Spinoza) and theological rationalism (Wolff), he represents the divine attributes as determinations of the process of divine self-constitution. Divine attributes concern less a given divine fullness than a process of coming to fullness.[20] Oetinger is not unconscious that this erotic reading is strictly speaking Boehmian, but he asserts it of the *sephirot*. He does so since, for him, to a large extent at least, Boehme can be regarded as the legitimate Christian realization of the Kabbalah, despite, or even because, he transforms constitutive commitments of the Kabbalah as originally Jewish texts.

(3) This brings us to a third consideration that bears on the prospects of the Kabbalah as the primary taxon for Boehmian narrative. This is the fairly formal, even methodological, issue of the ascriptive status of the Kabbalah when the basic context of the narrative discourse requiring taxonomic identification is Christian. To raise the issue, of course, is to entertain suspicions with

respect to the complex locution of "Christian Kabbalah." This locution is informative to the extent that it points to ways in which Kabbalistic discourse has historically been used to confirm and explicate the mysteries of the divine and creation within Christianity, and especially the mysteries of the Trinity and Christ. What is true in the Florentine Academy with Marcello Ficino and Pico della Mirandola,[21] is true also of the Kabbalah's German filiation from Reuchlin on. It should be said, however, that post-Reformation alchemical and apocalyptic resurgence, not to mention Luther's theology of the Cross, will add layers of complication beyond that prevalent in Florence's humanistic and Neoplatonic heyday. The locution is misleading to the extent that the adjective "Christian" functions to obscure the consequences to Jewishness of the transference of the Kabbalah from its native environment.

As Moshe Idel has pointed out, in this transition from one context to another the discourse of the Kabbalah undergoes a massive speculative simplification as it gets divorced from prayer and worship.[22] Moreover, in the transfer from one discursive context to another, the Kabbalah ceases to function as the supplement and amplification of the written Torah. It comes to define itself against Law and comes to legitimate a pneumatic-speculative alternative.[23] And, finally, on its new terrain, the anagogical function of interpretation is absolutized to the point that one does not read simply other than the literal and community sense of Scripture but against them.

In the Christian context the Kabbalah, therefore, is systemically an expropriated Jewish discourse. On the one hand, it is a Christian spoil, whose Jewishness is erased even before the Tetragrammaton is identified with the Father or Christ, or the correlations made between the Trinity and the first three *sephirot*. On the other, there is a sense that honorable gestures made with respect to the Hebrew language and scholarship notwithstanding (Boehme thinks of the Hebrew language as only inferior to the language of nature and spirit) as part of a speculative tapestry, the Kabbalah now defines itself against features that tropically define Judaism—that is, Law, worldliness, and commitment to the literal sense of things. This newly minted speculative discourse does not simply have a limited audience, as undoubtedly it would have in Judaism on grounds of intellectual and moral preparation, but it also seems to call forth an elite that defines itself against the faith of the community of Israel. What is true in the Florentine situation is even more true in a post-Reformation situation in which Judaism had come again to typify the Law, and the rigidity, obstinacy, and theological shortsightedness—a typification that can be transferred by post-Reformation pneumatic Christians to confessional Christianity itself. Within a Christian context in general, the Kabbalah functions as a speculative discourse that erases the specifically Judaic context of origin. Within a post-Reformation context, the Kabbalah functions as a critical instrument with respect to features that not only define Judaism but also standard forms of Christianity that are thought a regression into Judaism. Within the post-Reformation context the Kabbalah not only helps Christian discourse to contest discrete theologoumena, generated in large part in and through reflection on episodes of the biblical narrative (e.g., creation and fall, Genesis 1–3) but also contests basically the entire range of theologoumena that interpret the biblical narrative as a whole. Thus, in its appropriation of the Kabbalah post-Reformation discourse in the form provided by Boheme functions metaleptically vis-à-vis the biblical text as a whole, and not simply the Hebrew Scriptures.

9.1. Valentinian Enlisting of the Kabbalah

The above three considerations of (1) significant narrative differences, (2) the historical belatedness of influence, and (3) the transformation of the meaning and function of the Kabbalah argue against granting to the Kabbalah anything more than a supplemental taxonomic role with respect to Boehme's narrative. But this raises the issue once again: What kind of supplementarity, supplementarity in principle or in fact? The taxonomic stakes are clear at this juncture. A judgment of supplementarity in principle effectively means that no unitive explanation of Boehme's narrative can be offered. From the point of view of criteriology, such a judgment supposes that there are important elements of Boehme's narrative discourse so autonomous that they can only be explained by appeal to Kabbalah. A judgment of supplementarity in fact advances the weaker claim that while the presence of Kabbalistic elements in Boehme's narrative is real, these elements are not in fact autonomous, but are enlisted by a virtually constituted agonistic encompassing narrative. The three above considerations strongly suggest the probity of the weaker judgment, although again I assert that the major burden of the argument is carried by the first consideration.

Certainly, in line with what we have seen with respect to the discourses of apocalyptic and Neoplatonism, Kabbalistic discourse appears not only to be an enlistable discourse, but also to be a discourse that is actually enlisted. In the context of Boehme's narrative, the erotic gestures of the Kabbalah's interpretation of the move from divine hiddenness to manifestation are absolutized. Unequivocal assertions of the fullness and self-sufficiency of the divine abyss of YHWH are not tolerated in Boehme's scheme. Concerning the aboriginal will to manifestation, it becomes impossible to maintain that it is governed by divine excess that remains inaccessible to the giving of reasons. The Kabbalah may well suggest that the divine truly knows itself as personal only outside the context of the divine unity and nothing, but it takes Boehme to pronounce on the superior status of this knowledge relative to the undifferentiated knowledge the *En Sof* can be presumed to have of itself. The gesture toward the aporetics of representation is there in the Kabbalah, but it is redeemed only in the context of the metaleptic Christian discourse of Boehme.

The lack of support in Boehme's discourse for asserting that the anarchic divine is perfect means that his view of divine qualities is informed by Kabbalistic reflection on divine names only to the extent that such reflection does not challenge the fundamentally erotic tenor of the matrix of qualities. In Boehme's scheme the forms of divine expressivity and expression gradually overcome deficits inherent in the aboriginal depths of the divine. At the same time that the Kabbalistic *sephirot* gain admittance only under the rule of eros, they also have to submit to the rule that negative qualities are narratively anterior, positive qualities narratively posterior. Related to this rule, which does not apply in the case of the Kabbalah as such, is the rule for interpreting the divine force or forces that mediate between the negative and the positive bands. For Boehme, after Luther, but also after alchemy, it is the Cross that provides the image of the only form of mediation that is thinkable, a dramatic form that bears no analogy in the Kabbalah itself.[24] No more than in the case of the other enlisted discourses, however, is the Kabbalah devoid of reflexive effect on the enlisting Valentinian discourse. There are moments in which Boehme is prepared to insist on the sheer gratuity of vision. There are moments in which anagogic interpretation does not seem to set up a countertext that bleeds the authority of the texts commented on. And it is clearly the case that the narrative of the Kabbalah reinforces the agapaic notes struck by the other two enlisted discourses.

In any event, the supplementarity of the Kabbalah adds a further level of taxonomic complexification with regard to Boehmian narrative and invites reflection on the relation between this supplement and Valentinianism as the putative primary taxon, and between Kabbalah and the apocalyptic and Neoplatonic supplements. There are two ways of envisaging the relation, the first, topographical, the second, more abstractly grammatical or linguistic. Looked at topographically, or stratigraphically, one could say (a) that its level of correspondence with Boehme's narrative entitles the Kabbalah to a position at least as close to the narrative base as apocalyptic and Neoplatonism and (b) that although it risks elevating an aperçu of Bloom's into a construct, one could say that the Kabbalah mediates or intercallates between a Valentinian narrative base and the apocalyptic and Neoplatonic narrative strands by placing the symbolism of apocalyptic within a wider aesthetic frame, and by adding a voluntarist and erotic leaven to the dynamics of Neoplatonism's agapaic construal of the movement from divine mystery to manifestation.

Of course, the Valentinian narrative of divine fall and reconstitution, visualized at the base, is more or less a theoretical construct. When it comes to characterizing Boehme's discourse, one is talking about a virtual Valentinian entity, distinguished from classical Valentinian forms by its vastly greater teleological and erotic drive, although as open as those forms were to a multitude of symbolic and narrative discourses. The teleological and erotic potential, if in a sense already given, is at least in part realized through the instrumentality of apocalyptic, Neoplatonism, and Kabbalah to which Valentinian narrative is open.

As the case of psychoanalysis shows,[25] topographical models can at best be approximate, at the very least calling for more linguistic models to complement them. Thus, to envisage Valentinianism as a language or as a grammar is to envisage it as a horizon or field of force that is permissive about the lexical narrative elements, but not so with respect to the rules of formation, which are at the same time rules for the transformation of biblical narrative. Now, the topographical and linguistic ways of envisaging are more or less complementary. The topographical model presents in concrete fashion the continuity between Boehme's narrative and the classical Valentinian genres: it registers ways in which this Valentinian repetition is modified and modulated by other narrative discourses while not being changed into a non-Valentinian narrative discourse. The grammatical model is more abstract but offers an explanation rather than an image of how to view the relation between classical Valentinianism and modern narrative ontotheologies. It respects the plurality of classical Valentinian genres and allows for significant and systematic differences between classical Valentinian genres and what count as modern repetitions.

I have pointed out a number of these differences including a greater respect for world, time, and history, and the erotic-kenotic constitution complexion of the six-stage metaleptic narrative that is articulated by both. The systematic nature of these differences make a modern form of Valentinianism, such as I am claiming Boehme's discourse to represent, what I call a rule-governed deformation of classical Valentinian genres.

Concluding Remarks

In this third and final part I raised explicitly the issue of the best way to characterize Boehme's erotic-agonistic speculative narrative discourse. In chapter 6 I made a case for the probity of a Valentinian taxon. I recalled the narrative grammar revisioning of Valentinianism carried out in *Gnostic Return in Modernity*. I argued that Boehme's discourse observes the same rules of narrative formation instantiated in classical Valentinian texts such as *PSY*, the *Tractate*, and the *Gospel*. As with these classical texts, his narrative is a six-stage inclusive visionary narrative, fundamentally metaleptic in nature, that shows the facility of being compacted into a triadic narrative of divine perfection lost and divine perfection regained. Thus, Boehme's narrative is properly a lexical instance of Valentinian narrative grammar, despite the differences between his narrative and the classical instances.

Differences between Boehme's narrative and classical Valentinian genres should be expected for two reasons. First, differences are manifested in every instance of Valentinian grammar. This is true of the relations that abide between *PSY*, the *Tractate*, and the *Gospel*. Boehme's narrative is no exception to the rule. Second, there is another kind of difference, one that applies diachronically rather than synchronically. It would be unreasonable to expect over a millennium of Christian tradition from the time of Hellenistic Valentinianism to have no effect on Boehme's discourse. It would be equally unreasonable not to take account of the specific post-Reformation context of his discourse. None of these differences counts, therefore, against Boehme's discourse being a lexical instance of Valentinian narrative grammar.

Both the measure of continuity and discontinuity of Boehme's discourse from classical Valentinianism can be illuminated only by exhibiting the ways in which he repeats and departs from the classical Valentinian genres. In chapter 6 I explored the ways in which Boehme's discourse repeats features of all three classical Valentinian genres, and especially *PSY* and the *Tractate*. I argued that from the point of view of concrete details, especially the depiction of the faulting of divine perfection, Boehme's narrative is closer to *PSY* but that with respect to the narrative as a whole, it is closer to the *Tractate*, which justifies fall and introduces a teleological drift into the whole narrative. By comparison with both of these classical Valentinian genres, however, Boehme's narrative is radically teleological, thus theogonic. This specifies the major deviation of Boehme's discourse from, or his major deformation of, classical Valentinian genres. The deviation from, or deformation of, as I have already pointed out, is not such that it implies that Boehme's discourse breaks the rules of Valentinian narrative grammar. This teleological exacerbation is a possibility of Valentinian narrative grammar, since it is suggested at least in the *Tractate*.

The deviation of Boehme's discourse from, or its deformation of, these more classical discourses, is rule-governed since it is implied in Valentinian narrative grammar itself. Thus, the secondary characterization of Boehme's narrative discourse is that it is a rule-governed deformation of classical Valentinian genres. In chapter 6 I also suggested that a problem that is latent in the classical genres becomes truly explicit in Boehme's—that is, the problem of legitimate divine knowledge. This problem is resolved in favor of representation rather than infinite divine self-consciousness.

In chapter 6 I argued a case sufficient to demonstrate the plausibility of a Valentinian taxonomy of Boehme's narrative discourse. To demonstrate its validity, however, requires demonstrating the superiority of Valentinianism over rival taxons. I judged that there were three credible rival taxons. These were apocalyptic, Neoplatonism, and the Kabbalah. Devoting a chapter to each of these taxonomic rivals (chapters 7–9) I made the best possible case on their behalf. I agreed with each of their advocates that their preferential taxonomic discourse was a real presence in Boehme's discourse, and I conceded that it should be taken into account in any explanation of Boehme's visionary narrative discourse that pretended to be adequate. But I judged that neither apocalyptic, Neoplatonism, nor the Kabbalah really challenges Valentinianism in terms of taxonomic primacy. More, I concluded that the presence of none of the three discourses in Boehme's discourse functioned so autonomously that it merited the status of a principled taxonomic supplement. I did not disbar any of these discourses from supplying taxonomic supplementarity, but argued that their use to characterize Boehme's discourse was limited to pointing to the real presence of a non-Valentinian narrative, which for certain purposes it might be important to underscore. Indeed, I underscored how each of these discourses is coopted by an essentially Valentinian six-stage visionary narrative and how each is put to use in the systematic disfiguration-refiguration of the biblical narrative. In is in these chapters that the final of the four basic constructs of the 'Gnostic return' model—that is *Valentinian enlisting of non-Valentinian narrative discourses*—comes into operation. The other three are, of course, *Valentinian narrative grammar, rule-governed deformation of classical Valentinian genres*, and *metalepsis*. In speaking of *Valentinian enlisting*, I made sure not to neglect the fact that in such enlisting, the *enlisted* narrative discourse would exercise some reflexive effect on the *enlisting* discourse within its visionary, hermeneutic, and above all, narrative dimensions. Importantly, however, the reflexive effect has *not* the same force as the enlisting Valentinian form of discourse. With respect to the phenomenon of enlisting, the Valentinianism exhibited by Boehme's narrative discourse is continuous, as I showed in *Gnostic Return in Modernity*, with classical genres of Valentinianism. It is different from it only in being even more open to non-Valentinian narrative discourses and regulating them more thoroughly.

CONCLUSION

∼

Genealogical Preface

I have undertaken the analysis of Boehme's visionary discourse armed with the conviction that this post-Reformation discourse is still worthy of our attention in its struggles as well as its accomplishments. In this sense, I could not agree more with such great commentators on Boehme as Benz, Grunsky, Koyré, Stoudt, and Weeks. There is much to admire, since there is much that is profound and original in Boehme's vision of the dynamic of the being of beings, much that is philosophically probing in his questioning of Why something, why not nothing?[1] And why evil? And there is much that is theologically challenging in his elucidation of the living God of the Bible in developmental and agonistic terms that carry more than rhetorical freight.[2] If my analysis of Boehme's discourse does not exactly repeat any of his illustrious commentators in an exact way, nevertheless it is informed by them. It is so, even as I insist in a way that they do not on particular facets of Boehme's discourse—for example, on its inhabiting of an Eckhartian form of negative theology and its decidedly tensional relation to the thought of the Reformer.[3]

At a structural level, however, my analysis differs from all previous accounts—with the possible exception of David Walsh's—in its fairly relentless pursuit of the proper characterization of Boehme's discourse. In this sense, Part III of this text, in which I line up and examine the merits of the four viable candidates for a taxonomic characterization of Boehme's discourse—that is, Valentinianism, apocalyptic, Neoplatonism, and the Kabbalah—and decide in favor of Valentinianism, represents the telos of interpretation. Relative to this end, Part I essentially sets the table by suggesting that Boehme's visionary discourse, which is at once itself and more than itself (since it represents an *Aufhebung* of Paracelsian alchemy) has at its center a six-stage inclusive narrative that is the objective correlative of a self-certifying reason that transcends ratiocination and its argumentative responsibilities. This six-stage narrative mimics the biblical narrative but has as its subject matter divine self-development and its ineluctable narrative conditions. Part II contributes toward the taxonomic question in general, and

211

the Valentinian taxonomic conclusion in particular, by arguing that whatever the orthodox elements in Boehme's discourse, and whatever the deviations from the common theological tradition it shares with minority pre-Reformation and post-Reformation traditions, ultimately this narrative discourse represents a radical and comprehensive disfiguration-refiguration of the biblical narrative. Part II brings us to the threshold of Valentinian ascription, since it is disfiguration-refiguration, or metalepsis, that Irenaeus believed to be the peculiar mark of Valentinian haunting of appropriately biblically-informed Christian discourse.

I admit the complexity of my analysis, but plead that it corresponds to the complexity of the subject matter—that is, Boehme's visionary or apocalypse discourse. But even if this is granted me, I still have some explaining to do. Why deploy a sophisticated conceptual apparatus of general constructs such as *Valentinian narrative grammar, rule-governed deformation of classical Valentinian genres, metalepsis,* and *Valentinian enlisting of non-Valentinian narrative discourse,* and more specific constructs such as *apocalyptic inscription, apocalyptic distention, narrative deconstitution of negative theology,* and *aporetics of representation* on such a relatively arcane discursive specimen as Jacob Boehme. Even if we listen seriously to Boehme's commentators, hear what genealogists such as Baur, Staudenmaier, and Walsh have to say, and recall what Hegel said about the importance of a speculative thinker who with Bacon and Descartes contributes to the formation of specifically modern philosophical discourse, deployment of this conceptual apparatus looks like serious overkill. The style of interpretation in operation seems to amount to taking a machine gun to swat a fly. Although accurate characterization is a true good, Why hard-pedal in the way I do the following conclusions? Boehme's apocalypse discourse (1) represents an instance of Valentinian narrative grammar, (2) represents an erotic, kenotic, and agonistic deformation of classical Valentinianism that allows for much more positive estimates of world, time, history, and suffering, and (3) illustrates the phenomenon of Valentinian discourse sharing discursive space with three non-Valentinian visionary discourses—that is, apocalyptic, Neoplatonic and Kabbalistic discourses—but enlisting them for Valentinian purposes.

Boehme's apocalypse discourse, I believe, is intrinsically interesting. But is it interesting enough to justify the kind of conceptual as well as interpretive attention I have lavished on it here? If I answer in the negative, it is not that I think Boehme's discourse is at a major disadvantage with regard to appeal when set alongside other individual modern philosophical, mythopoetic, and theological discourses. Its speculative boldness makes most contemporary religious discourses—even the ones that advertise themselves as speculative—look timid and lacking in vision by comparison. Its comprehensiveness makes even the most wide-ranging of contemporary philosophical and theological discourses seem parochial. I answer no, because there still remains the issue of whether any individual discourse, no matter how singular, justifies in particular the kind of conceptual investment shown, especially in Part III of the text. But if not, What does justify the wading through symbolic swamps and mythological forests I referred to in the introduction? Foucault in his archeology might possibly be thought to provide a motive, since he more than many others sees Boehme's discourse as expressive of a larger figuration of a mode of thought different than the specifically modern mode of rational thought that makes for order and control. Foucault's historical rehearsal of premodern Paracelsian-Boehmian episteme suggests some critical or normative purchase with respect to the dominant way of thinking in the post-Enlightenment world. But the promise is not fulfilled.

First, the Paracelsian-Boehmian mode of thinking is irredeemably past. It functions both nostalgically and as an impossible hope for a form of knowledge—perhaps any form of knowledge—that would escape the hegemony of an all-controlling rationality. Second, Foucault's radical historicism forbids any discourse from having normative purchase over another. But beyond Foucault's dead end, there is an answer to the question, Why bother with a thinker who falls between the stools of theology and philosophy? The answer to this question I gave in the introduction, and I suggested throughout all three parts of my text the possibility that Boehme represents not only an instance of Gnostic or Valentinian return, but that he opens up a new line of Gnostic or Valentinian discourse in the modern period.

As I indicated in the introduction, and reminded the reader in chapter 6, there are three major genealogical accounts in which Boehme's discourse figures as the origin of an essentially Gnostic or Valentinian line of thought. Two belong to the nineteenth century. There is Baur's classic statement in *Die Christliche Gnosis*, and the reflections of Staudenmaier who agrees with Baur about the return of Gnosis and its proximate site, but Staudenmaier mourns its return every bit as much as Baur celebrates it. The third belongs to the twentieth century and is articulated in the work of David Walsh, who is indebted to Eric Voegelin's reflections on Gnosticism. While here, as well as in *Gnostic Return in Modernity*, I have adverted to the methodological and interpretive shortcomings of each of these proposals, it should be said that they provide both the inspiration for the pursuit of the genealogical question and offer useful tools for analysis. Still, what is necessary is the successful prosecution of a Valentinian taxonomy of Boehme's apocalypse discourse. Demonstrating this gets the Gnostic return program truly off the ground. If my text has succeeded in showing how Boehme's discourse is Valentinian, then the genealogist is in a position to ask the question, What discourses follow Boehme's in representing a repetition of Valentinianism, albeit a Valentinianism in a nonclassical mode?

In answering this question it is possible, of course, to stick to those visionary discourses of the seventeenth and eighteenth centuries that repeat Boehme's discourse in a very determinate way—for example, the Philadelphian Society and William Law in England, Pietism in Germany, Louis Claude de St. Martin in France, and Swendenborg in Sweden, and the theosophy societies of the twentieth century. As a tracing of a concrete history of effects, this approach is perfectly legitimate. My cavil with it begins when this approach becomes the exclusive one. For this will tend to suggest that Boehme's discourse disseminates only on the margins of high culture and Christianity. It ignores the possibility that Boehme's discourse secretes itself into high culture and putatively mainline versions of Christianity. At the same time (and more specifically) it takes the edge off the genealogy proposed initially by Baur—that is, that as Boehme's discourse represents a Valentinian return in the post-Reformation tradition, this Valentinian return inaugurated by Boehme becomes a staple throughout the post-Reformation period. More, it becomes a staple not in marginal but in relatively core post-Enlightenment discourses such as Romanticism and German Idealism. As I suggested in *Gnostic Return in Modernity* I want to explore Valentinian repetition in those discourses that continue to remain culturally pertinent in a way Boehme's discourse is not. This exploration, then, of Gnostic or Valentinian return in Romanticism and German Idealism is not merely of historical interest. In can be, and indeed should be, considered as nothing less than an intervention, insofar as it illuminates the contemporary theological scene by showing how in its dependence on these two major Western cultural discourses theology too is subject to Valentinian haunting.

While the ascription of Valentinianism to Romantic and Idealist discourses does not depend logically on a powerful recall of Boehme's discourse, it will be my contention that those Romantic and Idealist discourses that show significant measures of such recall provide by far the best candidates. In any event, it is Boehme's discourse that provides the model of what conditions need to be fulfilled by any *modern* (post-Reformation or post-Enlightenment) narrative discourse in order to justify Valentinian ascription. There are at least five conditions. (1) Whether the genre of the *modern* discourse is philosophical, mythopoetic, or theological, discourse is presumed to be revelatory or a form of apocalypse. This apocalypse discourse has as its central content a six-stage narrative of divine fall and recovery, which can, however, be synopsized or abbreviated for certain purposes. (2) The six-stage narrative has a theogonic drift, whose background is supplied by teleological optics, and whose foreground consists of erotic, kenotic, and agonistic figuration. (3) This six-stage narrative is a vehicle of absolute knowledge to the degree that no meaning or truth (a) remains outside it or (b) has the ability to fundamentally to contest it. (4) This narrative discourse is not only in tension with the biblical narrative, as interpreted by standard pre-Reformation and Reformation traditions, but bears a metaleptic relation to it. (5) The six-stage inclusive narrative is discursively complex. In addition to Valentinianism, it includes narrative discourses such as apocalyptic, Neoplatonism, and Kabbalah. Nonetheless, it is Valentinianism that regulates these discourses on the level of vision, interpretation, and above all narrative, while permitting some reflexive effect.

Needless to say, the general ideational context of the Enlightenment would be expected to have effect. Thus, if both Romantic and Idealist discourses dispute much that is proposed by the Enlightenment concerning the limits of knowledge, the value of symbol and narrative, and the legitimacy of God-talk, the ideational context of the Enlightenment would still be expected to show itself in what these post-Enlightenment discourses promote and reject. The Enlightenment's injunction against heteronomy, for example, would function as a given. As such it would make urgent the quest for alternative sources of authority to replace that of mainline Christianity and its canonic text. The menu of replacements would include individuals in their orientation to a focus of transcendence, the authority of conscience or the moral law, an organic community, or even the state conceived as a spiritual entity.[4] But it could equally encourage the more indirect tack of actually engaging in an act of displacing the authority of the biblical text and its narrative by interpreting its narrative and creating a kind of countertext. Of course, for this to make sense the biblical text and its narrative would have to be imagined as they functioned to pattern and sanction a world before the Enlightenment crisis.[5] I will have much to say in future volumes as to why one strategy was favored over another in particular Romantic and Idealist discourses, but the matter need not be gone into here.

Similarly, one might expect that as a major cultural event, the Enlightenment, would entail other modifications in Valentinian discourse in the post-Enlightenment period, should it be granted that Boehme has opened up a new line of Valentinian discourse. Given the Enlightenment's suspicion of narrative forms of discourse in general, and its suspicion with respect to the biblical narrative in particular, to the extent that Romantic and Idealist discourses support the value of narrative and believe that the biblical text and its narrative is illuminating in a way that the dogmatic traditions are not, narrative production is self-conscious and artificial. Its support of the biblical text and its narrative is hedged with qualification. At the same time, given that Romantic and Idealist discourses do not escape the concerns with knowledge, its limits and conditions, established in Enlightenment thought, it would not be surprising if Romantic and Idealist forms of narrative discourse are more clearly framed by the problem of knowledge than Boehme's post-Reformation discourse is.[6] This gets reflected in Romantic and Idealist renderings of the story of the fall and recovery of divine perfection. Recovery of divine perfection lost will in Romantic and Idealist discourses tend toward a more univocal epistemological register than was the case in post-Reformation narrative discourses. And finally, the high estimate of human being self-consciously asserted by Enlightenment thinkers, against the Christian tradition in its articulation of the doctrines of creation as well as fall, functions as an ineluctable for all post-Enlightenment thought, even the thought that desires to submit the Enlightenment to a fundamental questioning. Thus, one can imagine an even greater *anthropological displacement* from the divine onto the human than is evident in the post-Reformation milieu.

With respect to Romanticism's and Idealism's candidacy for Valentinian ascription, I will speak here only of the discourses of Hegel and Blake, since the next two volumes on German Idealism and Romanticism center in part or in whole around them. With respect to Hegel, in *God's Story: Hegel's Valentinian Curriculum,* I will sustain on internal as well as external grounds the importance of the Boehme-Hegel connection that has been to the fore in the genealogical reflections of Baur, Staudenmaier, and Walsh. I will, however, put this connection on a sounder methodological and interpretive footing. I will make two major moves.

In a first move, I will argue that Hegel's system as a whole fulfills all five conditions that need to be satisfied if his quintessentially modern discourse is to be classed as Valentinian. (1) Hegel's speculative discourse exceeds ratiocination and its limitation to empirical or merely formal reality. At a penultimate level it articulates a putatively Christian six-stage narrative of divine fall and recovery that can be justified and rehabilitated in the more adequate categories of philosophy. (2) The six-stage Valentinian narrative has an abiding teleological register and represents an erotic, kenotic, and agonistic rendition of Valentinianism that is fundamentally modern. (3) The six-stage narrative, which Hegel shows in his major texts can be trinitarianly synonopsized,[7] is neither a story that competes with other stories nor wins and loses by its ability to persuade. Rather it is an absolute story, what Blumenberg refers to as "absolute myth."[8] It brings all stories to an end, by including them as aspects of its story. The meaning and truth of all other stories is realized in the story of divine becoming. As the absolute story, Hegel's trinitarian rendition of a more complex six-stage story of divine fall and recovery is essentially invulnerable to contestation. This is all the more true in the elevation-preservation and disguise of narrative in the realm of philosophical concept. This invulnerability to contestation has been pointed to by critics as different from each other as Carl Popper and Jean François Lyotard.[9] It is only the latter, however, who questionably ties this property of invulnerability to the connection between Hegel's narrative and the biblical narrative. (4) Hegel's speculative discourse bears a metaleptic relation to the biblical narrative, and distorts the narrative as it takes antithetical positions on the Trinity, creation, the incarnation, suffering and death of Christ, the Resurrection, the Holy Spirit, the church, and the eschaton.[10] (5) Hegel's narrative discourse is discursively complex. In addition to Valentinianism, apocalyptic, Neoplatonism, and Kabbalah are all present. I argue, however, that these other narrative discourses are *enlisted* by the Valentinian discourse and subserve a Valentinian narrative program. I qualify this argument not only by admitting but by showing how these other three discourses have reflexive effect on the enlisting Valentinian discourse, helping Hegel's discourse to look more orthodox than it really is, and helping it become the rule-governed deformation of classical Valentinian genres I hypothesize it is.

In a second move, I will argue that Hegel's discourse realizes precisely the expectations about differences we thought might apply between post-Reformation and post-Enlightenment varieties of Valentinianism. Since the Enlightenment recognition of the impossibility of nonapologetic varieties of Christianity and the impossibility of the biblical text interpreting the world rather than being interpreted by its more value-free discourses functions more or less axiomatically, even in the discourses that contest the viability of the Enlightenment program(s), two paths are open. New sources of authority are found to replace the authority once invested in the biblical narrative that constituted particular forms of lives. Hegel will experiment with various communal and ethical alternatives that differ from the kind of individualistic alternatives posed by Romantics such as Hölderlin and Novalis, as well as by Schleiermacher. Hegel, however, also (and possibly primarily) takes a more indirect route in prosecuting the actual transfer of the authority of the biblical narrative—either actually or putatively enjoyed in the premodern period—to another text that articulates a different narrative, one that in fact bears a metaleptic relationship to the biblical narrative.

I will be more brief here in outlining Hegel's satisfaction of the three other expectations about the changes that get wrought on Valentinian discourses as they pass through the crucible of the fundamental principles and attitudes of the Enlightenment. If Hegel does not accept the Enlightenment's critique of narrative in general, and the biblical narrative in particular, nevertheless he is more self-conscious in his narrative construction, and more laissez-faire with respect to how to interpret the biblical text than Boehme was in the precritical environment of the seventeenth century. Moreover, epistemological exacerbation expected of discourse in its move from a post-Reformation to a post-Enlightenment environment is also evident. Hegel's discourse cannot be confined to the post-Kantian epistemological problematic, yet, as has been recognized by almost every commentator and critic, his major work is conditioned by this problematic and is inexplicable without it. Concretely, this means that while Hegel will reinstate narrative as a form of knowledge, narrative rendering, which has divine self-development as its object, has as its primary task that of setting forth the conditions of the possibility of knowledge. Arguing against the classical view of a kind of divine knowledge without the subject-object bifurcation, Hegel argues for the detour of representation, even for (or especially for) a grammatical subject that is infinite or divine. For Hegel, then, what I have referred to as the aporetics of representation is an even more central part of his problematic than was the case in Boehme.

Finally, in philosophical discourse, Hegel represents the emblematic version of the translation of a theogonic-agonic narrative into the becoming of the divine-human and the human-divine, that "between" that transcends the divine-human split. Hegel's position, therefore, is just as distant from Feurbach's position as it is from the standard pre-Reformation and Reformation theological traditions. Or in short, Hegel's discourse represents the example in a philosophical discourse of what I call *anthropological displacement*.

Making a Valentinian case with respect to Hegel's speculative discourse is not simply an application of an interpretive system. It is the result of a reading. Prosecuted against the background of the questioning of Enlightenment assumptions about knowledge, narrative, and the cultural viability of Christianity and its narrative, *God's Story: Hegel's Valentinian Curriculum* will chart the way from Kant to Hegel, through Fichte. On the more theological front, it will force important distinctions between the way the two Berliners, Hegel and Schleiermacher, revision the biblical narrative, such that if Hegel admits of Valentinian ascription, Schleiermacher cannot. This is essentially to correct Baur who, as I pointed out in the introduction, confounded the larger movement of pneumatic religion in the modern period with the more specific trajectory of ontotheological narrative. I will argue for more significant continuity between Schleiermacher and standard pre-Reformation and Reformation traditions, as these traditions interpret the biblical narrative, than that found in Hegel. Nevertheless, although I resist judging harshly the experiential turn in Schleiermacher,[11] I will want to emphasize the tendency toward a Marcionite contraction of Christian faith. Importantly, however, a Marcionite contraction is quite other than a Valentinian expansion, even if Marcionite assumption functions as the proximate background of Hegel's Valentinian escalation, as is shown most clearly in Hegel's earliest writings.[12]

With respect to Romanticism, I do not want to argue the totally improbable thesis that Romanticism in its widest spread represents Gnostic or Valentinian return. I am disbarred from making this claim on procedural grounds, since I will be considering only English and German Romanticism, and neglecting the French, Spanish, and American species. With this restriction to English and German species of Romanticism understood, *Deranging Narrative: Romanticism and its Gnostic Limit* will explore the tensional relationship between Romanticism and mainline varieties of Christianity—especially Reformation varieties—when Romanticism sets up literature as an authoritative discourse that replaces or displaces the biblical text. While all Romantics presume the importance of literary discourse that has been autonomous for some time, not all engage the biblical text. Yet in significant numbers English and German Romantics do. The typical form of such engagement is the attempt to syphon off the authority that once belonged to Scripture. The strategies are various and range from making selective retrieval of the biblical text to complementing its figures by other nonbiblical figures that are regarded as equally sublime. Looked at from the widest possible perspective, however, I will argue that in English and German Romanticism the basic form engagement takes amounts to a Marcionite contraction onto the New Testament, with the Old Testament being relegated to the negative presupposition for the liberating message and optimal form of life, illustrated by Christ, which has now taken up residence in poetry and the existence that it calls into being. I will read Novalis and Hölderlin on the German side, and the early Coleridge and Shelley on the English side as providing different and illuminating examples of the multiverse vocabulary of Marcionism in the post-Enlightenment period. Yet if Marcionism provides a useful label for Romanticism's general engagement with the biblical text, I will argue that at its limit, Romanticism's relation to the biblical text becomes defined by transgression. In short, Marcionism gives way to Valentinianism. This limit, I argue, is defined by William Blake, who is not only a major reader of Jacob Boehme, but fulfills in such mythic poems as *The Book of Urizen, Milton,* and *Jerusalem* all the criteria I have mentioned both for post-Reformation and more specifically post-Enlightenment Gnostic return.

Again, as in the case of Hegel, I argue that Blake's mythopoetic discourse satisfies all five general or post-Reformation criteria of Gnostic or Valentinian return. (1) As illustrated by his great mythic poems, Blake's discourse is a revelatory or apocalypse discourse with at least an equivalent authority to the biblical text. This discourse has as its content a six-stage narrative of the fall and recovery of a complex and differentiated state of divine perfection that is typical in Gnosticism or Valentinianism. (2) This six-stage narrative is theogonic, and represents an erotic, kenotic, and agonistic deformation of classical Valentinian genres. (3) Although the renderings are plural, Blake considers his mythic poems (a) to provide an unsurpassable viewpoint from which to look at reality and (b) to provide the most comprehensive account possible of the positive and negative states of existence. Reformation (specifically Reformed) positions and Enlightenment perspectives that would challenge his position are outmaneuvered by being placed within the inclusive story and registered as reflective of fallen forms of existence. Blake's poems, then, set up a fortress of irrefutability, which one sees sketched in Boehme and fully rendered in Hegel.

This brings me to (4). While Blake may avow allegiance to the biblical text and its narrative, his fidelity here is no more in evidence than it is with respect to the Reformed tradition, even the form it takes in Milton, whose poetic and prose discourses challenge Calvin's theological rendition of the biblical narrative. In fact, Blake's mythopoetic renditions constitute a metalepsis of the biblical narrative in which the standard interpretation of every episode of the biblical narrative is questioned—for example, the interpretation of the intradivine life, creation of the cosmos and human being, the fall of human being that is the result of pride and self-concern, Christ as the singular incarnate one and the salvific significance of his passion and suffering, the nature of church, and the nature of the eschaton and the identity of the redeemed. Blake shows that the limit of Romanticism is nothing less than a massive derangement of the biblical narrative.

(5) By consensus Blake's mythic poems set in action a multitude of symbols from a wide array of sources, some poetic, others belonging to the esoteric tradition of religious philosophy. But in telling and retelling the story of redemption by knowledge, it is also evident that his narrative discourse is similarly plural. As in the case of Boehme's and Hegel's discourse, in addition to Valentinianism these are apocalyptic, Neoplatonic, and Kabbalistic narrative strands. Underscoring the important role each discourse plays in resisting Reformed versions of Christianity and its Enlightenment extensions or alternatives, I argue that the presence of these discourses (a) does not undermine the narrative integrity of Blake's apocalypse discourse, (b) fundamentally challenge Valentinianism's taxonomic primacy, or (c) compromise that primacy by being a narrative strand that is not able to be accounted for by Valentinian narrative grammar. I argue that in Blake's complex visionary narrative discourse, Valentinianism asserts its dominance by enlisting all three discourses and essentially making them serve Valentinian visionary, hermeneutic, and narrative interests. At the same time, all three discourses exercise some measure of reflexive effect. Together they aid and abet the more erotic and agonistic configuration of Valentinian narrative and encourage more favorable estimates of matter, time, history, and suffering than those typical of classical Valentinian genres.

A final word should be said about Valentinian enlisting of non-Valentinian narrative discourses as these operate in Blake's mythic poems. In my account of Valentinian enlisting and the reflexive effect of the enlisted narrative discourses in Blake's mythic poems, I do not in principle privilege any one of the three non-Valentinian discourses. For a number of more or less contingent reasons, I highlight apocalyptic. The level of recall of biblical apocalyptic is high throughout the so-called Prophetic poems and is arguably much more obtrusive than the recall of Neoplatonism and the Kabbalah. Major commentators on Blake's work have thought this an appropriate designator, especially in the light of Blake's engagement with the biblical text.[13] To the degree that differences obtrude themselves between Blake's mythic poems and the biblical narrative, they can be held to the account of a radically apocalyptic version of Christianity. The conflict of interpretation is keenest here, and arguably the stakes are highest. For in speaking of the enlisting of apocalyptic by Valentinianism, I want to underscore not how the obvious apocalyptic modes of vision, interpretation, and narrative are controlled by a nonapocalypse form of discourse but rather by another form of apocalypse discourse, whose history shows the facility to engage precisely in such enlisting. In short, concerning the relation between apocalypse forms of discourse, I want to underscore an irony that surfaces in Blake's mythopoetic discourse, that also surfaces in Hegel's conceptual discourse, and whose modern template is provided by the theosophic discourse of Boehme.

Blake's apocalypse discourse, then, satisfies all five general post-Reformation criteria for Valentinian ascription. As I suggested above, there are also four more specific post-Enlightenment criteria. I will argue that no less than in the case of Hegel's discourse that Blake's discourse also fulfills these conditions. First, even more than is the case with Hegel, Blake presumes that a truly satisfying alternative to the biblical narrative can only come into being by negotiating with the biblical text. He rejects, therefore, the common Enlightenment move of simply looking for a form of reality or discourse that could adequately replace the role of the biblical canon. This negotiation represents a transfer of authority from the biblical text to texts of interpretation that essentially become a kind of Scripture. Second, against the backdrop of Enlightenment's dismissal of narrative (and of the biblical narrative in particular), Blake asserts their validity. He accepts the consequence, however, that narrative production is self-conscious, but he suggests that this has always been the case, since the origin of narrative is imagination or "poetic genius." And he considers that the biblical narrative is defensible, provided it is read in the light of vision rather than instrumenal rationality. Third, the epistemological index is as high as one might expect in a situation in which Lockean epistemology sets restriction to knowledge that provokes the response that Locke is not only wrongheaded but perverse in his limitation of vision to the eye and of the world to matter.

As is the case with Hegel's discourse, the third of the three major classical Valentinian paradigms (that is, the *Gospel*), begins to illuminate in a way it does not in the case of Boehme's post-Reformation discourse. As I showed in Part III, the classical Valentinian paradigms that best illuminated Boehme's apocalypse discourse are *PSY* and the *Tractate*. On the threshold of the knowing and the known is the issue of the aporetics of representation. The fundamental concept used to deal with the issue is that of imagination, which plays a similar but arguably even more central role in Blake's apocalypse discourse than it plays in Boehme's discourse, from which he borrows so much. And finally, more explicitly than Boehme, and every bit as conspicuously as in Hegel, I will maintain that the anthopological displacement of an essentially theogonic-agonistic narrative is in evidence. The development of the divine is the development of the "human form divine" that represents the overcoming both of a divine (that is either irresponsibly sovereign, distant, or both) and a human (that is defined by matter, sense, and a time that is not touched by eternity). Blake's mythopoetic productions render a humanized divine or a divinized humanity that bears only the most distant relation to what was asserted by even the most heterodox of Christian mystics.

Again, as is the case in the Hegel book, in *Deranging Narrative: Romanticism and its Gnostic Limit*, I will carry out the central sifting through of the double set of criteria for Gnostic or Valentinian return against the backdrop of uncoupling Valentinian expressions from other non-Valentinian narrative options that similarly question the Enlightenment, and centrally involve a non-community reading of the biblical text. Of course, as indicated already with respect to Hegel, the basic distinction I deploy is that between Marcionism and Valentinianism. The former category has significantly more range in Romanticism, and describes the general way in which Romantics respond to and appropriate the biblical text. By contrast, Valentinianism is a category that covers a single discourse, which is, nevertheless, made possible by the more pervasive attitude of the necessity for a reconstructed Christianity. In addition, however, I want to argue against the coupling of Milton and Blake that has come to be almost canonic in literary criticism.

Usually Milton is read as anticipating Blake, and thus at once as the grandfather of Romanticism and an inchoate realization of Blake, Romanticism's most extreme instance. Accordingly, Milton's Christianity gets read as being only a phenomenon of the surface; at a depth-level, he is involved, as Blake is, in a form of transgressive interpretation in which literature replaces the biblical text, and a creative retelling of the biblical narrative replaces the biblical narrative itself. Availing myself of Blake's own reading of Milton, I will contest this coupling and suggest that while there is much in Milton that swerves from the common tradition of interpretation, the Reformed tradition in particular, he does not authorize the metalepsis that is enacted in Blake's mythic poems. Thus, even if Milton's religious discourse has finally to be regarded as odd, given its debt to apocalyptic and to a lesser extent Neoplatonism and the Kabbalah, it is not haunted, as Blake's discourse is, by Valentinianism. Indeed, in what amounts to his enactment of implicit rules of symbolic and even narrative extension of the biblical rendering of fall and salvation, Milton's poetry, and especially *Paradise Lost*, might be regarded as a protest *avant la lettre* with respect to Blake's revisionings. In a narrow sense, I wish to show the irreducibility of Milton to Blake. In a more general sense, I wish to show how Milton's poetry sets norms for the relation between poetry and Scripture in general, and what can be classed as biblical poetry in particular. In doing so, Milton is made available as a resource for a generous orthodoxy that can include the imaginative extrapolations and improvisions on the biblical narrative that has more than its share of obscurities and silences.

Taking the story of post-Enlightenment forms of Valentinianism as told in *God's Story: Hegel's Valentinian Curriculum* and *Deranging Narrative: Romanticism and its Gnostic Limit* together, it becomes evident, I think, just how extraordinarily close Hegel's and Blake's discourses are. If the national and linguistic worlds from which they emerge are different, this is not to say that the relation of Blake to Hegel is not as deep as Blake's relations to Coleridge and Wordsworth, and the relation of Hegel to Blake is not as deep as Hegel's relation to Fichte and Schleiermacher. In a sense, therefore, these two volumes validate Altizer's brilliant intuition about their proximity, and arguably also, the proximity of poetic and philosophical forms of apocalypse.

As advertised in *Gnostic Return in Modernity*, other volumes on the general theme of the Gnostic or Valentinian complexion of modern discourses will follow the volumes on Hegel and Romanticism. I will continue my analysis of the German Idealists in a volume on Schelling. And there will be general volumes on nineteenth-century diagnosticians of Gnostic return and twentieth-century culprits. Description of these other texts can wait. It suffices to have given some indication of the direction of reflection with respect to two hugely important post-Enlightenment discourses. But *God's Story: Hegel's Valentinian Curriculum* and *Deranging Narrative: Romanticism and its Gnostic Limit* are still future. *Gnostic Apocalypse: Jacob Boehme's Haunted Narrative* and *Gnostic Return in Modernity* constitute the textual present. *Gnostic Apocalypse* represents the second beginning of the Gnosticism project, the properly genealogical beginning that complements and begins to actualize the first beginning, the story told in *Gnostic Return in Modernity* about the possibility of Gnostic return. *Gnostic Apocalypse* is the story about a discourse that is singular in summing up a broader tradition of discourse (philosophical alchemy), in being symbolically porous and discursively open, and being pregnant with future. It is a story about a form of apocalypse that bears the mark of Valentinian grammar and sends this grammar on its way as an opportunity for a discourse that at once maintains continuity with its Christian past and haunts it with its other as the grammar works its deranging of biblical narrative.

Notes

Introduction

1. The basis of all scholarship on Boehme is the *Sämtliche Schriften*, 11 vols. Edited by Will- Erich Peuckert and August Faust (Stuttgart: Frommanns, 1955–61). This is the facsimile reprint of the 1730 edition : *Theosophia Revelata: Das ist: Alle Göttliche Schriften des Gottseligen and Hocherleuchteten Deutschen Theosophi Jacob Böhmens*. Edited by Johann George Gichtel and Johann Wilhelm Ueberfeld. Amsterdam, 1730. Here I give the texts with the volume numbers that get cited in my own text. Vol. 1. *Aurora, oder Morgenröthe im Aufange* (1612); vol. 2. *De tribus principiis, oder Beschreibung der drey Principien Göttliches Wesens* (1619); vol. 3. *De tripici vita hominis, oder Vom dreyfachen Leben des Menschen* (1620).*Viertzig Fragen von der Seelen* (1620); vol. 4. *De incarnatione verbi, oder Von der Menchwerdung Jesu Christi* (1620). *Sex puncta theosophica, oder Von sechs theosophischen Puncten* (1620). *Sex puncta mystica, oder Kurze Erklarung von sechs mystischen Puncten* (1620). *Mysterium pansophicum, oder Grundlicher Bericht vom irdischen und himmlischen Mysterio* (1620). *Der Weg zu Christo* (1624); vol. 6. *De Signatura Rerum* (1622); *De electione gratiae, oder Von der Gnaden-Wahl* (1623); vol.7. *Mysterium Magnum, oder Erklärung uber das erste Buch Mosis (Kap. 1–43)* (1623); vol. 8. *Mysterium Magnum (Kap. 44–78)* (1623); vol. 9. *Quaestiones theosophicae, oder Betrachtung Göttlicher Offenbarung* (1624). *Clavis* (1624). *Epistolae theosophicae, oder Theosophische Sendbriefe* (1618–24). English titles include the following: *The Aurora*. Translated by John Sparrow. London, 1656. Edited by C.J. Barker and D. S. Hefner (London: John M. Watkins, 1914, reissued 1960). *Concerning the Three Principles of the Divine Essence*. Translated by John Sparrow. London, 1648). Reissued by C. J. Barker (London: John M. Watkins, 1909). *The High and Deep Searching Out of the Treefold Life of Man*. Translated by John Sparrow. London, 1650. Reissued by C. J. Barker (London: John M. Watkins, 1909). *The Forty Questions of the Soul and the Clavis*. Translated by John Sparrow. London, 1647. Reissued by C. J. Barker (London: John M. Watkins, 1911). *Of the Incarnation of Christ*. Translated by John Rolleston Earle (London: Constable, 1934). *De Electione Gratiae and Questiones Theosophicae*. Translated by John Rolleston Earle (London: Constable, 1930). *The Signature of All Things, With Other Writings*. No translator given (London: J. M. Dent 1912). Reissued (London: James Clark, 1969). *Six Theosophic Points and*

Other Writings. Translated by John Rolleston Earle (New York: Knopf, 1920). Reissued with introductory essay by Nicholas Berdyaev (Ann Arbor: University of Michigan Press, 1958). *Mysterium Magnum.* Translated by John Sparrow. London, 1654. Edited by C. J. Barker, 2 vols. (London: John M. Watkins, 1924; reprint 1965). *The Way to Christ.* Translated by Peter C. Erb (New York: Paulist Press, 1978). References throughout will be to the German edition, with the number on the right in brackets always referring to the paragraph number in the German edition. The second number from the right always refers to a book within the text. If there is a third number from the right, this will refer to a part of a text. It should be said, however, that by and large I limit myself to editing the existing translations rather than offering translations of my own.

2. See Ernst Benz, *Der Prophet Jakob Böhme: eine Studie über den Typus nachreformatorischen Prophetentums* (Mainz: Academie der Wissenschaften und Literatur, 1959); *Der vollkommene Mench nach Jakob Böhme* (Stuttgart: W. Kohlhammer, 1937); Hans Grunsky, *Jakob Böhme* (Stuttgart: Frommanns , 1956); *Jakob Böhme als Schöpfer einer germanischen Philosophie des Willens* (Hamburg: Hanseatische sanstalt, 1940); Alexandre Koyré, *La Philosophie de Jacob Boehme* (Paris: Vrin, 1929); John Joseph Stoudt, *From Sunrise to Eternity: A Study in Jacob Boehme's Life and Thought* (Philadelphia: University of Pennsylvania Press, 1957); and Andrew Weeks, *Boehme: An Intellectual Biography of the Seventeenth-Century Philosopher and Mystic* (Albany, N.Y.: SUNY Press, 1991).

3. For an account of the influence of Boehme, as well as other forms of esoteric thought, on Hegel and Schelling, see Ernst Benz, *Les sources mystiques de la philosophie romantique allemande* (Paris: Vrin, 1968); also Robert Schneider, *Schellings und Hegels schwäbische Geistesahnen* (Würzburg: Triltsch, 1938). For the influence of Boehme on Schelling, see Robert Brown, *The Later Philosophy of Schelling: The Influence of Boehme on the Works of 1809–1815* (Lewisburg, Pa.: Bucknell University Press, 1977); Kurt Leese, *Von Jakob Böhme zu Schelling: Eine Untersuchung zu Metaphysik des Gottesproblem* (Erfurt: Kurt Stenger, 1927). See also Frederick Kile, *Die theologische Grundlagen von Schellings Philosophy der Freiheit* (Leiden: Brill, 1965), where Boehme is pointed to as an important source of Schelling's later thought. For the relation between Hegel and Boehme, see G. W. F. Hegel, *Lectures on the History of Philosophy*, vol. 3, trans. E. S. Haldane and F. M. Simson (London: G. Routledge and Kegan Paul, 1963), 188–216; David Walsh, 'The Historical Dialectic of Spirit: Jacob Boehme's Influence on Hegel,' in *History and System: Hegel's Philosophy of History*, ed. Robert Perkins (Albany, N.Y.: SUNY Press, 1984), 15–35; 'The Esoteric Origins of Modern Ideological Thought'(Ph.D. diss., University of Virginia, 1978). See also Cyril O'Regan, *The Heterodox Hegel* (Albany, N.Y.: SUNY Press, 1994), esp.150–55, 180–87, 223–32, 279–85.

4. The interest in the relation of Boehme's reflections on nature and more mainline scientific thought has been considerable. Both Boehme's general ideology of the nature of knowledge, and his conviction of a centripetal force as basic have come in for discussion. It is difficult to determine how much exoteric science Boehme was acquainted with—although he seems to be familiar with the general outline of Copernicus's theory. But it is incontrovertible that he was read by scientifically-oriented philosophers such as Leibniz and the Cambridge Platonist Henry More, who, of course, also had theological interests. But what is more interesting, he was read by Isaac New-

ton whose appetite for matters esoteric, and especially alchemy and the Kabbalah, is a matter of public record. There is some dispute as to how much Newton owed to Boehme, with Karl R. Popp and Kurt Poppe giving a somewhat maximalist reading that is challenged by Stephen Hobhouse. See Popp, *Jakob Böhme und Isaac Newton* (Leipzig: Hirzel, 1935); Poppe, 'Uber den Ursprung der Gravitationslehre J. Bohmes, H. More, I. Newton,' in *Die Drei* 23 (1964): 313–40; and Hobhouse, ed., *Selected Mystical Writings of William Law: Edited with Notes and Twenty Four Studies in the Mystical Theology of William Law and Jacob Boehme and an Inquiry into the Influence of Jacob Boehme on Isaac Newton*, 2d ed. (New York: Harper, 1948).

    5. The fullest account of the influence of Boehme in eighteenth-century esoteric and mystical circles is offered by Nils Thune. See his *The Behemenists and the Philadelphians: A Contribution to the Study of English Mysticism in the 17th and 18th Centuries* (Uppsala: Almquist and Wiksells, 1948). For a view of Boehme's influence in the context of a broader pattern of esoteric influence, see Desiree Hirst, *Hidden Riches: Traditional Symbolism from the Renaissance to Blake* (New York: Barnes and Noble, 1964). It was the eighteenth-century French thinker Louis Claude de Saint Martin, the so-called *philosophe inconnu*, who translated Boehme into French, and whose own thought is saturated with the German mystic. In Catholic France, however, there was not much of an audience for Boehme. Saint Martin has been translated into English. See Arthur Waite, *The Unknown Philosopher: The Life of Louis Claude de Saint Martin and the Substance of his Transcendental Doctrine* (New York: Rudolph Steiner Publications, 1970).

    6. For a general account of the influence of Boehme's thought on German Pietism, see Emanuel Hirsch, 'Jakob Böhme und seine Einwirkung auf die Seitenbewegung der pietischen Ziet,' in *Geschichte der neuern evangelischen Theologie*, vol. 2 (Gütersloh: Bertelsmann, 1951), 208–55; also Arlene R. Miller, 'Jacob Boehme: From Orthodoxy to Enlightenment' (Ph.D. diss., Stanford University, 1971). Of course, Friedrich Christoph Oetinger, who both published digests of Boehme's work and appropriated his thought in his kabbalistic revisioning of evangelical thought, represents the high point of Boehme's influence. For explicit treatments of the relation between Boehme and Oetinger, see Sigrid Grossmann, *Friedrich Christoph Oetingers Gottesvorstellung: Versuch einer Analyse seiner Theologie* (Göttingen : Vandenhoeck und Ruprecht, 1979), 59–66; also Wilhelm Albert Hauck, 'Oetinger und Jakob Böhme,' in *Das Geheimnis des Lebens: Naturanshauung und Gottesauffassung Friedrich Christoph Oetingers* (Heidelberg: Winter, 1947), 159–79. But Boehme also had an effect on the pietistic strain in English thought in the eighteenth century, especially through his influence on William Law. Hobhouse's work, cited in note 4, represents the major contribution to the interpretation of the Boehme-Law relation. Not to be forgotten, however, is the fact that Law brought out an English edition of Boehme's works that are still consulted. In addition, see Peter Malekin, 'Jacob Boehme's Influence on William Law,' in *Studia Neophilosophica* 36 (1964): 245–60.

    7. See Franz von Baader, *Samtliche Werke*, ed. Franz Hoffman et al., vols. 2, 3, and 13 (Leipzig: Bethmann, 1851–1855) where Boehme is elucidated and recommended both as an aid toward a speculative renewal of an overly dogmatic Catholicism and as a bulwark against the invidious consequences of Hegel's speculative philosophy. At the

same time Baader is not wholly uncritical. For this point, see Antoine Faivre, 'La critique boehmienne de Franz von Baader,' [paper present at] Colloque Boehme, Paris, 1978; in *Jacob Boehme: ou, L'obscure lumière de la connaissance mystique: hommage a Jacob Boehme dans le cadre du Centre d'études et de recherches interdisciplinaires de Chantilly* (Paris: Vrin, 1979), 135–54. For Martensen, see Hans L. Martensen, *Jacob Boehme: Studies in his Life and Teaching*, trans. T. Rhys Evans (New York: Harper, 1949). The Lutheran Martensen is generally appreciative of Boehme. Boehme is not read as being antithetical to the main-line Lutheran tradition, even if the speculative tendency remains in tension with it.

8. For a general account of the influence of Boehme on Romanticism, and especially on Blake and Novalis, see Jacques Roos, *Les aspects littéraires du mysticisme philosophique et l'influence de Bœhme et de Swedenborg au début du romantisme: William Blake, Novalis, Ballanche* (Strasbourg: Heitz, 1951). For treatments of the influence of Boehme on Blake in addition to Hirst's outstanding *Hidden Riches*, see Bryan Aubrey, *Watchmen from Eternity: Blake's Debt to Jacob Boehme* (Lanham, Md.: University Press of America, 1986) and also Philip Clayton Richards, 'Visionary Mysticism: A Study of Visionary Mystical Experience as it Informs the Work of Jacob Boehme and William Blake and its Importance for the Philosophy of Religion' (Ph.D. diss., Claremont Graduate School, 1987). For Novalis, see Carl Pascheck, 'Der Einfluss Jakob Böhmes auf das Werk Friedrich von Hardenbergs (Novalis)' (Inaugural diss., University of Bonn, 1967). See also the still valuable work by Walter Feilchenfeld, *Der Einfluss Jakob Böhmes auf Novalis* (Berlin: Ebering, 1922). The important relation between Boehme and Coleridge has been documented. See Thomas McFarland, *Coleridge and the Pantheist Tradition* (Oxford: Clarendon Press, 1969), 320–32. W. B. Yeats's indebtedness to the traditions of Boehme and Swedenborg are almost too well known to deserve comment. Kathleen Raine in particular has underscored it. See her *Yeats the Initiate: Essays in Certain Themes in the Work of W. B. Yeats* (Mountrath, Ireland : Dolmen Press, 1986.), esp., 82–85.

9. Ferdinand Christian Baur, *Die christliche Gnosis: oder die christliche Religion-sphilosophie in ihrer geschichtlichen Entwicklung* (Tübingen: Ossiander, 1835).

10. Ferdinand Christian Baur, *Die christliche Lehre von der Dreieinigkeit und Menchwerdung Gottes in ihrer geschichtlichen Entwicklung*. Teil 3, *Die neuere Geschichte des Dogma, von der Reformation bis in der neueste Zeit* (Tübingen: Ossiander, 1843).

11. Franz Anton Staudenmaier, *Die Philosophie des Christentums oder Metaphysik der heiligen Schrift als Lehre von den göttlichen Ideen in ihrer Entwicklung in Natur, Geist und Geschichte*. 1. Bd. *Die Lehre von der Idee: In Verbindung mit einer Entwicklungs-geschichte der Ideenlehre und der Lehre von göttlichen Logos*, Unveränderter Nachdruck [der Ausg.] Giessen 1840 (Frankfurt am Main: Minerva, 1966). For Boehme, see 726–40; Hegel, 228–45, 798–810; Schelling, 176–216; *Zum Religiösen Frieden der Zukunft: mit Rücksicht auf die religiös-politische Aufgabe der Gegenwart*, 3 vols. (Freiburg: n.p., 1846–51). See esp. vol. 3, published in 1851, which has the following subtitle: *Die Grundfragen der Gegenwart mit einer Entwicklungsgeschichte der antichristlichen Principien in intellectueller, religiöser, sittlicher und social Hinsicht, von des Zeiten des Gnosticismus an bis auf uns herab*. For ancient Gnosticism, see esp.116–21; post-Reformation trajectory, 380ff. Hegel is regarded as a major courier. See esp. 144–53, 360–67.

12. David Walsh and Gerard Hanratty are two such admirers of Voegelin. See Walsh, *The Mysticism of Innerworldly Fulfillment: A Study of Jacob Boehme* (Gainsville, Fla.: University of Florida Press, 1983); Hanratty, *Studies in Gnosticism and the Philosophy of Religion* (Dublin: Four Courts, 1997). But non-Voegelinians have also thought Boehme's thought is Gnostic in its basic orientation. See Gerard Wehr, *Jakob Böhme in Selbstzugnissen und Bilddokumenten* (Reinbeck bei Hamburg: Rowohlt, 1971).

13. See Hans Urs von Balthasar, *The Glory of the Lord: A Theological Aesthetics*, vol. 1, *Seeing the Form*, trans. Erasmo Leiva-Merikakis (San Francisco: Ignatius Press, 1982), 49, 195; *The Glory of the Lord: A Theological Aesthetics*. vol. 2, *Studies in Theological Styles*, trans. Andrew Louth, Francis McDonagh, and Brian McNeil; ed. John Riches (San Francisco: Ignatius Press, 1984); *Theo-Drama. Theological Dramatic Theory*, vol. 2, *Dramatis Personae: Man in God*, trans. Graham Harrison (San Francisco: Ignatius Press, 1990) and vol. 3, *Dramatis Personae: The Person in Christ*, trans. Graham Harrison (San Francisco: Ignatius Press, 1992), 317. John Milbank, *Theology and Social Theory* (Oxford: Basil Blackwell, 1991), 148, 160, 184, 302.

14. See Cyril O'Regan, *Gnostic Return in Modernity* (Albany, N.Y.: SUNY Press, 2001).

15. See Hegel, *Lectures on the History of Philosophy*, vol. 3, 188–89.

16. See Baur, *Die christliche Gnosis*, 553.

17. Thomas Kinsella, *A Technical Supplement* (Dublin: Peppercannister, 1975), poem 19, lines 17–18.

18. When Claudel (1868–1955) thinks of language as a coagulated cyclone, he is thinking of language as creative, thus as exceeding the common redundancies of language, but also as interrupting the standard metaphoricity of poetry itself that depends upon form and clarity. At the same time, he believes that in this form of language that reality at its most dynamic and inexplicable is revealed. A good account of Claudel's understanding of "poetic" language, and the way in which it relates to classical and modernist conceptions, is to be found in Adrianna M. Paliyenko, *Misreading the Creative Impulse: The Poetic Subject in Rimbaud and Claudel, Restaged* (Carbondale: Southern Illinois University Press, 1997). See especially chapter 6, 111–32.

19. I here avail myself of John Rolleston Earle's translation in *Six Theosophic Points, and Other Writings* (Ann Arbor, Mich: University of Michigan Press, 1958), 181.

20. Both Hegel and Novalis are in different ways influential couriers of the picture of Boehme as both aboriginal and specifically German, with the former emphasizing the incipient rationality of his system, the latter the irrationality. In general Franz von Baader's portrait proceeds along the more nearly irrationalist front.

21. This is the case somewhat in Hegel's chauvinistic adoption of Boehme as the *philosopher teutonicus* in *Lectures on the History of Philosophy*, but more so in twentieth-century historiography, which perhaps owes more to the antirationalist, Novalis line of adoption. This particular view achieves new and dangerous levels in the work of Hans Grunsky. See in particular his *Jakob Böhmes als Schöpfer einer germanischen Philosophie des*

Willens, where Nietzsche's view of will represents the telos of Boehme's view. Andrew Weeks is particularly critical of this line of thought. See *Boehme*, 36–37.

22. In almost all his texts after *De Triplici Vita Hominis* (1619), with the exception of what might be called his edifying discourses that eventually constituted *The Way to Christ* (*Christosophia* [WC]), Boehme begins his text with trying to understand how a quiescient and immanifest divine turns to manifestation and relation with what is other than God. In his account Boehme unveils stages of divine evolution on the level of Trinity and Wisdom that are inadequate if the divine is to be the perfect divine confessed in Christian witness. He will then go on to describe the more adequately realized stage of divine development that includes description of the divine essence and qualities, and the agon between two principles. Account of the fall of the angels, the creation of human being, the fall of human being, the history of the battle between good and evil, the incarnation of Christ, and eschatological resolution follow. A synoptic account of this narrative, less Boehme's hesitancies between texts, is provided in chapter 1.

23. The importance of the perspectivalism of the Baroque is underscored by philosophers as different as Gilles Deleuze, Louis Dupré, and Karsten Harries. See Deleuze, *The Fold: Leibniz and the Baroque*, trans. Tom Comley (Minneapolis, Minn.: University of Minnesota Press, 1993); Dupré, *Passage to Modernity: An Essay in the Hermeneutics of Nature and Culture* (New Haven, Conn.: Yale University Press, 1993); Harries, 'The Infinite Sphere,' *Journal of the History of Philosophy* 13 (1975), 5–15. For both Dupré and Harries, it is Nicholas of Cusa who provides the most general expression.

24. I am thinking in particular of figures like Sebastian Frank (1499–1543), Caspar Schwenckfeld (1490–1561), and Valentin Weigel (1533–1588). In the substantive part of the text after the introduction, I will cite their works and give some notice of the relevant secondary literature. Here I would like to mention three works that provide synoptic introductions to these thinkers: Rufus M. Jones, *Spiritual Reformers in the 16th and 17th Centuries* (London: Macmillan, 1914; reprint, Boston: Beacon, 1959); Alexandre Koyré, *Mystiques, spirituels, alchemistes du xvi siècle* (Paris: Gallimard, 1961); Steven Osment, *Mysticism and Dissent* (New Haven, Conn.: Yale University Press, 1973).

25. Martin Heidegger, *Schelling's Treatise on the Essay of Human Freedom*, trans. Joan Stambaugh (Athens, Ohio: Ohio University Press, 1985).

26. See *Introduction to Metaphysics*, trans. Ralph Mannheim (Oxford: Basil Blackwell, 1967), where theological thought is regarded as the end of philosophy.

27. See *Schelling's Treatise on the Essay of Human Freedom*, 50ff. See also 'The Onto-Theological Nature of Metapysics,' in *Essays in Metaphysics: Identity and Difference*, trans. Kurt F. Leidecker (New York: Philosophical Library, 1960), 35–67; and *Hegel's Phenomenology of Spirit*, trans. Parvis Emad and Kenneth Maly (Bloomington, Ind.: Indiana University Press, 1988), 98–100, 124–26. If Schelling is not excused from the ontotheology charge, he is not guilty to the same extent as Hegel.

28. As is well known, Christ becomes a central figure in the Schelling of *Philosophy of Revelation* (1841–42) which articulated Schelling's putatively theistic alternative to Hegel's pantheism. When it comes to the Schelling of this period, it is not a ques-

tion of whether Schelling is theological in some general way, in that he identifies the ground of all reality with the highest entity, but whether his ruminations articulate Christian beliefs or not. Obviously, since Schelling's own day, there have been different estimates as to how Christian Schelling's articulation was, with Kierkegaard famously entering a negative verdict. Although Schelling still remains less read than Hegel in the twentieth century, arguably a greater proportion of his theologically interested readers have assumed that his Christian credentials are either not suspect, or at least not as suspect as Hegel's. In a later volume, I will argue against this view, and suggest that Schelling too can be included within the Valentinian line of discourse that begins with Boehme, to whose discourse he owes so much.

29. See note 5 for references to Hirst and Thune. For a representative contribution of Antoine Faivre, see *L'Ésotérisme au XVIIIe siècle en France et en Allemagne* (Paris: Sighers, 1973). For a contribution very much in the tradition of Faivre, see Arthus Versluis, 'Christian Theosophic Literature of the Seventeenth and Eighteen Centuries,' in *Gnosis and Hermeticism from Antiquity to Modern Times*, ed. Roelof van der Broeck and Wouter J. Hanegraff (Albany, N.Y.: SUNY Press, 1983), 217–37.

30. This represents a slightly emended version of Earle's translation. See *Six Theosophic Points*, 33.

31. See William A. Christian, *Doctrines of Religious Communities: A Philosophical Study* (New Haven, Conn.: Yale University Press, 1987); George Lindbeck, *The Nature of Doctrine: Religion and Theology in a Postliberal Age* (Philadelphia: Westminister Press, 1984); Joseph DiNoia, *The Diversity of Religions: A Christian Perspective* (Washington, D.C.: Catholic University Press of America, 1992); Paul Griffiths, *An Apology for Apologetics: A Study in the Logic of Interreligious Dialogue* (Maryknoll, N.Y.: Orbis, 1991).

32. See O'Regan, *Gnostic Return in Modernity*, ch. 2.1.

33. See *Work on Myth*, trans. Robert M. Wallace (Cambridge, Mass.: MIT Press, 1985).

34. In *Work on Myth*, Boehme's theogonic myth seems to be repeated in the 'aesthetic' myths of Romanticism and the "final" myths of Idealism.

35. For this point, see *The Legitimacy of the Modern Age*, trans. Robert M. Wallace (Cambridge, Mass.: MIT Press, 1983), 127–36, esp. 128.

36. In *The Legitimacy of the Modern Age*, 130, Gnosticism is read as supporting a static ontology in which wholeness (spiritual) is lost and restored. In *Work on Myth*, Jonas's theogonic view of the divine, in which the end is more than the beginning, is blithely called a modified Gnosticism. This theogonic registration of a narrative of divine becoming seems to be suggested also on pp. 529, 533, and 542.

37. Elizabeth Brient makes these criticisms of Blumenberg in 'The Immanence of the Infinite: A Response to Blumenberg's Reading of Modernity' (Ph.D diss., Yale University, 1995), 32-45. Blumenberg's apriorism is an object of criticism in David Walsh, *After Ideology: Recovering the Spiritual Foundations of Freedom* (San Francisco: Harper, 1990), 103–05.

38. In *The Legitimacy of the Modern Age,* Blumenberg opposes all forms of the secularization thesis, but especially the influential one prosecuted by Karl Löwith, *Meaning in History: The Theological Implications of the Philosophy of History.* See esp. 3–124.

39. See Baur, *Die christliche Lehre von der Dreieinigkeit* where the influence of Neoplatonism on modern narrative versions of the Trinity is recognized. For Staudenmaier, see *Die Philosophie des Christenthums,* 361–439, where Boehme, Hegel, and Schelling are thought to represent the culmination of a Neoplatonic trajectory that has its point of origin in Philo of Alexandria.

40. If Ernst Benz in his *Les sources mystiques de la philosophie romantique allemande* suggests this view, it is Robert Schulitz who provides what is required for a genealogical foundation in his probing analysis of the relationship between Boehmian and Kabbalistic discourse. See Robert Schulitz, 'Einheit in Differenz: Die kabbalische Metamorphose bei Jakob Böhme' (Ph.D. diss., University of Michigan, 1990).

41. Henri de Lubac, *La postérité spirituelle de Joachim de Fiore,* tome 1, *De Joachim à Schelling* (Paris: Lethielleux, 1979).

42. See esp. *Genesis and Apocalypse: A Theological Voyage Toward Authentic Christianity* (Louisville, Ky.: Westminister/John Knox Press, 1990); *The Genesis of God: A Theological Genealogy* (Louisville, Ky.: Westminister/John Knox Press, 1993).

43. In *Lectures on the History of Philosophy,* vol. 2, trans. E. S. Haldane and Francis H. Simson (London: Kegan Paul, Trench, Trübner, 1892–96), 374–453, where Hegel includes Gnosticism, Kabbalah, and Neoplatonism of a generic narrative of exit and return, which he also identifies with Neoplatonism, thus risking making 'Neoplatonism' a class of itself.

44. In *Die christliche Gnosis,* 626–68, Schleiermacher is plotted on the same line as Hegel (668–735) as a form of *Gnosis* that has its proximate origin in Boehme as the initiator of a new form of religious philosophy (557–611). And in *Die Lehre von der Dreieinigkeit,* with considerable sangfroid, Baur links Meister Eckhart and Boehme, thus making possible a Gnostic attribution to Eckhart.

45. See Hans Jonas, 'The Gnostic Phenomenon: Typological and Historical,' 90–108; Hans Urs von Balthasar, *The Glory of the Lord,* vol. 2, 31–94.

46. David Walsh, *The Mysticism of Innerworldly Fulfillment: A Study of Jacob Boehme* (Gainsville, Fla.: University Presses of Florida, 1983), 106ff.

47. 'Narrative' is basically a linguistic or discursive category, and does not imply that the reality referred to has intrinsically a story or developmental shape. 'Narrativity' is an ontological or ontotheological category and concerns reality itself precisely to the extent that it takes on such a story shape. For a basic discussion, see O'Regan, *The Heterodox Hegel,* 9–11.

48. See Harold Bloom, 'Lying against Time: Gnosis, Poetry, Criticism,' in *The Rediscovery of Gnosticism. Vol. 1. The School of Valentinus,* ed. Bentley Layton (Leiden, The Netherlands: Brill, 1980), pp. 57–72, and *Agon: Towards a Theory of Revisionism* (London: Oxford University Press, 1975).

49. I am here speaking of Irenaeus's figure of *metharmottein* or in Latin, *transfigura*. Irenaeus discusses the figure at two points in *Against Heresies*, bk 1.11, 1 and again at bk 1. 20, 2. The best discussion of the figure is found in Anne Marie McGuire, 'Valentinus and the Gnostike Hairesis: An Investigation of Valentinus's Position in the History of Gnosticism.' (Ph.D. diss., Yale University, 1983), 16-17. I discuss this figure in chapter 3 of *Gnostic Return in Modernity*.

50. In chapter 4.1 of *Gnostic Return in Modernity*, I discuss the ways in which Irenaeus suggests a grammatical rather than invariant interpretation of Gnosticism and Valentinianism. I specifically focus on Irenaeus's emphasis on the plurality, variety, and literary or creative character of Valentinian production.

51. When Ireneaus uses the figure of *metharmottein* in *Against Heresies*, it is used in connection with the image of mosaic, and how in and through Valentinian interpretation the picture of God (and thus God's relations to the world) are transformed or inverted. What is God in the properly Christian picture becomes "dog" in the Valentinian picture, what is "king" becomes "fox." We are meant to reject the transformation of the mosaic, and by implication, see the newly constituted "god" and "king" for what they are: a dog and a fox.

52. See chapters 2, 5, and 7 in particular.

53. *Apocalyptic distention* implies that there is both considerably greater articulation of the cosmic and particularly historical levels of existence that goes hand in hand with their greater importance vis-à-vis classical Valentinian paradigms. This is the crucial feature of *apocalyptic distention*. But I suggest in *Gnostic Return in Modernity*, and illustrate here, that there are also reflexive reflects on the level of vision and hermeneutics.

54. See in particular, Michel Foucault, *The Order of Things: An Archaeology of the Human Sciences*, no translator given (London: Tavistock, 1970), 29–33.

55. By "illuminist side of the Reformation" I mean to denote figures such as Sebastian Frank, Caspar Schwenckfeld, and Valentin Weigel, who are often labeled "spiritual reformers." See note 24.

56. Boehme first ran into trouble with the publication of *Aurora* (1612). This book provoked a writing ban on Boehme by the Lutheran pastor Gregor Richter, which Boehme obeyed until 1619 when he published *De Triplici Vita Hominis* (*Von dreyerley Zustandt des Menschen*). Thereafter in his extraordinarily fertile remaining years (1619–1624), Boehme and the Lutheran authorities were constantly at odds. The attacks on Boehme continued long after his death. Two persons, who wrote massive refutations with equally massive titles, are Johann Frick and Johann Christoph Holthausen: Frick, *Gründliche Undersuchung Jacob Boehmens vornehmster Irrthümer: So auss dessen eigenen Schrifften gezeiget und auss H. Schrift widerlegt werden: Vorrede Dr. Elias Veiels* (Ulm: zu finden bey Wolffgang Kraer Buchbindern druckts Ferdinand Manch, 1697); Holthausen, *Teutscher Anti-Barclajus, das ist, Aussführliche Untersuchung der gantzen Quackerey und Apologia Roberti Barclay* (n.p.: in Verlegung Johann David Zunners; Druckts Johann Dieterich Friedgen, 1691).

57. Heinrich Bornkamm, *Luther und Bornkamm* (Bonn: Marcus and Weber, 1925); also 'Renaissancemystik, Luther und Böhme,' in *Jahrbuch der Luther-Gesellschaft* 9 (1927): 156–97. For a point of view that sees the real continuities rather than discontinuities between Luther and Boehme, see Steven A. Haggemark, 'Luther and Boehme: Investigations of a Unified Metaphysics for Lutheran Theological Discourse' (Ph.D. diss., Luther Northwestern Theological Seminary, 1992).

58. As I will make clear in chapter 2, when I discuss a text of Paracelsus's such as *Philosophia Sagax*, this text, which is read by Foucault as a quintessential nature-philosophy text, is read much more persuasively by a Paracelsus scholar such as Weeks as being animated by broader metaphysical and theological interests.

Part I. Visionary Pansophism and the Narrativity of the Divine

1. Hegel, in *Lectures on the History of Philosophy*, vol. 3, refers to Boehme as "the first German philosopher." Of Boehme, but also Paracelsus, Blake asserted that from their writings that "any man of mechanical talents may produce ten thousand volumes of equal value with Swedenborg." See *The Poetry and Prose of William Blake*, ed. David Erdman (New York: Doubleday, 1965), 42. For Blake there is a hierarchy in the order of vision with Boehme being near the top. Yeats follows Blake in this respect. He agrees with Blake's general judgment on the visionary value of Paracelsus and Boehme, and thinks Blake belongs at least as much to this visionary tradition as the more nearly literary tradition of Spencer and Milton. Yeats seems to have been acquainted with Boehme from early on in his poetic career, possibly the early 1890s. For reflections on Boehme's status as a visionary, and a visionary precursor of Blake, see Kathleen Raine, 'Yeats's Debt to Blake,' in *Yeats the Initiate: Essays on Certain Themes in the Work of W. B. Yeats* (Mountrath, Ireland: Dolmen Press, 1986), 82–105, esp. 82, 85, 88. See also Allen Grossman, *Poetic Knowledge in the Early Yeats* (Charlottesville, Va.: University Press of Virginia, 1969), 68–69, 222.

2. The first experience in 1600 is of the actual shining of a pewter dish, which seemed to Boehme to be invested with significance. The second in 1612 is an actual experience of illumination, but again without a specific content, though it preceded the writing of Boehme's first book, *Aurora*. For accounts of Boehme's mystical experience, see Stoudt, *Sunrise to Eternity*, 56–67; and Weeks, *Boehme*, 4–10, 48–51.

3. Weeks, *Boehme*, 4–10. Interestingly, Weeks invokes the work of Steven Katz, who has been to the forefront of dismantling the notion that mystical experience is unmediated and transcultural. There are two sides to this correction: (1) experience is always mediated through symbols, thus always comes culturally and religiously interpreted; (2) a so-called peak experience in the traditions of mysticism is the motivating event, rather than the crowning height of mysticism, which is the discourse of explication and sometimes explanation. And often—and this is the case certainly in the monotheistic religions—mysticism takes the form of interpretation of sacred texts. See Katz, 'Language, Epistemology, and Mysticism,' in *Mysticism and Philosophical Analysis*,

ed. Steven Katz (New York: Oxford University Press, 1978), 22–74; 'The "Conservative" character of Mystical Experience,' in *Mysticism and Religious Traditions*, ed. Steven Katz (Oxford: Oxford University Press, 1983), 3–60.

4. For *Verstand*, see *Clavis* #99; *Mysterium Magnum* 11, 25; 35, 13. For *Vernunft*, see *De Signatura Rerum*, 8, 3, where Boehme thinks of this form of reason as the worldly spirit in human being. This distinction is fundamental to Boehme, as Benz points out in *Les sources mystiques de la philosophie romantique allemande*, 63. The contrast is, of course, operative in German Idealism, where *Vernunft* is identified as the higher synthetic power, and *Verstand* as the lower, discursive analytic power. Boehme is not only not original in making a distinction between two kinds of knowledge—this was in play throughout the entire German mystical tradition and was central in the influential fifteenth-century mystical text, the *Theologia Deutsch*—but also not original in his actual formulation. At the very least Boehme is preceded in this respect by Valentin Weigel (1533–1588). For this point, see Bernard Gorceix, *La mystique de Valentin Weigel 1533–1588 et les origins de la théosophie allemande* (Paris: Université de Paris, 1972), 109–12.

5. I make slight alterations to Sparrow's translation. I have put back in the word "unavoidable" for "necessary," and I replace "man" with the more inclusive "human being." While this makes for awkwardness in the passage, it does correspond more nearly to Boehme's view that Adam, or essential human being, is neither male nor female. It must be admitted, however, that as with his age in general, Boehme reinscribes the superiority of maleness by thinking of the feminine aspect as subservient to the masculine in their androgynous unity.

6. Will-Eric Peuckert, *Pansophia: Ein Versuch zur Geschichte der weissen und schwarzen Magie* (Berlin: Schmidt, 1976), 385ff. Others who emphasize the pansophistic aspect of Boehme's thought include Benz and Grunsky.

7. Scholem thinks that Boehme's mysticism and the Kabbalah are alike in this respect. Moreover, Scholem notes in passing actual connections between Boehme and the Kabbalah. See *Major Trends in Jewish Mysticism* (New York: Schocken Books, 1941), 1–39, 190, 237.

8. One such place is the preface to *De Signatura Rerum* (1622).

9. For this point, see Michel Henry, *The Essence of Manifestation*, trans. Girard Etzkorn (The Hague: Martinus Nijhoff, 1973), 107, 111.

10. Koyré underscores the importance of this question in his still unsurpassed twentieth-century commentary, *La philosophie de Jacob Boehme*, 248. This is also Nicholas Berdyaev's view in 'Unground and Freedom,' which introduces John Rolleston Earle's translation of *Sex Puncta Theosophica*.

11. Koyré, *La philosophie de Jacob Boehme*, 324.

12. Blumenberg argues that the traditional doctrine of the Trinity sets up the promise of story by breaking with metaphysical monism which completely rules it out, but betrays it by making the hypostases co-eternal and co-equal. Thus, the Christian Trinity represents a secondary repression of myth. See *Work on Myth*, trans. Robert M.

Wallace (Cambridge, Mass.: MIT Press, 1985), 259–60. Blumenberg does not explicitly reflect on the fact that the secondary nature of the repression makes the Trinity a prime locus for narrative breakout, though the breakthroughs of radical narrative he notes in Boehme and Hegel certainly support such an interpretation.

13. No reputable twentieth-century scholar denies the importance of Paracelsus (1490–1543) for Boehme. Benz, Grunsky, Koyré, Stoudt, and Weeks, for example, are in unison on this point. The main issue is whether Boehme's Paracelsian inheritance makes him derivative, or whether Boehme adds something fundamentally new. In line with most commentators on Boehme, I will adopt the second critical position, but not to the detriment of the theological subtlety of Paracelus, which is one of the more usual ways of securing the originality of Boehme.

14. Michel Foucault, *The Order of Things*, 20–33.

Chapter 1. Narrative Trajectory of the Self-Manifesting Divine

1. I speak of 'Immanent Trinity' in inverted commas because Boehme's *Ternarius Sanctus*—the cover-term for the intradivine Trinity in *Aurora*—is not the really real divine that grounds the activities of creation, redemption, and sanctification, as it is in more standard renditions of the Christian Trinity. See, for example, Aquinas, *Summa Theologiae*, I. qq. 36–43. This point has been made by a large number of Boehme commentators. One of the very first was the eighteenth-century emigré to London, Dionysius Andreas Freher. Freher's brilliant commentaries had a very limited private circulation. See Walton, *Notes for an Adequate Biography of William Law, 1854–61*, pp. 259–65. I made use of this difficult to find work at the National Library, Dublin, Ireland. For a similar view about the disturbance of the orthodox version of the Trinity, see Franz von Baader, *Fermente Cognitionis* in *Sämtliche Werke*, Bd. 2, 257, 319, 356; also Koyré, *La philosophie de Jacob Boehme*, 340–43.

2. If this symbol is not used in Boehme's earliest text, *Aurora* (1613), it is a dominant symbol in the later texts. Among the many instances of usage, see *MM* 1, 8; *EG*, 1, 8 ff; *SPT* 1. 1, 7–8. Berdyaev is just one of the many commentators who think of the Unground as the symbol for the ultimate reality in Boehme's mature texts. See his 'Unground and Freedom,' in *Six Theosophic Points*, v–xxxvii.

3. For a good discussion of Boehme's reading of the Unground as "nothing," see Koyré, *La philosophie de Jacob Boehme*, 321ff.

4. See Walton, *Notes for an Adequate Biography of William Law*, pp. 259ff.

5. See Berdyaev, 'Unground and Freedom,' xxxiv. See also Paul Tillich's use of this distinction in *Systematic Theology*, vol. 1 (Chicago: University of Chicago Press, 1951), 187.

6. Michel Henry sums up the importance of *Schiedlickeit* in *The Essence of Manifestation* when he writes : "The thought of Boehme was thoroughly influenced by the

idea of an opposition and a differentiation interior to the life of the Absolute and constitutive of this life precisely in so far as it is no more than a bringing to light of manifestation. The concept of consciousness is thought of by Boehme in its solidarity with the concept of otherness, mirror, splitting, namely in its unity with the ontological process of the internal division of being." 108.

7. The *contrarium* has the sense of differentiation that introduces contradiction and alienation into the divine. It was one of the more appealing aspects of Boehme's theosophical system as far as Hegel was concerned, and characterized the level of real dialectic. This was also one of the more appealing aspects of Boehme's system according to Blake, who avails of it in *The Marriage of Heaven and Hell* when he writes "without contraries there is no progression." See *The Poetry and Prose of William Blake*, 34. The *contrarium* has been much analyzed in the secondary literature. Hans Lassen Martensen made much of it in his book on Boehme, and regarded the distinction between contradiction and contrast as pivotal. See his *Jacob Boehme (1575–1624): Studies in his Life and Teaching*, trans. T. Rhys Evans, new rev. ed. (New York: Harper, 1949), 128. See also Koyré, *La philosophie de Jacob Boehme*, 362–63.

8. For excellent discussions of Wisdom as indicating a move beyond divine "nothing" and undifferentiated unity, see Stoudt, *Sunrise to Eternity*, 211–14; also 219–24. For other contributions to the understanding of Boehme's sophiology, see Koyré, *La philosophie de Jacob Boehme*, 344–48; also Freher in Walton, *Notes for an Adequate Biography of William Law*, p. 265. As Stoudt points out, however, *Gegenwurf* is not the only term used. Other terms used include *das Gefundene* (the discovered); *das Aufgeflössene* (emanated); *das Ausgehauchte* (breathed out), and *das Ausgesprochene* (spoken out).

9. Some of the more explicit associations of Wisdom and *mysterium magnum* are made in *Clavis* #19; *TL* 5, 45; and *SR* 2, 36. Freher in Walton's *Notes for an Adequate Biography of William Law*, cuts through Boehme's often confused statements about *mysterium magnum*, which associates in turn with the Unground and Eternal Nature, by maintaining their essential identity. Freher specifies as a condition for identification, however, that Wisdom is also connected with meontic will (p. 271). See also Koyré, *La philosophe de Jacob Boehme*, 312. Interestingly, in associating *mysterium magnum* with Eternal Nature, as he tends to do especially in *De Signatura Rerum*, Boehme is involved in a repetition of his Paracelsus's tendency to equate *mysterium magnum* with both ultimate and prime matter. I discuss Paracelsus's confusion in chapter 2.1. As the *mysterium magnum* Wisdom does introduce plurality into the oneness of the divine, even if this plurality is archetypal. See *MM* 1, 7; *DI* 1, 10–11.

10. See *Hymen zu Nacht*. For a convenient English translation, see *Hymns to Night*, trans. E. Passage (New York: Liberal Arts Press, 1960).

11. At one level the "heavenly virgin" reflects, for Boehme, the importance of Proverbs 8.22. At another level, one cannot rule out Catholic influence about Mary the "Mother of God," although Boehme's "heavenly virgin" has even more in common with *sancta sophia* of the Eastern Orthodox tradition. It is perhaps appropriate, therefore, that Boehme was an important figure in the sophiological movement in Russia at the end of the nineteenth century. As Koyré points out, however, there are major differences

between Boehme's usage and that of the Eastern Orthodox tradition, which Soloviev, Florenski, and Bulgakov take themselves to be reprising. Apart altogether from the fact that Sophia is never introduced into a theogonic narrative in the Eastern Orthodox tradition, Sophia is alway a mother, moreover a particular mother—that is the mother of the redeemer, Jesus Christ. Neither is the case in Boehme, where Sophia is not a true matrix, and where she is originary with respect to the totality of divine expression. See Koyré, *La philosophie de Jacob Boehme*, 213–14.

12. As I showed in *The Heterodox Hegel*, 107–40, there is nothing standard about Hegel's articulation of the Trinity. And the deviance is self-conscious. From the time of the *Phenomenology* (1807), Hegel is interested in both retrieving the Christian symbol of the Trinity and correcting it. Hegel presumes that the Christian Trinity is intrinsically tritheistic, involving the affirmation of three substances or subjects to the degree to which it affirmed three persons. In line with the *Phenomenology*, in *Lectures on the Philosophy of Religion* Hegel advocated a Trinity of moments rather than persons. But in doing so, he recalled Boehme who suggests a narrative revision of the standard view. Rahner does not elaborate a narrativized Trinity, but he is made anxious by the implications of the hypostatic and tripersonal view of the Trinity, arguing that pastorally at least it functions tritheistically. See Karl Rahner, *The Trinity*, trans. Joseph Donceel (New York: Herder and Herder, 1970).

13. After the work of Robert Brown, the influence of Boehme on Schelling hardly needs to be established. See his *The Later Philosphy of Schelling: The Influence of Boehme on the Works of 1809–1815* (Lewisburg, Pa.: Bucknell University Press, 1977). But, of course, ontotheological voluntarism is one of the forms this influence takes. Even as early as Schelling's voluntarist breakthrough in the *Essay on Human Freedom* in 1809 the influence of Boehme is apparent. For instance, when typifying will (*Wille*) in #350 Schelling uses adjectives like "unoriginated" (*unanfängliche*) and "groundless" (*ungründliche*) typical of Boehme's description. Schopenhauer's debt to Boehme is less obvious. But something like the anxiety of influence is indicated when in an important discussion of will, Boehme is introduced, only to be dispatched in a few sentences. See Arthur Schopenhauer, *The Fourfold Root of Sufficient Reason*, trans. E. F. J. Payne (La Salle, Ill.: Open Court, 1974), 22–23; also *The World as Will and Representation*, trans. E. F. J. Payne (New York: Dover Publications, 1966), 318–25. For the relation between Boehme and Schopenhauer, see Andrew Weeks, 'Schopenhauer and Boehme,' in *Schopenhauer-Jahrbuch* 73 (1992), 7–17; also *German Mysticism from Hildegard of Bingen to Ludwig Wittgenstein: A Literary and Intellectual History* (Albany, N.Y.: SUNY Press, 1993), 223, 230–32.

14. At the same time Boehme's commentators have been divided on this issue. For instance, Stoudt thinks that the binary scheme is primary. See *Sunrise to Eternity*, 212. Koyré, on the other hand, believes that the trinitarian scheme is primary. See *La philosophie de Jacob Boehme*, 335.

15. For meontological pull, see Michel Henry, *The Essence of Manifestation*, 108, 112.

16. I use this term advisedly. For if Boehme wishes to account for a divine movement whereby the divine undergoes an increase in being and knowledge, the divine also

undergoes an increase in what can be regarded as existential or experiential potential. At the level of the immanent divine, the divine cannot perceive or experience. Boehme brings this point out negatively in *Mysterium Magnum* (chs. 5–6) when he suggests that only insofar as the divine transcends the Quaternity does it have the ability to see, hear, smell, taste, and touch, all in a spiritual sense. Senses, or their conjoint operation that makes for a divine sensibility, are regarded as necessary for both knowledge of individual and for a vulnerability with respect to otherness.

17. The passage reads: *Mark es recht: Ich verstehe adhier mit Beischreibung der Natur die ewige, nicht die zeitliche.*

18. Another term that is used almost as often as *Sucht* is *Begierde* (hunger). The hunger is the hunger for being or *Wesen*.

19. Arguably, it is the emphasis on contractive or centripetal force that has led some commentators to postulate some real connection between Boehme and Newton's view of gravitation. An influence cannot be ruled out of hand, given that Boehme was read along with considerable amounts of other esoterica by Newton. There have been less and more moderate readings of influence. For maximalist readings, see Karl R. Popp, *Jakob Böhme und Isaac Newton* and Kurt Poppe, 'Über den Ursprung der Gravitationslehre J. Böhme, H. More, I. Newton.' For a more moderate reading, which acknowledges influence, while contesting the view that Newton's theory of gravitation is determined by Boehme, see Steven Hobhouse, *Selected Mystical Writings of William Law.*

20. Grunsky, *Jakob Böhme*, 125–36. For passages in which imagination is associated with darkness, see *SR* 13, 25; *IV* bk 2. 3, 14; *SPT* 1. 1, 62.

21. See *Biographia Literaria*, ch.13.

22. See Novalis, *Hymns to Night*, 9.

23. Not unlike his precursor Paracelsus who wrote in the vernacular, Boehme has a penchant for latinisms. For this binary pair, see *Mysterium Pansophicum* 34; *IV* bk 2. 3, 34 among others.

24. *Aurora* 8 reads: "Two qualities in nature. The one pleasant, heavenly and holy; the other fierce, wrathful, hellish, and thirsty"; 18 reads: "ever since the beginning the bad quality has wrestled with the good."

25. Other very similar passages on *contrarium* include *MM* 26, 27; *TL* 18, 21.

26. See also *EG* 2, 17 where wrath is taken to be the instrument of joy, and *MM* 5, 7 where darkness is regarded as the condition of manifested or self-reflected light. Schelling's *Weltalter* provides a brilliant gloss on this Boehmian point here by suggesting that while wrath and joy have "existential equality," there is also a "necessary sequence of revelation" that moves from wrath to joy. See *The Ages of the World*, trans. Frederick de Wolfe Bolman (New York: Columbia University Press, 1942; reprint, New York: AMS Press, 1967), 147, 200.

27. As the Greek-English lexicon defines it (p. 554), this patristic word, *enantio-dromia*, has as its verbal root *enantiodromein*, meaning "something running in the opposite direction." See Henry George Liddell and Robert Scott *A Greek-English Lexicon* (Oxford: Clarendon Press, 1968). Thus, it comes to mean the play of opposites, dark-light, death-life, etc. Importantly, the play is structural, with no sense of direction. As Jung interprets alchemy, however, while it continues to have a generic sense of the play of opposites, it comes to have directionality, for *enantiodromia* now names the essential part of the individuation process having to do with the sublation of the negative, imaged in alchemy by the *massa confusa*. For Jung, see Herbert Read, Michael Fordham, and Gerard Adler, eds., *The Collected Works of C. G. Jung* (London: G. Routledge & Kegan Paul, 1953ff.) vol. 12, *Psychology and Alchemy*, 83; vol. 5, *Symbols of Transformation*, 375, 438; vol. 13, *Alchemical Studies*, 245.

28. See Heidegger, 'Language in the Poem: A Discussion on Trakl's Poetic Work,' in *On the Way to Language*, trans. Peter D. Hertz (San Francisco: Harper & Row, 1971), 157–98, esp. 151–53, where there is a discussion of *Riss*.

29. I am here recalling the *Stauros* of *Ptolemy's System*, the scholastic Valentinian system that is presented by Irenaeus in *Against Heresies*. I will discuss the relation between Boehme's visionary narrative discourse and this particular classical Valentinian paradigm in some detail in ch. 6.

30. Berdyaev denies that Boehme's theogonic position is Manichean, and he thinks its unitive origin is emblematic for modern theogonies. See 'Unground and Freedom,' xxxiv. The non-Manichaean nature of the duality of the divine is underscored by Schelling in both the *Essay on Human Freedom* and in *The Ages of the Word*. Without a unitive point of origin, resolution of the agon is impossible. Resolution is constitutive for Schelling, if one is to speak of development in the divine, and if one is to have the possibility of a system.

31. See Koyré, *La philosophie de Jacob Boehme*, 247; Stoudt, *Sunrise to Eternity*, 83ff. The general connection between quality and pain is on the surface. *SPT* 3. 2, 6 is just one of the many examples. And, of course, pain or angst specifies the third quality in particular.

32. The fact that there are seven planets also influences the number of qualities. For on the basis of signatures, there should be a correspondence between the invisible and the visible. See *De Signatura Rerum* 9.8.

33. Still, these two streams are not fully separate. For instance, in *Aurora* the seventh quality is associated with "body," which is closely related to salt, and is called the *salitter* (16, 5 and 9). And in *Mysterium Magnum* while the sulphur, mercury, salt triad dominate, Boehme does not throw out his earlier associations. The first quality is "astringent," the second, "bitter" (6, 19).

34. See especially *De Electione Gratiae* 3, 31 (English 31, 33), where Boehme writes, "The sixth form is speech, namely the mouth of God, the sound of the powers, where the Holy Spirit in the love brings Himself out of the comprehended powers."

35. For a particularly good discussion of the *turba* in the secondary literature, see Steven A. Haggemark, 'Luther and Boehme,' 175ff.

36. For other texts, see *TF* 5, 2–6; 7, 2–7; *EG* 4, 29–31; *TL* 9, 38. The prideful nature of Lucifer becomes a trope that Milton picks up on in *Paradise Lost*. For a good discussion of this, see Margaret Lewis Bailey, *Milton and Jakob Boehme* (New York: Oxford University Press, 1914), 147.

37. See among other texts, *Forty Questions of the Soul* 15.4; *TL* 2, 53–54; *IV* bk 1. 6, 14.

38. See the famous lines of *Paradise Lost*: "A mind is its own place, and in itself / Can make a heav'n of hell, a hell of heav'n." In a future volume on Romanticism, I will explore the relationship between Boehme and Blake on the internality of heaven and hell, especially the latter.

39. In ch. 2 I will treat Boehme's debt to Paracelsus with respect to both the term, *astrum*, and its general understanding. Boehme, I will argue, stabilizes the distinction between the temporal and eternal dimensions of Principles prior to the physical world that are anything but stable in Paracelsus.

40. See Jacques Derrida's famous essay 'White Mythology,' especially the section called 'The Ellipsis of the Sun' in *The Margins of Philosophy*, trans. Alan Bass (Chicago: University of Chicago Press, 1982), 207–71, esp. 230–245.

41. See *Aurora* 25, 65ff. for an exemplary expression of Copernican allegiance. For Boehme's Copernicianism, see Stoudt, *Sunrise to Eternity*, 79, 93.

42. As with the Kabbalists, and Leibniz somewhat later, Boehme believes in a universal language. On the most general level, all of reality is a language, since in all of reality there are external means of expression of the inner core. Thus, there is a book of nature as well as Scripture. In a more specific sense, however, Boehme is interested in the basic units of meaning that will enable one to get at the truth of any sentence or statement or figure (Nimrod, Abraham, Hagar, etc.), scriptural or otherwise. Parallel to the Kabbalists, Boehme inaugurates a mystical phonetics in which he can explicate the meaning of words or sentences. One of these explications is his elucidation of the *Tetragrammaton* in *Mysterium Magnum* (36, 50–53) in which, like the Florentine Kabbalists Pico della Mirandola and Reuchlin, he shows that Jesus is an essential part of its definition. For a linguistically oriented analysis of Boehme's mystical phonetics, see Steven A. Konopacki, *The Descent into Words: Jakob Boehme: Transcendental Linguistics* (Ann Arbor, Mich.: Karoma Publications, 1979).

43. Søren Kierkegaard, *The Concept of Anxiety: A Simple Psychologically Orienting Deliberation on the Dogmatic Issue of Hereditary Sin*, ed. and trans. Reidar Thomte and Albert B. Anderson (Princeton, N.J.: Princeton University Press, 1980), 41ff. In the notes that accompany the text, it is obvious that Kierkegaard is aware of Boehme's views on the origin of sin and their influence in the Schellingian school (p. 187).

44. This position is most forcibly argued, however, in Boehme's antipredestination tract, *De Electione Gratiae* and his devotional tracts, gathered during his life into a single

volume. These texts have now been translated into English. See *The Way to Christ*, trans. Peter Erb (New York: Paulist Press, 1980). It was these devotional aspects of Boehme's work, rather than the more mythological ones, that exerted the greater influence on William Law.

45. For Eckhart, see Sermons 47 and 70 in the Quint edition of the German works: Meister Eckhart, *Die deutschen Werke*, ed. Joseph Quint (Stuttgart: W. Kohlhammer, 1958–).

46. See Peter Erb's introduction to *The Way to Christ*, 15–16.

47. This kind of language is used fairly freely by Boehme. See in particular *MM* 36. See also *The Way to Christ*, 118, 162, 164.

48. Interestingly, these include Abraham, whose faith is regarded as a form of seeing (*MM* 39, 8–9). Especially important is Abraham's vision of the three men, which, as in patristic interpretation, is taken as a type of the Trinity.

49. Speaking of Boehme's use of the symbol of the lilies, Franckenberg explains that it "evokes the paradise of God which will be manifest in the last time, when the end will return to the beginning, and when the circle will be closed." Cited by de Lubac in *Postérité spirituelle de Joachim de Fiore*, tome 1, 221.

50. The eschatological dimension of Sophia is perhaps that aspect of Boehme's sophiology found most attractive to Russian thinkers such as Soloviev, Florenski, and Bulgakov.

51. As Boehme points out on a number of occasions, at a very incipient level of divine life before the appearance of Eternal Nature, seeing is not fully real. In the act of 'seeing,' nothing or 'no something' is seen.

52. See G. W. F. Hegel, *Philosophy of Nature; being Part Two of the Encyclopaedia of the Philosophical Sciences (1830)*, trans. A. V. Miller from the Pöggeler's ed. (1959) and from the Zusätz in Michelet's text (1847) (Oxford: Clarendon Press, 1970–1975), #247 zu; #248 zu.

53. See O'Regan, *The Heterodox Hegel*, 43, 104, 106, 134.

Chapter 2. Discursive Contexts of Boehme's Visionary Narrative

1. For a more recent work that connects Boehme and Eckhart, see Gerald Hanratty, *Studies in Gnosticism and Philosophy of Religion* (Dublin, Ireland: Four Courts Press, 1997).

2. For the works of Paracelsus, see *Sämtliche Werke. 1. Abteilung: Medizinische, naturwissenschaftliche und philosophischen Schriften*, 14 vols., ed. Karl Sudhoff (Munich: Barth and Oldenburg, 1922–33; *Sämtliche Werke. 2. Abteilung: Theologische und religionsphilosophische Schriften*, ed. Kurt Golhammer (Stuttgart: Steiner, 1955–). Eight of fourteen projected volumes have appeared. This work is abbreviated *SW*. Only a portion of

Paracelsus's work has been translated. For an English translation of some of his scientific works, see Arthus Waite's dated *Hermetical and Alchemical Writings of Paracelsus*, 2 vols. (London: Eliot, 1914). For a taste of Paracelsus's voluminous religious output, see Jolando Jacobi, *Paracelsus: Selected Writings*, 2d ed. (Princeton, N.J.: Princeton University Press, 1958).

3. Trithemius (1467–1516) was a syncretistic thinker who joined together strands of Kabbalah, Neoplatonism, and Hermeticism. The Kabbalah in Trimethius, as it is in Paracelsus, is fairly tropic. It refers as much to the secret or occult dimension of natural and textual reality as the techniques that might be used to decode it. For the relationship between Trithemius and Paracelus, see Walter Pagel, *Paracelsus: An Introduction to Philosophical Medicine in the Era of the Renaissance*, 2d, rev. ed. (Basel: S. Karger, 1982), 227. For the relation between Paracelsus and Ficino, see ibid., 174ff.

4. This is the position adopted by a number of Paracelsus scholars. Kurt Goldammer, the editor of the religious and theological works, is just first among equals. See his *Paracelsus: Natur und Offenbarung* (Hannover: Theodor Oppermann, 1953); and *Paracelus in neuen Horizonten: Gesammelte Aufsätze Salzburger Beiträge zur Paracelsforschung* (Vienna: Verband der Wissenschaftlichen Gesellschaften Österreichs, 1986). See also Ute Gause, *Paracelsus: Genese und Entfaltung seiner frühen Theologie: Spätmittelalter und Reformation*, Neue Reihe, 4 (Tübingen: Mohr, 1993) and Andrew Weeks, *Paracelsus* (Albany, N.Y.: SUNY Press, 1996).

5. The first volume of the second division of the *Sämtliche Werk* , in which Christology is most to the fore has not yet appeared. The provisional title assigned by the editor for this volume is *Allgemeine zu 'seligen Leben.' Gott, Christus, Kirche*. For Paracelsus's views on the Trinity, see Harmut Rudoph, 'Kosmosspekulation und Trinitätslehre: Ein Beitrag zur Beziehung zwischen Weltbilt und Theologie bei Paracelsus,' in *Salzburger Beiträge zur Paracelsusforschung* (Vienna: Verband der Wissenschaftlichen Gesellschaften Östereichs, 1978).

6. The commentaries on the Psalms take up four volumes (vols. 4–7) of the second division of the *Sämtliche Werke*. Volumes 8 and 9 are on other Old and New Testament texts, the most prominent of which is the Gospel of Matthew. For reflection on Paracelsus's commentary on Matthew, see Arlene Miller-Guinsberg, 'Paracelsian Magic and Theology: A Case Study of the Matthew Commentaries,' in *Kreatur und Kosmos: internationale Beiträge zur Paracelsusforschung*, ed. Rosemarie Dilg-Frank (Stuttgart: Fischer, 1981), 125–39. For a more general reflection on Paracelsus's biblical hermeneutics, see Harmut Rudolph, 'Schriftauslegung und Schriftverständnis bei Paracelsus,' in *Kreatur und Kosmos*, 101–24.

7. Weeks points out that much early twentieth-century German historiography is marred by the Romantic myth of Paracelus as iconoclast and genius. Where this is not the case, as in the editor of the 'scientific' writings, that is, Karl Sudhoff, there is the attempt to gain respectability by making the religious marginal. See Weeks, *Paracelsus*, 21–29.

8. This prejudice can be seen even in fine Paracelsus scholars like Walter Pagel and Allen G. Debus. See Pagel, *Paracelsus*; and Allen G. Debus, *The French Paracelsians:*

The Chemical Challenges to Medical and Scientific Tradition in Early Modern France (Cambridge: Cambridge University Press, 1991).

9. See Weeks, *Boehme*, 27–31.

10. Foucault, *The Order of Things*, 20–33.

11. For reflection on the notion of image and imaging, see Weeks, *Paracelsus*, 101–28; 11 and 170.

12. Koyré, *Mystiques, spirituels, alchemistes*,106.

13. See Paracelsus's remarks on *mysterium magnum*, which is regarded as a kind of primal "stuff" in *Philosophia ad Athenienses* (*SW* 1. 13, pp. 390–93).

14. The three Principles inchoate in earlier texts such as *Von der ersten drei principiis* (*SW* 1. 3, pp. 1–11) are prominent in the *Opus Paramirum*, one of his most important texts. See *SW* 1. 9, pp. 40, 50, 83, 91, 95, 101, 105. For assertions of the cosmological (and not necessarily theological) importance of these three Principles, see among others, Pagel, *Paracelsus*, 218; also Ernst Kaiser, *Paracelsus* (Hamburg: Rowault, 1969), 103.

15. Other relative origins include the *yliaster*, a neologism concocted from *hyle*, the Greek word for matter, and *aster*, the Greek word for star. For Paracelsus, the *yliaster* is more basic than the *astrum*, which is the spiritual stuff of the physical universe. Boehme will avail himself of *mysterium magnum*, *yliaster*, and *astrum* in *De Signatura Rerum*, and he will bring clarity to their relationships, especially the relationship between *mysterium magnum* and *yliaster*, which is left unclear in Paracelsus.

16. The importance of the *Liber de Sancta Trinitate* has been underscored by both Rudolph and Weeks. See Rudolph, 'Kosmosspekulation und Trinitätslehre'; Weeks, *Paracelsus*, 82–83. My translation here essentially follows that of Weeks.

17. Blumenberg, *Work on Myth*, 260.

18. This is the thesis of Staudenmaier's *Die Philosophie des Christentums* (pp. 743–820) , where Hegel's Sabellianism is the culmination of a post-Reformation trajectory that includes Schwenckfeld, Weigel, and Boehme.

19. For Jung on Paracelsus, see *Alchemical Studies*, 110–181. See also Weeks, *Paracelus*, 83–84, 126–27, 149.

20. For this identification, see *SW* 1. 13, p. 391. This identification is also prominent in Paracelsus's *Das Buch der Mineralibus* (*SW* 1. 3, pp. 25–65. This is in effect a double confusion, for *prime matter* tends to be associated with the *astrum*, which is a tertiary rather than primary Principle. For a good account of Paracelsus's confusion, see Walter Pagel, 'The Prime Matter of Paracelsus,' in *Ambix* 9 (1961): 117–35.

21. *Archeus* is the source of differentiation or separation. Derived from *Ares*, the Greek God of the forge, *archeus* is necessary for the generation of particulars. See among other secondary works, Koyré, *Spirituels, mystiques, alchemistes*, 102; Pagel, *Paracelsus*, 91; also Jung, *Psychology and Alchemy*, 138. In Jung's analysis, *archeus* will also become a prin-

ciple of individuation of psyche. Boehme uses the term *archeus*, identified with spirit, in *De Signatura Rerum* (7), and locates it in the *yliaster*, which functions synonymously with Eternal Nature. Eternal Nature serves multiple functions: (i) it is a source of the multiplicity of real particulars; and (ii) the multiplicity of real particulars is a necessary condition for the individuation of the divine, since on the one hand, this authenticates the genuine creativity of the divine, and on the other, is a condition of the possibility of both perception and consciousness of the divine (subjective genitive), which in turn are conditions of the possibility of self-consciousness.

22. In *Confessions* bk 10. 11ff one hears echoes of Augustine's earlier *Commentaries on Genesis* that is directed against Manichaean interpretation of the chaos of Genesis as being a kind of primal stuff that is co-eternal, coeval, and thus co-divine. Aquinas, for instance, in the *Summa Theologiae* I, q. 41, art. 1 makes the judgment that the preposition "*ex*" or "from" should not be interpreted in a material sense, and suggests that it is better to interpret it as "after." His view that *creatio ex nihilo* means that something comes to be from no particular stuff, but solely according to the power of a first cause who requires nothing to work with, is basically representing a reprise of Augustine.

23. See Weeks, *Paracelsus*, 118.

24. While Sophia is distinct from the the trinitarian differentiation of divine essence, and in particular is not collapsed into the Son,one can only speak of hypostasis or person in an inverted-comma sense. Paracelsus seems to be dealing more nearly with ultimate Principles that ground the visible universe than with Persons worshiped in the religious community.

25. This is a real link between Boehme and Paracelsus, for the major deficit of Sophia is the lack of gyne-ontological potency. Sophia is a virgin, and virgins cannot give birth to a teeming multiplicity of a real world, which in turn serves as a condition of the possibility of divine personality and self-consciousness.

26. In *Mysterium Magnum* and *SPT* 2. 39, sulphur and the Son are closely related. On the one hand, sulphur with its combustibility is a transition element that defines the Son as the point of transformation from death to life and, on the other, the *sul* of sulphur is phonetically associated with *sol* or sun, which in turn is the natural image of the Son. In *Mysterium Magnum*, mercurius or mercury in the Second Principle is associated with the liveliness of mercury and speech. In *Mysterium Magnum*, Sophia as the Kingdom or "Body" of God (*MM* 6, 7) is associated with salt and is called the *Salitter*, a neologism that is already found in *Aurora* (1612).

27. For this identification, see Stoudt, *Sunrise to Eternity*, 215.

28. Boehme was aided in his distinguishing of the *yliaster* from *mysterium magnum*, on the one hand, and the *astrum* on the other, by those who tried to make Paracelsus more consistent with respect to his ultimate Principles. One thinker of special importance in this respect is Heinrich Khunrath (1560–1605), who thinks of the *yliaster* as the "world-orginary chaos" (*weltanfangliche Chaos*). This clarification is central in Khunrath's *Vom Hylealischen, das ist Prematerialischen Catholischen oder allgemeinen Natürlichen Chaos den naturgemässen Alchymie und Alchymisten* (Magdeburg: n.p., 1597).

29. The *astrum* theory is central to Paracelsus's opus as a whole, and enjoys particular prominence in the *Opus Paramirum*, the *Paragranum* (SW 1. 8, p. 71), and *Astronomica Magna*(*SW* 1. 12, pp. 13, 36, 304). As Pagel points out in *Paracelsus*, the *astrum* theory had been foreshadowed in the *Oculta Philosophia* of Agrippa von Nettesheim. For a good account of Agrippa, see C. C. Nauert, *Agrippa and the Crisis of Renaissance Thought* (Urbana, Ill.: University of Illinois Press, 1965).

30. See Weeks, *Paracelsus*, p. 179.

31. Another Paracelsus neologism which combines *astrum* with the Greek adjective *kaka*, meaning "bad." As Pagel points out in *Paracelsus* (p. 113), *cagastrum* signifies a reality that is far from the center, a reality corrupted and putrefying.

32. In Paracelsus himself Christ is not explicitly an androgynous figure. In Khunrath, however, who, as we have seen, clarified Paracelsus's hierarchy of ontological and cosmological grounds, the clearer association of Christ with the *lapis philosophorum*, and thus the identity of *sol* and *luna*, encourages an androgynous reading of Christ. In *Amphitheatrum* Khunrath writes: "Without blasphemy I say: in the book or mirror of nature, the stone of the philosophers, the preserver of the macrocosm, is the symbol of Jesus Christ crucified; savior of the whole race of men, that is, of the microcosm. From the stone you shall know in natural wise Christ and from Christ the stone." For this passage, see Jung, *Alchemical Studies*, 126-27. For a brief history of this particular text, see Lynn Thorndike, *History of Magic and Experimental Science*, vol. 5 (New York: Columbia University Press, 1958), 273–75.

33. See among other texts *De Generatione Hominis* (*SW* 1. 1, pp. 287–307); *Opus Paramirum* (*SW* 1. 9, pp. 37–231; *Virtute Imaginativa* and *Liber de Imaginibus* (*SW* 1, 13, pp. 304–21; 357–87).

34. Arguably, both Agrippa and Pico della Mirandola offered more searching accounts of imagination. Nevertheless, in their work imagination does not enjoy the prominence it has in Paracelsus. For a comparison of Paracelsus and his Renaissance precursors on this point, see Pagel, *Paracelsus*, 300.

35. For the connection of imagination with women under the general auspices of "defilement," see Jung, *Psychology and Alchemy*, 52–3.

36. See Weeks, *Paracelsus*, 111, 138–39.

37. Ibid., 161, 167–69.

38. The "light of nature" (*licht der Natur*) is commensurate to the *astrum*, which is superior to the physical universe. See *Paragranum* (*SW* 1. 8, p. 71) and *Astronomica Magna* (*SW* 1.12, 23, 36, pp. 304, 402). Nonetheless, there is a light beyond this which is the light of eternity. This light is not only beyond the light of nature, but also subtends it (*SW* 1. 11, p. 201). For a good discussion of the relation of the light of nature and the light of eternity with many of the more important passages cited, see Henry Maximilian Pachter, *Paracelsus: Magic into Science: Being the True History of the Troubled Life, Adventures, Doctrines, Miraculous Cures* (New York: Schuman, 1951), 208–12.

39. Alchemists in the Paracelsian tradition like Khunrath will be even more emphatic about this connection of Christ and light than Paracelus.

40. This contrast is central to Paracelsus, and is one of the ways Boehme parses the distinction between the two Principles, even after the heyday of Paracelsian influence—that is, in *De Signatura Rerum* (1622) is over. In Paracelsus's texts this contrast runs the gamut from empirical generalizations from the treatment of sick individuals to foundational Principles of reality. Alchemy, which is intrinsically tied to salvation, is the process by which the healthy life is separated from the poisonous life. For typical expressions of this point, see *SW* 1. 1, 123 and 190; 1. 4 pp. 200, 268, 270. This means, of course, that transformation is tied up with the force of separation, the *archeus*. Interestingly, digestion provides an image of this activity of separation, with evacuation being nothing more nor less than a separation of the unhealthy from the healthy. While Boehme does not give as much prominence to digestion as Paracelsus, as Weeks points out, he is extraordinarily interested in "waste" as a sign of evil (Weeks, *Boehme*, 33). It should be noted that as late as Hegel, German thinkers are recalling the waste, the *caput mortuum*, literally the "dead remains" left over in the retort after the alchemical operation. See Hegel, *Encyclopaedia of Philosophical Sciences*, #40. It should also be noted that in his discussion of animals in *The Philosophy of Nature* (*Encyclopaedia* #353–55), Hegel spends some time speaking of the power of assimilation and waste, and he makes it clear that his discussion is a metaphor for the process of dialect itself, which is the dialectic of absolute Spirit.

41. See esp. *SW* 1. 3, pp. 41–42; 1. 7, pp. 265–66.

42. Here I develop a position hinted at by Koyré who, noting in *La philosophie de Jacob Boehme* (p. 281) that there are real connections between Boehmian and Eckhartian *apophasis*, suggests that ultimately there is a world of difference. For Boehme, the divine "nothing," which in Eckhart is divine plenitude, is in Boehme the divine emptiness or indeterminacy.

43. When I speak of the privileging of divine unity, I have in mind the classical Neoplatonism of Plotinus and Proclus rather than the tradition of Christian Neoplatonism. In particular, I am not assuming that the Christian Neoplatonic tradition to which Eckhart was an heir, specifically the tradition of Pseudo-Dionysius and Eriugena, has monistic inclinations.

44. This is the point of view advanced by Ernst Benz in *Les sources mystiques*, 114–17.

45. *Divine Names* 1, 1–5 is typical in this respect. Pseudo-Dionysius uses such terms as "ineffable" (*arrhetos*), "inconceivable" (*adiannetos*), and "incomprehensible" (*aperileptos*). The unnameability and unknowability of the divine are constantly recurring themes in Eckhart's German sermons. See Meister Eckhart, *Die deutschen Werke*. For ineffability or unnameability, see Sermons 2, 17, 26, 29, 53, 58, 77. For unknowablility, see Sermons 3, 9, 57, 58, 59, 77. In Sermon 57 Pseudo-Dionysius is explicitly recalled.

46. It is hardly necessary to point out that for Eckhart, as with Dionysius and the whole Dionysian tradition, "unknowing" is a form of transnoetic experience of consum-

mate immediacy. Eckhart's particular version of unknowing has been brought into conversation with post-modern forms of thought by John Caputo and Reiner Schürmann. See especially, Caputo, 'Mysticism and Transgression: Derrida and Meister Eckhart,' in *Derrida and Deconstruction*, ed. Hugh J. Silverman (London: G. Routledge, 1989), 24–39 and Schürmann, *Meister Eckhart, Mystic and Philosopher: Translations with Commentary* (Bloomington, Ind: Indiana University Press, 1978).

47. For this recall, see Stoudt, *Sunrise to Eternity*, 199. For important points in Eckhart's work where he makes the distinction, see in particular Sermons 15, 22, 26 of *Die deutchen Werke*. Michel Henry is one thinker who has interpretively hard-pedaled this distinction. See his *The Essence of Manifestation*, 309–35, 424–38. Henry is aware of the different valorizations of God and Godhead made by Eckhart and Boehme.

48. For a good examination of the scholarly debate about the relative trinitarian and monistic tendencies in Pseudo-Dionysius, which finally comes down on the side of the trinitarian, see John Jones, 'Dionysian Mysticism: A Conversion to Christianity' (Ph.D. diss., Yale University, 1998), 217–67.

49. See, for example, Eckhart's Sermons 2, 10, 26, 67 in *Die deutschen Werke*, where there appears to be a fairly absolute distinction between the Godhead and Trinity. In addition, Sermons 13, 22, 29, and 65 put a heavy emphasis on unity prior to differentiation, trinitarian or otherwise. While these sermons do not prove conclusively that Eckhart is monistic (for one still has to square this emphasis with the emphasis on divine birth), a strong monistic tendency has to be granted. Thus, if Michel Henry overstates the case somewhat in *The Essence of Manifestation* in his insistence that this tendency be regarded as absolutely defining of Eckhart, nonetheless, it is a strong systematic tendency. It is one that is not adequately taken account of by speaking of heterodox-sounding trinitarian statements in Eckhart as merely rhetorical devices intended to freshen and enliven Christian faith by the use of paradoxical expressions. This is the view of Oliver Davies in his *Meister Eckhart: Mystical Theologian* (London: SPCK, 1991).

50. Sermons that identify God as "nothing" (*Nichts*) include 6, 23, 59, 71, and 82. Here Eckhart reprises a move first made by Eriugena in the apophatic tradition. See Michael A. Sells's chapter, 'The Nothingness of God in John the Scot Eriugena' in his *Mystical Languages of Unsaying* (Chicago: Chicago University Press, 1994), 34–62. The nonfecundity or barrenness of the Godhead is addressed in Sermon 59. The fecundity of the divine is of course closely tied up with the eternal birth of the Son, but obviously not totally constituted by it, since manifestation will also include the created order. For emphasis on the fecundity of divine self-manifestation, see Sermons 11, 12, 22, 47, 53, 59, 63, 68, 73. In these particular sermons the Neoplatonic principle of plenitude is valorized. The divine is self-diffusing and self-giving. However, Eckhart leaves it somewhat in doubt whether the self-diffusion of the divine is itself generative of the Trinity, rather than as in classical Christian Neoplatonism where the self-diffusing divine is understood to be a trinitarian divine.

51. This reading is essentially that prosecuted by John Caputo and Reiner Schürmann. See the latter's *Meister Eckhar*; also *Heidegger: On Being and Acting: From Princi-*

ples to Anarchy, trans, Christine-Marie Gros in collaboration with the author (Bloomington, Ind.: Indiana University Press, 1990).

52. Whether the One is without knowledge, or has a superior form of knowledge, is a classic conundrum of Neoplatonism. For instance, Plotinus in the *Enneads* at different points speaks of the One as too great to have knowledge (3.9.9, 6.7.4) and of having another kind of knowledge (*katanoesis*) or a superior kind of knowledge (*hypernoesis*). For a fine discussion of this conundrum, see John Rist, *Plotinus: The Road to Reality* (Cambridge: Cambridge University Press, 1967), 38–53.

53. See Meister Eckhart, *Parisian Questions and Prologues*, trans. A. Maurer (Toronto: Pontifical Institute of Medieval Studies, 1974) where Eckhart values *intelligere* over *esse*. In refusing to countenance Thomas's identity of being and knowing in the divine, Eckhart operates in terms of the Neoplatonic frame of thought in which being is correlated with thought of a conceptual kind. Thus, to go beyond being is to go toward a form of knowing that does not have the properties of discursive knowledge or the underlying division into subject-object.

54. Koyré, *La philosophie de Jacob Boehme*, 324.

55. For Michel Henry in *The Essence of Manifestation* (pp. 108 and 112), this point is crucial for defining Boehme's project. From his point of view, Boehme's decision that self-consciousness requires a form of consciousness that is necessarily finite not only separates Boehme from Eckhart, but also makes Boehme the precursor of German Idealism where this view is central. Needless to say, Boehme's position puts him at odds with the classical theistic position of Aquinas. For Aquinas in the *Summa Theologiae* (I, q. 14), divine knowledge is infinite without qualification.

56. On internal evidence it seems clear that Boehme had direct or indirect contact with the *Theologia Deutsch*, twice edited by Luther (1516, 1518). This text was obviously important for the early Luther. Although the reformer Luther came to be suspicious of mysticism, the *Theologia Deutsch* continued to have a place in Luther's affections. For a good account of the importance of this text in Luther, see Stephen Ozment, *Homo Spiritualis* (New Haven, Conn.: Yale University Press, 1967), 86ff. This was a text of tremendous importance in the sixteenth century, as Ozment and Rufus Jones point out, in their different ways. See Ozment, *Mysticism and Dissent*, 17–25; and Jones, *Spiritual Reformers in the Sixteenth and Seventeenth Centuries* (London: Macmillan, 1914), 141.

57. The *Gottesgeburt* is central, for example, in sermons 6, 10, 11, 19, 38, 46, 57, and 68. Almost every commentator thinks that the 'divine birth' is one of Eckhart's most important contributions. Heinrich Ebeling is typical in this respect. See his *Meister Eckharts Mystik* (Stuttgart: Scientia , 1941). The crucial issues that divide commentators of Eckhart with respect to the divine birth are (a) whether the divine birth is exclusively a soteriological trope, in which case it does not decide the issue of the relative theoretical priority of manifestation or immanifestation in the divine and (b) whether in the case that the divine birth not being exclusively soteriological, one can consistently assert the priority of the Godhead or the divine nothing.

58. As I have suggested already, this tendency is real. See Sermons 11, 12, 22, 47, 53, 63, 68, 73 in *Die deutschen Werke* of Eckhart.

59. This is evident in all the Eckhart sermons, cited in the previous note, where the emphasis falls on the giving of the plenitude and the superabundance of the self-communication of the divine. Even when Eckhart seems to compromise the note of graciousness when he talks about "must" (Sermon 81) with respect to divine manifestation, there is no suggestion that God fulfills Godself in manifestation. The must of manifestation is essentially aesthetic in that it is unimaginable how a superabundant divine reality would not communicate and invite participation. When Eckhart speaks of love, it does not appear to be erotic in the strict sense. For example, in Sermon 63 Eckhart talks about the love of the divine eliciting the responsive love of what is communicated by it. But this love of the divine (objective genitive) seems to be at one with its act of communication. This is also the case in Pseudo-Dionysius, and the love that it elicits is different in kind (*eros* in the strict sense) than the love which is the condition of its possibility (*agape*). In this particular sermon, Eckhart also seems anxious to present a form of divine love that has none of the trammels of creaturely love. Divine love has no must: it is pure gift.

60. See Meister Eckhart's commentary on the prologue in J. M. Clark and J. V. Skinner, *Meister Eckhart: Selected Treatises and Sermons* (London: Faber and Faber, 1958), 238.

61. The agapaic (as opposed to erotic) understanding of reality, and by implication divine reality, is central to the thought of William Desmond. See especially his *Being and the Between* (Albany, N.Y.: SUNY Press, 1995), 63, 166, 246–49, 260. Two statements from Desmond are particularly apropos in the present context. Contrasting Neoplatonic and more dialectical views of reality, Desmond stipulates that the "excess of the origin would not be an indigence but a marvel of infinite generosity that simply gives because it gives" (p. 257). Again arguing that supporting an agapaic origin rules out a view that reality comes to itself through the detour of the finite, Desmond is explicit about the theological correlative: "Put in theological language: God does not create himself in creating the world" (p. 260). An agapaic as opposed to an erotic understanding of divine reality is central also to the Jean-Luc Marion in his retrieval of Dionysian tradition. See his *God Without Being*, trans. Thomas A. Carlson, with a foreword by David Tracy (Chicago: University of Chicago Press, 1991). In that text, Marion thinks that the *bonum diffusivum sui* trope of Pseudo-Dionysius represents an adequate translation of the Johannine emphasis on love. Love and goodness are pure gift and have no teleological or economic weight (pp. 47–48).

62. See Friedrich Engels's 'Introduction to the English Edition of Socialism: Utopian and Scientific,' in *On Religion* (New York: Schocken Books, 1964), 287–315, esp. 291. But see also ch. 6 of Karl Marx's *The Holy Family; or, Critique of Critical Critique*. There the *Naturphilosophie* of Boehme is cited with favor. This work is found in Engels's *On Religion*; see in particular p. 64.

63. Benadetto Croce, *What is Living and what is Dead in the Philosophy of Hegel*, trans. Douglas Ainslie (New York: Russell & Russell, 1915), 36–37, 42.

64. See *Of Learned Ignorance*, trans. Jasper Hopkins, 2nd ed. (Minneapolis: Banning Press, 1985).

65. See *De Visione Dei* and *De Li non Aliud*. Both have been translated by Jasper Hopkins. See respectively *Nicholas of Cusa's Dialectical Mysticism*, 2d ed. (Minneapolis: Banning Press,1988) and *Nicholas of Cusa on God as Not-Other*, 3d ed. (Minneapolis: Banning Press, 1987). Chapter 14 of *De Visione Dei* is particularly eloquent on this matter.

66. See especially Khunrath in the Paracelsian tradition. Of course, the association of Christ and the philosopher's stone was made as early as the thirteenth century with Raymond Lull. In Khunrath, however, the association is made in the context of cosmogonic that was typical of the the Paracelsian and Weigelian traditions.

67. This view is elaborated in Schelling's *The Ages of the World*.

68. For this point, see Marc Lienhard, *Luther, Witness to Jesus Christ: Stages and Themes of the Reformer's Christology*, trans. Edison H. Robertson (Minneapolis: Augsburg Publishing House, 1982), 52.

69. Thomas J. J. Altizer, *Genesis and Apocalypse: A Theological Voyage Toward Authentic Christianity* (Louisville, Ky.: Westminster/John Knox Press, 1990), 163; *The Genesis of God: A Theological Geneaology* (Louisville, Ky.: Westminster/John Knox Press, 1993), 15–16, 108–9, 118.

70. Berdyaev, 'Unground and Freedom,' xviii.

71. Here I have particularly in mind Jan Ruusbroec. See *John Ruusbroec: Spiritual Espousals and Other Works*, trans. James Wiseman (New York: Paulist Press,1985). For a fine account of the way in which Ruusbroec modifies Eckhart, see Louis Dupré, *The Common Life: The Origins of Trinitarian Mysticism and its Development by Jan Ruusbroec* (New York: Crossroad, 1984), 29–33.

72. See Georges Bataille, *Inner Experience*, trans. Leslie Anne Boldt (Albany, N.Y.: SUNY Press, 1988), 43-61.

Part II. Metalepsis Unbounding

1. For Baur's assertion of relation between Boehme and the Spiritual Reformers, especially Franck and Schwenckfeld, see *Die christliche Lehre von der Dreieinigkeit*, 2, pp. 217–95. For the relation between Boehme and Hegel, see *Die christliche Gnosis*, 555ff.

2. In *Work on Myth* Blumenberg suggests that this myth is peculiarly prominent in modernity, and is so not only because it provides a lens through which to see reality and keep it at bay, but also because it is a myth of human self-legitimation. Interestingly, Blumenberg fails to reflect on the issue that so concerned him in *The Legitimacy of the Modern Age*, about whether modern culture could be conceived as something like a secularization of this myth, as religious thinkers like Hans Urs von Balthasar have proposed in texts like *Apokalyse der deutschen Seele* (Salzburg: Pustet, 1937).

Chapter 3. Nondistinctive Swerves

1. See James Samuel Preus's still valuable, *From Shadow to Promise: Old Testament Interpretation from Augustine to the Young Luther* (Cambridge: Harvard University Press, 1969). Preus points out that the hermeneutic situation prior to the mature Luther is not that allegory totally dominates, but that its authority is on a par with typology. The achievement of the mature Luther is to draw a decisive line of demarcation not drawn in the Western tradition of interpretation. What separates Luther from the Augustinian hermeneutic tradition is also what separates the later from the early Luther. Steven Ozment agrees with Preus on the issue of the early Luther's indebtedness to a hermeneutic tradition in which allegory was an essential element. See *Homo Spiritualis: A Comparative Study of the Anthropology of Johannes Tauler, Jean Gerson and Martin Luther (1509-16) in the Context of their Theological Thought* (Leiden: E. J. Brill, 1969), 86, where Ozment comments on Luther's reflection on the Psalms.

2. See especially the introduction to Book 3, where Augustine promises to discuss the ambiguity of Scripture and come to some solutions (*ad ambigua scripturam discutienda atque soluende*)(3.1.1). See *On Christian Doctrine*, trans. D. W. Robertson Jr. (New York: Liberal Arts Press, 1958), 78. Augustine's hermeneutic program does, however, permit allegorical interpretation, indeed demands it, if what appears to be the literal sense conflicts with the Christian sense of what God does and does not do.

3. Admitting that the Platonic split (*chorismos*) between the visible and invisible is operative in Clement and Origen, while acknowledging the Platonism of the Alexandrian Fathers, scholars like J. Daniélou, Henri de Lubac, and Hans Urs von Balthasar have been to the forefront in rejecting an excessively Platonic interpretation of the Church Fathers. See Daniélou, *Origène* (Paris: La Table Ronde, 1948); De Lubac, *Medieval Exegesis*, vol. 1, *The Four Senses of Scripture*, trans. Marc Sebanc (Grand Rapids, Mich.: W. B. Eerdmans, 1998); *Histoire et esprit. L' intelligence de l'écriture d'après Origène* (Paris: Aubier, 1950); von Balthasar, *Origen: Spirit and Fire: A Thematic Anthology of His Writings*, trans. Robert J. Daly (Washington: Catholic University of America Press, 1984).

4. For a good discussion of Valentinian hermeneutics, see David Dawson, *Allegorical Readers and Cultural Revision in Ancient Alexandria* (Berkeley: University of California Press, 1992), 127–82.

5. This point is made forcefully by Henri de Lubac in *Medieval Exegesis*, vol. 1.

6. See von Balthasar, *The Glory of the Lord: A Theological Aesthetic*, vol. 1, *Seeing the Form*, trans. Erasmo Leiva-Merikakis, ed. Joseph Fessio and John Riches (San Francisco: Ignatius Press, 1982), 138–39; 266–67.

7. With respect to noncanonic apocalyptic literature, I have especially in mind Fourth Esdra (Second Esdra in modern English translations) and the Enoch literature in general. This speculative form of apocalyptic literature exercises influence on Boehme that is especially apparent in *Mysterium Magnum*, with Fourth Esdra exerting direct influence. At the same time Enoch is the apocalyptic figure for Boehme. At one level this

may simply reflect late sixteenth-century apocalyptic expectation about the return of Enoch. On another level, given the speculative cast of Boehme's figuration, other sources cannot be ruled out, even Jewish sources. For a good account of the Enoch literature in its original setting, see Michael Stone, 'Enoch and Apocalyptic Origins,' in *Visionaries and their Apocalypses*, ed. Paul D. Hanson (Philadelphia: Fortress Press, 1983), 85–100.

8. As Gershom Scholem notes, the chariot was the dominant visionary form in Judaism from the third century to the emergence of Kabbalah at the end of the twelfth. For good accounts of *Merkabah* mysticism, see Scholem, *Major Trends in Jewish Mysticism* (New York: Schocken Books, 1995; originally published by Schocken in 1961, reprinted from the 3d rev. ed.), 40–79; *Jewish Gnosticism, Merkabah Mysticism, and Talmudic Tradition* (New York: Jewish Theological Seminary of America, 1960). See also Ithmar Gruenwald, *Apocalyptic and Merkabah Mysticism* (Leiden: E. J. Brill, 1980).

9. As is well known, one of the major works of Joachim is his interpretation of Revelation, *Expositio in Apocalypsim*. Other major works include *Liber concordie novie ac veteris testamenti*. The mediation of Joachim has been the subject of analyses by De Lubac, Marjorie Reeves, and Robin Barnes. See De Lubac, *La postérité spirituelle de Joachim de Fiore*; Reeves, *Joachim of Fiore and the Prophetic Future* (New York: Harper, 1977), 136ff.; and Barnes, *Prophecy and Gnosis: Apocalypticism in the Wake of the Lutheran Reformation* (Stanford: Stanford University Press, 1985), 25, 121, 281.

10. See Abraham Carlov, *Anti-Böhmius, in quo Docetur quid Habendum de Secta Jacobi Böhmen Satoris Görlicensis* (Wittenberg: Schrödter, 1684); also Johann Frick, *Gründliche Undersuchung Jacob Boehmens vornehmster Irrthümer* (Ulm: zu finden bey Wolffgang Kraer, 1697), 231–80, esp. 236–42. See also p. 67 where Carlov is recalled. Another major antipolemical text that sets sights on Boehme's scriptural interpretation—though also on substantive doctrines like creation and Trinity—is Abraham Hinckelmann, *40 Wichtige Fragen betreffende die Lehre so in Jacob Böhmens Schriften enthalten* (Hamburg: Schulssischen Buchladen, 1693).

11. For good accounts of Luther's fidelity to the literal sense and its practice, see Jaroslav Pelikan, *Luther the Expositor: Introduction to the Reformer's Exegetical Writings* (St. Louis: Concordia Publishing House, 1959). This is the companion volume to the *Collected Works of Luther*, ed. Jaroslav Pelikan (St. Louis: Concordia Press, 1955–1986). See also James Samuel Preus, *From Shadow to Promise*, 153–265.

12. For Pelikan this represents Luther's typical attitude toward allegorical interpretation. See *Luther the Expositor*, 28 and 89.

13. For a convenient English translation, see *Sebastian Franck—280 Paradoxes or Wondrous Sayings*, trans. E. J. Furcha (Lewiston, N.Y.: Edwin Mellen Press, 1986). # will indicate paradox number if the page number of the text is not supplied.

14. For insightful comments on Frank's exegesis, see Koyré, *Mystiques, spirituelles, alchemistes*, 27, 47–48; also Steven Ozment, *Mysticism and Dissent*, 60–61.

15. For brief accounts of the principles of Schwenckfeld's exegesis, see Rufus Jones, *Spiritual Reformers*, 77–81. See also Paul L. Maier, *Caspar Schwenckfeld on the*

Person and Work of Christ (Assen, the Netherlands: Royal van Gorcum, 1959), 26–27. See also Richard H. Grützmacher, *Wort und Geist: eine historische und dogmatische Untersuchung zum Gnadenmittel des Wortes* (Leibzig: A. Deichert, 1902), 158–73.

16. For an interesting account of this in Weigel, see Bernard Gorceix's magisterial *La mystique de Valentin Weigel 1533–1588 et les origins de la théosophie allemande* (Paris: Université de Paris, 1972), 369–70.

17. This is a point emphasized by both Koyré and Ozment. See Koyré, *Mystiques, spirituels, alchemistes*, 133; Ozment, *Mysticism and Dissent*, p. 209. For a similar opinion, see also Siegfried Wollgast in his introduction to Valentin Weigel's *Ausgewählte Werke* (Stuttgart: W. Kohlhammer, 1978), 17–164, esp. 73–74.

18. In the iconography that provided frontispieces for Boehme's works in the eighteenth century, all of Boehme's system from Unground to the completion of the heavenly body was enclosed in a circle that was regarded as a circle of vision, a circle there inchoately from the beginning in the emergence of Wisdom. The *philosophical globe* is thus subject as well as object of seeing and is absolutely inclusive. There are Neoplatonic and alchemical precursors of the philosophical globe or the encompassing eye. Something like this image can be found in the Florentine Neoplatonist, Ficino. See Edgar Wind, *Pagan Mysteries in the Renaissance* (London: Faber & Faber, 1958), 232 note. Also a version of this can be found in Paracelsus. See Jacobi, *Paracelsus: Selected Writings*, 231. Hermeticism, which experiences a revival in the Renaissance, also is a precursor. Désirée Hirst has drawn attention to the Hermetic antecedents of Boehme's philosophical globe. Together with the well-known adage that God is the reality whose center is everywhere, circumference nowhere, Hermeticism was especially ocular, with the *Poemander* being especially prominent in this respect. See *Hidden Riches: Traditional Symbolism from the Renaissance to Blake* (London: Eyre and Spottiswoode, 1964), 169. Hirst also notes that Boehme's philosophical globe has considerable life in the Philadelphian Society in the seventeenth century, especially in John Pordage. In Pordage's *Theologica Mystica* (London: n.p., 1683) the philosophical globe is a central image, with Pordage being aware that the philosophical globe is the mirror of Wisdom is a 'dilated' form.

19. See Barnes, *Prophecy and Gnosis*, 60–61.

20. The classic locus of the cosmogonic thrust of interpretation that operates within broad visionary contours is *Vom Ort der Welt*. This can be found in *Ausgewählte Werke*, 261–351.

21. See Barnes, *Prophecy and Gnosis*, 25, 121, 281.

22. Here there is something of a scholarly dispute between Koyré and Gorceix as to how much separation is enacted in Weigel between the Godhead and the Trinity. Gorceix acknowledges the influence of Eckhart, indeed believes scholars have underestimated it. Nevertheless, he does not think that the Godhead-Trinity distinction functions in a fully ontological way. See *La mystique de Valentin Weigel*, 197–98. In contrast, while not commenting on the question of whether Eckhart does or does not support an ontological distinction between the Godhead and Trinity, and the Godhead and God, Koyré adopts the more radical position that Weigel really anticipates Boehme in think-

ing of the distinction in a truly ontological fashion. See Koyré, *Mystiques, spirituels, et al-chemistes*, 164. Of course, Koyré's final position is complicated, for as *La philosophie de Jacob Boehme* makes clear, Koyré believes that at least to some extent the Unground is a placeholder for the real absolute, which is the ungrounded will to manifestation and self-reflexivity.

23. After a hermeneutic dispensation ruled by law-gospel binary opposition in which Luther's theology was antidogmatic in principle, in recent years there is new-found appreciation of the doctrinal depth of Luther's thought, trinitarian as well as christological. Prominent on the German side is Ulrich Asendorf. See, for example, his 'Die Trinitätslehre als integrales Problem der Theologie Martin Luthers,' in *Luther und trinitarische Tradition: Ökumenische und philosophische Perspektivan*, ed. Joachim Heubach (Erlangen: Martin Luthers , 1994), 113–30. Regin Prenter and Robert Jensen have been to the forefront of this renaissance in North America. Regin Prenter's *Spiritus Creator* (Munich: C. Kaiser, 1954) remains pivotal for John R. Loeschen's trinitarian apologia, *Divine Community: Trinity, Church, and Ethics in Reformation Theology* (Kirksville, Mis-souri: Sixteenth Journal Publishers: Northeast Missouri State University, 1981). See esp. pp. 15-71. For a fine recent work that synthesizes the best scholarship in Germany as well as North America, see Christine Helmer, *The Trinity and Martin Luther: A Study of the Relationship between Genre, Language and the Trinity in Luther's Late Works*, (1523–1546) (Mainz: Verlag Phillipp von Zabern, 1999).

24. For Luther the *Deus absconditus* and the *Deus revelatus* are two aspects of the same God who is hidden in his very revealedness. This dialectical relation Luther takes to be other than what he discovers in the more speculative branch of mystical theology—that is, the Dionysian branch—which he believes substantializes the hid-denness of the divine and takes the divine out of the circuit of revealedness that finds its axis and culmination in the crucified Christ. Thus the antipathy to Christ and the whole apparatus of negative theology that reaches its height in the language of "noth-ing." For what he regards as a Dionysian obfuscation, Luther has nothing but disdain. For a good account of this, see Anders Nygren, *Agape and Eros* (Philadelphia: Westmin-ister Press, 1953), 706.

25. I have mentioned Frick a number of times already. But Theodor Thummio was an important seventeenth-century critic of esoteric currents of thought, especially those of a *Naturphilosophie* kind. His *Impietas Wigeliana* (Tubingae: impensis Philiberti Brunni, 1650) went through a few editions (1628, 1650).

26. See Frick, *Gruendliche Undersuchung*, 587ff.; Thummio, *Impietas Wigeliana*, 66ff.

27. See Frick, *Gruendliche Undersuchung*, 238–42.

28. This is an important trajectory within the speculative theology tradition. The influence of Duns Scotus Eriugena, as perhaps one of the most radical thinkers in the Dionysian tradition, on Meister Eckhart is well established. The influence of Eckhart on Cusa is almost as well established. The most comprehensive and incisive account is still that of Herbert Wackerzapp. See his *Der Einfluss Meister Eckharts auf die ersten philosophischen Schriften des Nikolaus von Kues, 1440–1450*, ed. Joseph Koch (Münster:

Aschendorff, 1962). Some work has also been done with respect to the relation between Eriugena and Cusa. See Werner Beierwaltes, 'Eriugena und Cusanus,' in *Eriugena redivivus: zur Wirkungsgeschichte seines Denkens im Mittelalter und im Übergang zur Neuzeit: Vorträge des V. Internationalen Eriugena-Colloquiums, Werner-Reimers-Stiftung Bad Homburg, 26–30. August 1985*, ed. Werner Beierwaltes (Heidelberg: Carl Winter, 1987), 311–43. See also Dermot Moran, 'Pantheism from John Scotus Eriugena to Nicholas of Cusa,' in *American Catholic Philosophical Quarterly* 64 (1990): 131–52.

29. See *De Divisione Naturae*, bk 3, where Eriugena offers his account of the created natures inherence in the "primordial causes," which are eternal. While Eriugena stresses in bks 1 and 2 that the primordial causes are not to be confused with the Godhead and the Trinity, nonetheless, the emphasis on the dynamism of divine manifestation, which at one point is spoken of as "self-creation" suggests something less than an Augustinian ontological divide between the creator and the created order.

30. The denigration of the created order as created is a consistent theme in Eckhart. On the basis of deficits like materiality, mutability, and temporality, which are complaints common enough in Platonic Christianity, Eckhart speaks of the created order as being 'nothing.' While there is something hyperbolic in this evaluation, there is every reason to take it seriously, especially in situations in which God is identified with Being. For as Reiner Schürmann has pointed out in *Meister Eckhart: Mystic and Philosopher*, the breakdown of Thomistic analogy in Eckhart dictates that if God is identified with Being, then creation is nothing, and that if creation is identified with Being, then God is identified with nothing. For sermons where Eckhart explicitly speaks of the created order as "nothing," see Sermons 5A, 5B, 12, 45, 46, 59, 65, 71 of *Sämtliche Werke*. For sermons particularly emphatic on the point that not only the Son as such but also the self, qua Son, is a product of the trinitarian birth, see Sermons 2, 6, 10, 20A, 20B, 25 *inter alia*.

31. *De Docta Ignorantia* bk 2 chs. 3 and 4.

32. See Weigel, *Vom Ort der Welt*, ch. 14. If *Gnothi Seauton* is less oriented toward cosmogony than *Vom Ort der Welt*, nevertheless the influence of Paracelsian texts like *Philosophia Sagax* is just as evident.

33. Relative to *The Way to Christ*, *De Incarnatione Verbi* (1620) is speculative. This is especially true of the second part. Nonetheless, even in the most speculative second part of the text there are edifying reminders about Christ's dying and rising being the pattern of our existence (2.5; also 1.14).

34. The presence of the *German Theology* is evident throughout *Paradoxa* in its exemplarist christology, its view of the importance of *Gelassenheit*, and the possibility of deification. Ozment is convinced of its importance. See *Mysticism and Dissent*, 43. The text is no less important for Weigel. See Gorceix, *La mystique de Valentin Weigel*, 278–82, 296ff. The importance of the *German Theology* for the early Luther is underscored by Ozment. See *Mysticism and Dissent*, 18–25.

35. See Maier, *Caspar Schwenckfeld on the Person and Work of Christ*, 84–87.

36. The stand against imputed justice is particularly to the fore in Weigel's *Dialogus* (chs. 2–3). Two commentators who emphasize the importance of this resistance in Weigel are Gorceix, *La mystique de Valentin Weigel*, 70–72, 319; and Siegfried Wollgast, in his introduction to the *Ausgewählte Werke* of Valentin Weigel, pp. 121–26.

37. The assertion of the importance of free will is especially important in *Postille* 2 and in *Zwei nützliche Tractate*. See Gorceix, *La mystique de Valentin Weigel*, 327–38.

38. See Maier, *Caspar Schwenckfeld on the Person and Work of Christ*, 62, 67.

39. Eckhart is recalled with favor throughout Weigel's work. This is not surprising. Although soteriology may well be the ultimate mainspring of Eckhart's thought, he is also a speculative theologian whose formulations seem to go beyond the usual hyperbole of mystical writers. I have touched on the possibility that Weigel moves in a direction of announcing a structural and ontological distinction between the Godhead and the Trinity that is also a tendency in Eckhart's thought, but downplayed in the subsequent Flemish and German mystical traditions. See Gorceix, *La mystique de Valentin Weigel*, 88–89, 111–12, 279–82, 317–18, 325.

40. For a discussion of this passage and its subsequent trajectory, see Benz, *Les sources mystiques*, 27–31; Wolfram Malte Fues, *Mystik als Erkenntnis: Kritische Studien zur Meister Eckhart Forschung* (Bonn: Bouvier, 1981), 33–44. See also von Baader, *SW* 15, pp. 158ff.

41. See Weigel, *Der Güldene Griff*, ch. 16. For a good discussion, see Gorceix, *La mystique de Valentin Weigel*, 106–12.

42. See Weeks, *Boehme*, 22–6.

43. In the preface to the *De Electione Gratiae*, Boehme takes a stand against predestination. He argues that the notion of divine decree is anthropomorphic, and thus understandably popular. Conceding that there are indeed passages such as Romans 5 and 9, and the famous passage in Exodus that so exercised the Church Fathers about God hardening the heart of the pharoah, that support such a doctrine, he believes (a) others do not, and (b) all passages that appear to support predestination can, and indeed ought to be read, as supporting a view that God confirms finite creatures in their basic disposition or orientation (i.e., imagination) for good or evil. As early as *Aurora*, Boehme was anxious to exonerate God from evil. See the preface to *Aurora* #16 and 26 where God is good. Evil in the shape of Lucifer is God's other.

Chapter 4. Distinctive Swerves

1. Boehme is here anticipated by Weigel. See *Vom Ort der Welt*, ch. 14.

2. See Pelikan, *Luther the Expositor*, 102–3.

3. Though admitting that Boehme is original in his conception of the philosophical globe, in *Hidden Riches* Hirst argues successfully that it represents a development of Hermeticism.

4. I am here thinking of the Kabbalistic practice, taken over for Christian purposes by Pico della Mirandola, of *gematria*, where the nonobvious meaning of Scripture is decoded by synthesizing the numerical values assigned to letters in a word or phrase.

5. While Konopacki in *Descent into Words* does not make much of the distinction between Boehme and the Kabbalah on this point, his insistence of the linguistic aspects of Boehme's treatment of names and phrases (dentals, labials, dorsals, etc.) helps to separate Boehme decisively from Kabbalistic methodology. It is also worth pointing out, that Boehme focuses on the act of uttering German rather than Hebrew words.

6. This is particularly apparent in Eckhart's Latin works, especially his commentary on the Johannine prologue, where he speaks of Wisdom as an "unspotted mirror." Nonetheless, more conventionally than Boehme, Eckhart associates Wisdom with the Son. See Clark and Skinner, *Meister Eckhart*, 248.

7. There are two possibilities in Eckhart, both of which grant perfection to the Son. The first is qualified, the second unqualified. (1) If the Godhead-Trinity distinction is upheld, then the Son is the perfection of the manifest divine while being less than the immanifest divine. (2) If the divine birth is given priority over the immanifest divine, then the Son is perfect without qualification.

8. The best discussion of Luther's relation to late medieval nominalism and its keynote distinction of *potentia absoluta–potentia ordinata* is still Heiko Oberman, *The Harvest of Medieval Theology: Gabriel Biel and Late Medieval Nominalism* (Cambridge, Mass.: Harvard University Press, 1963).

9. In Nominalism and Luther, restriction of divine will by ethos is dependent on and specifies restriction of divine will by nature or essence.

10. See Scholem, *Major Trends in Jewish Mysticism*, 213–14; also *The Kabbalah and its Symbolism*, trans. Ralph Mannheim (New York: Schocken Books, 1969), where Scholem notes the general correlation between Boehme and the Kabbalah (pp. 98–100).

11. See Scholem, *Major Trends in Jewish Mysticism*, 214.

12. I especially have in mind *The Crucified God: The Cross of Christ as the Foundation and Criticism of Christian Theology*, trans. R. A. Wilson and John Bowden (London: SCM Press, 1974). There Jürgen Moltmann attempts a synthesis of Luther and Hegel, which will get qualified in later texts. Ironically, if *The Trinity and the Kingdom* represents such a qualification in which Moltmann is anxious to pass beyond monotheism or the metaphysical monism that infects trinitarian thought, it is also the text in which Moltmann is most explicit about his debt to Boehme's view about divine pathos. See *The Trinity and the Kingdom: The Doctrine of God*, trans. Margaret Kohl (San Francisco: Harper & Row, 1981), 34, 36. See also Moltmann's treatment of Berdyaev on pp. 42–47.

13. See Lienhard, *Luther, Witness to Jesus Christ*, 218–19, 335–66; Ian D. Siggins, *Martin Luther's Doctrine of Christ* (New Haven, Conn.:Yale University Press), 125ff.

14. See Annegrit Brunkhorst-Hasenclever, *Die Transformierung der theologischen Deutung des Todes bei G. W. F. Hegel: ein Beitrag zur Formbestimmung von Paradox und Synthese* (Bern: Herbert Lang and Peter Lang, 1970), 257–65.

15. See Heinrich Bornkamm, *Luther und Böhme* (Bonn: A. Marcus and K. Webers,1925), 131–56.

16. Weigel offers both clarifications of and a theological filter for Paracelsus's reflection on the imagination. Especially in his *Der güldene Griff* Weigel offers detailed reflections on the importance of objectification (*Gegenwurf*) for imagination. This idea becomes central to Boehme's ontotheology of the genesis of the divine subject and dominates his discussion of Wisdom both at the archeological and terminal levels of divine becoming.

17. See Frances A. Yates, *Giordano Bruno and the Hermetic Tradition* (Chicago: University of Chicago Press, 1964); Hirst, *Hidden Riches.*

18. See Blumenberg, *Work on Myth*, 260.

19. Ibid., 202, 542.

20. For example, Berdyaev believes that the orthodox tradition has fundamentally misinterpreted the biblical God. For Berdyaev, Boehme and his followers provide a more adequate version of the dynamic God of the Bible than theological orthodoxy with its static metaphysical assumption. See 'Unground and Freedom,' xi–xiii. Similarly, although Altizer understands his apocalyptic theology to be an epochal discourse, he also considers it to be a recovery of orginal Christianity distorted by orthodoxy with its view of a purely infinite God, neither defined by relationship nor exposed to becoming and change.

21. The binary symbolic pairs to which I will refer can be found in different kinds of Western religious texts. They can be found in the Bible, Marcionism, Manichaeism, and Gnosticism. Thus, they can be found in religious texts proper. But I want to suggest that they can also be found in philosophical texts that dramatize the position of the self. I am thinking especially of the texts of Plato, suffused as they are by Orphism, and obviously Neoplatonic texts where the "religious" problematic of fall and redemption is even more to the fore.

22. Blumenberg, *Work on Myth*, 557.

23. See Fritz Lieb for reflections on the importance of Weigel in the latter half of the sixteenth century and the texts, not written by him, that passed in his name. *Valentin Weigels Kommentar zur Schöpfungsgeschichte und das Schrifttum seines Schülers Benedict Biedermann: Eine literarkritische Untersuchung zur mystischen Theologie des 16. Jahrhunderts* (Zürich: EVZ- Verlag, 1962). For instance, *Studium Universale* was a text commonly attributed to Weigel. Lieb now thinks the text was composed by Biedermann in 1590, six years after Weigel's death. The issue of authentic Weigel and pseudo-Weigelian texts is not a purely academic issue. For example, in the argument between Koyré and Gorceix, about whether Weigel proposes an ontological divide between Godhead and Trinity, to support the positive case Koyré seems to accept *Studium Universale* as a text from Weigel. See *Mystiques, spirituels, alchemistes*, 164.

24. One can only agree with Robert Brown in *The Later Philosophy of Schelling* about the tremendous influence exerted by Boehme on Schelling that reflects itself not only in Schelling's thought but in his language. If *The Ages of the World* (1815) represents something of a crescendo of influence, this influence is just as much to the fore in the *Essay on Human Freedom* (1809) which reads in many places like a Boehmian paraphrase.

25. See *The Ages of the World* (1815).

26. I am thinking here especially of Anders Nygren's classic *Agape and Eros* (Philadelphia: Westminister Press, 1955).

27. This, of course, is axiomatic from the Heidelberg Disputations onward. For a representative reflection on this, see Walter von Loewenich, *Luther's Theology of the Cross*, trans. J. A. Bouman (Minneapolis, Minn.: Augsburg Publishing House, 1976).

28. See *Summa* I, q. 9, arts. 1 and 2 where impassibility is regarded as an implicate of divine simplicity in which no potency resides. For a comprehensive discussion of Thomas's position, see Michael J. Dodds, *The Unchanging God of Love: A Study of the Teaching of St. Thomas Aquinas on Divine Immutability in View of Certain Contemporary Criticism of this Doctrine* (Fribourg: Éditions Universitaires Fribourg Suisse, 1986).

29. See Siggins, *Martin Luther's Doctrine of Christ*, 125ff.; Lienhard, *Luther, Witness to Jesus Christ*, 112, 392.

30. See especially Lienhard, *Luther: Witness to Jesus Christ*, 218–19, 227, 230–31, 317.

31. This is the interpretation of Brunkhorst-Hasenclever in *Die Transformierung der theologischen Deutung des Todes bei G. W. F. Hegel*.

32. See Nygren, *Agape and Eros*, 724.

33. Augustine makes it clear in *The City of God* that the Adamic fall provides an opportunity for God to display power and mercy in Jesus Christ. To an extent, the very creation of human being in the wake of the fall of the angels also provides an opportunity for God to show power and goodness—although here the situation is complicated by Augustine's speculations about the perfect number, with human beings constituting an exact numerical replacement for the angels who fell. As those who depend for their very existence on the divine, angels and human beings are intended to reflect back divine glory. Doxological posture is the correlative of the display of divine glory in the theocentric matrix of *The City of God*.

34. Gregory of Nyssa is the Cappadocian whose thought is most determined by this idea. See *The Making of Man* in *A Select Library of Nicene and Post-Nicene Fathers of the Christian*, ed. Philip Schaff and Henry Wace *Church*, vol. 5, *Gregory of Nyssa* (Grand Rapids, Mich: W. B. Eerdmans, 1893), 387–427, esp. 411–14.

35. See Paul Ricoeur, *The Symbolism of Evil*, trans. Emerson Buchanan (Boston: Beacon Press, 1969), 327

36. For Altizer, see esp. *The Genesis of God*, 15–16, 108.

37. See Staudenmaier, *Die Philosophie des Christentums*, p. 809 for his most explicit assertion of the new form of Sabellianism. See also pp. 729–31 for his reflections on the heterodox nature of Boehme's trinitarian thought, which yet is different than ancient trinitarian heterodoxy.

38. Here I borrow Frank Kermode's felicitous phrase, which is the title of one of his best-known books. This book represents an application of the narrative of Scripture to the act of reading, though obviously the latter is in a sense confirmatory about the importance of the former. See *The Sense of an Ending: Studies in the Theory of Fiction* (London: Oxford University Press, 1967).

39. I am excepting the gender code here, for in Luther and Lutheran orthodoxy it does not appear to be in operation. One of the most violent disputes between Lutherans and Catholics concerned the role of Mary, who in Lutheran eyes was elevated into a divine mediatrix in Roman Catholicism. The denial that Mary has the effect of excluding the imaginability of a feminine aspect of the divine is something regretted later by the Romantic Novalis, and, in a very different dispensation, by Jung. The exclusion of femininity to the divine means that neither a masculine-feminine binary opposition, nor an opposition within the feminine between the pure and the impure feminine, can get set up. Of course, Paracelsus does not obey what amounts to an interdict. But, more interestingly, neither does Weigel, who sees himself as amplifying Lutheranism rather than, as is the case with Paracelus, of offering an alternative.

40. Here I am evoking Rodophe Gasché's *The Tain of the Mirror: Derrida and the Philosophy of Reflection* (Cambridge, Mass.: Harvard University Press, 1986). Though ostensibly a book on Derrida, Gasché shows how the mirror is covertly the dominant image of German Idealism, which announces itself as a speculative philosophy. For "speculation" has etymological roots in *speculum* or mirror. And since "speculation" is not other than "reflection" but rather its realization, then *speculative knowledge* means self-authenticating knowledge derived through the activity of mirroring. See esp. pp. 43–45. Though Gasché reflects on Hegel's early essay on *The Difference between Schelling's and Fichte's Systems of Philosophy* (1802), what he says has application to Boehme where the image of mirror is explicit rather than implicit as is the case in Hegel. Gasché's elaboration of the activity of mirroring in German Idealism tends to strengthen the ties between Hegel and Boehme at a systematic level. This is important, for on the surface the level of actual recall of Boehme in Schelling goes so far beyond that of Hegel that it is difficult to speak of the relationship between Boehme and Hegel, as if it is remotely of the same order as the relation between Boehme and Schelling.

41. If the suggestion here is that one might think of Boehme as offering a version of the ontological argument, then obviously this version is quite different than that of Anselm. First, one is dealing with more than conceptual explication in Boehme. In fact, one is dealing with an account of a real movement of divine becoming that is accessed in vision. Second, and correspondingly, the movement of becoming means the divine with which one begins—that is, the Unground—is poorer ontologically and gnoseologically than the fully actual personal divine that vision grasps as concluding a process of dramatic evolution. In contrast, in Anselm the ontological argument is prosecuted

against the assumption of the superabundant reality of the divine. Retrospective light is thrown on Boehme here by Hegel's attempt to rehabilitate Anselm in *Lectures on the Philosophy of Religion*. For a discussion of this rehabilitation, where Hegel ontologizes and narratizes Anselm, see O' Regan, *The Heterodox Hegel*, 323–26.

Chapter 5. Boehme's Visionary Discourse and the Limits of Metalepsis

1. See Hegel, *Lectures on the Philosophy of Religion*, vol. 1, 1824. Lectures, p. 123.

2. See the appendix in McFarland, *Coleridge and the Pantheist Tradition*, 320–33, which features Coleridge's annotation of Boehme's works.

3. See *Epistle* 22.

4. This has been recognized by most nineteenth- and twentieth-century commentators on Boehme. Martensen acknowledged Boehme's intentional orthodoxy, as did von Baader and Staudenmaier. See the latter's *Die Philosophie des Christenthums*, pp. 729–31. In their own ways Berdyaev, Walsh, and Haggemark acknowledge this point. See Berdyaev, 'Unground and Freedom,' xviii; Brown, *The Later Philosophy of Schelling*, 64ff.; Haggemark, 'Luther and Boehme,' 175ff.; and Walsh, *The Mysticism of Innerworldly Fulfillment*, 32–4.

5. Haggemark is especially critical of Walsh for imputing to Boehme a teleological logic that is fully realized in Hegel. Haggemark believes that Boehme is an eschatological rather than teleological thinker, and believes that the *turba* of the angels and human beings are events of rupture for which God compensates by the excess of mercy. They are not, as such, elements of a logic of divine becoming. See 'Luther and Boehme,' 175ff.

6. See *Essay on Human Freedom*, trans. James Gutman (Chicago: Open Court, 1936), p. 39. This text is vol. 7 of *Sämtliche Werke*, vol. 7, ed. K. F. A. Schelling (Stuttgart: Cotta, 1856–61). See also *Die Weltalter* in *Sämtliche Werke*, vol. 8, part 2, p. 54.

7. When I say "religiously" relevant, I have in mind the etymology of "religare" which means "bond." The immanifest Godhead is not as religiously relevant as the God of manifestation, since this is God considered outside relationality or bonding.

8. See O'Regan, *The Heterodox Hegel*, 43, 104, 106, 134.

9. For instance, one could think of Blake's famous "tyger" as representing such a coincidence.

10. Heinrich Bornkamm, *Luther und Böhme*, 131–33.

11. Staudenmaier, *Die Philosophie des Christenthums*, 228–45; 726–40; 798–810; *Zum religiösen Frieden der Zukunft*, Teil 1, 244–71 and Teil 3, 37–46, 360–67.

12. Walsh, *The Mysticism of Innerworldly Fulfillment*, 32–4.

13. See Paul Ricoeur, *The Symbolism of Evil*. If this typologically oriented text does not explicitly evaluate the merits of theogonic and Adamic myths of the origin of evil, it

is clear from other texts from the same period that on the theological level Ricoeur supports the Adamic view of origin. See 'Original Sin: A Study in Meaning,' and 'The Hermeneutics of Symbols and Philosophical Reflection, 1,' in *The Conflict of Interpretations*, ed. Don Ihde (Evanston, Ill.: Northwestern University Press, 1974), 269–86; 287–314.

14. See Ricoeur, *The Symbolism of Evil*, 327.

15. See von Balthasar, *Theo-Drama*, vol. 2, 35ff.

16. For Hegel, see von Balthasar, *Theo-Drama* , vol. 2, pp. 35, 50-51. For Gnosticism, see vol. 2, pp. 40, 140-49. For the connection between Boehme and Gnosticism, see vol. 2, p. 420.

Part III. Valentinianism and Valentinian Enlisting of Non-Valentinian Discourses

1. See *Against Heresies* bk 1. 20. The context of Irenaeus's use of *metharmottein* is iconic. He thinks of both orthodox Christianity and Gnosticism as having the same subject matter, the divine and its relations, but picturing, or expressly arranging the elements of the mosaic differently. In the case of Gnosticism, picturing differently is not accidental, for Gnosticism intends to arrange a mosaic contrarily to the arrangement of the Christian community that has an apostolic base. Yet given Irenaeus's depiction of the narratives of Gnosticism, which he assumes to be unfaithful to the biblical narrative that precedes his mentioning of *metharmottein*, and his elaboration in subsequent books of *Against Heresies* of the biblical narrative of a trinitarian divine that creates, redeems, and is a present with communities throughout history, it is not going too far to hypothesize that narrative rearrangement is implied at least in his figure. For a good discussion of *metharmottein* in a context of a sophisticated narrative elaboration of Valentinianism, see Anne Maguire, 'Valentinus and the Gnostike Hairesis' (Ph.D. diss., Yale University 1983), esp. 16–18.

2. See my 'Hegel and Anti-Judaism: Narrative and the Inner Circulation of the Kabbalah,' in *The Owl of Minerva* 28 (1997): 141–82.

Chapter 6. Boehme's Discourse and Valentinian Narrative Grammar

1. Gottfried Arnold, *Unparteiische Kirchen- und Ketzerhistorie : vom Anfang des Neuen Testaments bis auf das Jahr Christi 1688*, 2 vols. (Hildesheim : Georg Olms, 1967; originally published, 1697; reprint, Frankfurt am Main: T. Fritschens, 1729).

2. See Wehr, *Jakob Böhme*, 84, where the Ungrund is associated with the abyss and silence of *PSY*, as presented in *Against Heresies* bk 1. 1. As Wehr himself suggests, this association has a somewhat venerable pedigree. Without commenting on the connection implied by Baur, he mentions Schopenhauer as someone who stressed this

particular association. See Arthur Schopenhauer, *On the Fourfold Root of the Principle of Sufficient Reason*, trans. E. F. J. Payne (La Salle, Ill.: Open Court, 1974), 22–23.

3. That this is a structural difference between Boehme and *PSY* does not imply that this is a difference between Boehme and every classical Valentinian genre. For instance, the *Gospel* does speak of three kinds of human being, but emphasizes that nature or essence is a result of choice.

4. See especially the reservations of his his famous nineteenth-century admirers Baur and Hegel. See Baur, *Die christliche Gnosis*, 553; Hegel, *Lectures on the History of Philosophy*, vol. 3, 188– 89. One of his more able twentieth-century admirers, John J. Stoudt is also very conscious of this problem. See *Sunrise to Eternity*, 19ff.

5. See my discussion of the *Tractate* in *Gnostic Return in Modernity*, ch. 3.

6. For a good discussion of this aspect of the *Tripartite Tractate*, see Harold W. Attridge and Elaine Pagels, "*The Tripartite Tractate*" in *Nag Hammadi Codex I* [vol. 2]: *Notes*, ed. Harold W. Attridge (Leiden: E. J. Brill, 1985), 435–45.

7. Both the author of the *Tractate* and Boehme share negative views of the serpent. In *Mysterium Magnum* chs. 20–26 the serpent is excoriated as the physical symbol of Lucifer, though Lucifer in a satanic or deceiving mode. Their movement away from the biblical standard will not announce itself in the kind of tendentiousness that characterizes orphitic forms of Gnosticism, or interestingly, Hegel's rereading of Genesis in the *Encyclopaedia* #24 zu, where the serpent is straightforwardly supported as an emblem of knowledge at the expense of the transcendent divine who is exposed as both capricious and a liar.

8. In the *Tractate*, arguably, chaos has as much in common with the Platonic *chora* as the *tohu va bohu* of Genesis. This is consistent with the text overall which, as I indicated in *Gnostic Return in Modernity* (ch. 3), is greatly influenced by the available forms of Platonism.

9. At *Tractate* 56 the transcendent divine is spoken of as "invisible," "immutable," "unchangeable," "unvariable," "incomprehensible," "unknowable," "inscrutable," and "unbegotten." A little earlier in the text, however, the transcendent divine, referred to as "Father," is spoken of as "one," "unity," "root," "god," and "good" (53.6).

10. As I demonstrated in Part I, given Boehme's own assertions on the matter, one can speak of Sophia as a hypostasis in only an inverted comma sense.

11. As in *PSY* where the fall of Sophia precipitates a division into a lower and higher Sophia, where only the latter can be integrated into the pleroma, similarly in the *Tractate*, the fall of Logos issues in one aspect of Logos being emasculated (78) and in another aspect being elevated into the pleroma.

12. The *Tractate* suggests such a possibility at 118, 4, where it underscores the importance of kenosis in the context of the mimetic relation between Christ and the sufferings of the Logos.

13. Jonas, 'Delimitimation of the Gnostic Phenomenon'; von Balthasar, *The Glory of the Lord*, vol. 2, 59–61.

14. As I argued in *Gnostic Return in Modernity*, these differences in narrative are of two kinds: (1) differences between Valentinian texts within the Hellenistic field and (2) differences between modern Valentinian narratives and the classic paradigms of the Hellenistic field. Again, Ricoeur aids interpretation. He makes a distinction between the differences or deviations within a narrative field that constitutes distinct paradigms and the different deviations of later narrative forms with respect to the early paradigms, which in some cases at least amount to rule-governed deformations. See *Time and Narrative*, vol. 1, trans. Kathleen McLaughlin and David Pellauer (Chicago: University of Chicago Press, 1984), 69–70.

15. Amplifications include (1) opening up Baur's model to literary as well as religious and philosophical discourses, (2) accepting modern non-German as well as German discourses as plausible candidates for the ascription of Gnostic return, and (3) thinking of the Gnostic or Valentinian lines of discourse as projecting into the twentieth century. Corrections include both a critique of the *Urnarrative* predilection in *Die christliche Gnosis* and a tendency to overlook the specific ideational constellations of ancient Hellenistic narrative discourse as well as post-Reformation and post-Enlightenment narrative discourses.

16. One cannot reduce the incredible complexity of modern discourses to a few elements or transformations of elements. There is both wide variety between modern discourses and contingency with respect to their generation. As I indicated in *Gnostic Return in Modernity*, while grammar accounts for continuity across periods, it does not do so at the price of discontinuity. Discontinuity cannot be totally mastered. Or to use Ricoeur's language in *Time and Narrative*, syntagma cannot be mastered by paradigm.

17. These aspects of the *Gospel of Truth* is underscored by a number of scholars of Gnosticism. See especially Harold W. Attridge and George W. MacRae, "*The Gospel of Truth*" in *Nag Hammadi Codex I* [vol. 2]: *Notes*, 41–45; also 'The Gospel of Truth as an Exoteric Text,' in *Nag Hammadi, Gnosticism, and Early Christianity*, ed. Charles W. Hedrick and Robert Hodgson Jr. (Peabody, Mass.: Hendrickson Publishers, 1986), 239-55. See also William R. Schoedel, 'Gnostic Monism and the Gospel of Truth,' in *The Rediscovery of Gnosticism: Proceedings of the International Conference on Gnosticism at Yale, New Haven, Connecticut, March 28–31, 1978*, vol. 1, ed. Bentley Layton (Leiden: E. J. Brill, 1980), 379-80; also 'Typological Theology and Some Monistic Tendencies in Gnosticism,' in *Essays in Nag Hammadi: Texts in Honour of Alexander Böhlig*, ed. Martin Krause (Leiden: E. J. Brill, 1972), 88–108.

18. For an account of this synopsis, see *Gnostic Return in Modernity*, ch. 3.

19. This means, essentially also all that the Godhead is, since the *Gospel* exchanges "Father" for "Forefather" as the ultimate Principle of Origin. For a brilliant analysis of the relation between Father and Son from a Lacanian perspective, see J. Fineman, 'Gnosis and the Piety of Metaphor: The Gospel of Truth,' in *The Rediscovery of Gnosticism*, vol. 1, 289–318.

20. See David Dawson, *Allegorical Readers and Cultural Revision in Ancient Alexandria*, 127–82.

Chapter 7. Apocalyptic in Boehme's Discourse
and its Valentinian Enlisting

1. This is the phrase used by George A. Lindbeck to characterize the premodern regime of the functioning of Scripture. See *The Nature of Doctrine: Religion and Theology in a Postliberal Age* (Philadelphia: Fortress Press, 1984), 118. Here Lindbeck is undoubtedly influenced by Hans Frei's *The Eclipse of Biblical Narrative* (New Haven, Conn.: Yale University Press, 1973), which charts the demise of precisely such a reading. See also Bruce Marshall, 'Absorbing the World: Christian Unity and the Universe of Truths,' in *Theology and Dialogue: Essays in Conversation with George Lindbeck*, ed. Bruce Marshall (Notre Dame, Ind.: University of Notre Dame Press, 1990), 69–102.

2. Here I am accepting in part the necessity to take account of literary features of apocalyptic as has been suggested by John J. Collins, among others, but without assuming that a decision has to be made between literary and content considerations. See *Apocalyptic: Morphology of a Genre*, ed. John J. Collins (Missoula, Mont.: Scholars Press, 1975).

3. In *Mysterium Magnum* (ch. 30) the death of Christ is the beginning of the sixth or penultimate time—that is, the time of Jared that is foundational with respect to the final time, the time of revelation and judgment—that is, the time of Enoch.

4. Marjorie Reeves, for example, argues that Joachim's work is better conceived not as apocalyptic, but rather as a theology of history. See *Joachim of Fiore and the Prophetic Future*, 136ff. A contrary point of view is taken by Bernard McGinn who sees no reason why the label of 'apocalyptic' should be denied the work of Joachim, provided the reflective and hermeneutic aspects of Joachim's work are adequately recognized. See McGinn, *The Calabrian Abbot: Joachim of Fiore in the History of Western Thought* (New York: Macmillan, 1985). It is important for McGinn that central to Joachim's program is an interpretation of Revelation—that is, *Enchiridion super Apocalypsim*.

5. Certainly the close relationship between the Spirit and the state of being it augurates—that is, the state of a plenitude of intellect (*plenitudo intellectus*), as *Liber Concordia Novae ac Veteris Testamenti* refers to it—encourages the kind of immanentist reading offered by de Lubac in *La postérité spirituelle de Joachim de Fiore*.

6. De Lubac is in no doubt that Boehme has some contact with Joachim. See *La postérité spirituelle de Joachim de Fiore*, tome 1, 219ff. While Reeves does not discuss the case of Boehme, she shows convincingly in *Joachim of Fiore and the Prophetic Future* (pp. 136ff.) that Joachim remains a vital presence in the left wing of the Reformation.

7. For Boehme the number seven has a special significance, as witness his seven divine qualities. From a scriptural point of view, the importance of seven is underwritten by the mutual reinforcement provided by the seven candlesticks of Revelation and the seven days of creation. From a typological point of view, Boehme's view of the seven times recalls the Augustinian periodization of history. As *Mysterium Magnum* (ch. 30) presents it, there are seven periods or times, the times of Adam, Seth, Enosh, Kenan, Mahalaleel, Jared, and Enoch. At the same time, no absolute contrast can be drawn with Joachim on this score. Despite his trinitarian theology of history, Joachim also endorsed

a septenarian schematization. For Joachim, they are strictly complementary. For this point, see McGinn, *The Calabrian Abbot*, 153; also Winfrid H. J. Schachten, *Ordo Salutis: Das Gesetz als Weise der Heilsvermittlung: zur Kritik des hl. Thomas von Aquin an Joachim von Fiore* (Münster: Aschendorff, 1980), 24–25, 31.

8. Abraham von Frankenberg writes respecting the symbol that it "evokes the paradise of God that will be manifest in the last time, when the end will return to the beginning and when the circle will be closed" (Cited by de Lubac, *La postérité spirituelle de Joachim de Fiore*, tome 1, 221).

9. On the authority of the Enoch figure in the trajectory of Reformation thought, see Barnes, *Prophecy and Gnosis*, 121.

10. Johann Albrecht Bengel is a biblical theologian whose main concern is the proper exegesis of Revelation, which he regards as the text that unfolds God's relation to history. See especially his *Gnomon of the New Testament*, 5 vols., rev. and ed. Andrew R. Fausset (Edinburgh: T. & T. Clark, 1858). Bengel's mediation of Joachim has been underscored by a number of scholars. Perhaps the most persuasive of these has been Laurence Dickey. See *Hegel, Religion, Economics, and the Politics of Spirit, 1770–1807* (Cambridge: Cambridge University Press, 1987), 77–112; esp. 78, 82, 90, 95, 97, 103.

11. See 'The Education of the Human Race,' in *Lessing's Theological Writings*, trans. Henry Chadwick (Stanford: Stanford University Press, 1956), 82–98.

12. See de Lubac, *La postérité spirituelle de Joachim de Fiore*, tome 1, 359–93; Michael Murray, *Modern Philosophy of History: Its Origin and Destination* (The Hague: Martinus Nijhoff, 1970), 91; Henri Mottu, 'Joachim de Fiore et Hegel,' in *Storia e messagio in Gioacchino da Fiore: atti del I Congresso internazionale di studi gioachimiti, S. Giovanni in Fiore, Abbazia Florense, 19–23 settembre 1979* (S. Giovanni in Fiore: Centro di studi gioachimiti, 1980), 181–94.

13. See McGinn's rich discussion of this point in ch. 4 of *The Calabrian Abbot*, titled 'Intellectus Spiritualis: Joachim's Understanding of Scripture,' pp. 123–44, esp. 131–32, and De Lubac, *Exégèse médiévale*, vol. 1, 437–558. See also Henri Mottu, *La Manifestation de l'Esprit selon Joachim de Fiore: herméneutique et théologie de l'histoire d'après le Traité sur les quatre évangiles* (Neuchâtel: Delachaux & Niestlé, 1977), chs. 1–3.

14. As is well known, St. Thomas questioned the orthodoxy of Joachim and defended Peter Lombard against the criticism of Joachim that the Lombardian position was essentially Sabellian. See *Summa Theologica* I, q. 39, art. 5. For a measured account of the issues, see McGinn, *The Calabrian Abbot*, 164–66, 209–12.

15. Thomas's attack on Joachim on lack of christological grounding occurs in *Summa Theologica* I, q. 104. Reeves believes that the eschatological push in Joachim does indeed make the christological foundation of faith problematic. Ernst Benz essentially agrees with Reeves, but he remains entirely nonplussed. See his 'Joachim-Studien 2: Thomas von Aquin und Joachim de Fiore,' in *Zeitschrift für Kirchengeschichte* 53 (1934): 52–116. See also Mottu, *La manifestation de l'Esprit selon Joachim de Fiore*, 211–22; and Schachten, *Ordo Salutis*, 26–28. At the same time it should be remembered that the

battle lines were not simply drawn between the Franciscan Joachim and the Dominican Thomas, battle lines were also drawn within Franciscan theology itself. Bonaventure's resistance to Joachimite ideas was general, yet tended to focus on the way eschatology stressed Christology. See De Lubac, *La postérité spirituelle de Joachim de Fiore*, tome 1, ch.1; and McGinn, *The Calabrian Abbot*, 213–24; also Joseph Ratzinger, *The Theology of History of St. Bonaventure* (Chicago: Franciscan Herald Press, 1971).

16. See Schachten, *Ordo Salutis*, pp. 23ff. This point is even more to the fore in Schachten's *Trinitas et Tempora: Trinitätslehre und Geschichtdenken Joachim von Fiore* (Freiburg: n.p., 1975).

17. The redemptive activity of Christ in Luther obviously presupposes a fallen humanity, which in turn points back to creatureliness and createdness.

18. See O'Regan, *The Heterodox Hegel*, pp. 305–7.

19. See Bataille, *Inner Experience*, 43–61; and Jacques Derrida, 'From Restricted to General Economy: A Hegelianism without Reserve,' in *Writing and Difference*, trans. Alan Bass (Chicago: University of Chicago Press, 1978), 251–77.

20. Reeves underscores this point. See Reeves, *Joachim of Fiore and the Prophetic Future*, pp. 24–25.

21. Perhaps of all the features of apocalyptic, it is this feature that has the most contemporary currency. It is to the fore in Moltmann's philosophy of hope when he makes his famous distinction between *futurum* and *adventus*. The former indicates a teleological pattern, whereas the latter indicates the act of God outside the network of history, especially as history is understood in Hegelian fashion as progressive and developmental.

22. See Schachten, *Ordo Salutis*, 24–5, 31.

23. The Latin *distentio*, which makes a famous appearance in Book 11 of the *Confessions* when Augustine speaks of time as *distentio animi*, represents at least an indirect translation of the *diastasis* of *Enneads* bk 3. 7. Of course, Neoplatonic *diastasis* and *diastema* were also Christianly adopted and adapted in the Greek East. Gregory of Nyssa speaks of the *diastema* of the trinitarian persons, and the *diastasis* between the creator and the created.

24. Everyone would grant, I suspect, that Revelation is by far the most iconic of biblical texts. And it is plausible at least that many would agree with McGinn's judgment that Joachim is one of the most iconic thinkers within the Christian tradition. See *The Calabrian Abbot*, ch. 3, where he is called 'Joachim the Symbolist,' 101–22, esp. 113. Of course, for McGinn Joachim's symbolic mentality and the fact that Revelation is for him a text of mysteries to be unraveled is not accidental. In Joachim's case the iconic disposition is most thickly rendered in his *Liber della Figura*. For good discussions of the *figura*, see Mottu, *La manifestation de l'Esprit selon Joachim de Fiore*, pp. 173–77; also Majorie Reeves, 'The *Arbores* of Joachim of Fiore,' *Studies in Italian Medieval History Presented to Miss E. M. Jamison*, ed. Philip Grierson and John Ward Perkins (London: British School at Rome, 1956), 57–81.

25. See O' Regan, *The Heterodox Hegel*, 287–326.

Chapter 8. Neoplatonism in Boehme's Discourse
and its Valentinian Enlisting

1. At the very least, in *Die christliche Gnosis* Baur implies that modern narrative thought finds a precursor in Neoplatonism, for Neoplatonism is understood to exemplify "Gnosis" just as Valentinianism and Marcionism does. Thus the return of Gnosis in modernity is, among other things, the return of Neoplatonism. Baur is more explicit in *Die christliche Lehre von der Dreieinigkeit*, where Neoplatonism is understood to provide the ideational basis of modern trinitarian forms as it is does for ancient trinitarian thought. Similarly, in *Die Philosophie des Christenthums*, Staudenmaier thinks of Neoplatonism as providing the ideational basis of post-Reformation narrative thought that has its alpha in Boehme, its omega in Hegel.

2. In his book *Paracelsus: An Introduction to Philosophical Medicine in the Time of the Renaissance* Walter Pagel argues persuasively that while Paracelsus may modify his assumptive framework in important ways, this framework (which is the framework of his teachers, Agrippa von Nettesheim and Trithemius) is essentially Neoplatonic.

3. To speak of the intellectual nature of reality is to say more than that reality is intelligible, for Plato's theory of forms had already said as much. The advance of Neoplatonism is to think of intelligible reality as in some sense active, as thinking as well as thought. While classical Neoplatonism (as both Steven Gersh and Werner Beierwaltes point out) already makes this move, arguably the activity dimension is greater in the Christian Neoplatonism of Pseudo-Dionysius, but Eriugena especially represents an advance in this regard. See Gersh, *From Iamblichus to Eriugena: An Investigation of the Prehistory and Evolution of the Pseudo-Dionysian Tradition* (Leiden: E. J. Brill, 1978), and Beierwaltes, *Denken des Einen: Studien zur neuplatonischen Philosophie und ihrer Wirkungsgeschichte* (Frankfurt am Main: Klostermann, 1985).

4. Obviously the primary texts submitted to allegorical interpretation differ in the case of classical and Christian Neoplatonism, with Neoplatonism allegorizing old Greek myths, and Christian Neoplatonism allegorizing, at least on occasions, the biblical text.

5. In Blumenberg's mind the relation is positive insofar as a both discourses play important, if different, roles with respect to the development of discourses in modernity. The relation is negative, however, insofar as Bruno's demythologizing discourse depicts a divine that finds its term in the world, whereas Boehme's remythologizing discourse depicts a divine that in and through manifestation in the world finds its term in itself. In *The Legitimacy of the Modern Age* (pp. 549–96) Blumenberg is particularly effective in showing the originality of Bruno's view that the universe represents the real and complete expression of the divine, thus, on the one hand, displacing or interpreting the 'Son' and, on the other, eliminating transcendence at least to the extent that positing an excess of potential manifestation over actual manifestation serves as a guarantee.

6. Despite all Bruno's emphasis on the knowability of the divine that undergirds his cosmological speculation, in texts such as *De l'infinito universo et mondi* and *Spaccio de la bestia trionfante* indicate on a number of occasions how the One transcends knowledge, or

that it is graspable only through a form of blindness. A translation of the text, *De l'infinito universo et mondi* can be found appended to Dorothea Waley Singer's *Giordano Bruno, his Life and Work* (New York: Schuman, 1950); for a translation of Bruno's *Spaccio de la bestia trionfante* (Parigi [i.e., London]: n.p., 1584) see *The Expulsion of the Triumphant Beast*, trans. Arthur D. Imerti (Lincoln, Nebr.: University of Nebraska Press, 1992; originally published, New Brunswick, N.J.: Rutgers University Press, 1964).

7. The association of the One and the Good, the absolute First Principle of the *Parmenides* and the *Republic* is an achievement of classical Neoplatonism. This connection is prominent in the *Enneads*, especially in bk 1. 7 and bk 5. 5, but is pointed to throughout. See in addition bk 2. 9, 1; bk 3. 8, 11, bk 5. 4; bk 5. 9, 2; bk 6. 5, 1. At the same time, since the good is *epekeinai tes ousias*, it is also to some extent already *hyperagathon*. Proclus is already on the way to using this actual language that will enter Christian Neoplatonic circles through Pseudo-Dionysius, who uses this language in *Divine Names* 1 to characterize the superessential Godhead (*hyperousias thearchia*).

8. It is clear that in Neoplatonism the One can be existentially as well as ontologically, gnoseologically, and axiologically characterized. The existential characterization is often negative in kind, for instance, that the One is "impassible," but sometimes there are more positive avowals. In the *Enneads* one of the characterizations of the One is that the One exists or superexists in "holy repose." This "holy repose" is based on the One being without need (bk 6. 8, 7), and points to a self-satisfaction that is correlative to self-sufficiency.

9. See Staudenmaier, *Johannes Scotus Erigena und die Wissenschaft seiner Zeit Mit allgemeinen Entwicklungen der Hauptwahrheiten auf dem Gebiete der Philosophie und Religion, und Grundzugen zu einer Geschichte der speculativen Theologie* (Frankfurt am Main: Minerva, 1966; originally published, Frankfurt am Main: Andräische Buchhandlung, 1835).

10. See especially *Enneads* bk 6. 8, 9. See also John Rist, *Plotinus: The Road to Reality*, 66–83, esp. 77–78. The One is without compulsion (*ouk ex anankes*); it is what it wills to be (*ousan ho theles*). For a listing of passages in which Plotinus speaks of the One as existing necessarily but without compulsion, see Lloyd P. Gerson, *Plotinus* (London: G. Routledge, 1994), 28. *Enneads*'s 4, 3 and 4, 4 are especially important loci.

11. In speaking of "logical" notes, I mean to suggest that at least at an inchoate level Boehme implies that becoming belongs to the definition of a living God. Of course, it is only in a religious thinker like Hegel that one can say that this "logical" element is fully explicit.

12. For a detailed treatment of the *Eroici Furiori* in the Renaissance and specifically in a Neoplatonic framework of love, see John Charles Nelson, *Renaissance Theory of Love: The Context of Giordano Bruno's Eroici Furiori* (New York: Columbia University Press, 1958). See also Von Balthasar, *The Glory of the Lord*, vol. 5, 253 where, if Bruno is not blameless with respect to an immanentization of divine love, *eros* is not coextensive with *agapaic* divine diffusion.

13. The classical discussion of the *principle of plenitude* still remains Arthur Lovejoy's *The Great Chain of Being* (Cambridge, Mass.: Harvard University Press, 1936). See pp. 116–21 for Bruno.

14. In explicit assertion that nothing is held back by the divine, or that the divine would not be divine if anything were held back, Bruno distinguishes himself from previous softer renditions of the principle of plenitude. It would not be inaccurate to say that with Bruno, the principle operative in Neoplatonism from the beginning, and suggested at least in Plato's own texts, is asserted with full logical rigor.

15. For the cited passage of *De l'infinito universo* see Singer's *Giordano Bruno*, 260. The argumentive burden of the emptying of the divine into the world is often borne by the other side of the equation, the world which is not without the immanent presence of the divine. The aspect of divine immanence is especially prominent in *De la Causa*. See *Cause, Principle, and Unity*, trans. Jack Lindsay (Westport, Conn.: Greenwood Press Publishers, 1976). Both the formative and formed aspects, or *natura naturans* and *natura naturata*, of *De la Causa* (Dialogue 4), come in for discussion in Yates, *Giordano Bruno and the Hermetic Tradition*.

16. Thus the privative view of evil as nonbeing and as at best a *parahypothesis* (a not fully real mode of subsistence) that characterizes the discussion of Plotinus in *Enneads* bk 1. 8; bk 2. 9 and Proclus's texts on providence respectively.

17. In his treatment of providence in the *Enneads* Plotinus uses different images for the whole ranging from an image of the world as a picture that demands contrast, to an image of the whole as a symphony (bk 3. 2), to that of a complex woven fabric (bk 3. 3).

18. For Plotinus the key texts are bk 3. 2 and bk 3. 3 of the *Enneads*. For Proclus, see *On Providence and Fate* a translation of extracts from his treatise entitled *Ten Doubts Concerning Providence* in *The Six Books of Proclus, the Platonic Successor, On the Theology of Plato*, vol. 2, trans. Thomas Taylor (London: A. J. Valpry, printer; 1816), 414–577. It is in his commentary on the *Parmenides* (8, 35), however, that Proclus makes, perhaps, his most famous statement about the value of "cheap" and "insignificant" things. "Nothing," "Proclus writes, is "unworthy or rejected (*apobleton*)" when things are considered in relation to their divine origin.

19. See the Imerti translation of Bruno, *The Expulsion of the Triumphant Beast*, 136. See also p. 135.

20. Commentators on Boehme such as Berdyaev, Grunsky, and Koyré have all underscored this point that the interruption of manifestation is a condition of its possibility, and that such interruption brings the divine perilously close to a theogonic justification of evil. If Fichte provides the purest recapitulation of the necessity of interruption in his insistence on the necessity of *Anstoss* in the *Wissenschaftslehre*, in their different ways Hegel and Schelling—who have Boehme on their historical-intellectual screens in a way that Fichte does not—bring the discussion of contradiction and evil to a head. "Fell" is a word used by the victorian poet, Gerard Manley Hopkins.

21. See Ricoeur 'The Hermeneutics of Symbols and Philosophical Reflection, 1,' in *The Conflict of Interpretations*, 287–314, esp. pp. 301–2.

22. For a good discussion of how Bruno saw his own metaphysical construction in relation to the doctrine of the Trinity, see Emerti's introduction to *The Expulsion of the Triumphant Beast*, pp. 54–56.

23. For Cusa, see *De Docta Ignorantia* (Part III) and *De Visione Dei* (chs. 23–24).

24. This is the position adopted by Bruno, for example, in *The Expulsion of the Triumphant Beast*.

25. In *The Legitimacy of the Modern Age*, which provides Blumenberg's most extensive treatment of Bruno, he does not explicitly associate Bruno's deconstructive metaphysical position with the Promethean complex. *Work on Myth* (p. 553), however, does make such an association, as Blumenberg argues for the connection between Bruno and Goethe. A similar Promethean typing is provided by von Balthasar in *The Glory of the Lord*, vol. 5. It should be observed in passing that in *The Expulsion of the Triumphant Beast*, Bruno denies the absoluteness of the figure of Prometheus, who represents curiosity and a kind of linear intelligence that must give way to something superior that recognizes and embraces mystery.

26. This distinction is important, for were it the case that the narrative discourses of apocalyptic, Neoplatonism, or the Kabbalah exercised an equal amount of influence on the Valentinian narrative strand in Boehme's discourse, then the notion of *enlisting* would have to be surrendered.

Chapter 9. Kabbalah in Boehme's Discourse and its Valentinian Enlisting

1. Koyré, Stoudt, and Weeks all produce evidence of this. Von Frankenberg was, of course, Boehme's first biographer.

2. See Friedrich Christoph Oetinger, *Die Lehrtafel der Prinzessin Antonia*, ed. Reinhard Breymayer and Friedrich Häusermann, 2 vols. (Berlin: W. de Gruyter, 1977), esp. vol. 1, 131–44; 170–81. See also Sigrid Grossmann, *Friedrich Christoph Oetingers Gottesvorstellung*, 59–66.

3. See Benz, *Les sources mystiques*, 66–68; Stoudt, *Sunrise to Eternity*, 98ff.; also John Schulitz, *Jakob Böhme und die Kabbalah: eine vergleichende Werkanalyse* (Frankfurt am Main: Peter Lang, 1993). See also W. Huber, 'Die Kabbala als Quelle zur Anthropologie Jakob Böhmes,' in *Kairos* 13 (1971): 131–58; and W. Schulze, 'Jacob Böhme und die Kabbala,' in *Judaica* 11 (1959): 12–29.

4. For the multileveled nature of the Kabbalistic view of divine manifestation, see Scholem, *Major Trends in Jewish Mysticism*, 213ff.

5. The *raza de-mehemanutha* is the fourth and highest level of interpretation, having below it literal or historical interpretation (*Pashat*), homiletic interpretation (*De-*

rasha), and allegorical or philosophical interpretation (*Remez*). For a description of this the highest of four levels of interpretation—which fourfold sense of Scripture may represent some influence from Christianity—Scholem, *The Kabbalah and its Symbolism*, 52–57.

6. Benz articulates this position in *Der Prophet Jakob Böhme*.

7. Though a condition of the possibility of connection is to interpret the chaos of Genesis less as the nothing that the creation of the physical world overcomes than as a nothing or chaos in the divine itself. For a good account of this particular interpretation of chaos, see Schulitz, *Jakob Böhme und die Kabbalah*, 164ff.; also Scholem, *The Kabbalah and its Symbolism*, 101–3.

8. See *Zohar: Basic Readings from the Kabbalah*, ed. Gershom Scholem (London: Rider, 1977), 82.

9. See Scholem, *Major Trends in Jewish Mysticism*, 237ff.

10. For the image of 'root' with respect to the *En Sof*, see Scholem, *Major Trends in Jewish Mysticism*, 237.

11. See Scholem, *Major Trends in Jewish Mysticism*, 33–34.

12. Ibid., 221.

13. See Schulitz, *Jakob Böhme und die Kabbalah*, 54–60; Scholem, *Major Trends in Jewish Mysticism*, 221.

14. For a good account of this, see Grossmann, *Friedrich Christoph Oetingers Gottesvorstellung*, 177–80, 277–97. It should be said also that the connection was made prior to Boehme in the Renaissance in the Christian Kabbalah of Pico della Mirandola and Johann Reuchlin. The connection is made by Pico in the famous twelfth conclusion of his *Conclusiones Cabalisticae*. See Chaim Wirzubski, *Pico della Mirandola's Encounter with Jewish Mysticism* (Cambridge, Mass.: Harvard University Press, 1989), 106–8; also 162. The connection is made by Reuchlin in *De arte cabalistica*. See *On the Art of the Kabbalah*, trans. by Martin Goodman and Sarah Goodman (New York: Abaris Books, 1983). Through Reuchlin the Kabbalah comes into Christian circles in Germany in the sixteenth century.

15. Schulitz, *Jakob Böhme und die Kabbalah*, 64ff.

16. Ibid., 108.

17. Ibid., 109.

18. One might have to except the book *Bahir* in this respect. An important passage is the following: "there is in God a principle that is called 'Evil,' and it lies in the north of God, for it is written [Jeremiah 1.14]: 'Out of the north the evil shall break forth upon all the inhabitants of the land, that is to say, all evil that comes upon all the inhabitants of the land breaks forth out of the north. And what principle is this? It is the form of the hand [one of the seven holy forms which represent God as the original man], and it has many messengers, and all are named 'Evil,' . . . And it is they that fling the world into guilt, for the *tohu* is in the north, and the *tohu* means precisely the evil

that confuses men until they sin, and itis the source of all man's evil impulses."This passage is quoted by Scholem in *The Kabbalah and its Symbolism* (p. 92), where it gets read as upsetting longstanding rabbinic views about the anthropological origin of evil.

19. See Oetinger, *Die Lehrtafel der Prinzessin Antonia*, vol. 2, 133. See the introduction by Friedrich Häussermann in vol. 2, 31–50, esp. 32–44.

20. See Oetinger, *Die Lehrtafel der Prinzessin Antonia*, vol. 1, 150.

21. See Joseph L. Blau's still valuable *The Christian Interpretation of the Cabala in the Renaissance* (New York: Columbia University Press, 1944).

22. See Moshe Idel's introduction to *On the Art of the Kabbalah*, trans. Martin and Sarah Goodman, Bison Book ed. (Lincoln, Nebr.: University of Nebraska Press, 1993).

23. Idel thinks that this is the upshot of Christian adoption, a point possibly obscured by Scholem, who remains enthralled by the theosophic substance of Kabbalah, and who authorizes perhaps too great a distinction between exoteric and esoteric Torah. For Scholem's reflections on the Torah, see *The Kabbalah and its Symbolism*, pp. 32–86.

24. This point is perhaps not sufficiently emphasized by Schulitz in his treatment of the relationship between Boehme and the Kabbalah on the theodicy question. See *Jakob Böhme und die Kabbalah*, 131–60.

25. Freud's various topological models of superego, ego, id, or consciousness and unconsciousness, has come under attack both from psychologists and philosophers. On the psychological front, Jacques Lacan has been to the fore in recommending a linguistic translation of Freud's architectural view of the self. See *The Four Fundamental Concepts of Psychoanalysis*, ed. Jacques-Alain Miller, trans. Alan Sheridan, 1st American ed. (New York: W. W. Norton, 1978); *Écrits: A Selection*, trans. Alan Sheridan (New York: W. W. Norton, 1977). Powerful revisions of psychoanalysis have been launched by Louis Althusser, Jürgen Habermas, and Paul Ricoeur. See Louis Althusser, *Writings on Psychoanalysis: Freud and Lacan*, ed. Olivier Corpet and François Matheron, trans. Jeffrey Mehlman (New York: Columbia University Press, 1996). Athusser agrees with Lacan's modification of the topological model, and praises the theoretical emendation of thinking of the unconscious as a language. See esp. pp. 16, 22, and 26. For a more intersubjective and hermeneutic reading of Freud that, nonetheless, breaks with the topological model, see Jürgen Habermas, *Knowledge and Human Interests*, trans. Jeremy J. Shapiro (Boston: Beacon Press, 1971), 214–73, esp. 244–45, 252 and 256; Paul Ricoeur, *Freud and Philosophy: An Essay on Interpretation*, trans. Denis Savage (New Haven, Conn.: Yale University Press, 1970).

Conclusion: Genealogical Preface

1. Schelling's perspicuous version of the ontological question is "Warum ist uberhaupt Etwas, warum ist Nicht Nichts?" I am suggesting that this is the form of the ontological question deployed by Boehme. The account of the generation of something

(*Ichts*), or its possibility, is tied to the negation of nothing (*Nichts*) that is the divine as pure virtuality. For reference to Schelling's formulation, see Karl Jaspers, *Schelling* (Munich: Pieper, 1955), 124.

2. In his defense of the biblical God, Luther wishes to expose an alternative picture of God that contrasts with what he believes is the then current picture that has been fostered at least in part by the theological tradition in general, the medieval theological tradition in particular. This God is dynamic rather than the static God of the metaphysical tradition. More, it is a God that is dramatically present to the world and human beings. In offering a contrasting picture, Luther is best understood as offering a new rhetoric rather than a new concept of God. He does not explore the concept of God as dynamic and to what extent this involves or does not involve development. More, Luther will not want to say that the God of justice and the God of mercy fundamentally oppose each other, nor does he commit himself to the view that God, in some fundamental respect, suffers. In contrast, Boehme's view is ontological rather than rhetorical, indeed represents an ontological extrapolation or development of Luther's corrective rhetoric. Boehme wishes to speak of Luther's dynamic God undergoing development, of the ontological agon between the God of justice and the God of mercy, and of the divine as suffering, even suffering death.

3. I am not been original in underscoring this tensional relationship. This tensional relationship was pointed to by Heinrich Bornkamm over 70 years ago. See Introduction, note 57. In addition, Bornkamm provides a broad outline as to the narrative mechanisms in and through which Boehme distorts Luther's theology. Nevertheless, as I also point out in that note, the view that the relation between Boehme's speculative theology and Luther's kerygmatic theology is tensional is disputed by some scholars.

4. The early Schleiermacher provides the best example of the refocusing of authority on the individual orientation to transcendence not otherwise specified (God or nature). Kant and Rousseau provide two examples of the refocusing of authority in conscience. Hölderlin, the early Schelling, and the early Hegel provide good examples of refocusing authority in the community. And, of course, the mature Hegel infamously focused such authority in the state.

5. It is regarded as self-evident that conventional Christianity has lost cultural authority. The decision to be made is whether this is because of its inherent lack of intelligibility or because of Christianity's misinterpretation of itself. If the latter is accepted as the more plausible view, then the decision to be made is whether Christianity was realized at some time in the past or yet remains to be realized. Authentic Christianity, whether past or future, is not only protected from the standard criticisms of Christianity, but authentic Christianity itself can then be offered as an antidote to the misguided Enlightenment replacements of conventional Christianity.

6. At the same time I hope I have made clear in my interpretation that the epistemological issue is very much to the fore in Boehme's discourse. A central question guiding Boehme's reflection is how God as Nothing and One comes to know Godself adequately. The answer to the question is that God comes to self-consciousness only

through consciousness of the finite. But consciousness of the finite suggests as its subjective correlative a finitizing of an infinite consciousness that is purely notional.

7. See O'Regan, *The Heterodox Hegel*, chs. 2–6, where this point is central.

8. See Blumenberg, *Work on Myth*, 266–70.

9. See Karl R. Popper, *The Open Society and its Enemies. Volume 2. The High Tide of Prophecy: Hegel, Marx, and the Aftermath* (London: G. Routledge, 1945); Jean François Lyotard, *The Postmodern Explained: Correspondences, 1982–1985*, ed. Julian Pefanis and Morgan Thomas, trans. Don Barry et al. (Minneapolis, Minn.: University of Minnesota Press, 1993).

10. See O' Regan, *The Heterodox Hegel* for an extended analysis of each of these swerves. In that text, by contrast with *God's Story: Hegel's Valentinian Curriculum*, I merely pointed to the narrative infrastructure that accounts for the individual swerves; I did not attempt to identify this narrative infrastructure.

11. A particularly harsh verdicts of Schleiermacher is rendered in Lindbeck, *The Nature of Doctrine*, where Schleiermacher is dismissed as an "experiential expressivist."

12. R. Kendall Soulen, *The God of Israel and Christian Theology* (Minneapolis, Minn.: Fortress Press, 1996), 68–77.

13. These include Thomas Altizer, Harold Bloom, David V. Erdman, and Joseph Anthony Wittreich Jr. See Altizer, *The New Apocalypse: The Radical Christian Vision of William Blake* (East Lansing, Mich.: Michigan State University Press, 1967); Bloom, *Blake's Apocalypse: A Study in Poetic Argument* (Ithaca, N.Y.: Cornell University Press, 1970); *The Visionary Company: A Reading of English Romantic Poetry*, rev. ed. (Ithaca, N.Y.: Cornell University Press, 1971), 7–123; Erdman, *Blake, Prophet against Empire: A Poet's Interpretation of the History of his Own Times*, rev. ed. (Princeton, N.J.:, Princeton University Press, 1969); Wittreich, *Angel of Apocalypse: Blake's Idea of Milton* (Madison, Wis.: University of Wisconsin Press, 1975).

Index